Henry Wade Rogers

The Law of Expert Testimony

Henry Wade Rogers

The Law of Expert Testimony

ISBN/EAN: 9783744675369

Printed in Europe, USA, Canada, Australia, Japan

Cover: Foto ©Suzi / pixelio.de

More available books at **www.hansebooks.com**

THE LAW

OF

EXPERT TESTIMONY.

BY

HENRY WADE ROGERS.

Cuilibet in suâ arte perito est credendum.

ST. LOUIS, MO.:
WILLIAM H. STEVENSON,
LAW PUBLISHER AND PUBLISHER OF THE
CENTRAL LAW JOURNAL.
1883.

COPYRIGHT, 1883,
BY
HENRY WADE ROGERS.

St. Louis, Mo.: Printed by the Central Law Journal.

TO THE

HONORABLE THOMAS M. COOLEY, LL.D.
Of the Supreme Court of Michigan,

THIS BOOK IS INSCRIBED,

In appreciation of his friendship, and the virtues of his private life, as well as in recognition of his eminence as a jurist, and his fame as a judge.

PREFACE.

The purpose which the writer had in mind in the preparation of this monograph, was to furnish to the practitioner a more extended presentation of the law relating to expert testimony, than is afforded in the treatises on evidence. It seemed desirable that the law on this important subject should be set forth with more of detail than it has been found practicable to do in the general treatises of the law of evidence. The cases relating to expert testimony are so numerous and so diversified in character, that any attempt to bring them all together, and give to them that consideration which they merit in a work devoted to the general subject of evidence, would seem to be out of the question. Moreover, within the last few years, many and important cases on this subject have been decided by the courts, which have not yet found their way into the larger treatises on evidence. It was for the purpose of supplying this evident want that this work was undertaken.

HENRY WADE ROGERS.

TABLE OF CONTENTS.

CHAPTER I.

	SECTION.
The Admissibility in Evidence of Expert Testimony,	1–14

CHAPTER II.

The Competency of Expert Witnesses, . . . 15–23

CHAPTER III.

The Examination of Expert Witnesses, and the Weight of their Testimony, ... 24–42

CHAPTER IV.

Expert Testimony in Medicine, Surgery and Chemistry, 43–84

CHAPTER V.

Expert Testimony in the Science of Law, . . . 85–104

CHAPTER VI.

Expert Testimony in the Trades and Arts, . . . 105–127

CHAPTER VII.

Expert Testimony in Handwriting, ... 128–150

CHAPTER VIII.

VALUE, ... 151-165

CHAPTER IX.

THE RELATION OF SCIENTIFIC BOOKS TO EXPERT TESTIMONY, 166-186

CHAPTER X.

COMPENSATION OF EXPERTS, ... 187-196

APPENDIX.

OPINIONS ON THE VALUE OF EXPERT TESTIMONY.
ADDITIONAL CASES. . . . .

TABLE OF CASES CITED.

A.

Abbey v. Lill, 5 Bing. 299, p. 172.
Ayers v. Water Commissioners, 29 N. Y. 297, pp. 39, 44.
Abbott v. Coleman, 21 Kans. 250, p. 199.
Adams v. Dale, 29 Ind, 273, p. 218.
Adams v. Peters, 2 Car. & Kar. 722, p. 169.
Albright v. Corley, 40 Tex. 105, p. 155.
Allen v. Hunter, 6 McLean, 303, pp. 3, 116.
Allen v. State, 3 Hum. 367, p. 205.
Allis v. Day, 14 Minn., 516. p. 222.
Am. Life Ins. Co. v. Rosenagle, 27 P. F. Smith, 507, pp. 125, 133.
Anderson v. Anderson, 23 Tex. 639, p. 122.
Anderson v. Folger, 11 La. Ann. 26J, p. 122.
Andre v. Hardin, 32 Mich. 326, p. 49.
Anonymous, 37 Miss. 54, p. 20.
Anson v. Dwight, 18 Iowa, 244, pp. 212, 213.
Anthony v. Smith, 4 Bos. 503, pp. 54, 79.
Anthony v. Stinson, 4 Kans. 22.., pp, 59, 222.
Antomarchi v. Russell, 63 Ala., 356, p. 164.
Appleby v. Astor Fire Ins. Co., 54 N. Y. 253, p. 151.
Ardesco Oil Co., 63 Penn. St. 146, pp. 24, 175.
Armstrong v. Burrows, 6 Watts, 266, p. 184.
Armstrong v. Lear, 8 Peters, 52, p. 121.
Ashland v. Marlborough, 99 Mass. 48, p. 71.
Ashworth v. Kittridge, 12 Cush. 194, p. 250.
Atchison, etc. R. R. Co. v. United States, 15 Ct. of Cl. 126, pp. 10, 12, 60.
Atlantic, etc R. R. Co. v. Campbell, 4 Ohio St. 583, p. 211.
Attorney General Petitioner, 104 Mass. 537, p. 264.
Atwater v. Clancy, 107 Mass. 369, pp. 169, 172.
Atwood v. Cornwall, 28 Mich. 336, p. 205.
Aunick v. Mitchell, 82 Penn. St. 211, p. 193.
Aveson v. Kinnaird, 6 East, 18., p. 75.

B.

Babcock v. Babcock, 46 Mo. 243, p. 122.
Babcock v. Middlesex Sav. Bank, 28 Conn. 306, p. 4.
Bacon v. Charlton, 7 Cush. 581, p. 75.
Bacon v. Williams, 13 Gray, 535, pp. 183, 201.
Bailey v. McDowell, 2 Harr. 34, p. 121.
Bailey v. Pool, 13 Ired. 406, p. 4.
Baird v. Daly, 68 N. Y. 548, p. 142.
Baker v. Haines, 6 Whart. 281, p. 198.
Ball v. Franklinite Consol. Co., 32 N. J. Law, 102, p. 122.
Baltimore & Ohio R. R. Co. v. Glenn. 28 Md. 287, p. 123.
Baltimore, etc. R. R. Co. v. Shipley, 39 Md. 251, p. 48.
Baltimore, etc. R. R. Co. v. Thompson, 10 Md. 76, pp. 39, 155.
Bank of Commerce v. Bissell, 72 N. Y. 615, p. 168.
Bank of Commonwealth v. Mudgett, 44 N. Y. 514, p. 204.
Bank of Pennsylvania v. Jacobs, 1 Pa. 178, p. 193.
Barker v. Coleman, 35 Ala. 221, p. 80.
Barker v. Comins, 110 Mass. 477, p. 93.
Barnett v. Allen, 3 H. & N. 376, p. 165.
Baron De Bode's Case, 8 Ad. & Ellis (N. s.), 208, p. 127.
Barrick v. City of Detroit, 1 Mich. N. P. 135, p. 241.
Barrows v. Downs, 9 R. I. 453, p. 125.
Barkman v. Hopkins, 11 Ark. 168, pp. 123, 125.
Barnes v. Ingalls, 39 Ala. 193, pp. 163, 164.
Barnard v. Kellogg, 10 Wall. 383, p. 163.
Barlow v. Lambert, 28 Ala. 704, pp. 168, 169.
Barber v. Merriam, 11 Allen, 322, pp. 71, 75, 98.
Bates v. State, 63 Ala. 30, p. 237.
Baxter v. Abbott, 7 Gray, 71, pp. 70, 88.
Bayly v. Chubb, 16 Gratt. 284, p. 120.
Beaubien v. Cicotte, 13 Mich. 459, p. 92.
Bearss v. Copley, 10 N. Y. 95, pp. 8, 26.
Beauchamp v. Mudd, Hardin 163, p. 121.
Beach v. O'Riley, 14 W. Va. 55, p. 184.
Beaumont v. Perkins, 1 Phill. 78, pp. 189, 198.
Beckwith v. Sydebotham, 1 Camp. 117, p. 142.
Bedell v. Long Island R. R. Co, 44 N. Y. 367, pp. 216, 221.
Bedford v. Flowers, 7 Humph. 242, p. 169.
Beecher v. Denniston, 13 Gray, 354, p. 222.
Beekman v. Platner, 15 Barb. 550, p. 222.
Bellefontaine, etc. R. R. Co. v. Bailey, 11 Ohio St. 333, p. 146.
Beller v. Jones, 22 Ark. 92, p. 91.
Bellinger v. N. Y. Cent. R. R. Co., 23 N. Y. 42, p. 44.
Belnir v. the C. & N. W. R. R. Co., 43 Iowa, 667, p. 14.
Bennett v. Bennett, Deady, 299, p. 120.
Bennett v. Fail, 26 Ala. 605, pp. 77, 78.
Benedict v. City of Fon du Lac, 44 Wis. 496, pp. 4, 18, 159.

(b)

TABLE OF CASES CITED.

Benkard v. Babcock, 2 Robt. 175, p. 215.
Benaway v. Conyne, 3 Chand. 244, p 53.
Benson v. McFadden, 50 Ind. 431, p. 6.
Berckman v. Berckman, 16 N. J. Eq., 122, p. 4.
Berthon v. Loughman, 2 Starkie, 258, pp. 150, 151.
Berg v. Spink, 24 Minn. 138, p. 24.
Berry v. State, 10 Ga. 511, p. 91.
Berliner v. Waterloo, 14 Wis. 378, p. 120.
Bestor v. Roberts, 58 Ala. 331, p. 195.
Betts v. Clifford, 1 Warwick Lent Assizes, 1858, p. 261.
Beverly v. Williams, 4 Dev. & Batt. 236, p. 5.
Bierce v. Stocking, 11 Gray, 174, p. 115.
Biesenthrall v. Williams, 1 Duv. 330, p. 131.
Bills v. City of Ottumwa, 35 Iowa, 109, pp. 9, 153.
Birch v. Ridgway, 1 Fost. & Fin. 270, p. 190.
Bird v. Commonwealth, 21 Gratt. 800, pp. 2, 68 133.
Bishop v. State, 30 Ala. 34, p. 195.
Bishop v. Spining, 38 Ind. 113, pp. 39, 44.
Bissell v. Ryan, 23 Ill. 570, p. 169.
Bissell v. Wert, 35 Ind. 54, p. 211.
Bitner v. Bitner, 65 Penn. St. 347, p. 70.
Bixby v. Montpelier, etc. R. R. Co., 49 Vt. 125, p. 147.
Blackman v. Johnson, 35 Ala. 252, p. 81.
Blackwell v. State, 13 Rep. 271, p. 104.
Blanchard v. New Jersey Steamboat Co., 3 N. Y. Sup. Ct. 771, p. 144.
Blake v. People, 73 N. Y. 586, p. 6.
Blizzard v. Applegate, 61 Ind. 371, p. 223.
Blood v. Light, 31 Cal. 115, 171.
Blodgett Paper Co. v. Farmer, 41 N. H. 401, p. 173.
Blumenthall v. Roll, 24 Mo. 113, p. 158.
Board of Commissioners v. Chambers, 75 Ind. 403, p. 224.
Boardman v. Woodman, 47 N. H. 120, pp. 23, 25, 41, 86.
Bock v. Lauman, 12 Harris, 435, p. 139.
Bodfish v. Fox, 23 Me. 90, p. 169.
Boehfinck v. Schneider, 3 Esp. 58, p. 127.
Boies v. McAllister, 12 Mo. 310, pp. 81, 95.
Boingardner v. Andrews, 55 Iowa, 638, p. 40.
Booth v. Cleveland, 74 N. Y. 27, p. 172.
Borland v. Walwrath, 33 Iowa, 133, p. 63.
Boston, etc. R. R. Co. v. Montgomery, 119 Mass. 114, p. 246.
Boston, etc. R. R. Co. v. Old Colony, etc. R. R. Co., 3 Allen, 142, p. 211.
Bowditch v. Soltyk, 99 Mass. 138, p. 121.
Bowen v. Bowen, 74 Ind. 470, p. 226.
Bowman v. Woods, 4 G. Greene, 441, p. 238.
Bowles v. Eddy, 33 Ark. 645, p. 123.
Boydston v. Giltner, 3 Oreg. 118, pp. 97, 98.
Brabo v. Martin, 3 La. R. 177, p. 40.
Brabbitts v. Chicago & N. W. R. R. Co. 38 Wis. 289, p. 146.
Bragg v. Colwell, 19 Ohio, 412, pp. 196, 198.
Bradford v. Cooper, 1 La. Ann. 325, p. 118.
Brainard v. Boston, etc. R. R. Co., 12 Gray, 407, p. 229.
Brackett v. Norton, 4 Conn, 417, p. 121.
Branch, etc. R. R. Co. v. Nichols, 24 Kans. 242, p. 223.
Brantley v. Swift, 24 Ala. 390, p. 157.
Bremer v. Freeman, 10 Moore P. C. 306, p. 139.

Brehm v. Gt. Western R. R. Co. 34 Barb. 256, p. 59.
Briggs v. Briggs, 20 Mich. 34, p. 73.
Briggs v. Morgan, 3 Philim. 325, p. 100.
Bristol County Savings Bank v. Keavy, 128 Mass. 298, pp. 220, 230.
Brimhall v. Van Campen, 8 Minn. 13, p. 122.
Bristow v. Sequeville, 5 Exch. 275, p. 137.
Brown v. Brown, 1 Hagg. 523, pp. 100, 101.
Brown v. Brown, 10 Met, 573, p. 167.
Brown v. Chenoworth, 51 Tex. 469, p. 49.
Brown v. Foster, 113 Mass. 136, p. 163.
Brown v. Huffard, 69 Mo. 305, pp. 44, 223.
Brown v. Jackson, 2 Wash. C. C. 24, p. 169.
Brown v. Kennedy, 33 L. J. Ch. 71; 33 Beavan. 133, 40 J. & S. 217; p. 222.
Brown v. Leach, 107 Mass. 364, p. 174.
Brown v. Lester, Ga. Decis. Pt. 1, 77, p. 80.
Brown v. Mohawk & Hudson River R. R. Co., 1 How. Ct. App. Cas. 52, p. 23,
Brown v. Moore, 32 Mich. 254, p. 220.
Brown v. Prov. etc. R. R. Co., 12 R. I. 238, p. 208.
Brobston v. Cahill, 64 Ill. 358, p. 195.
Brookes v. Tichborne, 5 Exch. 929, p. 203.
Brooke v. Townshend, 7 Gill, 24, p. 92.
Bryant v. Kelton, 1 Tex. 434, p. 123.
Buchman v. State, 50 Ind. 1, pp. 254, 237.
Buckley v. Rice, 1 Plow. 125, p. 4.
Buffum v. Harris, 5 R. I. 250, pp. 2, 153, 159.
Buffum v. N. Y. Cen., etc. R. R. Co., 4 R. I. 221, pp. 203, 224.
Burdick v. Hunt, 43 Ind. 381, pp. 182, 195.
Burnham v. Mitchell, 34 Wis. 111, p. 92.
Burger v. Northern Pacific R. R. Co., 2 Minn. 343, pp. 204, 222.
Burns v. Welch, 8 Yerg. 117, p. 161.
Bush v. Jackson, 24 Ala. 273, p. 77.
Butcher v. Bank, 2 Kans. 70, p. 123.
Buxton v. Som. Pot. Works, 121 Mass. 446, pp. 37, 38.

C.

Cahwon v. Ring, 1 Clifford, 592, p. 163.
Caleb v. State, 39 Miss. 721, p. 85.
Calkins v. State, 14 Ohio St. 222, pp. 180, 190.
Callahan v. Stanley, 57 Ca'. 479, p. 166.
Campion v. Kille, 1 Mc. Carter, 229, p. 122.
Campbell v. Rickards, 2 Barn. & Ad. 840, pp. 8, 151.
Campbell v. Russe'l. 9 Iowa, 337, p. 166.
Cantling v. Hannibal etc. R. R. Co., 54 Mo. 385, pp. 209, 213.
Cannell v. Phoenix Ins. Co., 59 Me. 582, p. 161.
Carpenter v. Blake, 2 Lans. 206, pp. 34, 40, 44.
Carpenter v. Calvert, 83 Ill. 62, p. 270.
Carpenter v. Central Park R. R. Co., 11 Abb. Pr. 416. p. 148.
Carpenter v. Dexter, 8 Wall. 5 3, p. 122.
Carpenter v. Eastern Transportation Co., 71 N. Y. 574, pp. 38, 142.
Carpenter v. Wait, 11 Cush. 257, p. 155.
Carey v. Cincinnati etc. R. R. Co., 5 Iowa, 357. p. 121.
Carter v. Baker, 1 Sawyer, 512, p. 59.
Carter v. Boehm, 2 Burr. 1005, p. 151.
Carter v. Carter, 36 Mich. 207, p. 227.
Carter v. State, 2 Carter. 619, p. 238.
Carter v. Thurston, 58 N. H. 104, p. 212.

TABLE OF CASES CITED.

Cartwright v. Cartwright, 26 W. R. 684, p. 137.
Carew v. Johnston, 2 Sch. & Lef. 280, p. 92.
Castner v. Sliker, 33 N. J. Law, 95, S. C. Ibid. 507, pp. 5, 71.
Cavendish v. Troy, 41 Vt. 99, p. 9.
Central R. R. etc. v. Kelley, 58 Ga. 1 7, pp. 4, 211.
Central R. R. Co. v. Mitchell, 63 Ga. 173, pp. 30, 158.
Central Branch etc. R. R. Co. v. Nichols, 24 Kans. 242, p. 223.
Central Pacific R. R. Co. v. Pearson, 35 Cal. 247, p. 47.
Chaurand v. Angerstein, Peake N. P. C. 61, pp 8, 151.
Chamboret v. Cagnet, 3 J. & S. 474. p. 214.
Chamness v. Chamness, 53 Ind. 304. p. 213.
Champ v. Commonwealth. 2 Met. 18, p. 19
Chanoine v. Fowler, 3 Wend. 173, p. 131.
Chandler v. Grieves, 2 H. Bl. 606, p. 119.
Chandler v. Jamaica Pond Aqueduct, 125, Mass. 544. pp. 23, 159.
Chandler v. LeBarron, 45 Me. 534, p. 201.
Cha ce v. Indianapolis etc. Co., 32 Ind. 472, pp. 195, 136, 268.
Chase v. Lincoln, 31 Mass. 237, p. 90.
Chamberlain v. Maitland, 5 B. Monroe, 448, p. 131.
Cheek v. State, 38 Ala. 227, p. 151.
Chicago etc. R. R. Co. v. George, 19 Ill. 510, p. 80.
Chicago v. Greer, 9 Wall. 726, p. 161.
Chicago & Alton R. R. Co. v. Springfield, & Northwestern R. R. Co., 67 Ill. 105, pp. 22, 37.
Chorley v. Bolcot, 4 Term. 317, p. 224.
Choteau v. Pierre, 9 Mo. 3, p. 120.
Choice v. State, 31 Ga. 424, pp. 59, 91, 92, 269.
Church v Hubbard, 2 Cranch 187, p. 123.
Churchill v. Price, 44 Wis. 542, p. 21..
Cilley v. Cilley, 34 Me. 162, p. 90.
Cincinnati etc, Mut. Ins. Co. v. May, 20 Ohio, 211, pp. 37, 44.
Cincinnati etc. R. R. Co. v. Smith, 22 Ohio St. 227, p. 147.
City of Brownsville v. Cavazos, 2 Woods, 293 p. 120.
City of Decatur v. Fisher, 63 Ill 2 1, p. 39.
City of Parsons v. Lindsay, 26 Kans. 426, pp. 8, 17.
City of Chicago, v. McGiven, 78 Ill. 347, pp. 8, 9, 13, 17.
City of Ripon v. Bittel, 30 Wis. 614.
City of Indianapolis v. Scott, 72 Ind. 196, p. 158.
City of Washington, 92 U. S. 31, pp. 144, 168.
Clapp v. Fullerton, 34 N. Y. 190, p. 94.
Claggett v. Easterday, 42 Md. 617, p. 156.
Clague v. Hodgson, 16 Minn. 329, p. 155.
Clark v. Baird, 9 N. Y. 183, p. 229.
Clark v. Bruce, 19 Hun. 274, pp. 11, 187.
Clark v. Detroit Locomotive Works, 32 Mich. 348, pp. 37, 145.
Clark v. Fisher, 1 Paige Ch. 171, pp. 13, 66.
Clark v. Rhodes, 49 Tenn. 206, p. 195.
Clark v. Rockland Water Power Co. 52 Me. 68, pp. 9, 216.
Clark v. Perham, 2 Atk. 337, p. 80.
Clark v. State, 12 Ohio, 483, pp. 91, 270.
Clark v. Willett, 35 Cal. 534, p. 171.
Clark v. Wyatt, 15 Ind. 271, p. 180.
Clary v. Clary, 2 Ired. 78, p. 94.

Clason v. City of Milwaukee, 30 Wis. 316, p. 159.
Clay v. Alderson, 10 W. Va. 49, p. 195.
Clay v. Robinson, 7 W. Va. 348, p. 195.
Claxton's Adm'r. v. Lexington, etc. R. R. Co., 13 Bush, 636, p. 170.
Cleveland, etc. R. R. Co. v. Ball, 5 Ohio St. 568, pp. 8, 212.
Cleveland, etc. R. R. Co. v. Perkins, 17 Mich. 296, p. 233.
Clegg v. Fields, 7 Jones, 37, p. 157.
Clegg v. Levy, 3 Camp. 166, p. 127.
Clifford v. Richardson, 18 Vt. 620. p. 12.
Clinton v. Howard, 42 Conn. 294, p. 6.
Clussman v. Merkel, 3 Bosw. 402, p. 140.
Cobb v. City of Boston, 109 Mass. 438, pp. 208, 218.
Cobbett v. Kilminster, 4 Fos. & Fin. 490, pp. 190, 204.
Coburn v. Harvey, 18 Wis. 147, p. 120.
Cocks v. Purday, 2 C. & K. 269, p. 120.
Coffee v. Neely, 2 Heisk. 311, p. 122.
Cole v. Clark, 3 Wis. 323, p. 8.
Collender v. Dinsmore, 55 N. Y. 200, pp. 166, 168.
Collins v Godefroy, 1 Barn. & Adol. 930, p. 262.
Colt v. People, 1 Parker Cr. Cas. 611, p. 84.
Collier v. Simpson, 5 C. & P. 73, pp. 29, 211.
Colvill v. St. Paul, etc. R. R. Co., 19 Minn. 283, p. 212.
Commonwealth v. Brown, 14 Gray. 419, p. 95.
Commonwealth v. Brown, 121 Mass. 69, p. 95.
Commonwealth v. Cary, 2 Pick. 46, p. 205.
Commonwealth v. Choate, 105 Mass. 451, p, 171.
Commonwealth v. Dorsey, 103 Mass. 412, p. 6.
Commonwealth v. Fairbanks, 2 Allen, 511, p. 90.
Commonwealth v. Knowlton, 2 Mass. 534, p. 120.
Commonwealth v. Lenox, 3 Brew. 249, p. 83.
Commonwealth v. Mullins, 2 Allen, 296, p. 40.
Commonwealth v. Piper, 120 Mass. 185, p. 84.
Commonwealth v. Pope, 103 Mass. 440, p. 6.
Commonwealth v. Pomeroy, 117 Mass. 148, p. 89.
Commonwealth v. Rich, 14 Gray, 335, pp. 79, 86.
Commonwealth v. Rogers, 7 Met. 500, p. 86.
Commonwealth v. Sturtivant, 117 Mass. 122, pp. 6, 111, 114.
Commonwealth v. Timothy, 8 Gray, 480, p. 5.
Commonwealth v. Twitchell, 1 Brews. 562, p. 113.
Commonwealth v. Webster, 5 Cush. 295, pp. 50, 182.
Commonwealth v. Wilson, 1 Gray, 337, p. 240.
Commonwealth v. Williams, 105 Mass. 62, p. 5.
Comparet v. Jernegan, 5 Blackf. 375, p. 123.
Comstock v. Smith, 20 Mich. 338, p. 232.
Condit v. Blackwell, 19 N. J. Eq. 193, p. 132.
Conn. M. L. Ins. Co. v. Ellis, Adm'r. 89 Ill. 516, p. 245.

Conhocton Stone Road Co. v. Buffalo,
  etc. R. R. Co., 10 N. Y. 523, p. 45.
Continental Insurance Co. v. Delpench,
  82 Pa. St. 225, p. 4.
Continental Insurance Co. v. Horton,
  24 Mich. 173, p. 213.
Consolidated Real Estate & Fire Ins.
  Co. v. Cashow, 41 Md. 59, p. 125.
Concord R. R. Co. v. Greely, 3 Fos. 237,
  p. 13.
Cook v. Castner, 9 Cush. 266, p. 144.
Cooke v. England, 27 Md. 4, p. 157.
Cook v. State, 24 N. J. Law, 844, pp. 13,
  15, 94.
Cooper v. Bockett, 4 Moore P. C. 433, p.
  183.
Cooper v. Cent. R. R. Co., 44 Iowa, 140,
  p. 146.
Cooper v. Randall, 59 Ill. 317, pp. 212,
  213.
Cooper v. State, 23 Tex. 336, pp. 19, 77, 79,
  82.
Cooper v. State, 53 Miss. 393, p. 213, 222.
Corning v. Barden, 12 How. 252, p. 163.
Cornish v. Farm, etc. Fire Ins. Co., 74
  N. Y. 295, p. 151.
Corlis v. Little, 13 N. J. Law, p. 5, 232.
Corbett v. Underwood, 83 Ill. 324, p. 163.
Corby Ex'r. v. Weddle, 57 Mo. 452, p. 195.
Cottrill v. Myrick, 12 Me. 222, pp. 8, 173.
County of Cook v. Harms, 10 Bradw. 24.
Coughlin v. Poulson, 2 McArthur, 308,
  p. 88.
Covey v. Campbell, 52 Ind. 158, p. 223.
Cowan v. Beall, 1 McArthur, 270, p. 267.
Cowley v. People, 83 N. Y. 464, pp. 35, 9d.
Crane v. Crane, 33 Vt. 15, p. 91
Craig v. Gerrish, 58 N. H. (25 Alb. Law
  J. 498), p. 82.
Crawford v. State, 2 Ind. 132, p. 206.
Crawford v. Williams, 48 Iowa, 249, p.
  239.
Crawford v. Wolf, 29 Iowa, 168, p. 208.
Cresswell v. Jackson, 3 Fos. & Fin. 24,
  p. 190.
Crouse v. Holman, 19 Ind. 30, p. 223.
Crowell v. Kirk, 3 Dev. 358, p. 47.
Crowe Adm'r. v. Peters, 63 Mo. 429, p.
  91.
Cromwell v. Western Reserve Bank, 3
  Ohio St. 406, p. 8.
Culver v. Dwight, 6 Gray, 444, p. 6.
Cummins v. State, 58 Ala. 387, p. 4.
Cuneo v. Bessoni, 63 Ind. 524, pp. 59, 65.
Curtis v. Gano, 26 N. Y. 426, pp. 45, 160.
Curtis v. Martin, 1 Pennington, 290, p.
  122.
Curtis v. St. Paul, etc. R. R. Co., 20 Minn.
  28, p. 212.
Curry v. State, 5 Neb. 412, p. 81.

D.

Da'zell v. City of Davenport, 12 Iowa,
  437, p. 213.
Dalrymple v. Dalrymple, 2 Hagg. 54, p.
  127.
Dances v. Hale, 1 Otto, 13, p. 124
Dana v. Fiedler, 12 N. Y. 40, p. 167.
Daniells v. Aldrich, 42 Mich. 58, p. 40.
Daniels v. Hudson River Fire Ins. Co.,
  12 Cush. 416, p. 151-166.
Daniels v. Mosher, 2 Mich. 183, p. 4.
Danforth v. Reynolds, 1 Vt. 285, p. 123.
Dauphin v. United States, 6 Ct. of Cl.
  221, p. 135.
Davenport v. Ogg, 15 Kans. 363, p. 53.
Davis v. Mason, 4 Pick. 156, p. 157.
Davis v. Marlborough, 2 Swanst. 113, p.
  231.

Davis v. Rogers, 14 Ind. 424, p. 121.
Davis v. State, 38 Md. 15, pp. 8, 34, 84.
Davis v. State, 35 Ind. 496, pp. 23, 40, 46.
Dawson v. Callaway, 18 Ga. 573, p. 4.
Day v. State, 61 Ga. 667, p. 106.
Dean v. Aveling, 1 Robertson, 279, p. 100.
Dean v. McLean, 48 Vt. 4 2, p. 164.
DeArmand v. Neasmith, 32 Mich. 231; p.
  236.
Deer Creek, etc. Co. v. Salsaman, 67
  Penn. St. 415, p. 212.
Dekno v. Jopling, 1 Litt. 417, p. 120.
Delaware Steam Towboat Co. v. Starrs,
  69 Penn St. 36, pp. 23, 24, 58, 142.
Demerri t v. Randall, 116 Mass. 331, p.
  182.
Denton v. State, 1 Swan, 279, p. 75.
Dennis v. Weeks, 51 Ga. 24, p. 93.
Depue v. Place, 7 Penn. St. 429, p. 193.
Du Phue v. State, 44 Ala. 39, pp. 49, 68.
DeSobry v. Laistre, 2 H. & J. 191, p. 139.
Detwiler v. Groff, 10 Penn. St. 376, p. 156.
Detroit, etc. R. R. Co. v. Van Steinburgh,
  17 Mich. 99, p. 146.
Devenbagh v. Devenbagh, 5 Paige, 554,
  pp. 100, 101.
De Witt v. Baily, 17 N. Y. 344, p. 6.
Dewitt v. Barley, 9 N. Y, 371, pp. 99, 92.
Dexter v. Hall, 15 Wall. 9, pp. 37, 90.
Dickinson v. Barber, 9 Mass. 213, pp. 50,
  86.
Dickinson v. Fitchburg, 13 Gray, 546, pp.
  2, 39, 51.
Dickinson v. Gay, 7 Allen, 29, p. 163.
Dickie v. Vaubleck, 5 Redf. 231, p. 40.
Dieken v. Johnson, 7 Ga. 484, p. 91.
Dillard v. State, 58 Miss. 368, pp. 8, 13, 18,
  113.
Dillebar v. Home Life Ins. Co. (N. Y.),
  14 Cent. L. J. 158, p. 40.
Di Sora v. Phillips, 10 H. L. Cas. 624, p.
  165.
Division of Howard County, 15 Kans.
  194, p. 120.
Dixon v. Dunham, 14 Ill. 324, p. 169.
Dodge v. Coffin, 15 Kans. 277, p. 123.
Doe v. Eslava, 11 Ala. 1024, p. 120.
Doe v. Suckermore, 5 Ad. & El. 703, p.
  182.
Doe v. Tarver, R. & M. 141, p. 180.
Doe v. Wilson, 10 Moore P. C. 502, p. 204.
Dolph v. Barney, 5 Oregon, 191, p. 120.
Dole v. Johnson, 50 N. H. 452, pp. 25, 33,
  243.
Dolz v. Morris, 17 N. Y. Sup. Ct. 2 2, p. 37.
Donaldson v. the Mississippi, etc. R. R.
  Co., 18 Iowa, 291, pp. 231, 236.
Dorsey v. Dorsey, 5 J. J. Marsh. 280, p.
  128.
Dorsey v. Warfield, 7 Md. 65, p. 92.
Doster v. Brown, 25 Ga. 24, p. 157.
Dougherty v. Snyder, 15 S. & R. 84, p. 134.
Dove v. State, 52 Tenn. 348, p. 46.
Downs v. Sprague, 1 Abbott's Ct. of
  App. Decis. 550, p. 167.
Doyle v. N. Y. Eye & Ear Infirmary, 80
  N. Y. 631, p. 93.
Drake v. Glover, 30 Ala. 382, p. 121.
Drucker Simon, 4 Daly, 53, p. 220.
Du Bois v. Baker, 30 N. Y. 555, pp. 179,
  182, 183, 196.
Duchess Di Liora's Case, 10 Ill. Cases,
  640, p. 138.
Duchess of Kingston's Case. Hargr.
  State Trials, 243, p. 70.
Dunham's Appeal, 27 Conn. 193, p. 44.
Dunham v. Simons, 3 Hill, 609, p. 211.
Duntz v. Van Beuren, 12 N. Y. Sup. Ct.
  648, p. 81.
Durrell v. Hederly, Holt's N. P. Cases,
  283, p. 151.

TABLE OF CASES CITED. xiii

Dutcher v. Culver, 24 Minn. 584, p. 120.
Dyer v. Morris, 4 Mo. 214, p. 53.
Dyer v. Smith, 12 Conn. 384, p. 121.

E.

Eagle & Phœnix Manufacturing Co. v. Brown, 58 Ga. 240, p. 227.
Eagan v. Cowan, 30 Law Times, 223, p. 190.
Earl Nelson v. Lord Bridport, 8 Beav. 527, pp. 128, 138.
Eastman v. Amoskeag Manufacturing Co. 44 N. H. 143, p. 5.
East Pennsylvania R. R. Co. v. Hottenstine, 47 Penn. St. 30, p. 222.
Eaton v. Smith, 20 Pick. 156, p. 166.
Ebos v. State, 34 Ark. 520, pp. 19, 81.
Eborn v. Zimpleman, 47 Tex. 503, pp. 198, 201.
Eccles v. Bates, 26 Ala. 675, pp. 76, 79.
Edelin v. Sanders, Exr., 8 Md. 118, p. 184.
Edington v. Ætna Life Ins. Co., 77 N. Y. 564, p. 73.
Edie v. East India Co., 2 Burr, 1226, p. 119.
Edmonds v. City of Boston, 108 Mass. 535, p. 204.
Eggers v. Eggers, 57 Ind. 461, pp. 41, 65.
Eggier v. People, 56 N. Y. 642, p. 82.
Elfelt v. Smith, 1 Minn. 126, p. 224.
Ellingwood v. Bragg, 52 N. H. 488, p. 4.
Eltou v. Larkins, 5 C. & P. 385, p. 151.
Elting v. Sturtevant, 41 Conn. 176, p. 226.
Ely v. James, 123 Mass. 36, p. 139.
Emery v. Berry, 8 Foster, 473, p. 123.
Emerson v. Lowell Gas Light Co., 6 Allen, 146, pp. 34, 79.
Ennis v. Smith, 14 How. 400, p. 123.
Enright v. Railroad Co., 33 Cal. 230, p. 175.
Erd v. Chicago, etc. R. R. Co., 41 Wis. 64, p. 229.
Erickson v. Smith, 2 Abb. App. Decis., 64, p. 97.
Errisman v. Errisman, 25 Ill., 136, p. 54.
Erwin v. Clark, 13 Mich. 10, p. 164.
Estate of Brooks, 54 Cal. 471, p. 91.
Estate of Toomes, 54 Cal. 510, p. 87.
Evans v. Commercial Ins. Co., 6 R. I. 47, p. 166.
Evans v. Knight, 1 Add. 239, p. 260.
Evans v. People, 12 Mich. 27, pp. 6, 14, 80, 82.
Evans v. Reynolds, 32 Ohio St. 163, p. 122.
Evansville R. R. Co. v. Fitzpatrick, 10 Ind. 120, pp. 8, 211.
Evansville R. R. Co. v. Young, 28 Ind. 516, p. 163.
Exchange Bank v. Coleman, 1 W. Va. 69, p. 169.
Ex parte Dement, 53 Ala. 389, pp. 259, 261.
Ex parte Thistlewood, 19 Vesey, 245, p. 231.
Ex parte Whitehead, 1 Merivale, 127, p. 231.
Eyerman v. Sheehan, 52 Mo. 221, pp. 7, 171.

F.

Fairchild v. Buscomb, 35 Vt. 415, pp. 42, 47, 50, 70.
Fairchild v. M. C. R. R. Co., 8 Bradw. 591, p. 226.
Fairbank v. Hughson, 13 Rep. 8, p. 24.
Farrell v. Brennan, 32 Mo. 328, p. 47.
Farr v. Swan, 2 Pa. St. 245, p. 157.

Feabert v. Turst, Pre. Ch. 207, p. 121.
Fenwick v. Bell, 1 Car. & Kir. 311, p. 142.
Ferguson v. Hubbell, 26 Hun, 250, pp. 17, 154.
Ferguson v. Stafford, 53 Ind. 162, pp. 228, 229.
Fielder v. Collier, 13 Ga. 496, p. 91.
Filer v. N. Y. Cent. R. R. Co., 49 N. Y. 42, pp. 40, 79.
First Baptist Church v. Brooklyn Fire Ins Co., 28 N. Y. 154, p. 166.
First National Bank of Omaha v. Lierman, 5 Neb. 247, p. 196.
First National Bank v. Robert, 41 Mich. 709, pp. 195, 204.
Fish v. Dodge, 4 Denio, 311, p. 211.
Fitzgerald v. Hayward, 50 Mo. 516, p. 4.
Fleming v. Delaware, etc. Canal Co., 8 Hun, 358, p. 21.
Fletcher v. Seekel, 1 R. I. 267, p. 59.
Florey's Exrs. v. Florey, 24 Ala. 247, p. 91.
Flynn v. Wohl, 10 Mo. App. 582, p. 233.
Flynt v. Bodenhamer, 80 N. C. 205, pp. 23, 58, 62, 79, 268.
Fogg v. Dennis, 3 Humph. 47, pp. 195, 204.
Folkes v. Chadd, 3 Douglass, 175, pp. 8, 139, 163.
Foltz v. State, 33 Ind. 215, p. 6.
Forbes v. Caruthers, 3 Yeates, 527, pp. 4, 9, 157.
Forbes v. Howard, 4 R. I. 366, p. 208.
Forgery v. First National Bank, 66 Ind. 123, pp. 23, 27, 58, 195.
Forsyth v. Preer, 62 Ala. 443, p. 121.
Ford v. Tirrell, 9 Gray, 401, p. 162.
Foster v. Brooks, 6 Ga. 290, p. 91.
Foster v. Taylor, 2 Overton, 191, p. 122.
Foster's Will, 34 Mich. 21, p. 267.
Foster v. Ward, 75, Ind. 594, p. 213.
Fountain v. Brown, 38 Ala. 72, p. 81.
Frank v. Chemical National Bank, 37 N. Y. Sup. Ct. 30, p. 180.
Frantz v. Ireland, 66 Barb. 386, p. 172.
Fraser v. Tupper, 29 Vt. 409, pp. 17, 154.
Frazer v. Jennison, 42 Mich. 206, pp. 6, 40, 55, 250.
Frankfort, etc. R. R. Co. v. Windsor, 51 Ind. 238, p. 228.
Freemoult v. Dedire, 1 P. Wms. 430, p. 121.
Freeman v. People, 4 Denio, 9, p. 69.
Firth v. Barker, 2 Johns. 334, p. 169.
Frost v. Blanchard, 97 Mass. 155, p. 4.
Fulton v. Hood, 34 Penn. St. 365, p. 183.

G.

G. — v. G. — 2 Prob. & Div. 287, pp. 100, 102.
Galena, etc. R. R. Co. v. Haslem, 73 Ill. 494, p. 229.
Gartside v. Conn. Mut. Life Ins. Co., 8 Mo. App. 593, p. 74.
Garfield v. Kirk, 65 Barb. 464, p. 223.
Garrett's Case, 71 N. C. 58, p. 104.
Gardner v. Lewis, 7 Gill, 379, p. 123.
Gardner v. People, 6 Parker's Cr. Cas. 155, p. 64.
Gassenheimer v State, 52 Ala. 314, p. 5.
Gauntlett v. Whitworth, 2 C. & K. 720, p. 220.
Gavick v. Pacific R. R. Co. 49 Mo. 274, pp. 13, 14.
Gaylor's Appeal, 43 Conn. 82, p. 140.
Getchell v. Hill, 21 Minn. 464, p. 42.
Geylin v. Villerol, 2 Houston, 311, p. 165.
Gibson v. Budd, 32 L. J. Ex. 182, S. C. 2 H. & C. 92, p. 224.

TABLE OF CASES CITED

Gibson v. Cincinnati Enquirer, 5 Cent. Law J. 380, p. 165.
Gibson v. Gibson, 9 Yerg. 329, pp. 47, 86, 90
Gilbert v. Kennedy, 22 Mich. 117, p. 220.
Gilman v. Gard, 29 Ind. 291, p. 226.
Gilman v. Town of Strafford, 50 Vt. 725, p. 42.
Goldstein v. Black, 50 Cal. 464, pp. 180, 181.
Goldsmith v. Sawyer, 46 Cal. 209, p. 113.
Goodtitle v. Braham, 4 Term. 497, p. 182.
Goodyear v. Vosburgh, 63 Barb. 154, p. 182.
Gordon v. Price, 10 Ired. 385, p. 206.
Gossler v. Eagle Sugar Refinery, 103 Mass. 331, pp. 24, 115.
Gotlieb v. Hartman, 3 Col. 53, p. 39.
Graves v. Keaton, 3 Coldw. 8, p. 120.
Grand Rapids, etc. R. R. Co. v Martin, 41 Mich. 672, p. 66.
Grattan v. Metropolitan Life Ins. Co. 31 N. Y. Sup. Ct. 43, p. 73.
Grant v. Thompson' 4 Conn. 203, pp. 88, 90.
Great Western R. R. Co. v. Haworth, 39 Ill. 349, p. 161.
Green v. Aspinwall, 1 City Hall Recorder, 14, p. 236.
Green v. City of Chicago, 97 Ill. 372, p. 228.
Grigsby v. Clear Lake Wa'er Works Co., 40 Cal. 396, p. 159.
Griffith v. Spratley, 1 Cox Ch. 389, p. 231.
Griffin v. Town of Willow, 43 Wis. 509, pp. 4, 170.
Gueting v. State, 66 Ind. 94, pp. 40, 86.
Guiterman v. Liverpool, etc. Steamship Co., 83 N. Y. 358, pp. 37, 39, 44, 143.
Gulf City Ins. Co. v. Stephens, 52 Ala. 121, p. 23.

H.

H. v. P. 3 Prob. & Div. 126, pp. 100, 103.
Haas v. Choussard, 17 Tex. 592, p. 156.
Haggerty v. Brooklyn, etc. R. R. Co. 61 N. Y. 624, pp. 43, 48.
Hagadorn v. Connecticut Mut. Life Ins. Co. 29 N. Y. Sup. Ct. 251, pp. 42, 46.
Haight v. Kimbak, 51 Iowa, 13, p. 214.
Hall v. Costello, 48 N. H. 179, p. 134.
Hale v. Ross, 3 N. J. Law, 373, p. 132.
Haley v. State, 63 Ala. 89, p. 166.
Hamel v. Panet, 3 Quebec Law R. 173, p. 183.
Hames v. Brownlee, 63 Ala. 277, p. 4.
Hamilton v. Des Moines Valley R. R. Co. 36 Iowa, 31, p. 9.
Hamilton v. Nickerson, 13 Allen, 351, p. 169.
Hammond v. Woodman, 41 Me. 177, p. 155.
Hand v. Brookline, 126 Mass. 324, pp. 24, 34, 171.
Handley v. Gandy, 28 Tex. 211, p. 193.
Hanover Water Co. v. Ashland Iron Co. 84 Penn. St 284, p, 229.
Harnett v. Gurvey, 66 N. Y. 641, pp. 40, 222.
Harris v. Panama R. R. Co., 3 Bosw. 1, p. 241.
Harrison v. Harrison, 4 Moore P. C. 96, p. 103.
Hart v. Hudson River Bridge Co., 84 N, Y. 56, pp. 13, 158.
Hart v. Vidal, 8 Cal. 56, p. 223.
Hartford Protection Ins. Co. v. Harmer, 2 Ohio St. 452, p. 9, 149, 150.
Hartman v. Keystone, 21 Penn. St. 466, pp. 150, 151, 232.

Harland v. Lilienthal, 53 N. Y. 438, p. 223.
Hardy v. Merrill, 56 N. H. 227, pp. 90, 91.
Harford v. Morris 2 Hagg. 430, p. 27.
Harris v. Panama R. R. Co., 3 Bosw. 7, p. 117.
Harris v. Rathbun, 2 Abbott, 328, p. 166.
Harvey v. State, 40 Ind. 516, p. 219.
Haskins v. Hamilton Mut. Ins. Co., 5 Gray, 432, pp. 218, 219.
Hawkins v. Warren, 115 Mass. 514, p. 168.
Haskell v. Mitchell, 53 Mo. 466, p. 212.
Hastings v. Rider, 99 Mass. 625, p. 90.
Hastings v. Steamer Uncle Sam, 10 Cal. 341, p. 9.
Hathorn v. King, 8 Mass. 371, p. 80.
Hathaway's Adm'rs. v. National Life Ins. Co., 48 Vt. 333, pp. 40, 46, 70.
Haulenbeck v. Cronkright, 23 N. J. Eq. 413, p. 230.
Haverhill Loan Assoc. v. Cronin, 4 Allen, 141, p. 50.
Haver v. Tenney, 36 Iowa, 80, p. 161.
Hawkins v. Grimes, 13 B. Monr. 267, pp. 193, 195.
Hawkins v. State, 25 Ga. 207, p. 4.
Hawes v. N. E. Ins. Co., 2 Curtis, 229, p. 150.
Haycock v. Greup, 57 Penn. St. 438, p. 193.
Hayward v. Knapp, 23 Minn. 430, p. 164.
Haywood v. Rodgers, 4 East, 590, p. 151.
Hayes v. Ottawa, etc. R. R. Co., 54 Ill. 373, p. 229.
Hayes v. Wells, 34 Md. 513, p. 4.
Haynes v. Mosher, 15 How. Pr. 216, p. 253.
Hazleton v. Union Bank Co., 32 Wis. 34, p. 195.
Hazzard v. Vickery, 78 Ill. 64, p. 195.
Head v. Hargrave, 14 Cent. Law J. 388, pp. 61, 222.
Heald v. Thing, 45 Me. 392, pp. 1, 22, 34, 75, 267.
Hearne v. New England Mut. Ins. Co., 3 Clifford C. C. 318, p. 166.
Heath v. Gilson, 3 Oregon, 67, p. 97.
Heath v. Watts Prerog. 1 Cases in Eng. Ecc. Cts. 48, note 3, p. 189.
Heathcote v. Paignon, 2 Brown's Ch. 167, pp. 230, 231.
Heberd v. Myers, 5 Ind. 94 p. 123.
Hemphill v. Bank of Alabama, 6 Sm. & M. 144, p. 122.
Hempstead v. Reed, 6 Conn. 480, p. 121.
Hess v. Ohio, 5 Ohio. 6. p. 205.
Hewlett v. Wood, 55 N. Y. 635, p. 94.
Hicks v. Person, 19 Ohio, 426, p. 186.
Hickman v. State, 38 Tex. 191, p. 195.
Higgins v. Carlton, 28 Md. 115, pp. 4, 9.
Higgins v. Dewey, 107 Mass. 494, pp. 17, 154.
Highee v. Guardian Mut. Life Ins. Co., 66 Barb. 412, p. 71.
Highie v. Guardian Mut. Life Ins. Co.. 53 N. Y. 603, p. 80.
Hill v. Lafayette Ins. Co., 2 Mich. 476, pp. 9, 151.
Hill v. Portland, etc. R. R. Co., 55 Me. 444, pp. 37, 147.
Hill v. Sturgeon, 28 Mo. 323, p. 145.
Hills v. Home Ins. Co. 129 Mass. 345, pp. 22, 221.
Hinckley v. Kersting, 21 Ill. 247, p. 221.
Hinds v. Harbon, 58 Ind. 124, p. 175.
Hitchcock v. Clendinan, 12 Beav. 534, p. 130.
Hoard v. Peck, 56 Barb. 202, pp. 39, 77.
Houre v. Silverlock, 12 Ad. & El. 624, p. 165.
Hobby v. Dana, 17 Barb. 111, p. 151.

TABLE OF CASES CITED.

Hobbs v. Memphis, etc. R. R. Co., 56 Tenn. 874, p. 122.
Hoener v. Koch, 84 Ill. 408, pp. 97, 99.
Hoes v. Van Alstyne, 20 Ill. 202, pp. 123, 124.
Hoitt v. Moulton, 1 Forster, 586, p. 209.
Holliman v. Cabanne, 43 Mo. 568, p. 4.
Holman v. King, 7 Mer. 384, p. 139.
Holden v. Robinson, 63 Me. 216, p. 4.
Hollenbeck v. Rowley, 8 Allen, 473, p. 202.
Homer v. Dorr, 10 Mass. 26, p. 169.
Homer v. Taunton, 5 H. & N. 661, p. 163.
Hopper v. Commonwealth, 6 Gratt. 684, p. 53.
Hopper v. Ludlum, 41 N. J. Law, 182, p. 222.
Hopper v. Moore, 5 Jones Law, 130, pp. 125, 139.
Hook v. Stovall, 30 Ga. 418, p. 7.
Hook v. Stovall, 26 Ga. 704, p. 79.
Horne v. Williams, 12 Ind. 324, pp. 47, 51.
Hoslord v. Nichols, 1 Paige, 220, pp. 121, 122.
Hough v. Cook, 69 Ill. 581, pp. 208, 221.
House v. Fort, 4, Blackf. 293, p. 116.
Houston, etc. R. R. Co. v. Knapp, 51 Tex. 592, pp. 212, 218.
Houston, etc. R. R. Co. v. Smith, 52 Tex. 178, p. 5.
Hovey v. Chase, 52 Me. 304, p. 40.
Hovey v. Sawyer, 5 Allen, 554, pp. 13, 14.
Howard v. Patrick, 43 Mich. 128, p. 204.
Howard v. Providence, 6 R. I. 516, pp. 24, 58.
Howell v. Taylor, 18 N. Y. Sup. Ct. 214, p. 94.
Hoyt v. Long Island R. R. Co., 57 N. Y. 678, p. 147.
Hoyt v. McNeil, 13 Minn. 390, p. 122.
Hubble v. Osborn, 31 Ind. 249, p. 54.
Hudson v. Draper, 5 Fisher's Pat. Cas. 256, p. 163.
Hudson v. State, 61 Ala. 334, p. 229.
Huffman v. Click, 77 N. C. 55, pp. 241, 244.
Huff v. Nims, 11 Neb. 364, p. 204.
Humphries v. Johnson, 20 Ind. 190, pp. 8, 59, 64.
Hunt's Heirs v. Hunt, 3 B. Monr. 577, p. 91.
Hunt v. Lowell Gaslight Co., 8 Gray, 169, p. 38.
Hunt v. State, 9 Tex. Ct. of App. 166, pp. 39, 74.
Hurst v. The C. R. I. & P. R. R. Co., 49 Iowa, 76, pp. 40, 74.
Hynes v. McDermott, 82 N. Y. 41, pp. 132, 198, 199.
Hyde v. Woolfok, 1 Iowa, 159, pp. 27, 181, 198.

I.

Illinois Cent. R. R. Co. v. Sutton, 42 Ill. 438, p. 75.
Inge v. Murphy, 10 Ala. 885, p. 139.
Ingham v. Hart, 11 Ohio 255, p. 139.
Inglebright v. Hammond, 19 Ohio, 337, p. 169.
Inhabitants of West Newbury v. Chase, 5 Gray, 421, p. 212.
Innerarity v. Mims, 1 Ala. 660, p. 123.
In re Cliquot's Champagne, 3 Wall. 114, p. 233.
In re Fennerstein's Champagne, 3 Wall. 145, p. 233.
In re Springer, 4 Penn. Law J. 275, pp. 50, 59.
In re Todd, 19 Beav. 582, p. 135.

In the Goods of Hindmarch, 1 P. & M. 307, p. 184.
In the Matter of Roelker, 1 Sprague, 276, p. 237.
Irving v. McLean, 4 Blackf. 52, p. 121.
Isabella v. Peot, 2 La. Ann. 387, p. 123.

J.

Jacob's Case, 5 Jones, 259, p. 104.
Jackson v. Beling, 21 La. Ann. 377, p. 169.
Jackson v. Edwards, 7 Paige Ch. 386, pp. 231, 236.
Jackson v. N. Y. Cent. R. R. Co., 2 Sup. Ct. 653, p. 223.
James v. Bostwick, Wright, 142, p. 166.
James v. Hodsden, 47 Vt. 127, p. 160.
Jamieson v. Drinkald, 12 Moore, 148, pp. 37, p. 142.
Jarrett v. Jarrett, 11 W. Va. 627, p. 269.
Jarvis v. Furman, 25 Hun, N. Y 393, p. 230.
Jefferson Ins. Co. v. Cotheal, 7 Wend. 72, p. 151.
Jeffersonville R. R. Co. v. Lanham, 27 Ind. 171, pp. 147, 172.
Jerry v. Townshend, 9 Md. 145, p. 39.
Jevne v. Osgood, 57 Ill. 310, p. 222.
Jewell v. Center, 25 Ala. 498, p. 119.
Jewett v. Draper, 6 Allen, 434, p. 184.
Joe v. State, 6 Fla. 591, p. 110.
Johnson v. Chambers, 12 Ind. 112, p. 121.
Johnson v. State, 2 Ind. 652, p. 53.
Johnson v. Thompson, 72 Ind. 167, pp. 58, 220.
Jonau v. Ferrand, 3 Rob. 366, pp. 47, 222.
Jones v. Finch, 37 Miss. 468, p. 205.
Jones v. Laney, 2 Tex. 342, p. 122.
Jones v. Maffett, 5 S. & R. 523, pp. 131, 134.
Jones v. State, 11 Ind. 357, p. 206.
Jones v. State, 71 Ind. 66, p. 16.
Jones v. Tucker, 41 N. H. 547, pp. 2, 8, 10, 24, 25, 79.
Jones v. Trustees, Ind. R. 47, pp. 238, 249.
Jones v. White, 11 Humph. 268, pp. 2, 63, 79.
Jordan v. Osgood, 109 Mass, 457, p. 172.
Joyce v. Maine Ins. Co., 45 Me. 168, p. 151.
Judah v. McNamee, 3 Blackf. 269, p. 224.
Jumpertz v. People, 21 Ill. 374, p. 193.
Junction R. R. Co. v. Bank of Ashland, 12 Wall. 226, p. 120.
Jupitz v. People, 34 Ill. 516, p. 161.

K.

Kansas Pacific R. R. Co. v. Miller, 2 Col. 442, p. 6.
Keables v. Christie, 47 Mich. 535, p. 213.
Keith v. Lothrop, 10 Cush. 457, p. 50.
Keith v. Tilford, 12 Neb. 271, p. 153.
Keithsburg, etc. R. R. Co. v. Henry, 79 Ill. 290, pp. 58, 212, 229.
Keller v. N. Y. Cent. R. R. Co., 2 Abbott's App. Decis., 480, pp. 14, 37.
Kelly's Heirs v. McGuire, 15 Ark. 555, p. 92.
Kendall v. Gray, 2 Hilton, 302, p. 225.
Kendall v. May, 10 Allen, 59, p. 226.
Kennedy v. Brown, 13 C. B. (N. s.) 677, p. 222.
Kennedy v. People, 39 N. Y. 245, pp. 18, 83.

TABLE OF CASES CITED.

Kenny v. Clarkson, 1 Johnson, 385, p. 123.
Kenney v. Van Horne, 1 Johns. 394, p. 134.
Kermott v. Ayer, 11 Mich. 181, pp. 123, 232.
Kern v. South St. Louis Mutual Ins. Co., 40 Mo. 19, p. 157.
Kernin v. Hull, 37 Ill. 207, p. 193.
Kershaw v. Wright, 115 Mass. 361, p. 168.
Kessel v. Albetis, 56 Barb. 362, p. 120.
Key v. Thompson, 2 Hannay (N. B.), 224, p. 39.
Kilbourne v. Jennings, 38 Iowa, 533, p. 27.
Kilgore v. Cross, 1 Fed. Rep. 592, p. 92.
King v. Donahue, 110 Mass. 155, pp. 196, 204.
King v. N. Y. Cent. R. R. Co., 72 N. Y. 607, pp. 5, 170.
Kinley v. Crane, 34 Penn. St. 146, p. 157.
Kinne v. Kinne, 9 Conn. 102, p. 88.
Kinney v. Flynn, 2 R. I. 319, p. 193.
K pner v. Biebl, 28 Minn. ——, pp. 11, 17, 24, 154.
Kirksey v. Kirksey, 41 Ala., 626, pp. 190, 193.
Kline v. Baker, 99 Mass. 254, p. 139.
Kline v. The K. C., St. J, etc. R. R. Co., 50 Iowa, 656, p. 9, 15, 81.
Knapp v. Abell, 10 Allen, 85, p. 122.
Knapp v. Monell (N. Y. Sup. Ct.), 15 Cent. L. J. 281, p. 272.
Knox v. Clark, 123 Mass. 246,
Knoll v. State, The Reporter, 1882, p. 381, pp. 242, 271.
Koons v. St. Louis & Iron Mountain R. R. Co., 65 Mo. 592, p. 5.
Koons v. The State, 36 Ohio St. 195, p. 199.
Kopke v. People, 43 Mich., 41, p. 131.
Koster v. Noonan, 8 Daly, 232, p. 171.

L.

Lacon v. Higgins, 3 Starkie (N. P.) 178, p. 131.
Lake v. People, 12 N. Y. 358; s. c., 1 Parker Cr. Cas. 495, pp. 34, 41, 79, 89.
Lamoure v. Caryl, 4 Denio, 373, p. 216.
Lancaster v. Lancaster's Trustees, 78 Ky. 200, p. 232.
Lands v. Lands, 1 Grant, 248, p. 90.
Lane v. Wilcox, 55 Barb. 615, p. 154.
Lapham v. Atlas Ins. Co., 24 Pick. 1, p. 143.
Laros v. Commonwealth, 84 Penn. St. 200, p. 50.
Laughlin v. State, 18 Ohio, 99, p. 53.
Lawrence v. Boston, 119 Mass. 126, p. 23.
Lawrence v. Dana, 4 Clifford, 1, p. 163.
Lawrence v. Hudson, 59 Tenn. 671, p. 4.
Lawton v. Chase, 108 Mass. 238, pp. 23, 223.
Leathers v. Salvor Wrecking Co., 2 Wood, 680, p. 202.
Lee v. Mathews, 10 Ala. 682, p. 123.
Legg v. Drake, 21 Ohio, 286.
Legg v. Legg, 8 Mass. 99, p. 122.
Lehmicke v. St. Paul, etc. R. R. Co., 19 Minn. 464, p. 229.
Leighton v. Sargent, 11 Foster, 120, p. 16.
Leitch v. Atlantic Ins. Co., 66 N. Y. 100, pp. 144, 150.
Leopold v. Van Kirk, 29 Wis., 548, pp. 49, 174.
Lessee of Forbes v. Caruthers, 3 Yeates, 527, p. 3.

Lessee of Hoge v. Fisher, 1 Peters C. C. 163, p. 86.
Lester v. Pittsford, 7 Vt. 158; p. 9.
Lewis v. Brown, 41 Me. 448, p. 4.
Lincoln v. Battelle, 6 Wend. 475, p. 123.
Lincoln v. Inhabitants of Barre, 5 Cush. 591, pp. 23, 27, 158.
Lincoln v. Saratoga, etc. R. R. Co., 23 Wend. 425, pp. 8, 209, 211.
Lincoln v. Taunton Manufacturing Co., 9 Allen, 182, pp. 50, 115.
Lindsay v. People, 63 N. Y. 143 p. 82.
Line v. Mack, 14 Ind. 330, p. 123.
Linn v. Sigsbee, 67 Ill. 75, pp. 7, 13.
Lipscombe v. Holmes, 2 Camp. 441, p. 224.
Linton v. Hurley, 14 Gray, 191, p. 79.
Linz v. Mass. Mutual Life Ins. Co., 8 Mo. App. 369, p. 74.
Little v. Benzley, 2 Ala. 703, p. 193.
Littleda e v. Dixon, 1 Bos. & Pul. 151, p. 151.
Livingston v. Commonwealth, 14 Gratt. 592, pp. 34, 68, 77.
Llussman v. Merkel, 3 Bos. 402, p. 222.
Llussman v. Maryland Ins. Co., 6 Cranch, 274, p. 124.
Lockhart v. De Wees, 1 Texas, 535, p. 169.
Lodge v. Pipher, 11 S. & R. 334, p. 193.
Lonergan v. Royal Exchange Assurance, 7 Bing 725, p. 262.
Lord v. Beard, 79 N. C. 5, p. 88.
Low v. Connecticut, etc. R. R. Co., 45 N. H. 370, p. 209.
Loyd v. Hannibal, etc. R. R. Co., 53 Mo. 509, p. 108.
Luce v. Dorchester Ins. Co., 105 Mass. 297, pp. 149, 151.
Luning v. State, 1 Chandler, 178, pp. 38, 242.
Lus v. Jones, 39 N. J. Law, 708, p. 221.
Lush v. Druse, 4 Wend. 317, p. 235.
Lush v. McDaniel, 13 Ired. 485, pp. 79, 80.
Lyon v. Lyman, 9 Conn. 59, pp. 179, 196.

M.

Macer v. Third Ave. R. R. Co., 47 N. Y. Sup. Ct. 461, p. 82.
Machin v. Grindon, 2 Cas. Temp. Leg. 335, p. 189.
Macomber v. Scott, 10 Kan. 339, pp. 180, 195.
Maddox v. Fisher, 14 Moore P. C. 103, p. 119.
Maguire v. Labeaume, 7 Mo. App. 185, p. 220.
Malcomson v. Morton, 11 Irish Law, 230, p. 168.
Male v. Roberts, 3 Esp. 163, p. 121.
Manke v. People, 24 Hun, 416; s. c., 78 N. Y. 611, pp. 16, 18.
Marcy v. Barnes, 10 Gray, 161, pp. 24, 202.
Marcy v. Sun Ins. Co., 11 La. Ann. 748, p. 145.
Marshall v. Columbian Mut. Ins. Co., 7 Foster 157, pp. 9, 209.
Marshall v. Union Ins. Co., 2 Wash. C. C. 357, p. 151.
Martin v. Maguire, 7 Gray, 177, pp. 196, 198.
Martin v. Wallis, 11 Mass. 209, p. 196.
Mascheck v. St. Louis R. R. Co., 1 Mo. App. 600, p. 5.
Mask v. City of Buffalo, N. Y. Ct. of App. 1881, 13 Reporter, 251, p. 253.
Mason v. Fuller, 45 Vt. 29, p. 96.

TABLE OF CASES CITED. xvii

Mason, etc. R. R. Co. v. Johnson, 38 Ga. 409, p. 147.
Mason v. Wash, Breese, 39, p. 12.
Massachusetts Life Ins. Co. v. Erbelman, 30 Ohio St. 647, p. 5.
Masters v. Masters, 1 P. Wm. 425, p. 184.
Matter of Alfred Foster's Will, 34 Mich. 21, pp. 195, 201.
Matter of Robert's Will, 8 Paige, 446, p. 125.
Matteson v. N. Y. etc. R. R. Co., 62 Barb. 364, p. 79.
Matteson v. N. Y. etc. R. R. Co, 35 N. Y. 487, p. 97.
May v. Bradlee, 127 Mass. 414, p. 47.
May v. Dorsett, 30 Ga. 116, p. 205.
Mayor, etc. v. O'Neill, 1 Penn. St. 342, p. 170.
McAdory v. State, 59 Ala. 92, p. 5.
McAlister v. McAlister, 7 B. Monr. 270, p. 193.
McAllister v. State, 17 Ala. 434, p. 88.
McClackey v. State, 5 Tex. Ct. App. 320, pp. 91, 93.
McClintock v. Card, 32 Mo. 411, p. 47.
McCormick v. Hamilton, 23 Gratt. 561, p. 155.
McCracken v. West, 17 Ohio, 16, p. 178.
McCraney v. Alden, 46 Barb. 274, p. 121.
McDeed v. McDeed, 67 Ill. 545, p. 123.
McDougald v. McLean, 1 Winston, 120, p. 91.
McEwen v. Bigelow, 40 Mich. 217, pp. 23, 26.
McGill v. Rowand, 3 Penn. St. 452, p. 213.
McKee v. Ne son, 4 Cowen, 355, p. 6.
McKeone v. Barnes, 108 Mass. 344, pp. 183, 198.
McKnight v. State, 6 Tex. Ct. App. 162, p. 4
McLean v. State, 16 Ala. 672, pp. 53, 88.
McLeod v. Bullard, 84 N. Y. 515, p. 196.
McMahon v. Tyng, 14 Allen, 167, p. 163.
McMechen v. McMechen, 17 W. Va. 683, pp. 38, 43.
McNair v. National Life Ins. Co., 20 N. Y. Sup. Ct. 146, p. 78.
McNeill v. Arnold, 17 Ark. 154, pp. 123, 135.
McRae v Mattoon, 13 Pick. 53, p. 123.
Mead v. North Western Ins. Co., 3 Selden, 530, p. 162.
Melvin v. Easley, 1 Jones Law, 388, p. 241.
Mendum v. Commonwealth, 6 Rand. 704, pp. 26, 85.
Merkle v. State, 37 Ala. 139, p. 237.
Merriam v. Middlesex Ins. Co., 21 Pick. 162, p. 149.
Merrill v. Dawson, Hempstead, 563, p. 120.
Merritt v. Merritt, 20 Ill. 65, p. 123.
Merritt v. Seaman, 6 N. Y. 168, p. 4.
Mertz v. Detweiler, 8 W. & S. 376, pp. 97, 94.
Messer v. Reginnitter, 32 Iowa, 312, p. 157.
M'Fadden v. Murdock, 1 Irish R. 211, p. 64.
Middlebury Coll. v. Cheney, 1 Vt. 348, p. 122.
Middleton v. Janverson, 2 Hag. Cons. R. 437, p. 131.
Miles v. Loomis, 17 Hun. 372, p. 182.
Miles v. Loomis, 75 N. Y. 287, p. 180.
Millar v. Heinrick, 4 Camp. 155, p. 127.
Miller v. Eicholtz, 5 Col. 244, p. 195.
Miller v. Johnson, 27 Md. 30, pp. 193, 201.
Miller v. Jones, 32 Ark. 337, p. 195.
Miller v. Smith. 112 Mass. 476, pp. 34, 217.
Miller v. Stevens, 100 Mass. 518, p. 167.

Milton v. Rowland, 11 Ala. 732, p. 81.
Milwaukee, etc. R. R. Co. v. Eble, 4 Chand. 72, p. 229.
Milwaukee, etc. R. R. Co. v. Kellogg, 94 U. S. 469, pp. 9, 17.
Mins v. Swartz, 37 Tex. 13, p. 120.
M'Lanahan v. Universal Ins. Co., 1 Peters, 170, pp. 145, 151.
Minnesota Central R. R. Co. v. Morgan, 52 Barb. 217, p. 169.
Mish v. Wood, 34 Penn. St. 451, pp. 8, 213.
Mississippi River Bridge Co. v. Ring, 58 Mo. 492, p. 200.
Mitchell v. Allison, 29 Ind. 43, p. 211.
Mitchell v. State, 58 Ala. 418, pp. 78, 109.
Mobile R. R. Co. v. Blakeley, 59 Allen, 471, p. 147.
Mobile R. R. Co. v. Whitney, 39 Ala. 468, p. 121.
Mock v. Kelley, 3 Ala. 387, p. 224.
Molina v. United States, 6 Ct. of Claims, 269, p. 138.
Monroe v. Douglass, 5 N. Y. 447, p. 121.
Monroe v. Lattin, 25 Kan. 351, p. 8.
Monghon v. The State, 57 Ga. 102, p. 143.
Montgomery v. Deeley, 3 Wis. 700, p. 120.
Montgomery v. Gilmer, 33 Ala. 116, p. 162.
Montgomery v. Town of Scott, 34 Wis. 338, pp. 4, 18, 82.
Moody v. Rowell, 17 Pick. 490, pp. 179, 196.
Mooney v. Lloyd, 5 S. & R. 416, p. 224.
Moore v. Guyner, 5 Me. 187, p. 139.
Moore v. Leu's Admr., 32 Ala. 375, p. 184.
Moore v. State, 17 Ohio St. 521, pp. 39, 79.
Moore v. Westervelt, 9 Bos. 559, p. 143.
Moore v. United States, 91 U. S. 270, pp. 193, 194.
Morehouse v. Mathews, 2 N. Y. 514, p. 212.
Moreland v. Mitchell Co., 40 Iowa, 401, pp. 155, 173.
Morewood v. Wood, 14 East, 327, note a, p. 180.
Morris v. Davidson, 49 Ga. 361, p. 120.
Morrissey v. Ingham, 111 Mass. 63, p. 79.
Morrissey v. Wiggins Ferry Co., 47 Mo. 521, p. 122.
Morse v. Crawford, 17 Vt. 499, p. 91.
Morse v. State, 6 Conn. 9, p. 6.
Moses v. Delaware Ins. Co., 1 Wash. C. C. 385, p. 151.
Mostyn v. Farrigas, Cowper, 174, p. 121.
Mott v. Hudson River R. R. Co., 8 Bos. 345, p. 146.
Moulton v. McOwen, 103 Mass. 587, p. 161.
Moulton v. Scrutin, 39 Me. 288, p. 117.
Mowry v. Chase, 100 Mass. 79, p. 139.
Moye v. Herndon, 30 Miss. 115, pp. 184, 268.
Muldowney v. Illinois Cent. R. R. Co., 36 Iowa, 472, pp. 11, 14, 37.
Muldowney v. Ill. Cent. R. R. Co. 39 Iowa, 615, pp. 11, 40.
Mulry v. Mohawk Ins. Co., 5 Gray, 545, pp. 149, 151.
Munshower v. State, 55 Md. 11, p. 236.
Murphy v. Hagerman, Wright, 293, p. 179.
Murphy v. New York, etc. R. R. Co., 66 Barb. 125, p. 148.
Mutual Benefit Life Ins. Co. v. Brown, 30 N. J. Eq. 193, p. 268.
Mutual Life Ins. Co. v. Bratt, 55 Md. 200, p. 240.
Myers v. Murphy, 60 Ind. 282, p. 172.

(c)

xviii TABLE OF CASES CITED.

N.

Napier v. Ferguson, 2 P. & B. (N. B.) 415, pp. 79, 96.
Nashville, etc. R. R. Co. v. Carroll, 53 Tenn. 347, p. 13.
Naughton v. Stagg. 4 Mo. App. 271, pp. 13, 215.
Nave v. Tucker, 70 Ind. 15, p. 40.
Nave's Admr. v. Williams, 22 Ind. 366, p. 170.
Needham v. Ide, 5 Pick. 510, p. 90.
Nelson v. Bridport, 8 Beav. 527, pp. 121, 138.
Nelson v. Johnson, 18 Ind. 329, p. 184.
Nelson v. Sun Mut. Ins. Co., 71 N. Y. 453, pp. 2, 23, 167.
Nelson v. Wood, 62 Ala. 175, p. 174.
Newell v. Newell, 9 Paige 26, pp. 100, 101, 102, 135.
Newell v. Newell, 9 Miss. 58, p. 139.
Newton v. Cocke, 10 Ark. 169, p. 121.
Newmark v. Liverpool, etc. Ins. Co., 30 Mo. 163, p. 8.
New Albany, etc. R. R. Co. v. Huff, 19 Ind. 315, p. 4.
New England Glass Co. v. Lovell, 7 Cush. 319, pp. 9, 13, 142.
New Orleans, etc. R. R. Co. v. Albreton, 38 Miss. 242, p. 222.
Niagara Ins. Co. v. Greene, 77 Ind. 595, p. 153.
Nichols v. Gould, 2 Vesey, 423, p. 211.
Noblesville, etc. R. R. Co. v. Gause, 76 Ind. 142, p. 82.
Noonan v. Ilsley, 22 Wis. 27, p. 202.
Noonan v. State. 14 Reporter, 320, p. 95.
Norton v. Moore, 40 Tenn. 483, p. 81.
Norton v. Seton, 3 Phillemore, 147, pp. 100, 103.
Norman v. Morell, 4 Vesey Ch. 768, pp. 178, 184.
Norman v. Wells, 17 Wend. 136, pp. 8, 211.
Norment v. Fastnaght, 1 McArthur, 515, p. 158.
Norwood v. Morrow, 4 Dev. & Batt. 442, p. 88.
Nowell v. Wright, 3 Allen, 166, p. 175.

O.

O'Brien v. People, 36 N. Y. 276, p. 94.
Ogden v. Parsons, 23 How. 167, p. 143.
Ohio, etc. R. R. Co. v. Nickless, 71 Ind. 271, p. 211.
Oleson v. Tolford, 37 Wis. 327, p. 18.
O'Mara v. Commonwealth, 75 Penn. St. 424, p. 96.
Ordway v. Haynes, 50 N. H. 159, p. 243.
Ormsby v. Imhsen, 34 Penn. St. 462, p. 157.
Orr v. Mayor, etc., 64 Barb. 106, p. 217.
Otey v. Hoyt, 2 Jones Law, 70, p. 188.
Ott v. Soulard, 9 Mo. 58, p. 120.
Ottawa Gaslight Co. v. Graham, 35 Ill. 346, p. 212.
Ottawa University v. Parkinson, 14 Kans. 159, pp. 222, 223.
Owen v. Boyle, 15 Me. 147, pp. 121. 123.
Owings v. Hull, 9 Peters, 607, p. 121.

P.

P. & L. 3 Prob. Div. (L. R.) 73, p. 103.
Paddock v. Commonwealth, Ins. Co. 104 Mass. 52, p. 143.
Page v. Homans, 14 Me. 478, p. 196.
Page v. Parker, 40 N. H. 59, pp. 8, 174.

Page v. State, 61 Ala. 16, pp. 39, 81, 82.
Paige v. Hazard, 5 Hill, 604, pp. 7, 144, 210.
Paine v. Schenectady Ins. Co., 11 R. I. 411, p. 122.
Papin v. Ryan, 32 Mo. 21, p. 120.
Parker v. Boston, etc. Steamboat Co., 109 Mass. 449, p. 80.
Parker's Heirs v. Parker's Admr., 33 Ala. 459, p. 226.
Parnell v. Commonwealth, 86 Penn. St. 260, pp. 58, 269.
Parkinson v. Atkinson, 31 L. J. (N. S.) C. P. 199, p. 262.
Parsons v. Manuf. Ins. Co., 16 Gray, 463, p. 142.
Partridge v. Ins. Co., 15 Wall. 375, p. 168.
Patchin v. Astor Mutual Ins. Co., 13 N. Y. 268, p. 142.
Patterson v. Colebrook, 9 Foster, 94, p. 4.
Pate v. People, 3 Gilm., 644, p. 179.
Patten v. United States, 15 Ct. of Cl. 233. p. 210.
Pavey v. Pavey, 30 Ohio St. 600, pp. 196, 198.
Payson v. Everett, 12 Minn, 216, p. 205.
Peck v. Hibbard, 26 Vt. 698, pp. 123, 132.
Pelamourges v. Clark, 9 Iowa, 1, pp. 6, 8, 37.
Pennsylvania Coal Co. v. Conlan, 101 Ill. 93, pp. 13, 148.
Pennsylvania R. R. Co. v. Bunnell, 81 Penn. St. 428, p. 228.
Pennsylvania R. R. Co. v. Henderson, 51 Penn. St. 320, p. 232.
Pennsylvania R. R. Co. v. Holtenstine, 47 Penn. St. 30, p. 212.
People v. Badger, 1 Wheeler Cr. Cas. 543, p. 304.
People v. Boscovitch, 20 Cal. 436, p. 53.
People v. Brotherton, 47 Cal. 395, p. 188.
People v. Clark, 33 Mich. 112, p. 96.
People v. Checkee, 14 Rep. 582, p. 236.
People v. Donovan, 43 Cal. 162, p. 51.
People v. Eastwood, 14 N. Y. 562, p. 5.
People v. Finley, 38 Mich. 482, p. 91.
People v. Ganzalez, 35 N. Y. p. 114.
People v. Greenfield, 30 N. Y. Sup. Ct. 462, p. 113.
People v. Greenfield, 85 N. Y. 471, p. 113.
People v. Hewitt, 2 Parker Cr. Cas. 20, pp. 179, 182.
People v. Lake, 12 N. Y. 358, p. 94.
People v. Lambert, 5 Mich. 349, p. 123.
People v. McCann, 3 Parker Cr. Cas. 272, p. 88.
People v. McCoy, 45 How. Pr. 216, p. 106.
People v. Montgomery, 13 Abb. Pr. (N. S.) 207, pp. 88, 254.
People v. Morrigan, 29 Mich. 1, pp. 15, 172, 206.
People v. Olmstead, 30 Mich. 434, p. 81.
People v. Robinson, 2 Parker's Cr. Cas. 236, pp. 79, 109.
People v. Sanford, 43 Cal. 29, p. 91.
People v. Stout, 3 Parker's Cr. Cas. 670, pp. 71, 73.
People v. Thurston, 2 Parker's Cr. Cas. 49, p. 34, 41.
People v. Wheeler, 9 Pac. Coast L. J. 584, 235, 243.
People v. Wreden (Sup. Ct. Cal.), 12 Reporter, 682, p. 92.
Perkins v. Augusta, etc. Banking Co., 10 Gray, 312, p. 13.
Peters v. Stavely, 15 L. J. (N. S.) 151, p. 168.
Petterborough v. Jaffrey, 6 N. H. 462, p. 203.
Phillips v. Gregg, 10 Watts, 158, p. 134.

Phillips v. Starr, 26 Iowa, 351. p. 37.
Phillips v. Terry, 3 Abb. N. Y. Decis. 607, p. 154.
Pickard v. Bailey, 6 Foster, 169, p. 154.
Pidcock v. Potter, 68 Penn. St. 342, pp. 44, 70, 79, 91.
Pierson v. Baird, 2 G. Greene, 235, p. 120.
Pierson v. People, 79 N. Y. 434, p. 73.
Pierson v. People, 25 N. Y. Sup. Ct. 233, p. 73.
Pierson v. Wallace, 7 Ark. 262, p. 211.
Pierson v. Hoag, 47 Barb. 243, p. 117.
Pigg v. State, 43 Tex. 110, p. 80.
Pinney's Will, 27 Miss. 280, p. 92.
Pinney v. Cahill, 12 N. W. Reporter, 852, pp. 117, 240, 244.
Pitts v. State, 43 Miss. 472, pp. 78, 79, 260.
Pittsburgh, e c. R. R. Co. v. Rose, 74 Penn St. 368, p. 213.
Pleasant v. State, 15 Ark. 624, p. 53.
Plunket v. Bowman, 2 McCord, 139, p. 177.
Polhemus v. Heinman, 50 Cal. 438, p. 168.
Polk v. Coffin, 9 Cal. 56, p. 155.
Polk v. State, 36 Ark. 117, pp. 3, 4, 69, 78, 79, 109.
Pollard v. Wybourn, 1 Hagg. Ecc. 725, p. 103.
Pollen v. Le Roy, 10 Bosw. 38, p. 166.
Poole v. Richardson, 3 Mass. 330, p. 90.
Pope v. Filley, 9 Fed. Rep. 65, pp. 28, 164, 170.
Potts v. Aechternacht, 93 Penn. St. 142, pp. 215, 227.
Potts v. House, 6 Ga. 324, pp. 86, 90.
Pourcelly v. Lewis, 8 Mo, App. 593, p. 193.
Prather v. Rose, 17 Ind. 495, p. 166.
Pratt v. Rawson, 40 Vt. 183, pp. 58, 63, 268.
Price v. Hartshorn, 44 N. Y. 94, p. 144.
Price v. Powell, 3 N. Y. 322, pp. 45, 145.
Printz v. People. 42 Mich. 144, p. 213.
Public Schools v. Risley's Heirs, 40 Mo. 356, p. 158.
Pullman v. Corning, 9 N. Y. 93, p. 45.
Puryear v. Reese, 46 Tenn. 21, pp. 86, 91.

Q.

Quaife v. Chicago, etc. R R. Co., 48 Mo. 513, p. 76.
Queen v. Sheperd, 1 Cox Cr. Cas. 237, p. 182.
Quinn v. Nat. etc., Ins. Co., 1 Jones & Carey, 316, p. 151.
Quinsigimond Bank v. Hobbs, 11 Gray, 250, pp. 24, 183.

R.

Railroad Co. v. Frazier, 27 Kans. 463, p. 271.
Raisin v. Clark, 41 Md. 158, p. 169.
Ramagge v. Ryan, 9 Bing. 333, p. 19.
Rambler v. Tyron, 7 S. & R. 90, pp. 90, 91.
Randolph v. Adams, 2 W. Va. 519, p. 158.
Randolph v. Holden, 44 Iowa, 327, p. 109.
Randall v. Rotch, 12 Pick. 107, p. 168.
Rape v. Heaton, 9 Wis. 328, p. 122.
Rash v. State, 61 Ala. 90, p. 85.
Rawls v. Am. Mutual Life Ins. Co., 27 N. Y. 282, p. 152.
Rawles v. James, 49 Ala. 183.
Raynham v. Canton, 3 Pick. 29, pp. 123, 132.
Read v. Barker, 30 N. J. Law, 378; s. c., 32 Id. 477, p. 155.

Reading v. Menham, 1 Moo. & R. 234, p. 168.
Real v. People, 42 N. Y. 282, p. 94.
Reamer v. Nesmith, 34 Cal. 27, p. 66.
Reed v. Dick, 8 Watts, 479, p. 142.
Reed v. Richardson, 98 Mass. 216, p. 169.
Reed v. Timmins, 52 Tex. 84, p. 6.
Reese v. Reese, 90 Penn. St. 89, pp. 181, 183.
Regina v. Dent, 1 Clark, 96, p. 136.
Regina v. Neville, Crawf. & Dix, Ab. Not. Cas. 96, p. 92.
Regina v. Newman, 3 C. & K. 260, p. 53.
Regina v. Oxford, 9 C. & P. 525, p. 92.
Regina v. Still, 30 Upper Canada, C. P. 30, p. 95.
Regina v. Thomas, 13 Cox's Cr. Cas. 77, p. 237.
Regina v. Williams, 8 C. & P. 34, pp. 178, 183.
Reid v. Piedmont, etc. Life Ins. Co., 58 Mo. 426, p. 48.
Reilly v. Rivett, 1 Cases in Eng. Eccles. Cts. 43, note n., pp. 182, 189.
Revett v. Braham, 4 Term, 49, p. 179.
Rex v. Cator, 4 Esp. 127, p. 182.
Reynolds v. Jourdain, 5 Cal. 108, p. 168.
Reynolds v. Lounsbury, 6 Hill, 553, p. 23.
Reynolds v. Robinson, 64 N. Y. 589, pp. 37, 223.
Rice's Succession, 21 La. Ann. 614, p. 120.
Rich v. Jones, 9 Cush. 337, p. 34.
Richards v. Doe, 100 Mass. 524, p. 174.
Richards v. Murdock, 10 B. & C. 527, p. 151.
Richardson v. McGoldrick, 43 Mich. 476, p. 213.
Richardson v. Newcomb, 21 Pick. 315, p. 196.
Ripple v. Ripple, 1 Rawle, 386, pp. 122, 139.
Ritter v. Daniels, 47 Mich. 617, p. 227.
Roberts v. Commissioners of Brown County, 21 Kans. 248, pp. 8, 212.
Roberts v. Johnson, 58 N. Y. 613, pp. 26, 97.
Robertson v. Knapp, 35 N. Y. 91, p. 228.
Robertson v. Stark, 15 N. H. 109, pp. 8, 209.
Robinson v. Adams, 62 Me. 369, p. 90.
Robinson v Clifford, 2 Wash. C. C. 2, p. 123.
Robinson v. Fitchburg, etc. R. R. Co., 7 Gray, 92, p. 4.
Robinson v. N. Y. Cent. R. R. Co., Alb. Law J., 1881, 357, p. 250.
Rochester, etc. R. R. Co. v. Budlong, 10 How Pr. 289, pp. 9, 11, 12, 212.
Rochester v. Chester, 3 N. H. 364, pp. 1, 4, 209.
Rodgers v. Kline, 56 Miss. 818, p. 166.
Roe v. Roe, 40 N. Y. Sup. Ct. 1, p. 180.
Roe v. Taylor, 45 Ill. 486, p. 91.
Rogers v. Ritter, 12 Wall. 317, p. 196.
Roots v. Merriwether, 8 Bush. 401, p. 123.
Rouse v. Morris, 17 S. & R. 328, p. 224.
Rowe v. Rawlings, 7 East, 282, note a, p. 189.
Rowell v. City of Lowell. 11 Gray, 420, p. 82.
Rowley v. London, etc. R. R. Co, 3 Exch. 221, p. 231.
Rowland v. Fowler, 47 Conn. 348, p. 15.
Rowt, Admr., v. Kile's Admr., 1 Leigh 216, p. 193.
Rumsey v. People, 19 N. Y. 41, p. 97.
Runyan v. Price, 15 Ohio St. 14, p. 93.
Rush v. Megee, 36 Ind. 69, pp. 37, 91.

Russell v. Horn Pond, etc. Co., 4 Gray, 607, p. 229.
Russell v. State, 53 Miss. 367, p. 70.
Rutherford v. Morris, 77 Ill. 397, p. 270.

S.

S.—— v. A.——, 3 Prob. Div. (L. R.) 72, p. 103.
Sackett v. Sackett, 8 Pick. 359, p. 120.
Salvin v. North Branepeth Coal Co., 9 Ch. App. 705, p. 115.
Salvo v. Duncan, 49 Wis. 157, p. 164.
Sanchez v. People, 22 N. Y. 147, p. 89.
Sanderson v. Nashua, 44 N. H. 492, pp. 51, 79.
Saph v. Atkinson, 2 Eng. Ecc. R. 64, p. 189.
Sari v. Arnold, 7 R. I. 586, pp. 24, 50.
Sartorious v. State, 24 Miss. 602, p. 53.
Sasser v. State, 13 Ohio, 453, p. 205.
Sauter v. N. Y. Cent. R. R. Co., 14 N. Y. Sup. Ct. 451, p. 236.
Savings Bank v. Ward, 100 U. S. 195, p. 168.
Scattergood v. Wood, 79 N. Y. 263, p. 160.
Schell v. Plumb, 55 N Y. 598, p. 236.
Schenck v. Mercer Co.Mut. Ins. Co.,24 N. J L. 451, p. 152.
Schermerhorn v. Tyler, 11 Hun, 551, p. 210.
Schlenker v. State, 9 Neb. 250, p. 85.
Schmidt v. Herfurth, 5 Robertson, 124, p. 233.
Schomp v. Schenck, 40 N. J. L. 195, p. 222.
Schouv v. Peoria, etc. Ins. Co. 41 Ill. 296, p. 150.
Schroeder v. The C. R. I. & P. R. Co., 47 Iowa, 375, pp. 103, 107.
Schultz v. Lindell, 30 Mo. 310, p. 158.
Schuylkill Navigation Co. v. Thoburn, 7 S. & R. 411, p. 2 2.
Scraggs v. The Baltm., etc. R. R. Co., 10 Md. 268, p. 4.
Scripps v. Foster, 41 Mich. 742, p. 74.
Seaman v. Fonerau, 2 Strange, 1183, p. 151.
Seamans v. Smith, 46 Barb. 320, p. 153.
Seaver v. Boston, etc. R. R. Co., 14 Gray, 466, p. 146.
Seeley v. Brown, 15 N. J. I. 35, p. 222.
Seibles v. Blackwell, 1 McM. 57, p. 4.
Selfe v. Isaacson, 1 F. & F. 194, p. 53.
Semple v. Hagar, 27 Cal. 163, p. 120.
Sexton v. North Bridgewater, 116 Mass. 201, p. 212.
Sexton v. Lamb, 27 K ns. 426, p, 272
Shafer v. Dean's Adm'r. 29 Iowa, 144, pp. 223, 226.
Shafter v. Evans, 53 Cal. 32, p. 13.
Shattuck v. Stoneham Branch R. R. Co., 6 Allen, 116, p. 212.
Shattuck v. Train, 116 Mass. 206, p. 226.
Shaw v. City of Charleston, 2 Gray, 109, pp. 208, 212.
Shawneetown v. Mason, 82 Ill. 337, p. 80.
Shed v. Augustine, 14 Kans. 282, p. 121.
Sheldon v. Benham, 4 Hill, 129, pp. 165, 168.
Sheldon v. Booth, 50 Iowa, 209, pp. 100, 219.
Sheldon v. Warner, 45 Mich. 638, p. 186.
Shelton v. State, 34 Texas, 696, p. 78.
Shepard v. Ashley, 10 Allen, 542, p. 220.
Shepar t v. Pratt, 16 Kans. 209, p. 69.
Shriver v. Sioux City, etc. R. R. Co., 24 Minn. 506, p. 174.
Shulte v. Hennessy, 40 Iowa, 352, p. 162.
Sickles v. Gould, 51 How. Pr. 25, p. 153.

Sidwell v. Evans, 1 P. & W. (Penn.) 383, p. 139.
Sikes v. Paine, 10 Ired. Law, 282, pp. 23, 58, 144.
Silverthorne v. Fowle, 4 Jones, 362, p. 166.
Sims v. Maryatt, 17 Q. B. (79 E. C. L.) 232, p. 120.
Simmons v. Carrier, 68 Mo. 416, p. 220.
Simmons v. Means, 8 S. & M. 397, p. 224.
Simmons v. St. Paul, etc. R. R. Co., 18 Minn. 184, pp. 212, 229.
Simms v. Maryatt, 17 Q. B. 292, p. 120.
Simonson v. C. R. I. & P. R. R. Co., 49 Iowa. 87, p. 231.
Sinclair v. Roush, 14 Ind. 450, p. 211.
Sinnott v. Mullins, 82 Penn. St. 342, p. 20.
Sirrine v. Briggs, 31 Mich. 443, p. 234.
Sisson v. Conger, 1 N. Y. Sup. Ct. 569, p. 233.
Sisson v. Toledo, R. R. Co., 14 Mich. 489, p. 233.
Sizer v. Burt, 4 Denio, 426, p. 54.
Slais v. Slais, 9 Mo. App. 16, p. 269.
Slater v. Wilcox, 57 Barb. 604, pp. 9, 116.
Smalley v. Iowa Pacific R. R. Co., 36 Iowa, 571, p. 212.
Smith v. Frost, 42 N. Y. Sup. Ct. 87, p. 232.
Smith v. Gould, 4 Moore, P. C. 21, p. 121.
Smith v. Gugerty, 4 Barb. 619, p. 152.
Smith v. Tallapoosa Co., 2 Woods, 574, p. 121.
Smith v. Watson, 14 Vt. 332, p. 224.
Smith v. Wilcox, 4 Hun. 411, p. 220.
Snelling v. Hall, 107 Mass. 134, p. 168.
Snow v. Boston, etc. R. R. Co., 65 Me. 230, pp. 3, 9, 212.
Snowden v. Idaho Quartz Manuf. Co., 55 Cal. 450, pp. 23, 170.
Snyder v. Iowa City, 40 Iowa, 646, p. 254.
Snyder v. State, 70 Ind. 349, pp. 58, 60.
Snyder v. Western Union R. R. Co., 25 Wis. 60, pp. 212, 229.
Sorg v. First German Congregation, 63 Penn. St. 156, pp. 23, 24.
South, etc. R. R. Co. v. McLendon, 63 Ala. 266, p. 6.
South Western Freight, etc. Co. v. Stanard, 44 Mo. 71, p. 169.
Southey v. Nash, 7 C. & P. 632, p. 53.
Sowers v. Dukes, 8 Minn. 23, p. 8.
Sparrow v. Harrison, 3 Curteis, 16, p. 103.
Spaulding v. Vincent, 24 Vt. 501, pp. 123, 131.
Spear v. Bone (Miss.) 5 A. & E. 709, pp. 178, 182.
Spear v. Richardson, 34 N. H. 428, pp. 6, 117.
Spear v. Richardson, 37 N. H. 23, pp. 34, 39.
Speiden v. State, 3 Texas Ct. of App. 159, p. 79.
Spivs v. Stapleton, 38 Ala. 171, p. 154.
Springfield v. Worcester, 2 Cush. 52, p. 120.
Stacy v. Portland Publishing Co., 28 Me. 279, p. 5.
Stambaugh v. Smith, 23 Ohio St. 584, p. 170.
Stanford v. Pruet, 27 Ga. 243, p. 121.
State v. Ah Chuey, 14 Nev. 79, p. 105.
State v. Allen, 1 Hawk's Law and Eq., 6, p. 121.
State v Archer, 54 N. H. 465, p. 90.
State v. Baptiste, 26 La. Ann. 14, p. 78.
State v. Bowman, 78 N. C. 509, pp. 78, 108.
State v. Candler, 3 Hawks Law and Eq. 393, p. 205.
State v. Carr, 5 N. H. 369, p. 206.

TABLE OF CASES CITED. xxi

State v. Cheek, 13 Ired. 114, p. 206.
State v. Clark, 15 S. C. (N. S.) 403, pp. 2, 9, 68.
State v. Clark, 12 Ired. (N. C.) 152, pp. 9, 84, 85.
State v. Clinton, 67 Mo. 380, p. 195.
State v. Cook, 17 Kans. 334. pp. 104, 110.
State v. Cuellar, 47 Tex. 204, p. 134.
State v. Dollar, 66 N. C. 626, p. 233.
State v. Felter, 25 Iowa, 67, pp. 38, 85.
State v. Fitzsimmons, 30 Mo. 236, p 53.
State v. Folwell, 14 Kans. 105, pp. 5, 6.
State v. Geddis, 42 Iowa, 268, p. 90.
State v. Gedicke, 43 N. J. Law, 86, p. 76.
State v. Givens, 5 Ala. 754, pp. 190, 193.
State v. Glass, 5 Oregon, 73, p. 44.
State v. Graham, 74 N. C. 646, p. 105.
State v. Harris, 63 N. C. 1, pp. 82, 205.
State v. Harris, 5 Ired. Law, 287, p. 205.
State v. Hastings, 53 N. H. 452, pp. 196, 197.
State v. Hayden, 51 Vt. 296, pp. 34, 47, 91.
State v. Hinchman, 27 Penn. St. 479, p. 123.
State v. Hinkle, 6 Iowa, 159, pp. 27, 59, 110.
State v. Hooper, 2 Bailey Law, 37, pp. 50, 205.
State v. Hoyt, 46 Conn. 330, p. 248.
State v. Huxford, 47 Iowa, 16, p. 5.
State v. Jacobs, 6 Jones Law, 284, p. 170.
State v. Jarrett, 17 Md 309, p. 120.
State v. Jones, 68 N. C. 443, pp. 81, 83.
State v. Klinger, 46 Mo. 224, pp. 41, 91.
State v. Knapp, 45 N. H. 148, pp. 94, 95.
State v. Knight, 43 Me. 1, pp. 83, 112
State v. Lautenschlager, 22 Minn. 521, p. 42.
State v. Matthews, 66 N. C. 113, pp. 77, 81.
State v. Medlicott, 9 Kans. 289, p. 34.
State v. Miller, 53 Iowa, 84, p. 53.
State v. Miller, 47 Wis. 530, pp. 193, 195.
State v. Morphy, 33 Iowa, 272, pp. 81, 84.
State v. Morris, 84 N. C. 756, p. 6.
State v. Morris, 47 Conn. 179, p. 236.
State v. Murphy, 9 Nev. 394, p. 83.
State v. Newlin, 69 Ind. 108, p. 91.
State v. O'Brien, 7 R. I. 336, pp. 242, 245.
State v. O'Conner, 13 La. Ann. 486, p. 120.
State v. Owen, 73 Mo. 440, p. 196.
State v. Powell, 7 N. J. Law, 295, pp. 81, 82.
State v. Phair, 48 Vt. 366, pp. 2, 179.
State v. Pike, 49 N. H. 399, pp. 90, 92.
State v. Pike, 65 Me. 112, pp. 20, 78, 84.
State v. Porter, 34 Iowa, 131, pp. 21, 81.
State v. Reddick, 7 Kans. 143, p. 70.
State v. Reitz, 83 N. C. 634, p. 6.
State v. Salge, 2 Nevada, 321, p. 53.
State v. Secret, 80 N. C. 450. pp. 24, 26, 58, 190.
State v. Shinborn, 46 N. H. 497, pp. 6, 180.
State v. Slagh, 83 N. C. 630, p. 109.
State v. Smith, 32 Me. 370, pp. 78, 95.
State v. Smith, Phillips Law, 302, p. 94.
State v. Stoyell, 70 Me. 360, p. 81.
State v. Surtly, 2 Hawk's (N. C.) 320, p 122.
State v. Terrill, 12 Rich. 321, pp. 29, 79, 169.
State v. Tompkins, 71 Mo. 616, pp. 180, 195.
State v. Tutt, 2 Bailey (S. C. Law), 37, p. 205.
State v. Twitty, 2 Hawks, 248, p. 122.
State v. Ward, 39 Vt. 225, pp. 24, 178, 196.
State v. Watson, 65 Me. 74, pp. 16, 151, 152, 207.
State v. West, 1 Houston Cr. Cas. 94, p. 240.

State v. Windsor, 5 Harr. (Del.) 512, pp. 86, 88.
State v. Wood, 53 N. H. 484, pp. 29, 95.
State v. Zellers, 7 N. J. Law, 220, p. 53.
Staunton v. Parker, 26 N. Y. Sup. Ct. 56, p. 73.
Steamboat v. Logan, 18 Ohio, 375, pp. 143, 144.
Steam Packet Co. v. Sickles, 10 How. 419, p. 218.
Stearine v. Hentzman, 17 C. B. (N. S.) 56, p. 165.
Stephenson v. Bannis, 3 Bibb. 369, p. 121.
Stewart v. Redditt, 3 Md. 67, p. 92.
Stilling v. Town of Thorp, 54 Wis. —, p. 242.
St. Louis Mut. Life Ins. Co. v. Graves, 6 Bush. 290, p. 18.
Stokes v. Macken, 62 Barb. 145, pp. 106, 120.
Stonam v Waldo, 17 Mo. 489, p. 117.
Stone v. Covell, 29 Mich. 362, p. 223.
Stone v. Hubbard, 7 Cush. 595, p. 184.
Storer's Will, 28 Minn. 9, p. 271.
Storey v. Salomon, 6 Daly, 532, p. 168.
Story v. Maclay, 3 Mon. 480, p. 13.
Stoudenmeier v. Williamson, 29 Ala. 558, p. 237.
Stranger v. Searle, 1 Espin. 14, p. 181.
Strong v. Kean, 13 Irish Law R. 93, p. 39.
Strother v. Lucas, 6 Peters, 763, pp. 121, 190, 193.
Stuart v. State, 57 Tenn. 178, p. 41.
Stulz v. Locke, 47 Md. 562, p. 169.
Sturgis v. Knapp, 33 Vt. 486, pp. 12, 211.
Sturm v. Williams, 38 N. Y. Sup. Ct. 325, pp. 166, 221
Summer v. State, 5 Tex. Ct. of App. 374, pp. 254, 260.
Summers v. United States Ins. Co., 13 La. Ann. 504, p. 151.
Sussex Peerage Case, 11 Cl. & F. 85, pp. 128, 133.
Sutherland v. Hankins, 56 Ind. 343, p. 91.
Sutton v. Drake, 5 H. & N. 647, p. 236.
Swan v. Middlesex, 100 Mass. 173, pp. 212, 214.
Swan v. O'Fallen, 7 Mo. 231, p. 184.
Swartout v. N. Y. Cent. R. R. Co., 14 Hun, 575. p. 173.
Sweet v. Shumway, 102 Mass. 365, p. 167.
Swetser v. Lowell, 33 Me. 446, pp. 178, 180, 196.
Sydleman v. Beckwith, 43 Conn. 9, pp. 5, 6, 7, 8.
Syme v. Stewart, 17 La. Ann. 73, p. 122.

T.

Talbot v. Seeman, Cranch, 38, p. 121.
Tate v. M. K. & T. R. R. Co., 64 Mo. 149, p. 229.
Tatum v. Mohr, 21 Ark. 354, pp. 59, 79.
Taylor v. Cook, 8 Price, 650, p. 189.
Taylor v. Grand Trunk R. R. Co., 48 N. H. 304, p. 71.
Taylor v. Monnot, 4 Duer, 116, p. 16.
Taylor v. Runyan, 9 Iowa, 522, p. 121.
Taylor v. Town of Monroe, 43 Conn. 36, pp. 9, 11, 12, 18.
Taylor v. The French Lumbering Co., 47 Iowa, 662, p. 157.
Taylor's Will Case, 10 Abb. Pr. (N. S.) 300, p. 301.
Tebbetts v. Haskins, 16 Me. 283, pp. 9, 161, 208.
Teft v. Wilcox, 6 Kans. 46, pp. 39, 44.
Templeton v. People, 10 Hun, 357, p. 61.

Terpenning v. Corn Exchange Ins. Co., 43 N. Y. 279, pp. 8, 44, 211.
Terry v. McNeil. 58 Barb. 241, p. 233.
Terrett v. Woodruff, 19 Vt. 183, pp. 122, 123.
Thatcher v. Kaucher, 2 Col. 698, p. 213.
Thayer v. Davis, 58 Vt. 161, p. 34.
Thayer v. Providence Ins. Co., 70 Me. 539, p. 151.
The Queen v. Crouch, 1 Cox Cr. Cas. 94, p. 249.
The Clement, 2 Curtis, 363, p. 119.
The City of Washington, 92 U. S. 31, pp. 144, 168.
The Goods of Bonnelli, 1 Prob. & Div. 169, p. 137.
The Goods of Dost Ali Khan, 6 Prob & Div. 6, p. 135.
The Scotia, 14 Wall. 171, p. 120.
The Sussex Peerage Case, 11 Cl. & F. 85, pp. 128, 133, 137.
Thomas v. Mallinckrodt, 43 Mo. 65, pp. 228, 229.
Thomas v. State, 40 Tex. 36, pp. 4, 91, 268.
Thompson v. Lettrard, 23 Ark. 730, p. 80.
Thompson v. Bennett, 22 Upper Canada (C. P.), 3:2, p. 189.
Thompson v. Boyle, 85 Penn. St. 477, p. 223.
Thompson v. Dickhart, 66 Barb. 604, p. 211.
Thompson v. Riggs, 5 Wall. 663. p. 168.
Thompson v. Trevanion, Skinner, 402, p. 75.
Tingley v. Cowgill, 48 Mo. 294, p. 37.
Tinney v. New Jersey Steamboat Co., 12 Abbott's Pr.(N. S.) 1, pp. 64, 96.
Titlow v. Titlow, 54 Penn. St. 216, p. 40.
Tome v. Parkersburg R. R. Co., 39 Md. 38, p. 193.
Townsend v. Brundage, 6 Thomp., etc. 527, p. 220.
Townsend v. Pepperell, 99 Mass. 40, pp. 89, 90.
Townsdin v. Nutt, 19 Kans. 82, p. 82.
Toulandou v. Lacheumeyer, 1 Sweeny, N. Y. 45, p. 123.
Tracy Peerage Case, 10 Cl. & F. 154, p. 184, 267.
Transportation Line v. Hope, 95 U. S. 297, p. 142.
Travis v. Brown, 43 Penn. St. 9, pp. 3, 193.
Trelawny v. Colman, 2 Starkie, 168, p. 6.
Trimbey v. Vignier, 1 Bing. (N. s.) 158, p. 133.
Tucker v. Massachusetts Cent. R.R. Co., 118 Mass. 546, p. 23.
Tucker v. Williams, 2 Hilton, 562, p. 173.
Tullis v. Kidd, 12 Ala. 648, pp. 23, 26, 49.
Turner v. Cook, 36 Ind. 129, p. 5.
Turner v. Hand, 3 Wall., Jr. 88, p. 268.
Turner v. Turner, 5 Jur. (N. s.) 839, p. 262.
Turner v. McFee, 61 Ala. 468, p. 5.
Turner v. The Black Warrior, 1 McAlister, 181, p. 115.
Turnbull v. Dodds, 6 D. 901, pp. 178, 267.
Turnpike Co. v. Baily, 37 Ohio St. 104, p. 271.
Twogood v. Hoyt, 42 Mich. 609, p. 158.
Twombly v. Leach. 11 Cush. 405, p. 98.
Tyler v. State, 11 Tex. Ct. App. 388, p. 156.
Tyler v. Todd, 36 Conn. 222, pp. 22, 196, 204.
Tyler v. Trabue, 8 Mour. 306, pp. 122, 123.
Tyng v. Fields. 5 N. Y. Sup. Ct. 672, p. 219.

U.

Uhler v. Semple, 5 C. E. Green, 288, p. 122.
Underwood v. Waldron, 33 Mich. 232, p. 162.
Union Pacific Railway Co. v. Clopper (U. S. Sup. Ct.), p. 159.
United States v. Darnaud, 3 Wall., Jr. 143, p. 268.
United States v. De Coursey, 1 Pinney, 508, p. 120.
United States v. Howe, 12 Cent. Law J. 193, p. 258.
United States v. Jones, 10 Fed. Rep. 469, p. 193.
United States v. McGlue, 1 Curtis, 1, pp. 37, 59, 79.
United States v. Otega, 4 Wash. 533, p. 123.
United States v. Turner, 11 Howard, 663, pp. 120, 121.
United States v. Wigglus, 14 Peters, 334, p. 121.

V.

Van Atta v. McKinney, 16 N. J. L. 225, p. 222.
Van Buskirk v. Mulock, 18 N. J. Law, 184, pp. 122, 132.
Vander Donckt v. Thelusson, 8 Man. S. & S. (65 Eng. C. L.) 812, pp. 2, 26, 133.
Vandine v. Burpee, 13 Met. 288, p. 153.
Van Deusen v. Newcomer, 40 Mich. 120, p. 48.
Van Horn v. Keenan, 28 Ill. 440, p. 90.
Van Huss v. Rainbolt, 42 Tenn. 139, p. 90.
Van Wyck v. McIntosh, 14 N. Y. 439, p. 204.
Van Zandt v. Mut. Benefit Life Ins. Co., 55 N. Y. 179, p. 37.
Veerhusen v. Chicago, etc. R. R. Co., 53 Wis. 689, p. 13.
Vinton v. Peck, 14 Mich. 287, p. 185.

W.

Waco Tap R. R. Co. v. Shirley, 45 Tex. 355, p. 220.
Wade v. Dewitt, 20 Tex. 398, p. 249.
Wager v. Schuyler, 1 Wend. 553, pp. 231 236.
Wagner v. Jacoby, 26 Mo. 530, pp. 8, 180.
Walsh v. Dart, 12 Wis. 635, p. 122.
Walsh v. Sayre, 52 How. Pr. 334, p. 107.
Walsh v. Washington Marine Ins. Co., 32 N. Y. 427, p. 142.
Walker v. Fields, 28 Ga. 237, pp. 28, 34 156.
Walker v. Forbes, 31 Ala. 9, p. 124.
Walker v. Rogers, 24 Md. 297, p. 39.
Walker v. State, 7 Tex. Ct. App. 245, p. 105.
Walker v. State, 58 Ala. 393, p. 156.
Walker v. Walker, 14 Ga. 242, p. 91.
Wallace v. Finch, 24 Mich. 255, p. 229.
Wallace v. Goodell, 18 N. H. 439, p. 160.
Ware v. Ware, 8 Me. 42, p. 239.
Washburn v. Cuddihy, 8 Gray, 430, p. 193.
Washington v. Cole, 6 Ala. 212, pp. 22, 50, 69.
Washington Ice Co. v. Webster, 68 Me. 449, p. 213.
Waters v. Thorn, 22 Beav. 547, p. 266.
Watson v. Gresap, 1 B. Monr. 196, p. 206.
Watson v. Pittsburg, etc. R. R. Co., 37 Penn. St. 469, p. 212.

TABLE OF CASES CITED. xxiii

Waterbury Brass Co. v. N. Y. etc. Co., 3 Fisher's Pat. Cas. 43, p. 163.
Waters v. Waters, 35 Md. 531, p. 91.
Weane v. K. & D. M. R. R. Co., 45 Iowa, 246, p. 14.
Weaver v. Alabama, etc. Co., 35 Ala. 176, pp. 145, 175.
Webber v. Eastern R. R. Co., 2 Metc. 147, p. 230.
Webb v. Page, 1 Car. & K. 25, p. 261.
Webb v. State, 5 Tex. Ct. App. 596, pp. 34, 43.
Welde v. Welde, 2 Lee, 580, p. 100.
Welch v. Brooks, 10 Rich. 124, p. 79.
Wendell v. Troy, 39 Barb. 329, p. 97.
West Newbury v. Chase, 5 Gray, 421, p. 229.
West v. State, 22 N. J. L. 241, pp. 190, 193.
Western Ins. Co. v. Tobin, 32 Ohio St. 77, pp. 13, 142, 143.
Westlake v. St. Lawrence Ins. Co., 14 Barb. 206; s. c., 3 Bennett Fire Ins. Cas. 404, p. 218.
Wetherbee's Exr's v. Wetherbee's heirs, 34 Vt. 454. p. 75.
Whelan v. Lynch, 60 N. Y. 469, p. 233.
White v. Bailey, 10 Mich. 155, pp. 47, 86.
White v. Ballou, 8 Allen, 408, pp. 13, 16.
White v. Clemens, 39 Ga. 232, p. 170.
White v. Graves, 107 Mass. 325, p. 89.
White & Co. v. Sussman, 67 Penn. St. 415,
Whitesell v. Crane, 8 W. & S. 372, p. 213.
Whiteley v. Inhabitants of China, 61 Me. 199, p. 212.
Whitney v. Chicago & N. W. R. R. Co., 27 Wis. 327, p. 170.
Whitney v. City of Boston, 98 Mass. 315, p. 214.
Whitney v. Thacher, 117 Mass. 526, p. 233.
Whitesides v. Poole. 9 Rich. 68, p. 122.
Whitmore v. Bischoff, 5 Hun. 176, p. 211.
Whitmore v. Bowman, 4 G. Greene, 148, pp. 8, 212.
Whitman v. Boston, etc. R. R. Co., 7 Gray, 313, p. 229.
Whitbeck v. N. Y. etc. R. R. Co., 36 Barb. 644, p. 217.
Whitcomb v. State, 41 Tex. 125. p. 91.
Whiton v. Snyder, 88 N. Y. 299, p. 272.
Whittier v. Franklin, 46 N. H. 23, p. 6.
Whitfield v. Whitfield, 40 Miss. 352. p. 213.
Whittelsey v. Kellogg, 28 Mo. 404, p. 158.
Whittaker v. Parker, 42 Iowa, 586, p. 63.
Wiggins v. Wallace, 19 Barb. 338, p. 173.
Wilcox v. Hall, 53 Ga. 635, p. 115.
Wilcox v. Leake, 11 La. Ann. 178, p. 211.
Wilkinson v. Mosely, 30 Ala. 562, pp. 77, 81.
Wilkinson v. Pearson, 23 Penn. St. 117, p. 91.
Wilder v. Decou, 26 Minn. 10, p. 168.
Willings v. Consequa, 1 Peters C. C. 25, p. 123.
Willis v. Quimby, 11 Foster, 489, p. 117.
Willey v. Portsmouth, 35 N. H. 303, pp. 39, 79.

Williams v. Brown, 28 Ohio St., pp. 39, 40, 222.
Williams v. Lee, 47 Md. 321, pp. 90, 91.
Williams v. Poppleton, 3 Oregon, 139, pp. 97, 98.
Williams v. State, 61 Ala. 33, p. 204.
Williams v. Taunton, 125 Mass. 34, p. 115.
Williams v. Williams, 3 Beav. 547, p. 136.
Wilson v. Bauman, 80 Ill. 493, pp. 162, 168.
Wilson v. Beauchamp, 50 Miss. 24 p. 196.
Wilson v. Smyth, 13 Tenn. 399, p. 155.
Wilson v. State, 52 Ala. 2: 9, p. 53.
Wilson v. State, 41 Tex. 320. p. 97.
Willson v. Betts, 4 Denio, 201, p. 190.
Wilt v. Vickers, 8 Watts, 227, pp. 82, 99.
Winans v. N. Y. etc. R. R. Co., 21 How. 88, pp. 163, 266.
Winter v. Burt, 31 Ala. 33, p. 218.
Wogan v. Small, 11 S. & R. 141, p. 90.
Wood v. Brewer, 57 Ala. 515, p. 224.
Wood v. Chicago, etc. R. R. Co., 40 Wis. 582, p. 4.
Wood v. Sawyer, Phillips N. C. Law, 253, pp. 59, 75.
Woods v. Allen, 18 N. H. 28, p. 156.
Woodin v. People, 1 Parker Cr. Cas. 464, p. 94.
Woodbridge v. Austin, 2 Tyler, 364, p. 123.
Woodman v. Dana, 52 Me, 9, pp. 23, 196.
Woodcock v. Houldsworth, 16 M. & W. 124, p. 172.
Woodruff v. Imperial Fire Ins. Co., 83 N. Y. 133, p. 221.
Woodbury v. Obear, 7 Gray, 467, pp. 39, 44.
Woodrow v. O'Conner, 28 Vt.776, p. 122.
Woodward v. Bugsbee, 4 N. Y. Sup. Ct. 393, p. 225.
Woodward v. State, 4 Baxter, 322, p. 5.
Wright v. Hardy, 22 Wis. 348, pp. 42, 97, 98.
Wright v. Williams' Estate, 47 Vt. 222, pp. 25, 268.
Wyman v. Gould, 47 Me. 159, p. 90.
Wyman v. Lexington R. R. Co., 13 Met. 316, p. 213.
Wynne v. State, 56 Ga. 113, p. 173.

Y.

Yates v. Waugh, 1 Jones Law, 483, p. 184.
Yates v. Yates, 76 N. C. 142, pp. 27, 179, 196.
Yoe v. People, 49 Wis. 410, p. 251.
Young v. Makepeace, 103 Mass. 50, p. 97.
Young v. O'Neal, 57 Ala. 566, p. 153.

Z.

Zimmerman v. Hesler, 32 Md. 274, p. 123.
Zugasti v. Lamar, 12 Moore, 331, pp. 120, 142.

CHAPTER I.

THE ADMISSIBILITY IN EVIDENCE OF EXPERT TESTIMONY.

SECTION.
1. The Term Expert Defined.
2. The Practice of Admitting Expert Testimony an Ancient One.
3. Opinion Evidence—Non-Professional Witnesses.
4. Opinion Evidence—Non-Professional Witnesses—The Subject Continued.
5. Opinion Evidence—When Expert Testimony is Admissible.
6. When Expert Testimony is Admissible—The Subject Continued.
7. Meaning of the terms "Science" and "Art."
8. Expert Testimony—When Inadmissible.
9. Expert Testimony—When Inadmissible—The Subject Continued.
10. Expert Testimony—When Inadmissible—The Subject Continued.
11. Inadmissibility of Opinions founded on a Theory of Morals or Ethics.
12. Inadmissibility of Opinions on Abstract Questions of Science not Related to the Facts in Issue.
13. Inadmissibility of Opinions Based on Speculative Data.
14. Inadmissibility of the Testimony of Experts who have made *Ex Parte* Investigations.

§ 1. **The Term "Expert" Defined.**—Strictly speaking, an "expert" in any science, art or trade, is one who, by practice or observation, has become experienced therein. He has been defined as "a person of skill;"[1] as "a skillful or experienced person; a person having skill, experience, or peculiar knowledge on certain subjects, or in certain professions; a scientific witness."[2] "An expert" said Mr. Justice FOLGER, "is one instructed by experience,

[1] Rochester v. Chester, 3 N. H. 349, 365.
[2] Heald v. Thing, 45 Me. 392, 394.

and to become one, requires a course of previous habit and practice, or of study, so as to be familiar with the subject."[1] "All persons, I think," said Mr. Justice MAULE, "who practice a business or profession which requires them to possess a certain knowledge of the matter in hand, are experts so far as expertness is required."[2] And this language has been adopted by the court in Virginia.[3] In New Hampshire, we find Mr. Justice DOE declaring: "An expert must have made the subject upon which he gives his opinion, a matter of particular study, practice or observation, and he must have particular special knowledge on the subject."[4] While Mr. Chief Justice AMES, of Rhode Island, says: "Knowledge of any kind, gained for and in the course of one's business as pertaining thereto, is precisely that which entitles one to be considered an expert, so as to render his opinion, founded on such knowledge, admissible in evidence."[5] "An expert," says the court in Vermont, through Mr. Justice ROYCE, "is defined to be a person that possesses peculiar skill and knowledge upon the subject matter that he is required to give an opinion upon."[6] As defined by Mr. Chief Justice SHAW in Massachusetts, an "expert is a person of large experience in any particular department of art, business or science."[7] As stated by Mr. Justice REDFIELD in his edition of Greenleaf's Evidence, "The term 'expert' seems to imply both superior knowledge and practical experience in the art or profession; but generally, nothing more is required to entitle one to give testimony as an expert, than that he has been educated in the particular art or profession."[8] For persons are presumed to understand questions pertaining to their own profession or business.[9] As the

[1] Nelson v. Sun Mutual Ins. Co., 71 N. Y. 453, 460.
[2] Vander Donckt v. Thellusson, 8 Man. G. & S. (65 Eng. C. L.) 812.
[3] Bird v. Commonwealth, 21 Gratt. 800.
[4] Jones v. Tucker, 41 N. H. 546.
[5] Buffum v. Harris, 5 R. I. 250.
[6] State v. Phair, 48 Vt. 366, 377,
[7] Dickenson v. Fitchburg, 13 Gray, 546, 555.
[8] 1 Greenl. Evid., § 440.
[9] Jones v. White, 11 Humph. 268. And see State v. Clark, 15 S. C. (N. S.) 403, 408.

opinions of experts may rest either on their personal knowledge, or on facts testified of by other witnesses,[1] it is error to assume, as is done in one case,[2] that an expert is one who simply testifies from premises furnished by the testimony of other witnesses. In a matter of science, no individual can be considered an expert who does not thoroughly understand the sciences involved.[3]

§ 2. **The Practice of Admitting Expert Testimony an Ancient One.**—The practice of admitting the evidence of witnesses, who have become qualified by study and experience to express opinions upon questions of science and art, is by no means peculiar to modern times. By the Roman law, persons who were *artis periti* could be summoned by the *judex* at his discretion, in order to inform himself as to physical laws or phenomena.[4] And the celebrated criminal code framed by the Emperor Charles the Fifth, at Ratisbon in 1532, contained a formal enactment requiring the opinion of medical experts to be taken in all cases where death was supposed to have been occasioned by violent means.[5] In 1606, Henry the Fourth, of France, in giving letters patent to his first physician, conferred on him the power of appointing two surgeons in every city or important town, whose duty it should exclusively be to examine all wounded or murdered men, and report thereon. And in 1692, by an order of the Council of State, it was ordained that physicians should be associated with them.[6] While in England one of the early records shows,[7] that on an appeal of mayhem, the defendant prayed the court to see the wound for the purpose of determining whether there had been a maiming or not, but the court did not know how to decide,

---

[1] Snow v. Boston etc. R. R. Co., 65 Me. 230, 232; Lessee of Forbes v. Caruthers, 3 Yeates, 527; Polk v. State, 36 Ark. 117, 124, 125.
[2] Travis v. Brown, 43 Penn. St. 9, 13, 14.
[3] Allen v. Hunter, 6 McLean, 303, 310.
[4] L. 8, § 1, x. 1; L. 3, § 4, xl. 6; L. 3, Cod. fin. reg., iii. 39. Endeman, 243.
[5] See 2 Beck's Med. Juris. 896.
[6] Fodere, Introduction, Vol. I, p. 32.
[7] 28 Ass. pl. 5.

as the wound was new; and thereupon the defendant took issue, and prayed the court that the mayhem might be examined. A writ was accordingly sent to the sheriff to cause to come, *medicos chirurgicos de melioribus*, *London*, *ad informandum dominum regem et curiam de his, qua lis ex parte domini regis injungerentur*. And, in 1553, Mr. Justice Saunders is reported as saying: "If matters arise in our law which concern other sciences or faculties, we commonly apply for the aid of that science or faculty which it concerns, which is an honourable and commendable thing in our law, for thereby it appears that we don't despise all other sciences but our own, but we approve of them, and encourage them as things worthy of commendation."[1] Instances are recorded in the Year Books, where the courts received the opinions of witnesses learned in the sciences and arts.[2]

§ 3. **Opinion Evidence — Non-Professional Witnesses.** — The rule admitting the testimony of experts is exceptional,[3] for no principle of the law is better settled than that the opinions of witnesses are, in general, inadmissible in evidence.[4] They must state *facts*, and not opinions

---

[1] Buckley v. Rice, 1 Plowden, 125.
[2] 9 H. 7, 16; 7 H. 6, 11.
[3] Ellingwood v. Bragg, 52 N. H. 488; Polk v. State, 36 Ark. 117, 125.
[4] Continental Ins. Co. v. Delpench, 82 Penn. St. 225; Frost v. Blanchard, 97 Mass. 155; Hames v. Brownlee, 63 Ala. 277; Fitzgerald v. Hayward, 50 Mo. 516; Holden v. Robinson Co., 65 Me. 216; Thomas v. State, 40 Texas, 36; Lawrence v. Hudson, 59 Tenn. 671; Benedict v. City of Fon du Lac, 44 Wis. 495; Cummins v. State, 58 Ala. 387; Lewis v. Brown, 41 Me. 448; Scaggs v. Baltimore, etc. R. R. Co., 10 Md. 268; Higgins v. Carlton, 28 Md. 115; Hayes v. Wells, 34 Md. 513; Babcock v. Middlesex Savings Bank, 28 Conn. 306; McKnight v. State, 6 Tex. Ct. of App. 162; Seibles v. Blackwell, 1 McM. (S. C.) 57; Dawson v. Callaway, 18 Ga. 573; Hawkins v. State, 25 Ga. 207; Central Railroad, etc. v. Kelly, 58 Ga. 107; Rochester v. Chester, 3 N. H. 364; Patterson v. Colebrook, 9 Foster (N. H.) 94; Daniels v. Mosher, 2 Mich. 183; Griffin v. Town of Willow, 43 Wis. 509; Wood v. Chicago, etc. R. R. Co., 40 Wis. 582; Montgomery v. Town of Scott, 34 Wis. 338; Hollimau v. Cabanne, 43 Mo. 568; Bailey v. Pool, 13 Ired. (N. C.) 406; New Albany etc. R. R. Co. v. Huff, 19 Ind. 315; Robinson v. Fitchburg, etc. R. R. R. Co., 7 Gray (Mass.) 92; Forbes v. Caruthers, 3 Yeates, 527; Merritt v. Seaman, 6 N. Y. 168; Berckman v. Berckman, 16 N. J. Eq. 122

deduced from the facts; for it is the peculiar province of the jury to determine upon the inferences which are to be drawn from the facts. But to this general rule there are well recognized exceptions. Experience has demonstrated the difficulty which exists in certain cases, of stating the facts in detail to the jury in such a manner, that they shall produce the same impression upon the minds of the jurymen that they have legitimately produced upon the minds of the witnesses.[1] So that from the very necessities of the case, it is sometimes found essential that the opinions of ordinary witnesses should be received, as otherwise it would be impossible to arrive at any accurate conclusion as to the facts involved. Hence the opinions of witnesses, possessing no peculiar qualifications, have been received as to the identity of persons whom they have seen, or things which they have observed,[2] as well as to duration, distance, dimension, velocity, etc.[3] And a witness, without being an expert, may be asked whether a person appeared sober or intoxicated at the time he saw him,[4] and that without it being shown that the witness had any previous knowledge of the habits and conduct of such person.[5] And it does not seem to be necessary that a person should be an expert in order to make his opinion admissible as to the character of certain liquor, as to whether it was gin or not.[6] The

Corlis v. Little, 13 N. J. Law, 232; Massachusetts Life Ins. Co. v. Eshelman, 30 Ohio St. 647; Turner v. Cook, 36 Ind. 129; Shepard v. Pratt, 16 Kan. 209; Koons v. St. Louis & Iron Mountain R. R. Co., 65 Mo. 592; Mascheck v. St. Louis R. R. Co., 1 Mo. App. 600; Gassenheimer v. State, 52 Ala. 314; McAdory v. State, 59 Ala. 92; Houston, etc. R. R. Co. v. Smith, 52 Tex. 178.

[1] See Sydleman v. Beckwith, 43 Conn. 9.

[2] King v. N. Y. Central, etc. R. R. Co., 72 N. Y. 607; Woodward v. State, 4 Baxter (Tenn.) 322; Turner v. McFee, 61, Ala. 468; Beverly v. Williams, 4 Dev. & Batt. (N. C.) 236. In Commonwealth v. Williams, 105 Mass. 62, there was identification of a burglar by his voice.

[3] State v. Folwell, 14 Kans. 105; Eastman v. Amoskeag Manuf. Co., 44 N. H. 143.

[4] State v. Huxford, 47 Iowa, 16; People v. Eastwood, 14 N. Y. 562; s. c., 3 Parker Cr. Cas. 25; Stacy v. Portland Publishing Co. 68 Me. 279.

[5] Castner v. Sliker, 33 N. J. Law. 95; s. c., Ibid. 507.

[6] Commonwealth v. Timothy, 8 Gray (Mass.) 480. See also State v. Miller, 53 Iowa. 84.

opinions of witnesses have been received, that certain persons appeared attached to each other,[1] or that a person appeared to be sad,[2] or was of a certain age,[3] or seemed to be suffering and looked bad,[4] or was eccentric,[5] or was of a certain nationality.[6] So the opinions of ordinary witnesses have been admitted in evidence, that a horse appeared well and free from disease;[7] that a horse was safe and kind,[8] or that he had a sulky disposition,[9] and that a heap of stones in a highway was an object calculated to frighten horses of ordinary gentleness.[10] And a witness possessing no special qualifications has been permitted to express an opinion that certain shoes which he had seen appeared as if they had recently been washed,[11] and even that certain hairs were human,[12] and also that certain footprints corresponded with certain boots,[13] and that a certain wagon made certain tracks,[14] and that the sound of a wagon seemed to come from a certain point.[15] The opinion of a witness has been received that a certain estate was solvent.[16]

§ 4. **Opinion Evidence—Non-Professional Witnesses—Subject Continued.**— But the opinions of non-professional witnesses are never received, where the inquiry is into a

[1] Trelawney v. Colman, 2 Starkie R. 168; McKee v. Nelson, 4 Cowen (N. Y.) 355; Pelamourges v. Clark, 9 Iowa, 1, 17. See too, Evans v. People, 12 Mich. 27, 35; Blake v. People, 73 N. Y. 586.
[2] Culver v. Dwight, 6 Gray (Mass.) 444.
[3] Foltz v. State, 33 Ind. 215; Morse v. State, 6 Conn. 9; DeWitt v. Baily, 17 N. Y. 344; Benson v. McFadden, 50 Ind. 431; Kansas Pacific R. R. Co. v. Miller, 2 Col. 442.
[4] South, etc. Railroad Co. v. McLendon, 63 Ala. 266.
[5] Fraser v. Jennison, 42 Mich. 206, 215.
[6] Kansas Pacific R. R. Co. v. Miller, 2 Col. 442.
[7] Spear v. Richardson, 34 N. H. 428.
[8] Sydleman v. Beckwith, 43 Conn. 9.
[9] Whittier v. Franklin, 46 N. H. 23.
[10] Clinton v. Howard, 42 Conn. 294.
[11] Commonwealth v. Sturtivant, 117 Mass. 122.
[12] Commonwealth v. Dorsey, 103 Mass. 412.
[13] Commonwealth v. Pope, 103 Mass. 440; State v. Morris, 84 N. C. 756; State v. Reitz, 83 N. C. 634.
[14] State v. Folwell, 14 Kans. 105.
[15] State v. Shinborn, 46 N. H. 497.
[16] Reed v. Timmins, 52 Texas, 84.

subject matter, the nature of which requires some peculiar habit, study, or scientific knowledge to enable one to understand it and to form a correct judgment thereon.[1] This principle is more fully considered hereafter. It is, however, to be observed that in the case of non-professional witnesses, it is absolutely essential that they should have had the means of personal observation, and should have acquired a personal knowledge of the facts, as distinguished from a knowledge acquired from the testimony of others.[2] For no one but an expert can give testimony based on the testimony of others.[3] The Supreme Court of Massachusetts, in speaking of the admissibility of the opinions of non-professional witnesses, has laid down the law as follows: "The competency of this evidence rests upon two necessary conditions: first, that the subject matter to which the testimony relates cannot be reproduced or described to the jury precisely as it appeared to the witness at the time; and second, that the facts upon which the witness is called to express his opinion, are such as men in general are capable of comprehending and understanding.

When these conditions have been complied with or fulfilled in a given case, the court must then pass upon the question, whether the witness had the opportunity and means of inquiry, and was careful and intelligent in his observation and examination. It is not the mere qualification of the witness, but the extent and thoroughness of his examination into the specific facts to which the inquiry relates, and the general character of those facts, as affording to one, having his opportunity to judge, the requisite means to form an opinion. The same rule applies to this class of testimony, as to the testimony of experts, whether the expert is competent by his study or business, and whether he has qualified himself to testify, or had proper opportunity to examine, are preliminary questions for the court."[4]

[1] Linn v. Sigsbee, 67 Ill. 75.
[2] Eyerman v. Sheehan, 52 Mo. 221; Sydleman v. Beckwith, 43 Conn. 9.
[3] Paige v. Hazard, 5 Hill (N. Y.) 604; Hook v. Stovall, 30 Ga. 418.
[4] Commonwealth v. Sturtivant, 117 Mass. 122, 137.

While the general rule requires the witness first to state the facts upon which his opinion is based,[1] yet this is not always the case. For instance, in questions relating to identity of persons, the identification may be by the mere expression of the countenance, which cannot be described. And the witness may be correct although unable to describe a single feature, or to give the color of the hair, or of the eyes, or the particulars of the dress.[2]

§ 5. **Opinion Evidence — When Expert Testimony is Admissible.** — The rule is, that the opinions of experts or skilled witnesses are admissible in evidence in those cases in which the matter of inquiry is such, that inexperienced persons are unlikely to prove capable of forming a correct judgment upon it, for the reason that the subject matter so far partakes of the nature of a science, art or trade, as to require a previous habit, or experience, or study in it, in order to acquire a knowledge of it. When the question involved does not lie within the range of common experience, or common knowledge, but requires special experience, or special knowledge, then the opinions of witnesses skilled in the particular science, art or trade to which the question relates, are admissible in evidence.[3] "It is not because a man has a reputation for

---

[1] See § 61, and cases cited in note at end of that section.
[2] See Sydleman v. Beckwith, 43 Conn. 9, 13.
[3] Folkes v. Chadd, 3 Douglas, (26 Eng. C. L. 63) 175; Chaurand v. Angerstein, Peake N. P. C. 61; Campbell v. Ricards. 5 Barn. & Ad. 840; Davis v. State, 38 Md. 15, 38; City of Chicago v. McGiven, 78 Ill. 347; City of Parsons v. Lindsay, 26 Kans. 426, 432; Monroe v. Lattin, 25 Kans. 351; Roberts v. Commissioners of Brown county, 21 Kans. 248; Cromwell v. Western Reserve Bank, 3 Ohio St. 406; Cleveland etc. R. R. Co. v. Ball, 5 Ohio St. 568, 573; Page v. Parker, 40 N. H. 59; Jones v. Tucker, 41 N. H. 546; Sowers v. Dukes, 8 Minn. 23; Cole v. Clark, 3 Wis. 323; Cottrill v. Myrick, 12 Me. 222, 231; Humphries v. Johnson, 20 Ind. 190; Dillard v. State, 58 Miss. 368; Wagner v. Jacob, 26 Mo. 530; Newmark v. Liverpool etc. Ins. Co., 30 Mo. 165; Whitmore v. Bowman, 4 G. Greene, (Iowa,) 148; Pelamourges v. Clark, 9 Iowa, 1, 13; Bearss v. Copley, 10 N. Y. 95; Robertson v. Stark, 15 N. H. 109, 113; Norman v. Wells, 17 Wend. 136, 162; Lincoln v. Saratoga etc. R. R. Co., 23 Wend. 425, 432; Terpenning v. The Corn Exchange Ins Co., 43 N. Y. 279, 282; Evansville R. R. Co. v. Fitzpatrick, 10 Ind. 120; Mish v.

sagacity, and judgment, and power of reasoning," as Mr. Chief Justice SHAW has said, "that his opinion is admissible; if so, such men might be called in all cases, to advise the jury, and it would change the mode of trial. But it is because a man's professional pursuits, his peculiar skill and knowledge in some department of science, not common to men in general, enable him to draw an inference, where men of common experience, after all the facts proved, would be left in doubt."[1] And the rule admitting the opinions of experts in such cases, is founded on necessity,[2] for juries are not selected with any view to their knowledge of a particular science, art or trade, requiring a course of previous study, experience and preparation.[3] It, therefore, becomes matter of necessity, when questions arise which do not lie within the ordinary information of men in general, but fall rather within the limits of some art or science, that juries should have the benefit to be derived from the opinions of witnesses possessing peculiar skill in the particular departments of knowledge to which such questions relate. So that it may be said that the foundation on which expert testimony rests, is the supposed superior knowledge or experience of the expert in relation to the subject matter upon which he is permitted to give an opinion as evidence.[4] And it has been said that it is because all persons have not the leisure or capacity to master the principles of art or

Wood, 34 Penn. St. 451, 453; Snow v. Boston etc. R. R. Co., 65 Me. 230; Tebbetts v. Haskins, 16 Me. 283, 287; Forbes v. Caruthers, 3 Yeates, (Penn.) 527; Hastings v. Steamer Uncle Sam, 10 Cal. 341; Kline v. K. C., St. J. etc. R. R. Co., 50 Iowa, 656; Hamilton v. Des Moines Valley R. R. Co., 36 Iowa, 31; Bills v. Ottumwa, 35 Iowa, 107; Higgins v. Carlton, 28 Md. 115; Marshall v. Columbian etc. Ins. Co., 7 Foster, (N. H.) 157; Hill v. Lafayette Ins. Co., 2 Mich. 476, 481; Milwaukee etc. R. R. Co. v. Kellogg, 94 U. S. 469, 473; Lester v. Pitsford, 7 Vt. 158; Cavendish v. Troy, 41 Vt. 99, 108; Rochester etc. R. R. Co. v. Budlong, 10 How. Pr. 289, 291; Slater v. Wilcox, 57 Barb. 604, 608; Taylor v. Town of Monroe. 43 Conn. 36, 43; State v. Clark, 15 S. C. (N. S.) 403, 408.

[1] New England Glass Co. v. Lovell, 7 Cush. 319.
[2] State v. Clark, 12 Ired. (N. C.) Law, 152, 153; City of Chicago v. McGiven, 78 Ill. 347.
[3] Hartford Protection Ins. Co. v. Harmer, 2 Ohio St. 452, 457.
[4] Clark v. Rockland Water Power Co., 52 Me. 68, 77.

science; that those who are specially skilled in either, are allowed to give their opinions in evidence.[1]

§ 6. **When Expert Testimony is Admissible — The Subject Continued.** — The Supreme Court of New Hampshire, in declaring under what circumstances the testimony of experts may be properly received in evidence, has classified the cases under three heads, and declares that experts may give their opinions:

1. Upon questions of science, skill or trade, or others of like kind.

2. When the subject matter of inquiry is such, that inexperienced persons are unlikely to prove capable of forming a correct judgment upon it, without such assistance.

3. When the subject matter of investigation so far partakes of the nature of a science, as to require a course of previous habit or study, in order to the attainment of a knowledge of it.[2]

And a very satisfactory statement of the law upon this point, is to be found in a recent decision of the Supreme Court of Iowa, and is as follows: "It is often very difficult to determine in regard to what particular matters and points witnesses may give testimony by way of opinion. It is doubtful whether all the cases can be harmonized, or brought within any general rule or principle. The most comprehensive and accurate rule upon the subject, we believe to be as follows: That the opinion of witnesses possessing peculiar skill is admissible whenever the subject matter of inquiry is such, that inexperienced persons are not likely to prove capable of forming a correct judgment upon it, without such assistance; in other words, when it so far partakes of the nature of a science, as to require a course of previous habit or study in order to the attainment of a knowledge of it, and that the opinions of witnesses cannot be received when the inquiry is into a subject matter, the nature of which is not such as to require any particular habits of

---

[1] Atchison etc. R. R. Co. v. United States, 15 Ct. of Claims. 140.
[2] Jones v. Tucker, 41 N. H. 546.

study in order to qualify a man to understand it. If the relations of facts and their probable results can be determined without especial skill or study, the facts themselves must be given in evidence, and the conclusions or inferences must be drawn by the jury."[1] In a late case in Minnesota, it is said that the opinion of a witness possessing peculiar skill, is admissible whenever the subject of inquiry is such that inexperienced persons are unlikely to prove capable of forming a correct judgment upon it without such assistance.[2] While in New York it is said that "the opinions of experts are only admissible, when it appears from the nature of their avocations, or from their testimony concerning their experience, that the matter inquired about involves some degree of science or skill which they have made use of, so that from experience, they are fitted to answer the question propounded with more accuracy than others who may not have been called upon to employ science, or exercise skill on the subject."[3] And it is laid down that upon all questions, except those, the knowledge of which is presumed to be alike common to all men, whatever may have been their education or employment, the opinion of persons skilled in the particular subject to which the question relates, is admissible.[4] "The true test," says the Supreme Court of Connecticut, "of the admissibility of such testimony, is not whether the subject matter is common or uncommon, or whether many persons or few have some knowledge of the matter; but it is whether the witnesses offered as experts, have any peculiar knowledge or experience, not common to the world, which renders their opinions, founded on such knowledge or experience, any aid to the court or to the jury in determining the questions at issue."[5]

[1] Muldowney v. Illinois Central R. R. Co., 36 Iowa, 472.
[2] Kipner v. Biebl, (Sup. Ct. of Minn.) Alb. Law J., Sept. 3d, 1881.
[3] Clark v. Bruce, 19 Hun, 274, 276.
[4] Rochester etc. R. R. Co. v. Budlong, 10 How. Pr. 289, 291.
[5] Taylor v. Town of Monroe, 43 Conn. 36, 44.

§ 7. **Meaning of the Terms "Science" and "Art."**—It is sometimes laid down in a general way, that the opinions of experts are admissible only when the subject matter of inquiry relates to some "science" or "art." It is to be observed, however, that these words include all subjects on which a course of special study or experience is necessary to the formation of an opinion,[1] and that it is not necessary "that a specialty to enable one of its practitioners to be examined as an expert, should involve abstruse scientific conditions."[2] "Art, in its legal significance, embraces every operation of human intelligence, whereby something is produced outside of nature; and the term 'science' includes all human knowledge which has been generalized, and systematized, and has obtained method, relations and the forms of law."[3] So that, although it is generally laid down that the opinions of experts are limited to matters of science, art or skill, yet this limitation is not to be applied in any rigid or narrow sense.[4] And every business or employment, which has a particular class devoted to its pursuit, is said to be an art or trade, within the meaning of the rule.[5] As has been said in the Irish Exchequer Chamber by Pigot, C. B., "the subjects to which this kind of evidence is applicable, are not confined to classed and specified professions. It is applicable wherever peculiar skill and judgment, applied to a particular subject, are required to explain results, or trace them to their causes."[6]

§ 8. **Expert Testimony — When Inadmissible.**—Whenever the subject matter of inquiry is of such a character that it may be presumed to lie "within the common experience of all men of common education, moving in ordinary

[1] Stephen's Dig. of Law of Evid., Art. 49, p. 104.
[2] Story v. Maclay, 3 Mon. (Ky.) 480, 483.
[3] Atchison etc. R. R. Co. v. United States, 15 Ct. of Claims, 140, per Davis J.
[4] Clifford v. Richardson, 18 Vt. 620, 627; Sturgis v. Knapp, 33 Vt. 486, 531.
[5] Rochester etc. R. R. Co. v. Budlong, 10 How. Pr. 289, 291; and Taylor v. Town of Monroe, 43 Conn. 36, 43.
[6] 1 Irish R. (Com. L.) 211, 218.

walks of life," the rule is that the opinions of experts are inadmissible, as the jury are supposed in all such matters to be entirely competent to draw the necessary inferences from the facts testified of by the witnesses.[1] The testimony of experts is inadmissible upon a matter concerning which, with the same knowledge of the facts, the opinion of any one else would have as much weight. It is only admissible when the facts to be determined are obscure, and can only be made clear by and through the opinions of persons skilled in relation to the subject matter of inquiry.[2] "If the jury can be put in possession of all the facilities for forming a correct opinion that the witness had, they must come to their conclusions unembarrassed by the opinions of others."[3] "It is only where the matter inquired of lies within the range of the peculiar skill and experience of the witness, and is one of which the ordinary knowledge and experience of mankind does not enable them to see what inferences should be drawn from the facts, that the witness may supply opinions as their guide."[4] So that the testimony of experts is inadmissible in regard to matters upon which one individual can form a judgment as well as another, both having equal knowledge of the circumstances.[5] As expressed in a recent case, the opinions of witnesses, though experts, are not admissible as to matters which do not so far partake of the nature of a science as to require a course of previous habit or study in order to an attainment of a knowledge of them.[6] While there is no doubt as to

[1] New England Glass Co. v. Lovell, 7 Cush. (Mass.) 319; Shafter v. Evans, 53 Cal. 32; City of Chicago v. McGiven, 78 Ill. 347; Naughton v. Stagg, 4 Mo. App. 271; Cook v. State, 24 N. J. Law, 843, 852; Dillard v. State, 58 Miss. 368; Gavick v. Pacific R. R. Co., 49 Mo. 274; Concord Railroad Co. v. Greely, 3 Foster (N. H.) 237, 243; Nashville, etc. R. R. Co. v. Carroll, 53 Tenn. 347; Linn v. Sigsbee, 67 Ill. 75; Veerhusen v. Chicago, etc. R. R. Co., 53 Wis. 689, 694; White v. Ballou, 8 Allen, 408; Hovey v. Sawyer, 5 Allen, 554; Perkins v. Augusta, etc. Banking Co., 10 Gray, 312; Clark v. Fisher, 1 Paige, Ch. 171; s. c., 19 Am. Decis. 402.
[2] Western Ins. Co. v. Tobin, 32 Ohio St. 77, 96.
[3] Dillard v. State, 58 Miss. 368, 388.
[4] Kennedy v. People, 39 N. Y. 245.
[5] Hart v. Hudson River Bridge Co., 84 N. Y. 56, 60, 61.
[6] Pennsylvania Coal Co. v. Conlan, 101 Ill.

the general rule, it is often found exceedingly difficult to determine whether the facts to be examined are to be considered as beyond the range of ordinary intelligence. It is, therefore, not surprising to find the courts declaring that " the decisions are by no means clear or satisfactory upon the distinctions " between the facts that lie within the range of common experience and ordinary intelligence, and those that lie beyond them. And that " the principles on which the authorities rest are more consistent than the attempts to apply them." [1]

In illustration of the general principle that the opinions of experts will not be received as to facts within the common experience of men, we shall notice the following cases. It has been held that the opinion of one whose occupation was the braking and switching of cars, was inadmissible on the question of whether it would be prudent for a man to stand any other way than flatwise in making a coupling of cars, and whether it was considered safe or unsafe among brakemen to stand facing the draft iron while making the coupling.[2] That a railroad expert could not be asked whether the time which a railroad train stopped at a station was sufficient to enable passengers to get off.[3] That a railroad conductor could not be asked whether a person would have been thrown from the cars, if, at the time of the cars striking, he had been holding on to the brakes, and exercising ordinary care and prudence in his own protection and preservation.[4] That an experienced railroad man could not be asked the following question: " Suppose there was a man standing by the side of a switch that night, and holding a lantern, such as you have described, a foot or two from the ground, how far away from the target could the man see the top of the target, or any part of the target above the lantern?" [5]

---

[1] Evans v. People, 12 Mich. 27.
[2] Belair v. The C. & N. W. R. Co., 43 Iowa, 667; Muldowney v. Illinois Cent. R. R. Co., 36 Iowa, 472.
[3] Keller v. N. Y. Central R. R. Co., 2 Abbott (Ct. of App.) 480.
[4] Gavisk v. Pacific R. R., 49 Mo. 274.
[5] Weane v. K. & D. M. R. Co., 45 Iowa, 246.

§ 9. Expert Testimony — When Inadmissible — The Subject Continued. — That a medical expert who had testified as to the injury of the plaintiff's fingers being very severe — that the fingers were badly mashed — that the middle finger was quite stiff, and forefinger permanently stiff — could not answer the following questions:

"I will ask you to state to what extent the injury impairs the usefulness of that hand for any skilled occupation, or any occupation requiring a quick and ready use of the hand?"

"State the degree to which the usefulness of that hand would be impaired for skilled labor, requiring a quick and ready use of the fingers, such as coupling and braking cars on the railroad?"[1]

That a physician could not testify as to the possibility of a rape having been committed in a particular manner, described by the prosecutrix. "No peculiar knowledge of the human system was necessary to answer it. It was a mere question of relative strength or mechanical possibility, which an athlete or a mechanic could have answered as well as a physician, and every man upon the jury as well as either."[2]

That brokers and bankers could not be asked whether brokers and bankers would discount a note of the appearance of the one in question, without a wilful failure to inquire into the circumstances under which it was obtained—the note was written on tracing paper.[3]

That detectives could not express an opinion as to whether it was possible to commit a robbery in the manner charged.[4] That a surveyor could not express an opinion as an expert as to where the highest part of a hill was.[5] That an innkeeper

---

[1] Kline v. The K. C., St. J. & C. B. R. Co., 50 Iowa, 656.
[2] Cook v. State, 24 N. J. Law, 843.
[3] Rowland v. Fowler, 37 Conn. 348.
[4] People v. Morrigan, 29 Mich. 1. "If experts were allowable on questions of criminal science, the professors and practitioners of that science would naturally be the experts needed."
[5] Hovey v. Sawyer, 5 Allen (Mass.), 554.

could not express an opinion as to whether it was safe for a guest to keep his money in a locked trunk.[1]

That firemen, long connected with a city fire department— to whom had been presented a plan of the buildings, with a statement of the distances between them, the materials of which they were constructed, the direction of the wind, the state of the weather, and the fact that no water was used on the fire — could not be asked whether or not in their opinion the dwelling house and connected buildings would take fire from the barn; whether or not it was a common occurrence for fire to be communicated from leeward to windward across a space greater than twenty-six feet; whether or not, in their experience, large wooden buildings or large fires made their own currents, frequently eddying against the prevailing wind.[2]

§ 10. Expert Testimony — When Inadmissible — The Subject Continued.— That an expert accustomed to the use of fire-arms could not be asked whether a certain piece of paper had been used as wadding, and as such shot from a loaded gun.[3] That the question whether the deceased, seated at or near a window, through which he was shot, could have seen and recognized the person on the outside who inflicted the wound, was not one of skill or science, and that, therefore, experiments made by others, and the results thereof, and opinions founded thereon, were inadmissible.[4]

It has been held that the testimony of experts was incompetent to show whether the placing of wet staves upon the outside of an arch, in which a fire was kindled, was a safe and prudent method of drying them.[5]

---

[1] Taylor v. Monnot, 4 Duer (N. Y.) 116.
[2] State v. Watson, 65 Me. 74.
[3] Manke v. People 24 Hun (N. Y.), 316; s. c., 78 N. Y. 611. The court said it could have been determined by a jury from a description of the facts touching the appearance of the paper when found, such as the manner in which it was folded, whether it appeared to have been partially burned, whether it bore upon its creases traces of powder stains, etc.
[4] Jones v. State, 71 Ind. 66.
[5] White v. Ballou, 8 Allen, 408.

That the opinion of a person experienced in clearing land by fire was inadmissible, as to the probability that a fire set under the circumstances described by the witnesses, would have spread to the adjoining land.[1] But the opinion of a person experienced in prairie fires has been received in answer to the question: "How many feet in width in plowing do you think would be necessary to stop a fire on stubble land?"[2] The court held that it was not a matter of common knowledge, as to how far a fire in the stubble might be carried in the air or might "jump." The jury could not be presumed as well able to form an opinion as could a witness who had had actual experience in such matters. And in a case lately decided in New York it has been decided that a witness experienced in clearing land, could express an opinion as an expert as to whether a fire was set at a proper time. "A man who had never cleared up land, or worked a farm, might be unable to determine whether the time was proper for burning, even after he had been informed of all the facts."[3]

It has been held that the question of what is the proximate cause of an injury is not a question of science, or of legal knowledge, but is a fact to be determined by a jury from surrounding circumstances.[4] Whether glass placed in a sidewalk to afford light to the area below is unsafe, by reason of the too great smoothness or slipperiness of its surface, is not a question of science or skill such as to render the opinions of witnesses admissible.[5] So it has been said that whether a street crossing is unsafe and dangerous is not a question of science or skill, upon which it is proper to receive the opinions of witnesses.[6] On the other hand, it has been held that professional road builders may be examined as experts

---

[1] Higgins v. Dewey, 107 Mass. 494. And see Fraser v. Tupper, 29 Vt. 409.
[2] Kippner v. Biebl (Sup. Ct. of Minn.), Alb. Law J., Sept. 3, 1881.
[3] Ferguson v. Hubbell, 26 Hun, 250.
[4] Milwaukee, etc. R. R. Co. v. Kellogg, 94 U. S. 469.
[5] City of Chicago v. McGiven, 78 Ill. 347.
[6] City of Parsons v. Lindsay, 26 Kan. 426, 432.

as to the safety of a road, and the necessity of a railing along an elevated part of the road. "If this case," say the court, "falls pretty near the line, we think it is clearly on that side of the line that permits expert testimony."[1] In Wisconsin it is said that "possibly there might be cases in which the opinions of experts might be admissible upon matters going to the sufficiency of a highway. Generally, however, it is a pure question of fact, not of science or skill."[2]

It is evident, therefore, that to make the opinions of experts admissible in evidence it is necessary:

First. That the subject matter of inquiry should be within the range of the peculiar skill and experience of the witness.

And, *Second.* That it should be one of which the ordinary knowledge and experience of mankind does not enable them to see what inferences should be drawn from the facts.

If either of these two requisites are wanting, the subject of inquiry is not such as to admit of the introduction of expert testimony.[3] And all the cases recognize the rule that it is for the court to determine whether the subject matter is one of science, art or trade, or whether it is a matter of common experience.[4]

§ 11. **Inadmissibility of Opinions Founded on a Theory of Morals or Ethics.** — The opinion of a witness, not founded on science, but as a theory of morals or ethics, is inadmissible in evidence, whether given by professional or unprofessional witnesses. Hence, where the question was whether a man who had committed suicide was sane or insane, the opinion of a physician that no sane man would commit suicide in a Christian country, was held inadmissible, as being founded, not on the phenomena of mind, but rather on a theory of morals, religion and a future state.[5]

---

[1] Taylor v. Town of Monroe, 43 Conn. 36, 44.
[2] Benedict v. City of Fond du Lac, 44 Wis. 496. And see Oleson v. Tolford, 37 Wis. 327; Montgomery v. Scott, 34 Wis. 338.
[3] Manke v. People, 24 Hun (N. Y.), 416; s. c., 78 N. Y. 611.
[4] Dillard v. State, 58 Miss. 368, 388.
[5] St. Louis Mutual Life Ins. Co. v. Graves, 6 Bush, (Ky.) 290.

And the opinions of medical practitioners are inadmissible on the question whether a physician has honorably and faithfully discharged his duty to his medical brethren.[1]

§ 12. Inadmissibility of Opinions on Abstract Questions of Science, not Related to the Facts in Issue. —The opinions of professional witnesses cannot be asked upon mere abstract questions of science, having no proper relation to the facts upon which the jury are to pass. The opinion of an expert, to be admissible, must always be predicated upon, and relate to the facts disclosed by the evidence in the case.[2]

§ 13. Inadmissibility of Opinions Based on Speculative Data. —The rule is, that the opinions of experts are not admissible when based on merely speculative data.[3] On a trial for murder, where the question was asked whether the deceased was not addicted to the excessive use of snuff and violent fits of passion, the evidence being desired as a basis for the introduction of expert testimony, to prove that such habits and temperament indicated the probable presence of a condition from which sudden death might well have resulted, without reference to the blow given by the prisoner, it was held that such expert testimony could not be received, as no evidence had been introduced, and none offered, to prove that the deceased was in a violent fit of passion, or had taken an overdose of snuff at the time the blow was struck. The court ruled the testimony inadmissible, as being speculative in its nature.[4] And where it did not appear that the medical witness had been present at the *post mortem* examination, or that he had any knowledge of the case, or the kind, or extent of the examination needed, the court refused to allow him to answer the following question : " For the purpose of arriving at a correct conclusion in the case of the death of a person, where you don't know to your own satisfaction what caused the death, how

---

[1] Ramadge v. Ryan, 9 Bing. 333.
[2] Champ v. Commonwealth, 2 Met. (Ky.) 18.
[3] Cooper v. State, 23 Texas, 336, 337.
[4] Ebos v. State, 31 Ark. 520.

long a time should two men give to a *post mortem* examination? And would four hours be sufficient?"[1] So an engineer has not been permitted to express an opinion as to the original purpose in view, in building a wall which had been standing between twenty or thirty years.[2] The Supreme Court of Mississippi has held it to be incompetent to show by the testimony of professional persons, in impeachment of the mother's testimony, in a prosecution for bastardy, that it was highly improbable that impregnation could be produced by the first act of coition.[3] Such testimony was said to be too uncertain, indefinite, and hypothetical to form the basis of judicial action. "The courts, in our opinion," it is said, "have gone quite far enough in subjecting the life, liberty and property of the citizen to the mere speculative *opinions* of men claiming to be *experts* in matters of science, whose confidence, in many cases, bears a direct similitude and ratio to their ignorance. We are not disposed to extend this doctrine into the field of hypothetical conjecture and probability, and to give certainty as evidence, to that which, in its very nature, must be wholly uncertain and unsatisfactory; dependent on circumstances and conditions entirely secret, hidden and unknown, as facts, and without a knowledge of which, neither science nor experience, however great, could afford us the remotest information."

§ 14. **Inadmissibility of the Testimony of Experts who have made Ex Parte Investigations.**—It is important in many cases that notice should be given to the opposing interest of the intention to have experts make an investigation of the facts involved. For instance, if it is proposed to make an examination of blood on clothing, or of the stomach of a deceased person in cases of alleged poisoning, there are strong reasons why such an examination should be undertaken after notice has been given, in order that the adverse interest might be properly represented at such an

[1] State v. Pike, 65 Me. 111.
[2] Sinnott v. Mullin, 82 Penn. St. 342.
[3] Anonymous, 37 Miss. 54.

examination. And it has been laid down that there can be no question that when the matter comes fairly up, such examinations, when taken flagrantly *ex parte*, at a time when there could readily have been notice to the opposite side, will be ruled out as inadmissible.[1] The principle does not apply, however, to investigations conducted by a public officer immediately after the commission of a crime, for the public action of such a functionary is said to be adequate notice to all parties that the proceeding is taking place. Neither does the principle apply in those cases in which the investigation or examination could not be enhanced in accuracy or authoritativeness by being preceded by notice.[2]

When a *post mortem* examination of a deceased person is made, the admissibility of the testimony of the physicians who made it, does not at all depend on the thoroughness of the examination which they made.[3] In the case cited, the question was whether death had been caused by internal disease or external violence. And the physicians were allowed to express an opinion thereon, although their examination had not been sufficiently thorough to enable them to state that no other cause existed than the one they assigned, to which the death could be attributed.

[1] 2 Wharton & Stelle's Medical Jurisprudence, Pt. II., § 1246.
[2] Ibid., § 1247.
[3] State v. Porter, 34 Iowa, 131, 134.

CHAPTER II.

THE COMPETENCY OF EXPERT WITNESSES.

SECTION.
15. The Competency of Expert Witnesses must First be Shown.
16. Their Competency a Question for the Court.
17. Whether a Witness Possesses the Qualifications of an Expert, is a Question of Fact.
18. Preliminary Examination of the Expert.
19. No exact Test for Determining Amount of Experience Expert should Possess.
20. Competency of Experts whose Knowledge is derived from Study.
21. Competency of Experts whose Knowledge is derived from Study —The Subject Continued.
22. Competency sometimes dependent on whether the Expert has Heard the Testimony.
23. Competency of Experts in Particular Cases.

§ 15. **The Competency of Expert Witnesses must First be Shown.**—If the subject matter of inquiry is such that the opinion of an expert may be properly received in evidence, then the question arises, when the witness is offered as an expert, whether he possesses the requisite qualifications to entitle him to testify in that character. And that he possesses such qualifications, peculiar skill and experience in the particular department of inquiry, must appear in evidence before he can properly be asked to express any opinion in the case.[1] "That an expert must have special and peculiar knowledge or skill, is as definite a rule as that the search for a lost paper, or subscribing witness, must be

[1] Chicago & Alton R. R. Co. v. Springfield & Northwestern R. R. Co., 67 Ill. 142; Heald v. Thing, 45 Me. 392; State v. Secrest, 80 N. C. 450; Washington v. Cole, 6 Ala. 212; Tullis v. Kidd, 12 Ala. 648; State v. Ward, 29 Vt. 225, 236; Tyler v. Todd, 36 Conn. 218, 221.

diligent and thorough."[1] Whether the witness has that knowledge, is as much a question of fact to be determined preliminary to the reception of his testimony, as the question whether the search for a lost paper has been diligent and thorough. And if his testimony is called for before his qualifications have been shown, it has been held sufficient to interpose the general objection, that the testimony is "illegal and improper," without interposing the special objection that his competency as an expert has not been shown.[2]

§ 16. **Their Competency a Question for the Court.**— The question whether the witness possesses the necessary qualifications to render him competent to testify in the character of an expert, is a preliminary question addressed to the court, which should be satisfied upon that point, by the presentation of proper evidence.[3] The question must be determined by the court, and cannot be referred by it to the jury.[4] And in determining whether the witness is a person of skill in the particular department, or subject matter in which his opinion is desired, the rule is, that very much is left to the discretion of the presiding judge,[5] and

[1] Jones v. Tucker, 41 N. H. 546.
[2] Brown v. Mohawk & Hudson R. R. R. Co., 1 Howard's Ct. of App. Cas., 52, 124.
[3] Nelson v. Sun Mutual Ins. Co., 71 N. Y. 453, 460; Lincoln v. Inhabitants of Barre, 5 Cush. 591; Flynt v. Bodenhamer, 80 N. C. 205, 207; Gulf City Ins. Co. v. Stephens, 52 Ala. 121; Forgery v. First National Bank, 66 Ind. 123; Davis v. State, 35 Ind. 496; Boardman v. Woodman, 47 N. H. 120, 135; Sorg v. First German Congregation, 63 Penn. St. 156; Reynolds v. Lounsbury, 6 Hill, (N. Y.) 534; Sikes v. Paine, 10 Ired. (N. C.) Law, 282; State v. Secrest, 80 N. C. 450; Washington v. Cole, 6 Ala. 212; Tullis v. Kidd, 12 Ala. 648; Woodman v. Dana, 52 Me. 9, 13; Delaware etc. Steam Towboat Co. v. Starrs, 69 Penn. St. 36; Jones v. Tucker, 41 N. H. 546; Snowden v. Idaho Quartz Manuf. Co., 55 Cal. 450; McEwen v. Bigelow, 40 Mich. 217; State v. Ward, 29 Vt. 225, 236.
[4] Fairbank v. Hughson, 13 Reporter, 8. In this case the Supreme Court of California reversed a judgment, because the trial court allowed a book-keeper in a bank to testify, (having been offered as an expert in handwriting,) with the remark, "I shall hold it is for the jury to say how much he knows about it. I will admit the testimony."
[5] Hills v. Home Ins. Co., 129 Mass. 345; Chandler v. Jamaica Pond Aqueduct, 125 Mass. 544, 551; Tucker v. Massachusetts Central R. R. Co., 118 Mass. 546; Lawrence v. Boston, 119 Mass. 126; Lawton v.

his decision will not be overruled, except in a clear and strong case.[1] An objection to the ruling of the court, upon the sufficiency of the proof in such cases, must be made at the time of the trial, as it cannot be raised in the first instance in the court above.[2] And the decision of the trial court, as to the qualifications of a witness introduced as an expert, will be deemed conclusive in the court above, unless the entire evidence upon that point is reported, and appears to present a question of law.[3] If it appears that the witnesses offered had any claim to the character of experts, the court will not reverse on the ground that their experience was not sufficiently special.[4]

§ 17. **Whether a Witness Possesses the Qualifications of an Expert is a Question of Fact.**— An examination of the cases in which the courts have passed on the competency of experts, shows a lamentable confusion and mixing up of matter of fact with matter of law, it has been judicially commented on as leading to most unsatisfactory results, and unnecessarily obscuring the true aspect of the law on this subject by the diversity of practice which has prevailed in the judicial tribunals. The subject of the competency of experts has been ably considered by the Supreme Court of New Hampshire, and the principle which should govern so clearly and succinctly laid down, that much confusion will be avoided by keeping it clearly in mind in such cases. The principle, although " a perfectly, clear, fixed, and certain condition of the law upon the subject," has been lost sight of in many cases. As ex-

---

Chase, 108 Mass. 238, 241; Berg v. Spink, 24 Minn. 138. 139; Howard v. Providence, 6 R. I. 516; Ardesco Oil Co. v. Gilson, 63 Penn. St. 146, 152; Kipner v. Biebl, Sup. Ct. of Minn. (Alb. Law J., Sept. 3d, 1881); Sarle v. Arnold, 7 R. I. 586; Delaware etc. Steam Towboat Co. v. Starrs, 69 Penn. St. 36.

[1] Sorg v. First German Congregation, 63 Penn. St. 156.
[2] Hand v. Brookline, 126 Mass. 324.
[3] Gossler v. Eagle Sugar Refinery, 103 Mass. 331, 335; Quinsigamond Bank v. Hobbs, 11 Gray, 250, 258; Marcy v. Barnes, 16 Gray, 161; Sarle v. Arnold, 7 R. I. 586.
[4] Delaware etc. Steam Towboat Co. v. Starrs, 69 Penn. St. 36.

pressed by Mr. Justice Doe, the rule is as follows: "When a witness is offered as an expert three questions necessarily arise: 1. Is the subject concerning which he is to testify, one upon which the opinion of an expert can be received? 2. What are the qualifications necessary to entitle a witness to testify as an expert? 3. Has the witness those qualifications? The first two questions are matters of law; the third is matter of fact. * * *

As to the third question, while it is settled, as matter of law, what qualifications are requisite, the possession of those qualifications is equally well settled to be a question of fact, purely within the discretion of the judge before whom the witness is offered. His decision concerning the matter is not subject to revision. It would not be wise to adopt a different rule. The ability or disability of a witness to testify, under the legal requirements for the admission of opinion, is a matter most conveniently and satisfactorily determined at the trial, upon personal examination of the witness. It can, indeed, be determined in no other way." [1] Or, as the Supreme Court of Vermont has expressed it, "So long as the evidence of facts do not constitute or conclusively show the skill, and such skill is matter of fact to be inferred from such evidence or facts, the finding of the court in that respect is not revisable as being error in law." [2]

§ 18. **Preliminary Examination of Expert.**—For the purpose of determining the competency of the witness, a preliminary examination takes place, in which the witness may be asked to state his acquaintance with the subject matter in reference to which his opinion is desired, and what he has done to qualify himself as an expert in that particular department of inquiry.[3] The court is also at liberty to examine other witnesses as to whether he is qualified to draw correct conclusions upon questions relating to the science or trade in relation to which he is to be

---

[1] Jones v. Tucker, 41 N. H. 547; Dole v. Johnson, 50 N. H. 452. 458.
[2] Wright v. Williams' Estate, 47 Vt. 222, 233.
[3] Boardman v. Woodman, 47 N. H. 120, 135.

examined.[1] On this preliminary examination the court simply decides upon proof of the opportunities which the witness has had for acquiring special knowledge and experience in the subject matter, that the jury may hear his opinion as a person of science and skill.[2] In passing upon the competency of the witness, however, the fact should be borne in mind that the law does not require that a witness skilled in a particular art or trade, should be actually engaged in its practice at the time of the trial.[3] So one who, at the time he was offered as a witness was a student at law, has been allowed to testify as an expert in the tanning business, he having formerly been employed in that trade.[4] "There was nothing in the change of employment, from tanning hides to the study of the law, which would necessarily deprive him of the skill acquired in his original trade." But it has been held no error to hold that a witness who had not been engaged in the occupation of a plumber for twenty years, could not testify as an expert in matters pertaining to that trade. "This was a long time to be out of a business," said the court, "that must have changed so greatly in that time, and we cannot say that the ruling was clearly erroneous. The court must exercise a judicial discretion regarding the reception of evidence purporting to be that of experts; and presumptively there must in a business like this be much better expert evidence than that of a person so long out of the business."[5] It is evident that in all such cases the question of competency must depend largely on the nature of the trade or occupation, as well as on the length of time since the witness abandoned it. It is also to

---

[1] Mendum v. Commonwealth, 6 Rand. 704, 710; Tullis v. Kidd, 12 Ala. 648.

[2] State v. Secrest, 80 N. C. 450, 457.

[3] Vander Donckt v. Thellusson, 8 Man. G. & S. (65 Eng. C. L.) 812. "Whatever the line of business he now follows, if he was an expert before, he can hardly be said to be less so now," per Mr. Justice Maule. See, too, Roberts v. Johnson, 58 N. Y. 613; Tullis v. Kidd, 12 Ala. 648, 650.

[4] Bearss v. Copley, 10 N. Y. 93.

[5] McEwen v. Bigelow, 40 Mich. 217.

be borne in mind on such preliminary examinations, that while there are various grades of experts, it is not considered necessary that the witness should possess the highest degree of skill to qualify him to testify in the character of an expert.[1] But his peculiar skill, knowledge, or experience should have been acquired by him in some trade or profession.[2]

§ 19. **No Exact Test for Determining Amount of Experience Expert should Possess.**—"We find no test laid down," says the Supreme Court of Indiana, "by which we can determine with mathematical precision, just how much experience a witness must have had, how expert, in short, he must be, to render him competent to testify as an expert."[3] But it is for the court to decide within the limits of a fair discretion whether the experience of the supposed expert has been such as to make his opinions of any value.[4] Mere opportunities for special observation are not sufficient to render a witness competent to testify as an expert. For example, a painter by trade who had worked at his calling for twenty years, and who swore that his experience as a painter had enabled him to judge of the quality and character of carpenter work and material, was held incompetent to testify as an expert respecting the workmanlike manner in which the carpenter and joiner work was done upon a house on which he did the painting.[5] So a miller is not a

[1] Yates v. Yates, 76 N. C. 142, 149; Hyde v. Woolfolk, 1 Iowa, 159, 166; State v. Hinkle, 6 Iowa, 159, 166.
[2] Lincoln v. Inhabitants of Barre, 5 Cush. 591.
[3] Forgery v. First National Bank, 66 Ind. 123, 125.
[4] McEwen v. Bigelow, 40 Mich. 215, 217.
[5] Kilbourne v. Jennings, 38 Iowa, 533. "A painter, in virtue of the special knowledge and skill acquired in his employment of painting," said the court, "could learn nothing of the proper mode of framing together materials for the construction of a building. Whatever knowledge he acquires respecting carpenter and joiner work, must be gained from mere observation and attention. But any observant man, whose attention has been specially directed to buildings in process of erection and erected, could have equal means of knowledge, and could be equally qualified to give an opinion. But the opinion of a witness is not to be received merely because he has had some experience, or greater opportunity of observation than others, unless the experience relates to mat-

competent witness to give an opinion as to the skillfulness of work done on a mill, that the construction of its machinery was improper, although a millwright would be a competent witness in such an inquiry.[1] And where the investigation relates to the quality of iron, it has been held that a witness must show himself to be skilled in the business of manufacturing iron, and that "a clerk or book-keeper, although he may have been long employed in an iron foundry, and may have seen the business, is not competent to testify as an expert, unless he shows by his testimony that he has given the subject of examining and testing iron special attention and study, and has had experience in that art. If it appears that he relies upon the decision of others, or upon the marks on the iron, he is not an expert."[2]

§ 20. **Competency of Experts whose Knowledge is derived from Study.**—A witness is not incompetent to testify as an expert by reason of the fact that his special knowledge of the particular subject of inquiry, has not been derived from experience or actual observation, but from the reading and study of standard authorities. We are not to understand, however, that a person may qualify himself to testify as an expert in a particular case, merely by devoting himself to the study of authorities for the purposes of that case, when such reading and study is not in the line of his special calling or profession, and is entered upon to enable him to testify in the case. A lawyer would not be competent to express an opinion on a question of medical science, from information which he might acquire from reading medical authorities bearing on such question. Neither would a physician be qualified to express an opinion on a question of

---

ters of skill and science. It is true the witness in question could tell whether a joint was a close or an open one. And any observant person, without special instruction or skill could do as much. But it is apparent that, to admit as an expert every person who had availed himself of an opportunity to observe a structure, and who had acquired a knowledge as to the closeness of the joints, would overturn entirely the rule respecting expert testimony."

[1] Walker v. Fields, 28 Ga. 237.
[2] Pope v. Filley, 9 Fed. Rep. 65, 66.

foreign law, from information which he might acquire by an examination of legal authorities. While the opinion of either would not be inadmissible on a question lying within the domain of their particular department of science, merely because such opinion was based on information acquired from books. In the English case of *Collier v. Simpson*,[1] Mr. Chief Justice Tindal laid down the doctrine, that an expert could be asked whether in the course of his reading he had found so and so laid down, and that his judgment and the grounds of it could be founded in some degree on books as a part of his general knowledge. And the authority of that case has been recognized and followed in this country. The Supreme Court of New Hampshire has held that a physician may state his knowledge of a particular subject in medical science, although such knowledge was not derived from experience or actual observation, but from what he had learned merely from reading and studying medical authorities; and that upon his cross-examination, he may be asked, whether in his general reading he has not found particular theories laid down, conflicting with the theory he had advanced.[2] So, too, in North Carolina the courts have said that medical witnesses, testifying as experts, are not to be confined to the expression of opinions derived from their own observation and experience, but may state opinions based on information derived from books.[3] And in a case recently decided in the Supreme Court of Georgia, where an expert, who was a civil engineer, stated the rules for the construction of cuts and embankments as such rules are found in standard works on engineering, and added: "I give these rules solely from what I recollect of the books. These rules are found in Mahan, Gillespie and Gilmore, and many others." The court held that "the expert was competent to testify. Every expert derives much of his knowledge from books as

[1] 5 Carr & Payne, 73 (24 Eng. C. L. 219.)
[2] State v. Wood, 53 N. H. 484.
[3] State v. Terrill, 12 Rich. (N. C.) 321; Melvin v. Easley, 1 Jones (N. C.) Law, 388.

well as from experience, and can give his opinion based upon the knowledge acquired from both sources."[1]

§ 21. **Competency of Experts whose Knowledge is derived from Study—The Subject Continued.**—In a case decided in the Supreme Court of New Hampshire in 1870, the law as to the qualifications of witnesses without practical experience, but who have devoted themselves to special study and reading of authorities, was laid down by Mr. Justice Foster with such force and clearnesss, as to warrant its repetition in this connection, notwithstanding its length. A Mr. Waite, as editor of a stock journal, who had read extensively on the subject of " foot-rot," but who was without practical experience as to the treatment of the disease, had been called as an expert on the question whether the " foot-rot " is ever a spontaneous disease, or is bred only by contact. Mr. Justice Foster, speaking for the court, said: " Mr. Waite had no *skill* whatever, 'no practical experience in the treatment of sheep for any disease ;' that he must then have had *special* and *peculiar* knowledge ; that he must have been *really* a man of science, in order to be qualified to give an opinion, would seem to be a settled and definite rule of law. The extent of Mr. Waite's qualification is thus described: ' As editor of a stock journal, he had read extensively on the subject of foot-rot.' The object of all testimony in courts is to place before the jury a knowledge of *facts* pertaining to the case under consideration, and it is a serious departure from this purpose ever to admit, instead of actual knowledge, mere opinion, however correct it may probably be, and therefore, opinion, if admitted at all, should be as nearly approximated as possible to the actual knowledge of fact for which it is substituted ; and it should always be required of an expert, that he should, at least, be sufficiently acquainted with the subject matter of his testimony to *know* what its laws are, and not merely to conjecture or to have an idea about it. That is, he should be *really* a man of *science*. The *science*, (especially in the

[1] Central R. R. Co. v. Mitchell, 63 Ga. 173; s. c. 1 Am. & Eng. R. R. Cases, 145.

absence of *skill*,) which an expert should be required to possess and employ on a given subject, implies that special and peculiar knowledge acquired only by a course of observation and study, and the expenditure of time, labor and preparation, in a particular employment and calling of life. The matter of our present consideration is of vast importance. 'In the multiplication of interests connected with the application of the laws of science, which are daily growing more and more numerous and refined, it is hardly possible to dispense with the aid of experts in determining the rights of parties;' but it is greatly to be feared that an unwise generosity and liberality of construction have sometimes permitted the admission of this kind of evidence to an extent outside the bounds of discretion and safety, and that perhaps a more scrupulous regard for and estimation of the great importance of the office of an expert in the ascertainment of truth, than has sometimes been exercised, has become necessary, not only for the vindication of justice itself, but also for strengthening the confidence of the public in its ministers and instrumentalities.

"We admit the wisdom of the rule which, permitting a man of genuine science to give as his opinion the results of study and research into books of acknowledged authority, yet will not allow such books to be read in court to the jury. The rule is founded partly in the delay which would thus be occasioned to the business of courts, and partly in the idea that it is safer, on the whole, to trust to the judgment of learned men, acquired by study, observation and skill, than to the imperfect deductions of jurors, hastily derived from readings not familiar to them, unassisted by study, examination and comparison of kindred subjects (though we must confess that, in a particular case we may have little doubt that a page from Youatt or Morrell would be a safer guide for the jury than the opinion of such a witness as Mr. Waite). But so long as the opinions of the most distinguished and most learned authors in the world, expressed through the direct and pure *media* of their celebrated works, are thus excluded from the jury, surely it can be neither wise nor prudent to admit opinions unsustained by the slightest experience or even observation, the deductions of readings at best scanty and superficial, because not pertaining to the *special study and business* of the reader. * * *

"Of course, it must be admitted that the testimony of knowledge and opinion, obtained from mere reading, without *study*, reflection, or observation, is no more than a relation by the witness of that which the policy of the law excludes, namely, the books themselves which the witness has read.

"The limit of safety in this direction is reached, it would seem, when we admit, as the practice in this State is, the opinions of medical men, for instance, with regard to a disease which in actual practice they may not have treated, but concerning which the science and skill of long experience in the affinities and analogies of the subject have prepared them to speak with confidence, from a knowledge of the rules and laws governing the special subject of inquiry. * * *

"And so the practice in this State permits the skilled practitioner, who has made himself familiar with the science of medicine or surgery by a long course of study and practical experience with kindred subjects, to testify as an expert; and common sense demands that such a man shall have respect given to his opinion, though he may have had no practical experience in a particular case.

"But how is it in the case of this witness? He was not a veterinarian, nor any other kind of a physician or surgeon. 'He had had no practical experience in the treatment of sheep,' nor of any person or thing 'for *any* disease.' He was the editor of a newspaper, devoted, not to the special consideration of this, nor even of kindred subjects, but embracing the very large class of matters ordinarily included in a stock journal. His newspaper was, probably, the ordinary collection of miscellaneous literature and news items, concerning all the diverse matters embraced within the range of such a production, its editor having and making no pretension to veterinary skill and practice.

"It being evident, too, that in the line of his comprehensive reading and study the subject of the diseases of animals was by no means a specialty, the element of editorship has in reality nothing to do with the party's qualifications. 'As an editor,' it is said 'he had read extensively on the subject of foot-rot.' So, as a lawyer, prosecuting or defending a man charged with murder, I, who am not a doctor, may have read extensively on the subject of the effects of strychnine and its manifestations after death, and, as the result of my reading, I might well form the opinion that enough of strychnine might be administered to cause death, without a possibility that a medical man or chemist could be able to detect it in the stomach or blood of the deceased; but, it is to be hoped, my opinion upon this subject would not be allowed. And, as a lawyer, also, in the examination of this case, I have, in fact, read extensively on the subject of foot-rot, the books of Morrell, Youatt and Clock. * * *

"As the result of *my* reading, I should, perhaps, be inclined to believe the disease is *not* contagious, but my opinion is no more admissible than the books themselves of these authors. They are men of acknowledged science and skill. The witness in this case can have examined no better authority. Why should his opinion, without practical skill and experience, be received, and theirs rejected?

"In view of all these considerations, and of the evidence reported by the case submitted to us, we are strongly of the opinion that the witness, having confessedly no veterinary skill nor practice, having also no professional education, not being in any true sense a man of science, because not instructed and prepared by a long course of habit of study concerning the diseases of domestic animals, did not possess the legal qualifications of an expert."[1]

§ 22. **Competency Sometimes Dependent on whether the Expert has Heard the Testimony.**— An expert either

---

[1] Dole v. Johnson, 50 N. H. 452, 455.

states general facts, which are the results of scientific knowledge or general skill, or else he testifies to opinions.[1] If he testifies to opinions, his testimony is founded either on personal knowledge of the facts, or else it is based on facts shown by the testimony of others.[2] If his opinion is desired on facts testified to by other witnesses, it should appear that he has reliable information or knowledge of what those facts are.[3] But even in such cases it is not always necessary that the witness should have been present, and heard *all* the evidence.[4]

It is sufficient if it appears that he has heard all the testimony which is material to the subject of inquiry.[5] And he should have heard the evidence as actually given, and not as it appears on the minutes of the testimony as taken by counsel. When an expert had not heard the evidence as given on the trial, and counsel offered to read to him their minutes of the testimony, it was held that this could not be allowed.[6] Of course the necessity for the witness to have heard the testimony does not exist if the *whole* of the evidence is embraced in a hypothetical question submitted to him.[7]

§ 23. **Competency of Experts in Particular Cases.**—We have thus confined our attention to the general principles relating to the competency of experts, and have left the consideration of the competency of experts in particular cases to be considered in subsequent chapters. For instance, the competency of physicians and surgeons to testify as ex-

---

[1] Emerson v. Lowell Gas Light Co., 6 Allen, 146.
[2] Spear v. Richardson, 37 N. H. 23, 34; Livingston v. Commonwealth, 14 Gratt. (Va.) 592; Walker v. Fields, 28 Ga. 237.
[3] Heald v. Thing, 45 Me. 392; Lake v. People, 12 N. Y. 358; *s. c.*, 1 Parker Cr. Cas. 495; People v. Thurston, 2 Parker Cr. Cas. 49.
[4] Miller v. Smith, 112 Mass. 470, 475.
[5] Carpenter v. Blake, 2 Lans. (N. Y.) 206; State v. Medlicott, 9 Kans. 289; Rich v. Jones, 8 Cush. (Mass.) 337; Hand v. Brookline, 126 (Mass.) 324; Davis v. State, 38 Md. 15, 40; State v. Hayden, 51 Vt. 296.
[6] Thayer v. Davis, 38 Vt. 163.
[7] See Webb v. State, 9 Texas Ct. of App. 490.

perts, is considered in the chapter relating to expert testimony in medicine, surgery and chemistry. So the qualifitions of experts in handwriting have been considered in the chapter relating to expert testimony in handwriting.

CHAPTER III.

THE EXAMINATION OF EXPERT WITNESSES, AND THE WEIGHT OF THEIR TESTIMONY.

SECTION.
24. Mode of Examination of Expert Witnesses.
25. The Hypothetical Question.
26. The Hypothetical Question—The Subject Continued.
27. When Questions need not be Hypothetical.
28. The Hypothetical Question on the Cross-examination.
29. Questions to Experts should not embrace Questions of Law.
30. Questions to Experts as to Particular Cases.
31. An Expert cannot be asked for an Opinion on Facts not Stated.
32. Latitude of Inquiry in the Examination of Experts.
33. Some General Rules Governing the Examination of Witnesses.
34. Excluding Experts from the Court Room during the Examination of Witnesses.
35. Right of the Court to Limit the Number of Expert Witnesses.
36. By whom Expert Witnesses are Selected.
37. Weight of Expert Testimony a Question for the Jury.
38. Right of the Jury to Exercise an Independent Judgment.
39. Instructions to the Jury as to the Nature and Weight of Expert Testimony.
40. Instructions to the Jury as to the Nature and Weight of Expert Testimony—The Subject Continued.
41. Instructions to the Jury as to the Nature and Weight of Expert Testimony—The Subject Continued.
42. The Value of Expert Testimony.

§ 24. **Mode of Examination of Expert Witnesses.**—It being determined by the court, that the subject matter of inquiry is one upon which the opinion of experts may properly be received in evidence, and that the witness introduced possesses special skill in the subject matter of inquiry, the examination of the witness is next in order, and it becomes important that such examination should proceed strictly in accordance with the rules, which it has been found necessary to establish in relation to the admission of expert testimony. It is necessary in the examination of all such witnesses, that questions should be so framed as not to call on the witness for a critical review of the testimony given by the other witnesses, compelling the expert to draw inferences or conclusions of fact from the testimony, or to pass on the credibility of the witnesses,[1] the general rule being that an expert should not be asked a question in such a manner as to cover the very question to be submitted to the jury.[2] As expressed in one of the opinions, "a question should not be so framed as to permit the witness to roam through the evidence for himself, and gather the facts as he may consider them to be proved, and then state his conclusions concerning them."[3] And the language in another case is as follows: "The questions to him must be so shaped as to give him no occasion to mentally draw his own conclusions from the whole evidence, or a part thereof, and from the conclusion so drawn, express his opinion, or to decide as to the weight of evidence or the credibility of witnesses; and his answers must be such, as not to involve

[1] Jameson v. Drinkald, 12 Moore, 148; Guiterman v. Liverpool etc. Steamship Co., 83 N. Y. 358, 366; United States v. McGloin, 1 Curtis C. C. 1, 9; Buxton v. Somerset Potters Works, 121 Mass. 446; Reynolds v. Robinson, 64 N. Y. 589; Phillips v. Starr, 26 Iowa, 351; Van Zandt v. Mutual Benefit Life Ins. Co., 55 N. Y. 179; Dexter v. Hall, 15 Wall. 9; Cincinnati etc. Mutual Ins. Co. v. May, 20 Ohio, 211, 224; Rush v. Megee, 36 Ind. 1. "Le Medicin ne doit jamais donner un avis sur le difficulté même, que les juris ont à resoudre; par exemple, sur le point de savoir si l'accusé est irresponsable, mais simplement faire connaitre son opinion sur l'existence ou le degré d'influence de certain faits." Dr. Mittermaier's Traité de la Procedure Criminelle.

[2] Chicago & Alton R. R. Co. v. Springfield & Northwestern R. R. Co., 67 Ill. 142; Tingley v. Cowgill, 48 Mo. 294; Muldowney v. Illinois Central R. R. Co., 39 Iowa, 615; Pelamourges v. Clark, 9 Iowa, 1. 16; Hill v. Portland etc. R. R. Co., 55 Me. 444; Keller v. N. Y. Central R. R. Co., 2 Abbott's App. Decis. (N. Y.) 480, 490; Clark v. Detroit Locomotive Works, 32 Mich. 348.

[3] Dolz v. Morris, 17 N. Y. Sup. Ct. 202.

any such conclusions so drawn, or any opinion of the expert, as to the weight of the evidence or the credibility of the witnesses."[1] "The object of all questions to experts," says the Supreme Court of Massachusetts, "should be to obtain their opinion as to the matter of skill or science which is in controversy, and at the same time to exclude their opinions as to the effect of the evidence in establishing controverted facts. Questions adapted to this end may be in a great variety of forms. If they require the witness to draw a conclusion of fact, they should be excluded."[2] It is not the duty of an expert to reconcile conflicting evidence.[3] In illustration of this principle that an expert cannot be asked an opinion which requires him to pass upon the evidence, the following question may be cited as having been held to be an improper one, for the reason that it practically put the expert in the place of the jury: "From the facts and circumstances stated by previous witnesses, and from those testified to by still other witnesses, relating to the homicide, and from defendant's conduct on the trial, is it your opinion that the defendant was sane or insane when he committed the act?"[4] For the same reason an engineer has not been allowed to answer the question whether "the plaintiff in oiling that pulley, could have been injured unless he was careless."[5] So it has been held improper to ask: "In your opinion as a canal boatman, did Mr. C. in any way omit or neglect to do anything which he might have done to save his boat?" He could be asked whether certain acts assumed to be proven were seamanlike and proper, but he could not be allowed to express an opinion as to what was or was not done as a matter of fact.[6] And in an action against a physician for neglect and non-attendance in a case of frost bite, it has been held that a

---

[1] McMechen v. McMechen, 17 W. Va. 683, 694.
[2] Hunt v. Lowell Gas Light Co., 8 Gray, 169.
[3] Luning v. State, 1 Chandler, (Wis.) 178.
[4] State v. Felter, 25 Iowa, 67, 74.
[5] Buxton v. Somerset Potters Works, 124 Mass. 446.
[6] Carpenter v. Eastern Transportation Co., 71 N. Y. 574.

medical witness, to whom the evidence was read, could not be asked: From the evidence before the court, to what do you ascribe the loss of the plaintiff's fingers and toes?[1]

§ 25. **The Hypothetical Question.**—As an expert is not allowed to draw inferences or conclusions of fact from the evidence, his opinion should be asked upon a hypothetical statement of facts.[2] Mr. Chief Justice SHAW well stated the law as follows: "In order to obtain the opinion of a witness on matters not depending upon general knowledge, but on facts not testified of by himself, one of two modes is pursued: either the witness is present and hears all the testimony, or the testimony is summed up in the question put to him; and in either case the question is put to him hypothetically, whether, if certain facts testified of are true he can form an opinion, and what that opinion is."[3]

Counsel in framing the hypothetical question, may base it upon the hypothesis of the truth of all the evidence, or on a hypothesis especially framed on certain facts assumed to be proved for the purpose of the inquiry.[4] If framed on the assumption of certain facts, counsel may assume the facts in accordance with his theory of them, it not being essential that he should state the facts as they actually exist.[5]

"The claim is," says Chief Justice FOLGER, in the case last cited, "that a hypothetical question may not be put to

---

[1] Key v. Thompson, 2 Hannay, (N. B.) 224.
[2] Strong v. Kean, 13 Irish Law R. 93; Polk v. State, 36 Ark. 117, 124, 125; Spear v. Richardson, 37 N. H. 23; Teft v. Wilcox, 6 Kan. 46; Pidcock v. Potter, 68 Pa. St. 342; Woodbury v. Obear, 7 Gray (Mass.). 467; Williams v. Brown, 28 Ohio St. 547, 551; Moore v. State, 17 Ohio St. 526; Jerry v. Townshend. 9 Md. 145; Baltimore & Ohio Railroad Co. v. Thompson, 10 Md. 76; Walker v. Rogers, 24 Md. 237; Page v. State. 61 Ala. 16; Willey v. Portsmouth, 35 N. H. 303; Bishop v. Spining, 38 Ind. 143; Dexter v. Hall, 15 Wallace, 9; Ayers v. Water Commissioners, 29 N. Y. Sup. Ct. 297; Guiterman v. Liverpool, etc. Steamship Co., 83 N. Y. 358, 366; Hunt v. State, 9 Tex. Ct. of App. 166; Hoard v. Peck, 56 Barb. (N. Y.) 202; City of Decatur v. Fisher, 63 Ill. 241.
[3] Dickenson v. Fitchburg, 13 Gray. (Mass.) 546, 556.
[4] Gotlieb v. Hartman, 3 Col. 53.
[5] Cowley v. People, 83 N. Y. 464.

an expert, unless it states the facts as they exist. It is manifest, if this is the rule, that in a trial where there is a dispute as to the facts, which can be settled only by the jury, there would be no room for a hypothetical question. The very meaning of the word is that it supposes, assumes something for the time being. Each side, in an issue of fact, has its theory of what is the true state of the facts, and assumes that it can prove it to be so to the satisfaction of the jury, and so assuming, shapes hypothetical questions to experts accordingly. And such is the correct practice."[1] The fact that counsel make an error in their assumption, does not render the question objectionable, if it is within the possible or probable range of the evidence.[2] But the testimony should tend to establish every supposed fact embraced in the question.[3] For if the hypothetical question is clearly exaggerated and unwarranted by any testimony in the case, an objection to it will be sustained.[4] As declared in the Supreme Court of Michigan, counsel should not be, permitted to embrace in a hypothetical question "anything not proved or offered to be proved."[5] And if it turns out that the question includes circumstances which are neither proved, nor as to which there is any tendency of proof, then the court is to instruct the jury to disregard the opinion based upon it.[6] But where there is any evidence tending to prove the facts assumed, it is for the jury to weigh

---

[1] See to the same effect Davis v. State, 35 Ind. 496; Guetig v. State, 66 Ind 94; Filer v. N. Y. Central R. R. Co., 49 N. Y. 42; Carpenter v. Blake, 2 Lans. (N. Y.) 206.

[2] Harnett v. Garvey, 66 N. Y. 641; Nave v. Tucker, 70 Ind. 15.

[3] Bomgardner v. Andrews, 55 Iowa, 638; Hathaway's Admr. v. National Life Ins. Co., 48 Vt. 335; Hurst v. The C. R. I. &. P. R. Co., 49 Iowa, 76; Gueting v. State, 66 Ind. 94; Daniells v. Aldrich, 42 Mich. 58; Dillebar v. Home Life Ins. Co. (N. Y. Ct. of App., Nov. 1881), 14 Cent. L. J. 158.

[4] Williams v. Brown, 28 Ohio St. 547, 551, 552; Muldowney v. Illinois Central R. R. Co., 39 Iowa, 615; Dickie v. Vanbleck, 5 Redf. (N. Y.) 284, 294.

[5] Fraser v. Jennison, 42 Mich. 206, 227.

[6] Commonwealth v. Mullins, 2 Allen (Mass.), 296; Gueting v. State, 66 Ind. 94; Hovey v. Chase, 52 Me. 304.

the evidence, and determine whether the supposed facts so stated actually correspond with the facts as proved.[1] The opinion of an expert cannot be considered of material value, unless the hypothetical case put to him is fully sustained by the evidence; but an exception to the rule arises where the hypothetical case is susceptible of division, and a part of it only is sustained by the evidence.[2] In putting the hypothetical case the facts of the actual case should be fairly represented.[3]

§ 26. **The Hypothetical Question — The Subject Continued.** — It is to be noted, however, that if there is no dispute as to the facts on which the expert is to base his opinion, it is proper to require that the question to the expert shall embrace *all* the facts, and that the witness shall take them all into consideration.[4] The doctrine as to the proper form of the hypothetical question, has been very ably set forth by the Supreme Court of Vermont in an opinion, from which we quote as follows: "A study of the various cases will show that the form of the question is modified and shaped by the courts; whether it states facts, or puts facts hypothetically, or refers to the testimony of witnesses as being true, so as to give the witness no occasion or opportunity to decide upon the evidence, or mingle his own opinion of the facts, as shown by the evidence, with the facts upon which he is to express a professional opinion. This is the important point, and to secure this, various forms of inquiry have been adopted. Hypothetical questions may be so put as to require the witness to decide upon the evidence, to determine which side preponderates, and to find conclusions from the evidence, in order to reconcile conflicting facts. Such questions, though hypothetical, are as clearly improper as if they directly sought the opinion of the witness on the merits of the case. Hence, in framing

---

[1] Boardman v. Woodman, 47 N. H. 120, 135; Lake v. People, 1 Parker's Cr. Cas. 495; People v. Thurston, 2 Parker's Cr. Cas. 49.
[2] Eggers v. Eggers, 57 Ind. 461.
[3] Stuart v. State, 57 Tenn. 178, 189.
[4] Davis v. State, 35 Ind. 496.

such questions, care should be taken not to involve so much, or so many facts in them, that the witness will be obliged in his own mind to settle other disputed facts, in order to give his answer. * * In some cases, all the facts bearing on the issue might be summed up in a single question. But when facts on one side conflict with facts on the other, they ought not to be incorporated into one question, but the attention of the witness should be called to their opposing tendencies, and if his skill or knowledge can furnish the explanation which harmonizes them, he is at liberty to state it. Then the jury can know all the facts and grounds on which the opinion is based."[1] It is not always necessary that a hypothetical question should be asked in a formal manner. Where a medical expert had read the deposition of the plaintiff, detailing minutely the injuries and bodily condition claimed to have resulted to him from an injury which he related, it was held proper to ask him "from the knowledge gained by reading the deposition," his opinion as to the plaintiff's condition at the time the deposition was made, and as to the cause of that condition. The court said that where an expert heard or read the evidence, there was no reason why he might not form as correct a judgment based upon such evidence, assuming it to be true, as if the same evidence had been submitted to him in the form of hypothetical questions, and that it would be an idle and useless ceremony to require evidence with which he was already familiar, to be repeated to him in that form.[2] It has been held proper to ask the expert, "supposing the testimony of the witness to be truthful," what is your opinion?[3] This is said to be a convenient mode of stating a hypothetical case, permissible in the discretion of the court.[4] In a recent case in Texas, where the opinion of an expert was asked on the testimony of one of the witnesses,

[1] Fairchild v. Bascomb, 35 Vt. 415.
[2] Gilman v. Town of Strafford, 50 Vt. 726.
[3] Wright v. Hardy, 22 Wis. 348. But see Hagadorn v. Connecticut Mutual Life Ins. Co., 29 N. Y. Sup. Ct. 251.
[4] State v. Lautenschlager, 22 Minn. 521; Getchell v. Hill, 21 Minn. 464.

the Court of Appeals declared that an opinion could not be predicated on anything less than the entire testimony, whether actually or hypothetically presented.[1] And it has been said that the advantage of the usual hypothetical question, including the substance of the whole testimony, is so great, that it should only be sacrificed when the circumstances of the case plainly call for it.[2] The hypothesis should be clearly stated, so that the jury may know with certainty upon precisely what state of facts the expert bases his opinion.[3] We give in the note below an illustration of the hypothetical question, the question being the one propounded by the defence to the experts in the trial of Guiteau,[4] that propounded by the prosecution in the same case, being of too great length to permit of its reproduction in these pages.

§ 27. **When Questions need not be Hypothetical.**— There are two exceptions to the general rule requiring that

[1] Webb v. State, 9 Texas Ct. of App. 490.
[2] Haggerty v. Brooklyn etc. R. R. Co., 61 N. Y. 624.
[3] McMechen v. McMechen, 17 W. Va. 683, 698.
[4] Q. Assuming it to be a fact that there was a strong hereditary taint of insanity in the blood of the prisoner at the bar; also that at about the age of thirty-five years his own mind was so much deranged that he was a fit subject to be sent to an insane asylum; also that at different times after that date during the next succeeding five years, he manifested such decided symptons of insanity, without simulation, that many different persons conversing with him and observing his conduct, believed him to be insane; also that in or about the month of June, 1881, at or about the expiration of said term of five years, he became demented by the idea that he was inspired of God to remove by death the President of the United States; also that he acted on what he believed to be such inspiration, and as he believed to be in accordance with the Divine will in the preparation for, and in the accomplishment of such a purpose; also that he committed the act of shooting the President under what he believed to be a Divine command which he was not at liberty to disobey, and which belief made out a conviction which controlled his conscience and overpowered his will as to that act, so that he could not resist the mental pressure upon him: also that immediately after the shooting he appeared calm and as if relieved by the performance of a great duty; also that there was no other adequate motive for the act than the conviction that he was executing the Divine will for the good of his country—assuming all of these propositions to be true, state whether, in your opinion, the prisoner was sane or insane at the time of shooting President Garfield?

the opinions of experts should be asked upon an assumed state of facts.

First. A distinction is taken between cases in which there is a conflict of evidence upon the material facts, and those in which no such conflict exists. In the former class of cases the question must be framed hypothetically, but in the latter class there is no such necessity.[1]

Second. It is not necessary to assume a state of facts in those cases in which the expert is personally acquainted with the material facts in the case.[2]

For instance, a medical witness who has no personal knowledge of the prisoner, cannot be asked: "From the facts and circumstances stated by previous witnesses, and from those testified to by still other witnesses, relating to the homicide, and from defendant's conduct on the trial, is it your opinion that the defendant was sane or insane when he committed the act? * * * But if a physician visits a person, and from actual examination or observation becomes acquainted with his mental condition, he may give an opinion respecting such mental condition at that time — that is, he may, under such circumstances, state to the jury his opinion as to the sanity or insanity of the person at the time when he thus observed or examined him."[3] So, where a medical expert had made a personal examination of the uterus of a deceased woman, it was proper to ask him, "What, in your opinion, caused the death of the person from whom the uterus was taken?"[4] And an expert having personal knowledge of the facts has been permitted to testify that a machine was constructed in a workmanlike

[1] Cincinnati, etc. Mut. Ins. Co. v. May, 20 Ohio, 211, 224; Tefft v. Wilcox, 6 Kan. 46; Page v. State, 61 Ala. 16; Woodbury v. Obear, 7 Gray, 467; Pidcock v. Potter, 68 Penn. St. 342; Bishop v. Spining, 38 Ind. 143; Guiterman v. Liverpool, etc. Steamship Co., 83 N. Y. 358, 366; State v. Klinger, 46 Mo. 224; Carpenter v. Blake. 2 Lans. (N. Y.) 206.

[2] Bellefontaine, etc. R. R. Co. v. Bailey, 11 Ohio St. 333, 337; Transportation Line v. Hope, 95 U. S. 297, 298; Brown v. Huffard, 69 Mo. 305; Ayres v. Water Commissioners, 29 N. Y. Sup. Ct. 297; Bellinger v. N. Y. Cent. R. R. Co. 23 N. Y. 42, 46; Dunham's Appeal, 27 Conn. 193.

[3] State v. Felter, 25 Iowa, 67, 74, 75, per Dillon, C. J.

[4] State v. Glass, 5 Oregon. 73.

manner;[1] that a wall was properly and compactly constructed;[2] that the abutments of a bridge were properly and skillfully placed, and sufficient to discharge water in time of flood;[3] that an article was properly stowed in a vessel.[4]

In relation to this subject we cannot do better than quote from the opinion of Lord Chief Justice TINDAL, delivered in the House of Lords, in the celebrated McNaughten case: "The question lastly proposed by your Lordships is: 'Can a medical man conversant with the disease of insanity, who never saw the prisoner previous to the trial, but who was present during the whole trial and the examination of all the witnesses, be asked his opinion as to the state of the prisoner's mind at the time of the commission of the alleged crime, or his opinion whether the prisoner was conscious at the time of doing the act that he was acting contrary to law, or whether he was laboring under any and what delusion at the time?' In answer thereto, we state to your Lordships, that we think the medical man, under the circumstances supposed, cannot in strictness be asked his opinion in the terms above stated, because each of those questions involves the determination of the truth of the facts deposed to, which it is for the jury to decide, and the questions are not mere questions upon a matter of science, in which case such evidence is admissible. But where the facts are admitted or not disputed, and the question becomes substantially one of science only, it may be convenient to allow the question to be put in that general form, though the same cannot be insisted on as matter of right."[5] Whenever a hypothetical question is put in such a form that the answer to it depends on what the recollections and impressions of the witness are as to the evidence

---

[1] Curtis v. Gano, 26 N. Y. 426.
[2] Pullman v. Corning. 9 N. Y. 93.
[3] Conhocton Stone Road Co. v. Buffalo, N. Y. & Erie R. R. Co., 10 N. Y. 523.
[4] Price v. Powell. 3 N. Y. 322.
[5] 10 Cl. & Fin. 200, 211.

which he has heard, it is improper, and goes beyond the limits of questions to experts.[1]

It may be remarked as well in this connection as any other, that answers to hypothetical questions are not objectionable because they include considerations not referred to in the questions, as constituting the basis of the opinion given, and such as the testimony tends to prove, and as might properly have been included in the questions.[2]

§ 28. **The Hypothetical Question on the Cross-examination.**— After counsel have propounded to an expert a hypothetical question, based on the facts assumed to have been proved in accordance with their theory of the case, opposing counsel may propound the same question to the same witness based on the facts assumed in the opposing theory.[3] In the case cited, the court below had sustained an objection to such method of examination, on the ground that it was not legitimate cross-examination. This ruling was reversed on appeal, the court expressing itself as follows: "We think that when such a witness has expressed an opinion based on facts assumed by the party introducing him to have been proved, or upon a hypothetical case put by such party, the other party may cross-examine him by taking his opinion based on any other set of facts assumed by him to have been proved by the evidence, or upon a hypothetical case put to him."

Upon the trial of a person indicted for murder, where the defence was insanity, it was held no error to require the defendant to submit his hypothetical case to his professional witnesses, before the rebutting evidence of the State was heard on the question of sanity. The court declaring that if evidence materially varying the hypothetical case was afterwards introduced, the defendant must ask leave to re-examine as to new matter.[4]

[1] Hagadorn v. Connecticut Mutual Life Ins. Co., 29 N. Y. Sup. Ct. 251.
[2] Hathaway's Admr. v. National Life Ins. Co., 48 Vt. 335.
[3] Davis v. State, 35 Ind. 496.
[4] Dove v. State, 52 Tenn. 348.

§ 29. **Questions to Experts should not Embrace Questions of Law.**—It is not proper to so frame a question to an expert as to call for an expression of an opinion as to the law of the case. For instance, it is improper to ask a medical expert whether a person possessed sufficient mental capacity to enable him to make a will.[1] The question should be so framed as to require him to state the degree of intelligence or imbecility of the person, in the best way he can, by the use of such ordinary terms as will best convey his own ideas of the matter.[2] Or the witness may be asked whether the testator's mind and memory were sufficiently sound to enable him to know and understand the business in which he was engaged at the time he executed the will.[3]

§ 30. **Questions to Experts as to Particular Cases.**— While the opinion of experts may be based on their observation and experience in similar cases, yet the principle is well settled that such witnesses cannot, on their direct examination, be questioned concerning the particular cases which have happened to come within their observation, and which have no connection with the case in hand.[4] The reason for the rule is manifestly to prevent the introduction of innumerable side issues, which might render the trial of a cause interminable, distract the attention of the jury from the real issue, and render the costs in the case unnecessarily burdensome and enormous. Different experts might have different theories, and each theory might be founded on the observance of several and distinct cases, each of which the opposite party would have a right to controvert. And inasmuch as a party would be unable to anticipate the cases which the experts on the other side would mention, he

---

[1] Farrell v. Brennan, 32 Mo. 328; McClintock v. Card, 32 Mo. 411; May v. Bradlee, 127 Mass. 414; Gibson v. Gibson, 9 Yerg. 329; White v. Bailey, 10 Mich. 155.

[2] Fairchild v. Bascomb, 35 Vt. 416, 417; State v. Hayden, 51 Vt. 304; Crowell v. Kirk 3 Dev. (N. C.) 358.

[3] McClintock v. Card, 32 Mo. 411.

[4] 1 Greenl. Ev. § 448; Clark v. Willett, 35 Cal. 534, 544; Central Pacific R. R. Co. v. Pearson, 35 Cal. 247; Jonau v. Ferrand, 3 Rob. (La.) 366; Horne v. Williams 12 Ind. 324.

would be unable to prepare for their investigation, and would, therefore, be unable to properly avail himself of his right to controvert them.

§ 31. **An Expert cannot be Asked for an Opinion on Facts not Stated.**— An expert, testifying from personal knowledge, cannot be asked for an opinion based on facts which he has not given in evidence. He should be first asked as to the facts, and then allowed to state his opinion. This is necessary to enable the correctness of the opinion expressed to be tested by calling other experts, and obtaining their opinion upon the same state of facts. It is equally necessary to enable the jury to have the means of determining whether the facts upon which the opinion is predicated, were correct or not. Hence it has been held improper to ask a physician " whether a person was in good health, and free from any symptoms of disease," he not having testified to any facts from which it could be seen upon what his opinion was based.[1] For the same reason the following question has been held improper : " From what you found at the time, in the examination of her, from your knowledge of her during the years previous, and from the symptoms which you observed at that time, paralysis or trouble with her limbs, and the other difficulties under which she is laboring, what in your opinion produced the condition that you then found her in?"[2] So it has been held improper to ask experts who saw a railroad accident, whether, in their opinion after having seen the accident, anything could have been done by the conductor to prevent it? It called for an opinion not derived from the testimony, but simply what was seen at the time of the occurrence.[3]

The opinion of an expert is inadmissible if based on facts which he has heard outside the court room, and which he believes to be credible.[4] An exception exists in the case

[1] Reid v. Piedmont, etc. Life Ins. Co., 58 Mo. 425.
[2] Van Deusen v. Newcomer, 40 Mich. 120.
[3] Haggerty v. Brooklyn, etc. R. R. Co., 61 N. Y. 624.
[4] Polk v. State, 36 Ark. 117, 124; Baltimore, etc. R. R. Co. v. Shipley, 39 Md. 251.

of physicians whose testimony is based in part on declarations of patients, but that is elsewhere considered.[1]

§ 32. Latitude of Inquiry in the Examination of Experts.—The rule is laid down that in the examination of experts, considerable latitude of inquiry is to be indulged, and that counsel are not to be limited by any narrow or stringent rules, either in obtaining their opinions upon the facts disclosed, or in ascertaining their skill and competency, or the want of them.[2] "There must be some limit to such an inquiry, and from the nature of the case, no definite limit can be prescribed as a rule of law. The court ought to permit the inquiry to proceed far enough to enable the jury to judge of the reasonableness of the witness' pretentions to skill, so far as such an inquiry can afford the means."[3] But it is to be observed that after a witness has been admitted to testify as an expert, evidence cannot be given to the jury of the opinion of other experts in the same science, that the witness was qualified to draw correct conclusions on the science on which he had been examined,[4] the general rule being, that after such a witness has been adjudged competent by the court, his reputation can only be sustained after it has been impeached.[5] Any different rule, it has been said, "would lead to anything but a satisfactory result. Another witness might then be called to give his opinion as to the capacity of him just examined, to form a correct opinion on the degree of weight which was due to the testimony of the first, and so on. The jury are to judge of the weight due to the opinion of medical men on the disease, from the facts detailed by them, and the reasons given in support of their conclusions, not from the opinion others may form of their capacity."[6] It has been held competent, however, for one expert to testify as to the

---

[1] §§ 47 48.
[2] Leopold v. Van Kirk, 29 Wis. 548, 555; Brown v. Chenoworth, 51 Tex. 469.
[3] Andre v. Hardin, 32 Mich. 326.
[4] Tullis v. Kidd, 12 Ala. 648.
[5] De Phul v. State, 44 Ala. 39.
[6] Brabo v. Martin, 3 La. R. 177.

skill of another, where the knowledge of the witness was derived from personal observation, as distinguished from an opinion based on such expert's general reputation.[1] In the case cited, one expert was allowed to testify as to the correctness of the tests used by another expert in testing for arsenic. A witness called as an expert cannot be asked on cross-examination whether he considers himself as good a judge of the matter in dispute, as other witnesses who have testified as experts, for the reason that such a question is simply an attempt to get the opinion of the witness as to the value of the testimony of the experts on the other side.[2] When a witness has been adjudged competent upon the preliminary examination, opposing proof going to his incompetency is to be addressed to the jury to affect the value of his testimony, and not to the court for the purpose of excluding his opinion.[3] And it has been held, therefore, no ground for objection, that counsel was not permitted on the preliminary examination of the expert, to cross-examine him for the purpose of testing his competency, he having an opportunity on the cross-examination in chief to test and impeach his skill,[4] for the extent of an expert's acquaintance with the subject matter, may always be inquired into, to enable the jury to estimate its weight,[5] and counsel have a right in every case to the reasons upon which the opinion of the expert is based.[6] In an early case in Massachusetts, the depositions of medical experts on the question of a person's sanity, were rejected because the experts did not state the reasons for their opinion.[7] "Whenever the opinion of any living person is deemed to be relevant, the grounds on which such opinion is based are also deemed to

[1] Laros v. Commonwealth, 84 Penn. St. 200, 209.
[2] Haverhill Loan etc. Ass. v. Cronin, 4 Allen (Mass.)141.
[3] Washington v. Cole, 6 Ala. 212.
[4] Sarl v. Arnold, 7 R. I. 586.
[5] Davis v. State, 35 Ind. 496.
[6] State v. Hooper, 2 Bailey (S. C.) Law, 37; Fairchild v. Bascomb, 35 Vt. 398, 406; Lincoln v. Taunton Manufacturing Co., 9 Allen, (Mass.) 182, 191, 192; Keith v. Lothrop, 10 Cush. (Mass.) 457; In re Springer, 4 Penn. Law J. 275; Commonwealth v. Webster, 5 Cush. (Mass.) 295.
[7] Dickinson v. Barber, 9 Mass. 218.

be relevant."[1] Neither judge nor jury can know what credence to give to a mere opinion, unless the reasons on which it is founded are set forth. The opinion of an expert may be contradicted, by showing that at another time he had expressed a different opinion,[2] and he may be asked as to the grounds upon which the change of his opinion had been brought about.[3] While the inquiry into the grounds and reasons of the opinion of an expert is more frequently made on the cross-examination of the witness, yet there is no objection to its being made on the direct-examination.[4] Where an expert was called and asked if he concurred in the statement of another expert witness, and if not, to state wherein he differed, the court held this method of examination to be erroneous. "The mode sought to be adopted in eliciting the opinion of this witness, may have the merit of being expeditious, but it might be attended with some unfairness toward the witness himself, as well as to the opposite party. Witnesses called upon to testify professionally, should be left free to give their own individual opinion upon the facts involved, unconnected with, and untrammeled by the opinions of others who may have been examined."[5]

§ 33. **Some General Rules Governing the Examination of Witnesses.**—It would be foreign to our purpose to consider in detail those rules of evidence regulating the examination of witnesses, which are alike applicable to the examination of professional and non-professional witnesses. Yet a concise statement of the more important principles to be observed in such cases, may be found of convenience in this connection.

I. Evidence should be confined to the points in issue, and evidence of collateral facts which are incapable of affording

---

[1] Stephen's Dig. of Ev., Art. 54.
[2] Sanderson v. Nashua, 44 N. H. 492.
[3] People v. Donovan, 43 Cal. 162.
[4] Dickenson v. Fitchburg, 13 Gray, 546, 557.
[5] Horne v. Williams, 12 Ind. 324.

any reasonable presumption as to the principal matter in dispute, should not be received.[1]

(a) Evidence of collateral facts may, however, be received where the question is a matter of science, and where the facts proved, though not directly in issue, tend to illustrate the opinions of scientific witnesses.[2]

II. Leading questions should not be asked on the direct, but may be asked on the cross-examination of a witness.[3]

(a) The above rule may be relaxed when made necessary by the complicated nature of the matter concerning which the witness is interrogated.[4]

(b) And the rule does not apply when the witness appears to be hostile to the party producing him.[5]

III. In England the rule is that the examination *and cross-examination* of a witness, must relate to the facts in issue, or relevant or deemed to be relevant thereto, while the re-examination must be directed to an explanation of the matters referred to in the cross-examination.[6] But in this country, the weight of authority is said to be in favor of confining the cross-examination of the witness to the facts testified to in chief.[7]

IV. On the cross-examination, a witness may be asked any question tending, (1) to test his accuracy, veracity or credibility, or, (2) to shake his credit by injuring his character. And he may be compelled to answer the same, unless such answer would tend to criminate himself.[8]

V. If, on the cross-examination, a witness is asked a question which is relevant only in that it may tend to shake his credit by injuring his character, his answer cannot be contradicted unless, (1) he has denied facts tending to show

---

[1] 1 Taylor Evid., § 316; 1 Greenl. Evid., § 52; 1 Wharton's Evid., § 29.
[2] 1 Taylor Evid., § 337.
[3] 2 Best Evid., § 641; 1 Greenl. Evid., § 434; 1 Wharton's Evid., § 499.
[4] Stephens' Evid., Art. 128; 2 Best Evid., § 642.
[5] 2 Taylor Evid., § 1262 A; 1 Greenl. Evid., § 435; 1 Wharton's Evid., § 500.
[6] Stephens' Evid., Art. 127.
[7] 1 Greenl. Evid., § 445; 1 Wharton's Evid., § 529.
[8] Stephens' Evid., Art. 129; 1 Wharton's Evid., § 562.

that he is not impartial, or, (2) he has been asked and has denied or refused to answer whether he has been convicted of some criminal offence.¹

VI. On the cross-examination, a witness may be asked as to any former statements which he may have made, and which are inconsistent with his present testimony. If he denies having made them, they may be proven against him.²

VII. The court in its discretion, may permit a witness to be recalled for further examination. If permission is granted for further examination-in-chief, or further cross-examination, the parties have the right of further cross-examination and of further re-examination respectively.³

VIII. A party is entitled to the cross-examination of a witness who has been, (1) examined-in-chief, or, (2) according to the English rule, if he has been intentionally sworn.⁴

§ 34. **Excluding Experts from the Court Room during the Examination of Witnesses.**—The principle is well settled that the judge, on the application of either party, may, at his discretion, order a separation of ordinary witnesses, in order that they may be prevented from hearing the testimony of the witnesses as given in the court room.⁵ And this practice was established at an early period, being referred to with approbation by Fortescue, in his work *De Laudibus Legum Angliæ*.⁶ It is evident that in the case of

¹ Stephens' Evid., Art. 130; 1 Wharton's Evid., § 559; 1 Greenl. Evid., §§ 418, 449.
² Stephens' Evid., Art. 131; 1 Wharton's Evid., § 551; 1 Greenl. Evid., § 462.
³ Stephens' Evid., Art. 126; 1 Wharton's Evid., §§ 572, 575.
⁴ Stephens' Evid., Art. 126.
⁵ Nolfe v. Isaacson, 1 F. & F. 194; Southey v. Nash, 7 C. & P. 632; Regina v. Newman, 3 C. &. K. 260; McLean v. State, 16 Ala. 672; Wilson v. State, 32 Ala. 299; Pleasant v. State, 15 Ark. 624, 633; People v. Boscovitch, 20 Cal. 436; Johnson v. State, 2 Ind. 652; Errisman v. Errisman, 25 Ill. 136; Davenport v. Ogg. 15 Kans. 363; Sartorious v. State, 24 Miss. 602; Dyer v. Morris, 4 Mo. 214; State v. Fitzsimmons, 30 Mo. 236; State v. Zellers, 7 N. J. L. 220; Laughlin v. State, 18 Ohio, 99; State v. Salge, 2 Nev. 321; Hopper v. Commonwealth, 6 Gratt. (Va.) 684; Benaway v. Conyne, 3 Chand. (Wis.) 214.
⁶ "Et si necessitas exegerit dividantur testes hujus modi, donec ipsi de posuerint quicquid velint, ita quod dictum unius non docebit aut concitabit eorum alium ad consimiliter testificandum." C. 26.

the expert witnesses an exception should be made. As they are to be examined as to opinions based on facts testified to by other witnesses, they should be allowed to remain in court and hear the evidence relating to the facts. But when the testimony as to the facts is closed, and the expert testimony commences, the judge may, in his discretion, order a separation of the expert witnesses. Such is the practice in Scotland, where it has been the usual practice to exclude medical witnesses as soon as the medical experts commence testifying concerning matters of opinion.[1] In England the rule is laid down that " medical or other professional witnesses, who are summoned to give scientific opinions upon the circumstances of the case, as established by other testimony, will be permitted to remain in court until this particular class of evidence commences, but then, like ordinary witnesses, they will have to withdraw, and to come in one by one, so as to undergo a separate examination."[2] And in this country the principle is similarly stated.[3]

§ 35. **Right of the Court to Limit the Number of Expert Witnesses.**—The number of expert witnesses, whose testimony will be received in any particular case, rests in the sound discretion of the trial court. In the old Roman law, the power of the court to limit the number of experts who could be sworn, and even to select two or three from those proposed by the parties, excluding the others, was conceded to exist.[4] And in this country, the right of the court to decline to permit certain witnesses to be sworn as experts, after a sufficient number have already been examined, has been maintained in several cases.[5] But it would not be proper for the court to limit a party to one witness on any vital point.[6] In France the number of experts who

---

[1] Alison's Practice of Crim. Law of Scotland, 542.
[2] 2 Taylors's Evid., § 1259. And see Tait. Evid. 420.
[3] 1 Wharton's Evid., § 492.
[4] Bartol in L. 1, pr. de ventr. insp. no. 5; Bald. in L. 20, cod. de fide inst.
[5] Sizer v. Burt, 4 Denio, 426; Anthony v. Smith, 4 Bos. (N. Y.) 503, 508; Fraser v. Jennison, 42 Mich. 206, 223.
[6] See Hubble v. Osborn, 31 Ind. 249.

may be examined in questions of handwriting, seems to be limited to three,[1] while in Kansas the opinions of at least three experts are required by law, to establish the genuineness of a disputed writing.[2] In a recent case in Michigan, involving testamentary capacity, the trial court, after listening to the testimony of five experts called by the contestants of the will, declined to permit a sixth expert to be examined. The Supreme Court sustained the action of the court below, and Mr. Justice Cooley said: "If testamentary cases are ever to be brought to a conclusion, there must be some limit to the reception of expert evidence, and that which was fixed in this case, was quite liberal enough. To obtain such evidence is expensive, since desirable witnesses are not to be found in every community; but an army may be had if the court will consent to their examination; and if legal controversies are to be determined by the preponderance of voices, wealth, in all litigation in which expert evidence is important, may prevail almost of course. But one familiar with such litigation, can but know that for the purposes of justice, the examination of two conscientious and intelligent experts on a side, is commonly better than to call more. And certainly when five on each side have been examined, the limit of reasonable liberality has in most cases been reached. The jury cannot be aided by going farther. Little discrepancies that must be found in the testimony of those even who in the main agree, begin to attract attention and occupy the mind, until at last, jurors, with their minds on unimportant variances, come to think that expert evidence, from its very uncertainty, is worthless. This is not a desirable state of things, and it can only be avoided by confining the use of expert evidence within reasonable bounds."[3]

§ 36. **By whom Expert Witnesses are Selected.** — In France experts are officially delegated by the court, to in-

---

[1] Code de Procedure civile. Part I, l. 2. tit. 10. s. 200.
[2] Gen. Stat. (1868) p. 854. § 216.
[3] Fraser v. Jennison, 42 Mich. 206, 223, 224.

quire into the facts, and report thereon.[1] But in Germany even greater care has been taken to provide, that only those who are in every way qualified by their learning and experience, shall be permitted to testify in the character of experts. The courts of that country are not granted the power of appointment, nor allowed to pass upon the qualifications of the witnesses, but the experts, in criminal cases, first summoned are exclusively those whom the State, after prior examination of their competency and skill in such particular inquiries, has duly authorized to testify in such cases. In addition to this, provision is made for an appeal to a tribunal of experts, to which the opinions of the expert witnesses can be referred.[2] In Prussia it was the practice for the State to appoint as experts, a physician and surgeon for every county. A medical college was established for each province, to which men of peculiar knowledge in medical jurisprudence were assigned. And if a difference of opinion existed between the county experts, or the parties desired an appeal, the case could be brought before this medical college of the province. In addition to this an appellate medical commission for the whole Monarchy existed.[3] In England and in this country, as all know, the practice has been entirely different from that adopted in either France or Germany. Both here and in England the parties usually select their own experts, and pay them their compensation. The adoption in this country of the German system of governmental experts, has been advocated by a distinguished writer on medico-legal questions,[4] who proposes that there should be selected after an adequate competitive examination, a medical expert for each county in a State, to whom should be referred all questions of medical science that might arise in a litigation. It is proposed that

---

[1] Code de Procedure civile, Part I, l. 2, tit. 10, s. 200. And see Best on Evidence, § 515.

[2] Casper's Gericht Med., Berlin, 1871, I, § 3. See 2 Wharton & Stillé's Med. Juris. (Part II) § 1249.

[3] Rechts lexicon, Leipzig, 1870, I, 478.

[4] 2 Wharton & Stillé's Medical Jurisprudence, Pt. II, § 1250.

it should be his duty to take testimony bearing on such questions, and hear counsel thereon, and after having judicially heard the case, should certify his opinion to the court, by whom the reference was made. In proper cases an appeal could be taken from such an opinion to a Supreme Court of governmental experts appointed by the State at large. In this way it is thought that the expert would be free from the embarrassment of any personal relations to the parties. "He will have no client to serve, and no past partisan extravagances to vindicate. He will render his opinion as the advocate neither of another nor of himself. When he speaks, he will do so judicially, as the representative of the sense of the special branch of science which the case invokes, governed by the opinion of the great body of scientists in this relation, and advised of the most recent investigations. When this is done, we will have expert evidence rescued from the disrepute into which it has now fallen, and invested with its true rights as the expression of the particular branch of science for which it speaks." The appointment of a board of State experts certainly has much to commend it to judicial approval. By the adoption of some such system, the mature judgment of the best minds could be obtained, and the superficial opinions of quacks and mountebanks would not be thrust upon the jury to their confusion, and to the hinderance of justice. Whether the experts are appointed by the court or by the State, in either case there would be eliminated the embarrassment caused by having the experts appear in the case as the interested partisans of the party by whom they are called and specially paid. But while we should under the system proposed be rid of some of the embarrassments we now labor under, there are certain disadvantages connected with it which seriously detract from its practicable value. Men eminent in one branch of their profession often have but a superficial knowledge of other branches, and a physician who may be very able and learned in certain subjects connected with his profession, may be quite ignorant of certain intricate questions of medical science. So that if all questions of medical science, for instance, have to be referred to a board of governmental experts, suitors would be practically prohibited from availing themselves of the testimony of other experts, who might be much better qualified by their special knowledge on that particular subject, to form a correct and accurate opinion.

Another distinguished writer,[1] has expressed the opinion that it would be better to take away from counsel the examination of experts, and devolve it upon the court. "It would be better," he says, "were it possible, for the court alone to examine experts upon those points on which their professional opinions are needed, rather than to hand them over to counsel, each of whom has an interest in making their testimony aid his own side, and to that extent forcibly impressing upon it a unilateral character." He overlooks the fact that it is necessary to a thorough and enlightened examination of an expert witness on an intricate question of medical, or other science, that the examiner should have made himself as familiar as possible with the subject matter of inquiry. To prepare himself for the examination of an expert witness, counsel often spend days and even weeks in the careful investigation of the scientific question involved. This the court cannot do, both for want of time, and for want of knowledge of the questions which will be raised. It is the part of wisdom that the inquisitorial and judicial functions should be so far as possible kept distinct.

§ 37. **Weight of Expert Testimony a Question for the Jury.**—But while the court determines the competency of the witness to testify as an expert, the weight to be accorded to the testimony which he may give, is a question for the jury to determine.[2] "There is no rule of law that

[1] Ordonaux's Jurisprudence of Medicine, § 104, p. 123.
[2] Mitchell v. State, 58 Ala. 418; Delaware etc. Steam Towboat Co. v. Starrs, 69 Penn. St. 36, 41; Sikes v. Paine, 10 Ired. (N. C.) Law, 282; Davis v. State, 35 Ind. 496; Forgery v. First National Bank, 66 Ind. 123; Howard v. Providence, 6 R. I. 516; Parnell v. Commonwealth, 86 Penn. St. 260, 269; Snyder v. State, 70 Ind. 349; Johnson v. Thompson, 72 Ind. 167; Flynt v. Bodenhamer, 80 N. C. 205; State v. Secrest, 80 N. C. 450, 57; Keithsburg etc. R. R. Co. v. Henry, 79 Ill. 290; Pratt v. Rawson,

requires jurors to surrender their judgments implicitly to, or even to give a controlling influence to the opinions of scientific witnesses, however learned or accomplished they may be, and however they may speak with conceded intelligence and authority, aided by the accumulated results of a long experience."[1] The testimony of experts is to be considered like any other testimony, and is to be tried by the same tests, and receive just so much weight and credit as the jury may deem it entitled to, when viewed in connection with all the circumstances.[2] Their testimony is given, it is said, for the purpose of enlightening the jury, and not for the purpose of controlling their judgment.[3] "It must have its legitimate influence by enlightening, convincing and governing the judgment of the jury, and must be of such a character as to outweigh, by its intrinsic force and probability, all conflicting testimony. The jury cannot be required by the court to accept, as matter of law, the conclusions of the witnesses instead of their own."[4] Upon the jury rests the responsibility of rendering a correct verdict, and if the testimony of the experts is opposed to the jury's convictions of truth, it is their duty to disregard it.[5] They should take into consideration the expert's means of knowledge, and the reasons he assigns for the opinion he has given, and give or withhold credence to his testimony, as they may find his qualifications sufficient, and his reasons satisfactory or otherwise.[6] The value of an opinion does not depend upon the skill and knowledge *professed* by the expert, but upon the skill and knowledge which he actually possesses, and of

---

40 Vt. 183, 188; Tatum v. Mohr, 21 Ark. 354; Humphries v. Johnson, 20 Ind. 190.

[1] Brehm v. Great Western R. R. Co., 34 Barb. 256, 272.

[2] Carter v. Baker, 1 Sawyer (U. S. C. C.) 512, 525; Cuneo v. Bessoni, 63 Ind. 524.

[3] Fletcher v. Seekel, 1 R. I. 267; Choice v. State, 31 Ga. 424, 481.

[4] Anthony v. Stinson, 4 Kans. 221.

[5] United States v. McGlue, 1 Curtis C. C. 1, 9.

[6] State v. Hinkle, 6 Iowa, 380; Wood v. Sawyer, Phillips (N. C.) Law, 253, 276; Fairchild v. Bascomb, 35 Vt. 398, 406; In re Springer, 4 Penn. Law J. 275.

the accuracy of such knowledge the jury must judge.[1] It has been said, however, that "an expert's opinion on a question of art or science, is a fact which must be accepted by a jury, if uncontradicted."[2]

§ 38. **Right of the Jury to Exercise an Independent Judgment.**—The right of the jury to determine the weight to be accorded to the testimony of experts, is well illustrated in a case but recently decided in the Supreme Court of the United States, where it was held that the following instruction was erroneous, in an action brought to recover for professional services as attorneys at law: "You must determine the value of the services rendered from the evidence that has been offered before you, and not from your own knowledge and ideas as to the value of such services." The opinion of the court was delivered by Mr. Justice Field, in the course of which he says: "It was the province of the jury to weigh the testimony of the attorneys as to the value of the services, by reference to their nature, the time occupied in their performance, and other attending circumstances, and by applying to it their own experience and knowledge of the character of such services. To direct them to find the value of the services from the testimony of the experts alone, was to say to them that the issue should be determined by the opinions of the attorneys, and not by the exercise of their own judgment of the facts on which those opinions were given. The evidence of experts as to the value of professional services, does not differ in principle, from such evidence as to the value of labor in other departments of business, or as to the value of property. So far from laying aside their own general knowledge and ideas, the jury should have applied that knowledge and those ideas to the matters of fact in evidence, in determining the weight to be given to the opinions expressed; and it was only in that way that they could arrive at a just conclusion. While they cannot act in any case upon particular facts material to its disposition resting in their private

[1] Snyder v. State, 70 Ind. 349.
[2] Atchison etc. R. R. Co. v. United States, 15 Ct. of Cl. 140.

knowledge, but should be governed by the evidence adduced, they may, and, to act intelligently, they must judge of the weight and force of that evidence by their own general knowledge of the subject of inquiry. If, for example, the question were as to the damages sustained by a plaintiff from a fracture of his leg by the carelessness of a defendant, the jury would ill perform their duty, and probably come to a wrong conclusion, if controlled by the testimony of the surgeons, not merely as to the injury inflicted, but as to the damages sustained, they should ignore their own knowledge and experience of the value of a sound limb. * * They should not have been instructed to accept the conclusions of the professional witnesses in place of their own, however much that testimony may have been entitled to consideration. The judgment of witnesses, as a matter of law, is in no case to be substituted for that of the jurors."[1]

§ 39. **Instructions to Jury as to the Nature and Weight of Expert Testimony.**—While the jury must determine the credibility of the experts and the weight of their testimony, and to this end must be left at liberty to exercise their own judgment, independent of any positive direction of the court, yet it has been held that a mere expression of opinion as to the weight of the evidence, which still allows the jury to be guided and governed by their own convictions, forms no proper ground for an exception.[2] In the case last cited, Mr. Justice Daniels says: "That may be proper, and even necessary under certain circumstances, to enable the jury to give appropriate consideration to evidence requiring their judgment. The evidence of witnesses who are brought upon the stand to support a theory by their opinions, is justly exposed to a reasonable degree of suspicion. They are produced, not to swear to facts observed by them, but to express their judgment as to the effect of those detailed by others, and they are selected on account of their ability to express a favorable opinion, which there is great reason

---

[1] Head v. Hargrave, 14 Cent. Law J. 388, 389.
[2] Templeton v. People, 10 Hun, (N. Y.) 357.

to believe, is, in many instances, the result alone of employment, and the bias arising out of it. Such evidence should be cautiously accepted as the foundation of a verdict, and it forms a very proper subject for the expression of a reasonably guarded opinion by the court. That is often necessary to prevent the jury from being led astray, by giving too much weight to evidence really requiring to be suspiciously watched, and which, in many instances, has induced unwarranted verdicts, discreditable to the administration of justice, as well as exceedingly detrimental to the public interest." The following instruction, however, was held in this case to be erroneous: "There is no more reliance to be placed upon it (the testimony of the expert) than upon the testimony of any other person in this case. I regard you gentlemen of the jury as equally skilled, and as able to decide from the evidence, whether or not the prisoner was insane as Dr. Clymer." In a recent case in North Carolina, an instruction was sustained, charging the jury that the law attached peculiar importance to the opinions of medical men who have had opportunity of observation upon questions of mental capacity.[1]

§ 40. **Instructions to the Jury as to the Nature and Weight of Expert Testimony — The Subject Continued.** — In Iowa the following instruction has been sustained: "Evidence of this character (comparison of handwriting by experts) has been introduced in the case at bar, and it will be for you to say how much weight shall be given to such testimony, taking into consideration the amount of skill possessed by the witnesses. But while it is proper to consider such evidence, and to give to it such weight as you may think it justly entitled, yet it is proper to remark that it is of the lowest order of evidence, or evidence of the most unsatisfactory character. It cannot be claimed that it ought to overthrow positive and direct evidence of credible witnesses who testify from their personal knowledge, but it is most useful in cases of conflict between witnesses as corrob-

---

[1] Flynt v. Bodenhamer, 80 N. C. 205.

orating witnesses." Counsel claimed that the above instruction was erroneous, as it practically destroyed expert evidence, by taking from it the force and weight given to it by law. But in sustaining the instruction the court says: "The observation and experience of daily life, as well as in the administration of justice in the courts of law, must be applied by judges and jurors to enable them to decide to what extent the mind should be influenced by evidence submitted to them. * * * The effect, then, which all evidence has upon the mind is determined by observation and experience, the only original instructors of wisdom. These teach that the evidence of experts is of the very lowest order, and of the most unsatisfactory character. We believe that in this opinion experienced laymen unite with members of the legal profession."[1] And in Vermont the Supreme Court of that State declared, that if the trial judge had "told the jury, what to be sure is unusual, as expressed in an early case, that it (testimony of experts in handwriting) was entitled to but little weight as proof of the disputed fact, but, after all leaving it for them to weigh and consider, it would not have been an error."[2] So, in a case which involved a question as to the permanency of a person's loss of vision, where one of the experts testified that in his examination of the eye he had not used the opthalmoscope, or stereoscope, while the other had employed both instruments and reached a different conclusion, it was held to be error to refuse the following request to charge: "Considering the extraordinary character of the injuries alleged in this case, and the great difficulty attendant upon their proper investigation, great weight should be given by the jury to the opinion of scientific witnesses, accustomed to investigate the causes and effect of injuries to the eye, and a distinction should be made in favor of the opinion of those accustomed to use the most perfect instruments and processes, and who are acquainted with the most

[1] Whittaker v. Parker, 42 Iowa, 586. See, too, Borland v. Walwrath, 33 Iowa, 133.
[2] Pratt v. Rawson, 40 Vt. 183, 188.

recent discoveries in science, and most approved methods of treatment and investigation." [1]

§ 41. **Instructions to the Jury as to the Nature and Weight of Expert Testimony — The Subject Continued.** — The following has been held an erroneous instruction: "That in questions involving science and skill, the opinions of scientific men in professions or pursuits, to which such questions may pertain, are authoritative, and in all doubtful cases in which such questions are involved should control the jury." The Supreme Court in reviewing the instruction declared that "such opinions are to be received and treated by the jury like any other evidence in the cause." [2] The same court in a subsequent case held the following instruction erroneous. It illustrates the other extreme to which trial courts are apt to go: "Some persons have been introduced as experts on the question of unsoundness (of testator's mind). These witnesses gave opinions based upon hypothetical cases. These opinions are of no value, unless the hypothetical cases put to the experts are fully sustained by the evidence given in the cause. If the hypothetical cases are fully proved by the evidence, and the experts understand the subject upon which their opinions are given, those opinions ought to have some weight, but the testimony of experts is usually of very little value in determining the sanity or insanity of a party. The opinions of experts are not so highly regarded now as formerly; for, while they sometimes afford aid in the determination of facts, it often happens that experts can be found to testify to any theory, however absurd; and they frequently come with biased minds, prepared to support the cause in which they are embarked. I do not wish to be understood that the witnesses called in this case are biased. You are the judges of that matter."

The court held that this instruction underrated too much the value of the testimony of experts as a class. And it declared its belief that the trial court was mistaken in say-

[1] Tinney v. New Jersey Steamboat Co., 12 Abbott's Pr. (N. S.) 1.
[2] Humphries v. Johnson, 20 Ind. 190.

ing that "the testimony of experts is usually of very little value in determining the sanity or insanity of a party." As to the value of expert testimony, the court declares it "depends as much upon all the facts and circumstances connected with each particular case as that of any other class of witnesses. It is for the court first to decide whether a witness is competent to testify as an expert; but when permitted to testify, an expert stands substantially on the same footing as any other witness as to credibility. His testimony may be valuable, or it may not be, depending upon the manner in which it may be able to withstand the usual tests of credibility which may be app ied to it." [1] And the same court in a still more recent case has also held the following instruction erroneous, as giving too much prominence to experience: "The less experience a professional witness has, and the less satisfactory the reasons for his opinion, the less weight should the opinion have. As to all the witnesses, whether medical or not, you are the exclusive judges of the weight to be given to the evidence." [2]

§ 42. **The Value and Weight of Expert Testimony.**—We have collected in the appendix the expressions of judicial opinion as to the value attaching to the testimony of experts. It is evident that the value of expert testimony depends on the learning and skill of the expert, and on the nature of the subject of investigation. If the subject of inquiry relates to the cause, nature or effect of disease, for instance, the opinions of eminent or learned physicians would be entitled to the very highest consideration. If, on the other hand, the subject of inquiry is the genuineness of a disputed signature, great importance cannot always be attached to the testimony of the experts. The value of the testimony varies with the circumstances of each case, and of those circumstances the jury must be the judges. They must determine whether great or little weight is to be accorded it. But in all cases, the testimony of experts is to be received and

[1] Eggers v. Eggers, 57 Ind. 461.
[2] Cuneo v. Bessoni. 63 Ind. 524.

weighed with great caution. As a judge in one of the Irish courts has expressed it, "such evidence ought, as all evidence of opinion ought, to be received and considered with narrow scrutiny, and with much caution."[1] And no error would be found with an instruction which should merely caution the jury as to such evidence. Indeed, it would seem to be the duty of the trial court in all cases, to give the jury to understand that they must consider all such testimony with caution. It would seem to be as proper in such cases to caution the jury, as it is conceded to be to caution them as to the testimony of detectives and police officers, or as to the testimony of the relatives of an accused person. It may also be highly proper, too, in many cases, to remind the jury that the weight of the testimony of experts does not depend so much on the number of the witnesses, as upon their capacity, their opportunities for observation, the unprejudiced state of their minds, and the nature of the facts.[2] But cautions to a jury against the testimony of witnesses should, in all cases, be very guarded, as they may easily become erroneous and misleading.[3] .

[1] M'Fadden v. Murdock, 1 Irish R. (C. L.) 211, 218.
[2] Clark v. Fisher, 1 Paige, Ch. (N. Y.) 171; s. c. 19 Am. Decis. 402.
[3] See Grand Rapids etc. R. R. Co. v. Martin, 41 Mich. 672.

CHAPTER IV.

EXPERT TESTIMONY IN MEDICINE, SURGERY AND CHEMISTRY.

SECTION.
43. Competency of Physicians to Testify as Experts.
44. Competency of Physicians to Testify as Experts — The Subjec Continued.
45. Disqualifications Arising from Information Acquired while Attending Patient.
46. Cases in which Physicians may Testify, notwithstanding the Prohibitory Statutes.
47. Opinions Based on Statements made out of Court, and not under Oath.
48. Opinions of Physicians Based in part on Declarations of Patients.
49. Opinions as to the Condition of a Patient.
50. Opinions as to Cause of Death.
51. The Nature and Symptoms of Disease.
52. Who are Competent to Express Opinions in such cases.
53. Nature and Effect of Wounds.
54. Character of Instrument with which Wound was Produced.
55. Who are Competent to Express Opinions as to Instrument used.
56. Opinions of Medical Experts as to Mental Condition.
57. The Rule in Massachusetts.
58. Roman Catholic Priest an Expert as to Sanity.
59. Mode of Examination as to Sanity.
60. Evidence Bearing on Question of Insanity.
61. Opinions of Non-Professional Witnesses as to Mental Condition.
62. This Subject Continued.
63. Rape, Abortion and Pregnancy.
64. Opinions in Miscellaneous Cases.
65. Opinions of Medical Experts in Malpractice Cases.
66. Right to Order an Examination of the person by Medical Experts in cases of alleged Impotency.
67. Who should be Appointed to make the Examination.
68. When Compulsory Examination in such cases will not be ordered.
69. Summoning Experts to Assist in Determining the Proper Interrogatories.

70. The Subject of Inquiry. Structural Defect. Impracticability of Consummation.
71. The Testimony of the Experts in such Cases to be Received with Caution.
72. Defraying the Expenses of the Examination by the Expert.
73. Compulsory Examination in Criminal Cases.
74. Compulsory Examination in Criminal Cases — The Subject Continued.
75. Compulsory Examination in Actions for Damages.
.76. Detection of Poisons by Chemists.
77. Chemical Analysis of Poison not necessary when.
78. Chemical Analysis of Contents of Stomach.
79. Order of Research in Analysis for Poisons.
80. Chemical and Microscopic Examination of Blood.
81. Whether Ordinary Witnesses may Testify as to Blood Stains.
82. Blood Stains—Proper Question Concerning.
83. Other Cases in which the Opinions of Chemists have been received.
84. Diseases in Animals—Qualifications of Expert.

§ 43. **Competency of Physicians to Testify as Experts.** —The principle is well established that physicians and surgeons of practice and experience, are experts in medicine and surgery, and that their opinions are admissible in evidence upon questions that are strictly and legitimately embraced in their profession and practice.[1] Persons are presumed to understand questions appertaining to their own profession.[2] As expressed in a recent case in South Carolina a physician is "in law an expert as to all matters embraced within the range of his profession."[3] In the absence of any statutory provision to the contrary, it does not seem to be necessary that they should be graduates of any medical college, or have a license to practice from any medical board, in order to render them competent to testify as experts in relation to matters connected with their profession.[4] If it is shown that the witness is a practicing physician or surgeon, it is sufficient evidence that he is competent to express an opinion upon

[1] Hathaway Adm'r v. National Life Ins. Co., 48 Vt. 335, 351; De Phue v. State, 44 Ala. 39; Livingston v. Commonwealth, 14 Grattan (Va.) 592; Bird v. Commonwealth, 21 Grattan (Va.) 800.
[2] Jones v. White, 11 Humph. (Tenn.) 268.
[3] State v. Clark, 15 S. C. (N. S.) 403, 408.
[4] New Orleans etc. R. R. Co. v. Allbritton, 38 Miss. 242.

a medical question.[1] But in Wisconsin, the legislature has interposed, and enacted a law providing that "no person practicing physic or surgery shall have the right * * to testify in a professional capacity as a physician or surgeon in any case, unless he shall have received a diploma from some incorporated medical society or college, or shall be a member of the State or some county medical society, duly organized in this State."[2] The mere fact, that a person was by education a physician, is not deemed in itself sufficient to justify his admission as an expert, provided he never practiced his profession.[3] His competency, it is said, should be shown "from his study and experience in medicine."[4] But it is not to be supposed that a physician and surgeon, who shows himself otherwise qualified, is to be considered as disqualified by the fact that at the time of giving his testimony, he is not in full practice. That merely goes to his credit, and is for the consideration of the jury in weighing his testimony.[5] Hence, a witness was held competent to testify as a medical expert, who stated that he had attended a course of medical lectures, had obtained a license from the State, and had practiced as a physician for a year, when he abandoned the medical profession for that of the law, which had been his profession for the last sixteen years, but that he had continued to read medical works, had kept up with the improvements made in the science of medicine, and felt competent to express a medical opinion upon the subject of inquiry.[6] Although the witness had once practiced medicine, it appears that the court in this case inclined to the opinion that he would have been competent had that fact not been shown, for they say: "If one asserts an ability to give correct opinions upon any art or science, from an

---

[1] Wisconsin Rev. Stat. (1878) p. 440, § 1436.
[2] Livingston v. Commonwealth, 14 Gratt. (Va.) 592; Washington v. Cole, 6 Ala. 212.
[3] Fairchild v. Bascomb, 35 Vt. 410.
[4] Polk v. State, 36 Ark. 117, 123.
[5] Roberts v. Johnson, 58 N. Y. 613.
[6] Tullis v. Kidd, 12 Ala. 648, 650.

acquaintance with the subject, acquired by observation and study, we cannot perceive on what ground he can be rejected because he has not been in the actual practice of his profession." It is not necessary that a physician should have made the particular disease involved in any inquiry, a specialty, in order to make his testimony admissible as being that of an expert.[1] But if he has devoted himself exclusively to one branch of his profession, and has had no practical experience in that subject matter to which he is called to testify, as if an oculist is called to testify as an expert in insanity, his testimony would be inadmissible.[2] Hence, it has been held that a physician was incompetent to express an opinion upon the question of insanity, whose habit it had been, when his patients required medical treatment for insanity, to call in the services of a physician who had made a special study of mental diseases, or to recommend their removal to a hospital for the insane.[3]

§ 44. **Competency of Physicians to Testify as Experts— The Subject Continued.**—So in a recent case in Mississippi, the court declared, that a medical practice confined to the treatment of ordinary diseases, does not qualify a physician to testify as an expert upon insanity upon hypothetical interrogations as to supposed facts, of which he had no personal knowledge.[4] But his testimony is admissible if he has a personal knowledge of the facts,[5] or if he has studied somewhat the subject of psychological medicine.[6] It has been held that a physician who had been in practice for several years, but who had no experience as to the effect upon health of breathing illuminating gas, could not testify in relation thereto, as an expert.[7] The fact that he was a

[1] Hathaway v. National Life Ins. Co., 48 Vt. 335, 351; State v. Reddick, 7 Kans. 143.
[2] Fairchild v. Bascomb, 35 Vt. 410.
[3] Commonwealth v. Rice, 14 Gray (Mass.), 335.
[4] Russell v. State, 53 Miss. 367.
[5] Baxter v. Abbott, 7 Gray (Mass.), 71.
[6] State v. Reddick, 7 Kans. 143; Davis v. State, 35 Ind. 496. See too Bitner v. Bitner, 65 Penn. St. 347, and Pidcock v. Potter, 68 Penn. St. 347.
[7] Emerson v. Lowell Gas Light Co., 6 Allen, 146.

physician, it was said, did not necessarily give him any knowledge of gas and its effects upon health; and an experience in attending other persons who were alleged to have been made sick by breathing gas from the same leak, was pronounced insufficient. It has been held in New Jersey, that a physician may be examined as to injuries done to the eyes of a party by violence, although he may not be a surgeon or an oculist.[1] The case was decided upon the statute of that State, which requires all physicians to be skilled in both medicine, surgery and anatomy. A practicing physician whose knowledge of the particular subject of inquiry was derived from study alone, has been held competent to express an opinion as an expert.[2] When a medical witness declines to express an opinion on the ground of the want of sufficient information, it is improper to ask him for his "impressions."[3]

§ 45. **Disqualifications Arising from Information Acquired while Attending Patient.**—In the absence of any statutory provision to the contrary, it is well settled that a physician or surgeon may be compelled to disclose any communications made to him in professional confidence.[4] A physician, therefore, would not be incompetent at the common law, to testify to a professional opinion based on facts which may have been learned by him from such communications.

But in several of the States statutes have been enacted which have abrogated the common law rule on this subject. In Wisconsin the statute is that "no person duly authorized to practice physic or surgery, shall be compelled to disclose any information which he may have acquired in attending

[1] Castner v. Sliker, 33 N. J. L. 95; s. c., ib. 507.
[2] Taylor v. Grand Trunk R. R. Co., 48 N. H. 304. The opinion expressed in this case, was that injuries from railroad accidents were more severe than from other causes, although bearing the same external appearance.
[3] Higbee v. Guardian Mutual Life Ins. Co., 66 Barb. 462, 467.
[4] Stephens' Dig. of Evidence, Art. 117; Dutchess of Kingston's Case, Hargr. St. Tr. 243, 20 How. St. Tr. 613, 614; Ashland v. Marlborough, 99 Mass. 48; Barber v. Merriam, 11 Allen, 322; People v. Stout, 3 Parker Cr. Cas. 670.

any patient in a professional character, and which information was necessary to enable him to prescribe for such patient as a physician, or to do any act for him as a surgeon."[1] This provision is distinguished from the ones adopted in New York,[2] Michigan,[3] Iowa,[4] Minnesota,[5] Missouri,[6] Ohio,[7] Indiana,[8] and Nebraska,[9] in which it is provided that the witness shall not be competent, or shall not be *allowed* to make the disclosure, while in Wisconsin the language is that he shall not be *compelled* to make the disclosure. But in Iowa, Indiana and Minnesota, his testimony may be received with the consent of the patient; and in Minnesota the prohibition is confined to civil cases.

§ 46. **Cases in which Physicians may Testify Notwithstanding the Prohibitory Statutes.**— The statutory provisions noticed in the preceding section were undoubtedly designed for the exclusive protection of the patient, and although the statutes declare that the physician "shall not be allowed" to make the disclosure, it is not believed that they will be construed so as to prejudice the public interests, provided the disclosure to be obtained manifestly works no injustice to the spirit and intent of the law. In a recent case in New York, where a prisoner was charged with murder committed by the administration of arsenic, the State called as a witness the physician who attended the deceased in a professional capacity, and inquired of him concerning the symptoms exhibited by the deceased, and what he had learned concerning his condition during the time of his attendance upon him. Counsel for the prisoner objected that the examination was contrary to the statute, but the Supreme Court overruled the objection for the reason that it

---

[1] Wisconsin Rev. Stat. (1878) p. 992, § 4075.
[2] Code, § 834,
[3] Comp. Laws, § 5943.
[4] Code of 1873, p. 565, § 3643.
[5] Stat. of 1878, p. 793, § 10.
[6] 1 Rev. Stat. (1879) p. 690, § 4017.
[7] 2 Rev. Stat. (1880) p. 1278, § 5241.
[8] 2 Rev. Stat. (1876) p. 134, § 2.
[9] Gen. Stat. (1873) p. 582, § 333.

was not within the spirit and intent of the statute, although within the letter."¹

The matter was taken to the Court of Appeals, and the judgment of the Supreme Court affirmed, the court saying: "That the purpose for which the aid of this statute is invoked in this case, is so utterly foreign to the purposes and objects of the act, and so diametrically opposed to any intention which the legislature can be supposed to have had in the enactment, so contrary to and inconsistent with its spirit, which most clearly intended to protect the patient, and not to shield one who is charged with his murder, that in such a case the statute is not to be so construed as to be used as a weapon of defense to the party so charged, instead of a protection to his victim."²

The same subject was under discussion in a subsequent case which involved the mental capacity of a testator. The surrogate excluded the testimony of a physician who attended the testator, and who stated that all his knowledge was derived from what he observed while attending deceased professionally. The Supreme Court held that the testimony was admissible. That it did not involve the disclosure of any confidential information acquired in his professional capacity, but of facts which were open to the observation of any person who had seen or conversed with the testator.³ The same question has been considered in Michigan, where an objection was made against allowing the proponents of a will to examine a physician, for the purpose of showing the condition of the decedent while he was treating him professionally. The court held⁴ that while the statute covered information acquired by observation while the physician was in attendance upon his patient, as well as communications made by the patient to him,⁵ yet the rule it

---

¹ Pierson v. People, 25 N. Y. Sup. Ct. 239.
² Pierson v. People, 79 N. Y. 434.
³ Staunton v. Parker, 26 N. Y. Sup. Ct. 56. See also People v. Stout, 3 Parker Cr. Cas. 670; Grattan v. Metropolitan Life Ins. Co., 31 N. Y. Sup. Ct. 43.
⁴ Fraser v. Jennison, 42 Mich. 206, 224.
⁵ Briggs v. Briggs, 20 Mich. 34.

established was one of privilege for the protection of the patient, which he might waive if he saw fit;[1] and that what he might do in his lifetime, those who represented him after his death might also do for the protection of the interests they claimed under him. In a case in the St. Louis Court of Appeals, arising under the Missouri statute, that court declared that objective signs, which are obvious on an observation of a patient by the physician, but which imply no disclosure on the part of the patient, as well as symptoms which are apparent before the patient submits himself to any examination, are not to be excluded under the statute. "It is not an objection," remarked the court, "that the trained eye of the physician might thus detect sure signs of a given disease."[2] The same court in another case, has declared that where the whole testimony of a physician is excluded on the ground that he could not separate the impressions received by him, growing out of the relation of physician and patient, and those received by observation of the patient when that relation did not exist, it is necessary that the facts justifying such exclusion should appear. The statement of the physician that he is unable to distinguish between such impressions, is not sufficient. And the fact that such discrimination can be made by the witness, may be developed on a proper cross-examination.[3]

§ 47. **Opinions Based on Statements made out of Court and not under Oath.**— The rule is that an expert cannot be allowed to give his opinion based upon statements made to him by parties out of court and not under oath.[4] His opinion to be admissible, must be founded either on his own personal knowledge of the facts, or else upon an hypothetical question.[5] Hence the opinion of a physician, called in consultation with the attending physicians, cannot be received if based upon declarations made to him by such

[1] Scripps v. Foster, 41 Mich. 742.
[2] Linz v. Mass. Mut. Life Ins. Co., 8 Mo. App. 369.
[3] Gartside v. Conn. Mut. Life Ins. Co., 8 Mo. App. 593.
[4] Hurst v. The C. R. I. & P. R. R. Co., 49 Iowa, 76, 79.
[5] Hunt v. State, 9 Tex. Ct. of App. 166.

physicians, or by the wife and nurse of the patient as to his previous symptoms or condition.[1]

§ 48. **Opinions of Physicians Based in part on Declarations of Patients.**—But the principle stated in the preceding section, does not apply to the opinions of a physician or surgeon, based *in part* on statements made by the *patient* himself to the physician, to enable the latter to determine upon the proper course of treatment. Upon this point the Supreme Court of Massachusetts says: "The opinion of a surgeon or physician is necessarily formed in part on the statements of his patient, describing his condition and symptoms, and the causes which have led to the injury or disease under which he appears to be suffering. This opinion is clearly competent as coming from an expert. * * The existence of many bodily sensations and ailments which go to make up the symptoms of disease or injury, can be known only to the person who experiences them. It is the statement and description of these which enter into, and form part of the facts on which the opinion of an expert, as to the condition of health or disease, is founded."[2] In a case in the Supreme Court of Illinois, it was said that a physician must necessarily, in forming his opinion, be, to some extent, guided by the statements of his patient; and that the opinion of an expert, founded in part upon such *data*, may be received in evidence.[3] In the same case, the court held that the physician might state what the patient said in describing his condition, if spoken under circumstances freeing it from suspicion of having been spoken with reference to future litigation. A similar ruling has been lately made in New Jersey, it being held that the declarations made to a physician of bodily feelings and symptoms of pregnancy, at the time of his examination, were admissi-

[1] Heald v. Thing, 45 Me. 392; Wood v. Sawyer. Phillips Law (N. C.) 253; Wetherbee's Exr's v. Wetherbee's Heirs, 38 Vt. 454; Hunt v. State, 9 Tex. Ct. of App. 166.

[2] Barber v. Merriam, 11 Allen, 322, 324. See also Thompson v. Trevanion, Skinner, 402; Aveson v. Kinnaird, 6 East. 188, 195, 197; Bacon v. Charlton, 7 Cush. 581, 586; Denton v. State, 1 Swan (31 Tenn.) 279.

[3] Illinois Central R. R. Co. v. Sutton, 42 Ill. 438.

ble evidence as a part of the facts on which his opinion was founded.[1] The jury should have these declarations, in order that they may know whether the physician's conclusions are careful, skillful and reliable. In a case in Alabama, the court say that the physician may state the declarations of the patient as to his symptoms and condition during previous similar attacks, when they form the predicate of his opinion, in whole or in part, as to the duration and character of the disease.[2] Upon this general subject, a very interesting case was decided by the Supreme Court of Wisconsin in 1879,[3] and as it is worthy of careful consideration, a somewhat detailed statement of it may not be deemed inappropriate. The action was brought to recover damages for an injury sustained by the negligence of the defendant, the plaintiff claiming to be lame in her hip and to suffer pain there, and that she was unable to use her limb as she had used it before the accident. That it was still so weak and painful as to render it unsafe for her to attempt to walk without the aid of a crutch. At the suggestion of the defendant, the plaintiff submitted to an examination by experts for the purpose of testing the truthfulness of the claim, and of placing before the jury her real condition. The result of the examination was that the experts found no such appearances as would indicate lameness or pain. As one of the experts testified, "the general opinion was that we could not find anything. The only way I could tell that she ached, was by *what she said, and how she looked and appeared.*" Counsel for the defendant claimed that an error was committed in permitting one of the experts, who testified as above, to answer the following questions:

"*Question.* Do you think that you could tell whether or not she suffered pain by the movement of the hip, judging from all the examination, including what she said? *Answer.* I think I could. *Q.* Now go on and state whether, in your

---

[1] State v. Gedicke, 43 N. J. L. 86.
[2] Ecles v. Bates, 26 Ala. 655.
[3] Quaife v. Chicago etc. R. R. Co., 48 Wis. 513.

opinion, she did suffer pain? *A.* She gave every indication of suffering pain. *Q.* In your opinion, did she suffer pain? *A.* Yes, sir; that is my opinion, that she did."

It was claimed that this was in effect, asking the witness whether he believed the statements of the plaintiff that she suffered pain. The Supreme Court held that the questions were proper. That as the plaintiff insisted upon the fact of lameness and pain, it was a question for the experts whether such pains and lameness were imaginary, feigned or real; and that to determine this, it was necessary to resort to other evidences than those to be derived from the limb itself. "And in such case, we think it is clearly competent for the expert to give an opinion from the general appearance, actions and looks of the patient, and what she says at the time in regard to her condition."

§ 49. **Opinions as to the Condition of a Patient.**—A physician may give his opinion as to the actual condition of a patient whom he has visited,[1] or whose symptoms and condition have been described by others.[2] He may state his belief that a woman had been delivered of a child within three or four days, and state his opinion as to the condition of her mind at the time of giving birth to the child.[3] And he may state what effect certain drugs would have upon a person in a particular condition.[4] But it has been held that he cannot be asked his opinion, from the condition of a person whom he had not seen, as described by witnesses whose testimony was conflicting, whether the attention of a physician was necessary.[5]

§ 50. **Opinions as to Cause of Death.**—The opinions of physicians are also received as to the cause of the death of any particular person; such opinion being founded either upon

---

[1] Bush v. Jackson, 24 Ala. 273; Bennett v. Fail, 26 Ala. 605.
[2] Livingston v. Commonwealth, 14 Gratt. 592; Cooper v. State, 23 Texas. 336, 340.
[3] State v. Matthews, 66 N. C. 113.
[4] Hoard v. Peck, 56 Barb. (N. Y.) 202, 210. That the opinions of physicians are admissible as to the ordinary effect of medicines, see also Cooper v. State, 23 Texas, 336, 340.
[5] Wilkinson v. Mosely, 30 Ala. 562.

a personal knowledge of the facts of the case, or upon a statement of the symptoms of the disease as detailed by others.[1] If such opinions were not received, it would be impossible in many cases to prove the cause and manner of death; especially in those cases where there was no one present at the time of death. In such cases the opinions of physicians and surgeons who have made a *post-mortem* examination of the deceased, seem to be necessary in order to ascertain the facts and clear up the mystery. And where the attending physicians were dead at the time of trial, it was held competent for the wife of the deceased to state the declarations made to her at the time by the physicians, as to the cause of death. The declarations made by them were in the ordinary line of their professional duty, and as such were receivable in evidence to establish the fact that they entertained such opinion as they stated.[2]

In a recent case in Arkansas, where the subject of inquiry was as to the cause of death, the court considered the mode of examination which should be pursued in such cases. The case was one of alleged poisoning, and it was held not erroneous to ask a physician to describe the symptoms of strychnine in the human system, and stop and allow the jury to compare the symptoms testified to by the witness with those given by the expert, as to the usual effects of strychnine, as affording some tendency to prove the manner of death. "But," said the court, "although not erroneous, such a course of examination is eminently unsatisfactory, and liable to mislead. The proper course is to take the opinion of the expert upon the facts given in evidence, not as to the merits of the case, or the guilt or innocence of the prisoner, but as to the cause of the death, so that the jury may first determine whether any crime has been committed by any one at all."[3]

[1] Pitts v. State, 43 Miss. 472; State v. Bowman, 78 N. C. 509; Shelton v. State, 34 Tex. 666; State v. Baptiste, 26 La. An. 134, 137; State v. Smith, 32 Me. 370; Mitchell v. State, 58 Ala. 418; State v. Pike, 65 Me. 111, 114; Polk v. State, 36 Ark. 117; 124.

[2] McNair v. National Life Ins. Co., 20 N. Y. Sup. Ct. 146. See, too, Stephen's Dig. of Evidence, Art. 27, p. 33.

[3] Polk v. State, 36 Ark. 117, 124.

§ 51. **The Nature and Symptoms of Disease.**—The opinions of witnesses skilled in the science and practice of medicine, are admissible as to the nature of the disease a person is afflicted with,[1] and as to how long he has probably been afflicted with it.[2] Their opinions are also received as to the severity and ordinary duration of the disease,[3] as well as to the probability of its recurrence,[4] and the effects upon the general health.[5] They are also permitted to testify as to the cause of the disease and the remedy for it,[6] and to describe the symptoms of any particular disease,[7] explaining its characteristics,[8] and that it is contagious.[9] And an attending physician may be asked whether he ever saw any appearance of a certain disease in the family of a particular person,[10] and that before a certain injury he considered the person to be a hearty and vigorous man.[11]

[1] Napier v. Ferguson, 2 P. & B. (New Bruns.) 415; Polk v. State, 36 Ark. 117, 124; Tatum v. Mohr, 21 Ark. 354; Hook v. Stovall, 26 Ga. 704; Flynt v. Bodenhamer, 80 N. C. 205, 208; Jones v. White, 11 Humph. (Tenn.) 268; Pidcock v. Potter, 68 Pa. St. 342, 344; Lush v. McDaniel, 13 Ired. (N. C.) 485; Washington v. Cole, 6 Ala. 212; Linton v. Hurley, 14 Gray (Mass.), 191; Cooper v. State, 23 Tex. 336, 340; State v. Terrill, 12 Rich. (S. C.) 321.

[2] Lush v. McDaniel, 13 Ired. (N. C.) 485; Bennett v. Fail, 26 Ala. 605; Edington v. Ætna Life Ins. Co., 77 N. Y. 564, 568; Tatum v. Mohr, 21 Ark. 354; Eckles v. Bates, 26 Ala. 655.

[3] Linton v. Hurley, 14 Gray (Mass.), 191; Willey v. Portsmouth, 35 N. H. 303, 308.

[4] Filer v. N. Y. Central R. R. Co., 49 N. Y. 42.

[5] Pidcock v. Potter, 68 Penn. St. 344, 342; Flynt v. Bodenhamer, 80 N. C. 205, 208; Filer v. N. Y. Central R. Co., 49 N. Y. 42; Anthony v. Smith, 4 Bos. (N. Y.) 503.

[6] Matteson v. N. Y. etc. R. R. Co., 62 Barb. (N. Y.) 364; Jones v. Tucker, 41 N. H. 546; Cooper v. State, 23 Tex. 336, 340; Napier v. Ferguson, 2 P. & B. (New Bruns.) 415.

[7] Welch v. Brooks, 10 Rich. (S. C.) 124; State v. Terrill, 12 Rich. (S. C.) 321; United States v. McGlue, 1 Curtis C. C. 1, 9; Napier v. Ferguson, 2 P. & B. (New Bruns.) 415; Pitts v. State, 43 Miss. 472; People v. Robinson, 2 Parker Cr. Cas. (N. Y.) 236; Lake v. People, 1 Parker Cr. Cas. (N. Y.) 495.

[8] Jones v. White, 11 Humph. (Tenn.) 268, Washington v. Cole, 6 Ala. 212.

[9] Moore v. State, 17 Ohio St. 521, 526.

[10] Morrissey v. Ingham, 111 Mass. 63.

[11] Sanderson v. Nashua, 44 N. H. 492.

§ 52. Who are Competent to express Opinions in such Cases.— A physician may testify that a certain disease prevailed in a certain neighborhood at a certain time.[1] But it has been held that one not an expert cannot testify whether there was any case of a particular disease in the neighborhood in question.[2] And the general rule seems to be that one who is not skilled in the science or practice of medicine, is not competent to express an opinion that a person is afflicted with a particular disease.[3] But any person of ordinary understanding is competent to form an opinion, whether one whom he has had an opportunity of observing, and with whom he has been acquainted, appeared to be sick or well.[4] It has been held, too, that a person who is not a physician may testify whether it was necessary for a party to receive medical assistance, and the length of time such assistance was necessary. "But, in a question of this kind, any person of intelligence is capable of judging of the necessity of medical advice and services. It is universally acted upon by all classes of mankind, and we are not disposed to lay down a rule that none but a physician is competent to prove that a person is sick, or so sick as to require medical advice."[5] A non-professional witness may also testify that a person was decidedly worse at one time than he was at another, and could not do so much work as before — his testimony being based on facts within his observation.[6]

[1] Lush v. McDaniel, 13 Ired. 485.
[2] Evans v. People, 12 Mich. 27.
[3] Lush v. McDaniel, 13 Ired. (N. C.) 485; Thompson v. Bertrand, 23 Ark. 730; Chicago, etc. R. R. Co. v. George, 19 Ill. 510, 516; Shawneetown v. Mason, 82 Ill. 337, 339.
[4] Bennett v. Fail, 26 Ala. 605; Barker v. Coleman, 35 Ala. 221; Stone v. Watson, 37 Ala. 279; Higbie v. Guardian Mutual Life Ins. Co., 53 N. Y. 603; *s. c.*, 66 Barb. 462; Shawneetown v. Mason, *supra*; Brown v. Lester, Ga. Decis. Part I, 77; See Thompson v. Bertrand, 23 Ark. 730.
[5] Chicago, Burlington & Quincy R. Co. v. George, 19 Ill. 510.
[6] Parker v. Boston, etc. Steamboat Co. 109 Mass. 449. This case distinguishes Ashland v. Marlborough, 99 Mass. 48 (which held that one not an expert could not testify that another "did not appear like a well man"), upon the ground that the witness in the latter case had not testified to any appearances which indicated disease, such as weakness or inability to labor.

But such a witness cannot testify that he thought a person was going to die.[1] In an action on a warranty of a slave, a person who was not an expert has been permitted to testify as to his opinion of the soundness of the slave, stating the facts upon which his opinion was founded.[2] So a wife has been permitted to testify that her husband had a rupture; the testimony being received upon the theory that it was not a fact resting in opinion, and its determination did not involve any question of science or skill.[3] But where the question was whether a woman had been pregnant, the opinions of unprofessional witnesses were held to be inadmissible.[4] In Alabama it is laid down that any person may speak of the existence of disease in another, when the disease is perceptible by the senses.[5] In a case in Michigan it is said, that "no witness, medical or otherwise, can be allowed to give testimony from his observation concerning the nature of a person's illness or its causes, without proof both of a sufficient examination, and such knowledge or experience as will qualify him to offer an opinion."[6]

§ 53. **Nature and Effect of Wounds.**—The opinions of physicians and surgeons are admissible as to what would be the natural and probable results of wounds,[7] and whether they were sufficient to cause death.[8] In a recent case, where it was objected that the physician who made the *post-mortem* examination of the deceased, could not express an opinion that death resulted from concussion of the brain, unless he had opened the head and examined the brain, the court

[1] Blackman v. Johnson, 35 Ala. 252.
[2] Norton v. Moore, 40 Tenn. 483.
[3] Duntz v. Van Beuren, 12 N. Y. Sup. Ct. 648.
[4] Boies v. McAllister, 12 Me. 310.
[5] Milton v. Rowland, 11 Ala. 732; Fountain v. Brown, 38 Ala. 72; Wilkeson v. Mosely, 30 Ala. 562.
[6] People v. Olmstead, 30 Mich. 434; *s. c.*, 1 Hawley's Cr. R. 301.
[7] Curry v. State, 5 Neb. 412; State v. Porter, 34 Iowa, 131; Page v. State, 61 Ala. 16; Kline v. The K. C., St. J. etc. R. Co., 50 Iowa, 656, 660; State v. Stoyell, 70 Me. 360.
[8] State v. Powell, 7 N. J. Law, 295; Livingston v. Commonwealth, 14 Gratt. (Va.) 592; State v. Morphy, 33 Iowa, 273; Ebos v. State, 34 Ark. 520; State v. Jones, 68 N. C. 443; State v. Matthews, 66 N. C. 113.

said: "We are aware of no law that required him to open the skull and examine the brain, before he could be permitted to express such an opinion to the jury. Of course, the opinion of a medical witness in such case would have more or less weight with the jury, according to the extent of the examination, the professional rank and character of the witness."[1] They are allowed to give their opinion as to whether the effects of the wound are permanent in their nature,[2] and as to the probable effect of the wound on the general health of the injured person, whether in consequence of it he is liable to any particular disease.[3] The opinion of an expert has been received as to which of two wounds, either by itself necessarily fatal, actually caused the death of the deceased.[4] The opinion of such a witness has been received, too, as to whether the fracture of a skull was recently made, the body having been found six months after the person's disappearance.[5] And it is not necessary that the expert should have actually seen the wound, provided he has heard it described.[6] He may express an opinion that a wound was inflicted after death.[7] It has been held that a non-professional witness, who had seen the wounded person, could describe the wound as inflamed and tender to the touch, and could testify that such person complained of stiffness in the fingers, and in the neck and in the jaws, and that since the injury the witness had observed that the wounded man could not use his arm as he could before.[8] And one need not be an expert to testify as to the condition of a person's health and body before and after an injury.[9] It has been held that a physician or

[1] Ebos v. State, *supra.*
[2] Wilt v. Vickers, 8 Watts, (Penn.) 227; Rowell v. City of Lowell, 11 Gray (Mass.), 420; Noblesville etc. R. R. Co. v. Gause, 76 Ind. 142; Maeer v. Third Avenue R. R. Co., 47 N. Y. Superior Ct. 461.
[3] Montgomery v. Town of Scott, 34 Wis. 338.
[4] Eggler v. People, 56 N. Y. 642.
[5] Lindsay v. People, 63 N. Y. 143.
[6] State v. Powell, 7 N. J. Law, 295; Page v. State, 61 Ala. 16.
[7] State v. Harris, 63 N. C. 1; Shelton v. State, 34 Texas, 666.
[8] Craig v. Gerrish, to appear in 58 N. H.; *s. c.* 25 Alb. L. J. 498.
[9] Townsdin v. Nutt, 19 Kans. 282.

or surgeon may testify as to the amount of force required to break a person's skull, his opinion being based on his familiarity with anatomy, and his knowledge of the structure, thickness and strength of the human skull generally.[1] It has been held, too, that one having a knowledge of gun shot wounds, may be asked as to the posture and position of the deceased at the time he was shot,[2] and whether, if he was in a stooping position at the time he was struck, the ball would have taken the course which it did.[3] But it has been held that a physician or surgeon is not an expert as to the manner of giving blows upon the head, and is, therefore, incompetent to express an opinion as to the position of the body when struck. "The form, nature, extent, depth, length, width and direction of the wound being given, and its precise location on the head, with a general statement of the amount of force requisite, and the probable shape of the instrument, the jury can judge as well as any one, in what position the head or the body probably was when the blow was given."[4] For the purpose of explaining and rendering his evidence intelligible to the jury, an expert may be allowed, in describing wounds, to make use of plates and diagrams, although not claimed to be strictly accurate, and not intended to be used as evidence.[5] In the trial of a person indicted for murder, counsel for the prisoner insisted that experts should have been summoned to show that the wound inflicted was dangerous, or mortal, or caused death. The court held that no such testimony was necessary, as it appeared that the deceased was a strong and apparently healthy man, who took to his bed immediately after the wound, suffered intensely for two days, and then died.[6] And on the trial of an indictment for murder, where a witness testified that he had made certain experi-

[1] Kennedy v. People, 39 N. Y. 245.
[2] State v. Jones, 68 N. C. 443.
[3] Commonwealth v. Lenox, 3 Brewster, 249.
[4] Kennedy v. People. 39 N. Y. 245, 256.
[5] State v. Knight, 43 Me. 1, 130.
[6] State v. Murphy, 9 Nevada, 394.

ments upon a dynamometer, an instrument for measuring the force of blows and the weight of falling bodies, by striking it with a bat of substantially the same form and weight as that with which the government contended the murder was committed, it was held that the court might, in its discretion, properly reject such testimony, unless the experiments were shown to have been made under conditions the same as those existing in the case on trial.[1]

§ 54. **Character of Instrument with which Wound was Produced.**—A practicing physician or surgeon may be asked his opinion as to the kind of instrument used in inflicting wounds,[2] as whether a wound was produced with a blunt or a sharp instrument;[3] and whether the fractures on the skull of the deceased, produced in court, were caused by blows from a gun shown to the witness;[4] also whether the skin of a person's throat had been cut by a sharp instrument, or torn.[5] It has been held proper to show that the corner of a hatchet's edge, if held by a person standing in front of the deceased while he was on his feet, exactly fitted the hole in the skull.[6] A surgical expert who had examined the wound, has been allowed to testify, whether, from its form and appearance, it could have been produced by a razor;[7] and whether certain injuries to the head could have been produced at the same time, and by one blow;[8] also whether the wounds could have been inflicted accidentally;[9] and whether the wound could have been produced by coming in contact with a body of hard material, where there were no sharp angles or points.[10] A physician and surgeon of experience with gunshot wounds, may testify whether a

---

[a] Commonwealth v. Piper, 120 Mass. 185.
[1] Davis v. State, 38 Md. 15, 35; State v. Porter, 34 Iowa, 131.
[2] State v. Morphy, 33 Iowa, 272.
[3] Gardner v. People, 6 Parker Cr. Cas. 155.
[4] State v. Clark, 12 Ired. Law (N. C.) 152.
[5] Colt v. People, 1 Parker Cr. Cas. 611, 620.
[6] State v. Knight, 43 Me. 1, 130.
[7] Commonwealth v. Piper, 120 Mass. 185.
[8] Davis v. State, 38 Md. 15, 37.
[10] State v. Pike, 65 Me. 111, 114.

wound was inflicted by a shot from a gun,[1] and he may explain to the jury why the wound looks smaller than the ball which caused it.[2]

§ 55. Who are Competent to Express Opinions as to the Instrument Used.—It seems that one who is not skilled in the science of medicine or surgery, is not competent to express an opinion as to whether a wound was made by a gunshot, or by a knife or other sharp instrument, no matter what may have been his experience and observation.[3] But a physician or surgeon, although he has never seen a wound made by a knife or dirk, is competent to express an opinion, if he states that from his general acquaintance with the human body, and his knowledge of the practice and principles of surgery, he believes he can successfully distinguish and form a correct opinion in the case.[4]

§ 56. Opinions of Medical Experts as to Mental Condition.— The general rule undoubtedly is that the opinions of medical experts are admissible, where the question involved relates to soundness or unsoundness of mind. If a physician visits a person, and from actual examination or observation becomes acquainted with his mental condition, there would seem to be no good reason why he should not state to the jury his opinion as to such person's sanity or insanity, mental soundness or unsoundness, at the time he thus observed him. As Mr. Chief Justice DILLON expressed it, in a case in Iowa: "There is no more reason why he may not do this, than why he might not testify that he saw a certain person at a certain time, and that he was then laboring under an epileptic fit, or under an attack of typhus fever, or had been stricken down and rendered unconscious by an apoplectic stroke."[5]

It is not to be supposed, however, that it is at all essential that a physician should have seen the person, and made

[1] Rash v. State, 61 Ala. 90; Colt v. People, 1 Parker Cr. Cas. 611, 620.
[2] Schlencker v. State, 9 Neb. 250.
[3] Caleb v. State, 39 Miss. 721; Rash v. State, 61 Ala, 90.
[4] Mendum v. Commonwealth, 6 Rand. (Va.) 704. See too, State v. Clark, 12 Ired. (N. C.) Law, 152.
[5] State v. Felter, 25 Iowa, 67. 75.

a personal examination of the case, in order to make him competent to express an opinion as to his mental condition. On the contrary, the rule is that his opinion is admissible, whether it is founded on facts within his personal observation, or upon a hypothetical case based on the testimony of others.[1] But where he has made a personal examination it is necessary for him to describe the symptoms observed, and state the circumstances from which he has drawn his conclusions.[2]

§ 57. **The Rule in Massachusetts.**— In Massachusetts greater strictness prevails as to the competency of witnesses to express opinions upon the subject of mental disease. The rule is in that State to receive the opinions of professional men who are conversant with insanity, who have made a specialty of mental diseases, and had experience with the insane. Such witnesses are permitted to express their opinions, and it is not necessary that they should have made any personal examination of the individual concerned.[3] But it seems that a physician who has not made a specialty of mental diseases, is not competent to express an opinion, unless he was the person's attending physician, in which case his opinion is received, as "It is his duty to make himself acquainted with the peculiarities, bodily and mental, of a person who is the subject of his care and advice."[4]

§ 58. **Roman Catholic Priest as an Expert as to Sanity.**— A very interesting case was decided in the Supreme Court of California in 1880, which involved the question whether a Roman Catholic priest could express an opinion as to the sanity of a testator, such opinion being

---

[1] Potts v. House, 6 Ga. 324; Boardman v. Woodman, 47 N. H. 120, 135; State v. Windsor, 5 Harr. (Del.) 512; Pigg v. State, 43 Tex. 110; Gueting v. State, 66 Ind. 94; Cooper v. State, 23 Tex. 336, 340; Lessee of Hoge v. Fisher, 1 Peters C. C. 163, 164.

[2] Puryear v. Reese, 46 Tenn. 21; Gibson v. Gibson, 9 Yerg. (Tenn.) 329; White v. Bailey, 10 Mich. 155; Hathorn v. King, 8 Mass. 371; Dickinson v. Barber, 9 Mass. 225.

[3] Commonwealth v. Rogers, 7 Metcalf, 500.

[4] Hastings v. Rider, 99 Mass. 625. But see Commonwealth v. Rich, 14 Gray, 335.

given by him in the character of an expert. The court, overruling the decision of the trial court, held that he was competent to testify as an expert. The evidence showed that he had been regularly educated for the priesthood in a college in Spain, that he had officiated as a priest for ten years, that it was part of his preparatory education to become competent to pass upon the mental condition of communicants in his church, and that for that purpose physiology and psychology were branches of his study. It appeared, said the court, "That previous to officiating as a priest it was requisite that he should be skilled in determining the mental condition of those who sought the sacraments. That in every case of the administration of the rites of his church to invalids or dying persons, it was necessary for the priest to make an examination of the mental condition of the recipient, to ascertain if his mind was in a proper state to reason or act of its own volition. That the sacrament could only be administered after such a preliminary examination, and that therefore as a priest he was daily required to exercise and pass his judgment on the mental condition of persons."[1]

§ 59. **Mode of Examination as to Sanity.**— We have elsewhere considered the mode of examination to be pursued in the case of expert witnesses.[2] The principles there stated are, of course, as applicable to the examination of experts in mental diseases, as to the examination of any other class of experts, and it is not necessary to make any reference to that subject in this connection, farther than to call attention to the mode of inquiry, which has been suggested in New York as proper to be pursued in the examination of medical witnesses testifying as to sanity. First inquire of the witness, said Judge HARRIS, as to the particular symptoms of insanity, asking whether all or any, and which of the circumstances spoken of by the witnesses upon the trial are to be regarded as such symptoms. Then in-

[1] Estate of Toomes, 54 Cal. 510.
[2] See Chapter III.

quire of him whether any and what combination of these circumstances would, in his opinion, amount to proof of insanity.[1]

§ 60. **Evidence Bearing on Question of Insanity.**—The opinions of experts are received as to the causes tending to the development of mental unsoundness. For instance, the opinions of experts have been received showing that paralysis in old persons has a tendency to impair the mind.[2] As bearing upon the question of a person's insanity, or tendency to insanity, evidence is received that such person's father or mother were of unsound mind,[3] or that his uncle,[4] or brother,[5] or other relations suffered from mental disease.[6] And reputation in the family of the insanity of some of the members of the family, is admissible on the same principle which admits such reputation as to deaths, births, genealogies, etc.[7] But it is highly important that evidence should not be received as suggesting insanity, unless it has some legitimate tendency to prove it. "We are pursuaded that much wrong has unwittingly been done in many cases, by allowing misfortunes, family calamities and personal peculiarities, to go to the jury as having some necessary tendency to unsettle the mind, and therefore, some bearing on the issue of mental soundness."[8] It is proper to inquire as to the person's state of mind, both before and after the time concerning which the the particular inquiry is directed.[9] "Upon the question of sanity

---

[1] See People v. McCann, 3 Parker Cr. Cas. 272, 298.
[2] Lord v. Beard, 79 N. C. 5.
[3] Coughlin v. Poulson, 2 McArthur, 308; Baxter v. Abbott, 7 Gray, (Mass.) 71.
[4] Baxter v. Abbott., *supra*.
[5] Fraser v. Jennison, 42 Mich. 206, 228.
[6] People v. Montgomery, 13 Abb. Pr. (N. S.) 207, 250; State v. Windsor, 5 Harr. (Del.) 512.
[7] State v. Windsor, *supra*.
[8] Fraser v. Jennison, 42 Mich. 206, 227.
[9] McAllister v. State, 17 Ala. 434, 436; McLean v. State, 16 Ala. 672; Grant v. Thompson, 4 Conn. 203, 208; Kinne v. Kinne, 9 Conn. 102; Norwood v. Morrow, 4 Dev. & Batt. 442, 451; State v. Felter, 25 Iowa,

at the time of committing an offence," says the Supreme Court of Massachusetts, "the acts, conduct and habits of the prisoner at a subsequent time, may be competent as evidence in his favor. But they are not admissible, as of course. When admissible at all, it is upon the ground, either that they are so connected with, or correspond to evidence of disordered or weakened mental condition preceding the time of the offence, as to strengthen the inference of continuance, and carry it by the time to which the inquiry relates, and thus establish its existence at that time; or else that they are of such a character as of themselves to indicate unsoundness to such a degree, or of so permanent a nature, as to have required a longer period than the interval for its production or development."[1] It is admissible to give in evidence particular acts of madness.[2] But it is not competent to introduce the *doubt* of an expert as to a person's sanity.[3] And a record of the condition and treatment of a patient in a hospital, produced at a trial forty years after its date by the superintendent of the hospital, of which he is the official custodian, and which purports to have been contemporaneously made by the attending physicians, of all cases there treated, and which it was their duty to make, has been held in Massachusetts to be admissible in evidence, as a foundation for the opinion of an expert as to whether it indicated mental disease of the patient, and that without identifying the person who made it.[4] In a case where the sanity of a testatrix was questioned, and positive evidence of her insanity had been given, upon its being proved that she had a paralytic attack shortly before the execution of the will, it was held improper to prove by an expert that, in nine cases out of ten, paralysis did not pro-

67, 75; Lake v. People, 1 Parker Cr. Cas. 495; Freeman v. People, 4 Denio, 9.
[1] Commonwealth v. Pomeroy, 117 Mass. 148. See too, White v. Graves, 107 Mass. 325.
[2] Clark v. Periam, 2 Atk. 337, 340.
[3] Sanchez v. People, 22 N. Y. 147.
[4] Townsend v. Pepperell, 99 Mass. 40.

duce any effect upon the mind.[1] If it could have been shown that it in no case affected the mind, the ruling would, of course, have been different.

§ 61. Opinions of Non-Professional Witnesses as to Mental Condition.—There seems to have been no dispute as to the right of the subscribing witnesses to a will, to testify concerning the actual mental condition of the testator, but their opinions have been received as fully as those of medical experts. The fact that they were present at the time the will was signed, makes them competent to speak upon the subject, whether they "happen to be the attending physicians, nurses, children, or chance strangers."[2] And it does not seem to be necessary that they should state the facts upon which their opinions are predicated.[3] But a marked difference of opinion has existed as to the right of persons, who are neither the subscribing witnesses to the will, nor experts in mental diseases, to express any opinion whatever as to a person's sanity or insanity, soundness or unsoundness of mind. It has been held in a number of cases, that the opinions of such witnesses cannot be received.[4] Such opinions were excluded upon the theory, that special knowledge and skill was required to judge intelligently of the mental condition of another, and that if the

[1] Lands v. Lands, 1 Grant (Penn.), 248.
[2] Hardy v. Merrill, 56 N. H. 227, 243; Poole v. Richardson, 3 Mass. 330; Chase v. Lincoln, 31 Mass. 237; Needham v. Ide, 5 Pick. 510; Potts v. House, 6 Ga. 324; Van Huss v. Rainbolt, 42 Tenn. 139; De Witt v. Barley, 9 N. Y. 371; Williams v. Lee, 47 Md. 321; Boardman v. Woodman, 47 N. H. 120, 134; Grant v. Thompson, 4 Conn. 203; Wogan v. Small, 11 S. & R. (Penn.) 141; Rambler v. Tyron, 7 S. & R. (Penn.) 90, 92; Cilley v. Cilley, 34 Me. 162; Robinson v. Adams, 62 Me. 369; Logan v. McGinnis, 12 Penn. St. 27; Titlow v. Titlow, 54 Penn. St. 216; Gibson v. Gibson, 9 Yerg. (Tenn.) 329.
[3] Williams v. Lee, 47 Md. 321; Van Huss v. Rainbolt, 42 Tenn. 139.
[4] Wyman v. Gould, 47 Me. 159; Hickman v. State, 38 Texas, 191; State v. Archer, 54 N. H. 465; Boardman v. Woodman, 47 N. H. 120; Commonwealth v. Fairbanks, 2 Allen (Mass.), 511; Townsend v. Pepperell, 99 Mass. 40; Hastings v. Rider, 99 Mass. 624, 625; Commonwealth v. Wilson, 1 Gray, 337; State v. Pike, 49 N. H. 399; Van Horn v. Keenan, 28 Ill. 445, 449; De Witt v. Barley, 9 N. Y. 371; State v. Geddis, 42 Iowa, 268.

witnesses gave a detailed account of the acts and conduct of the person whose mental capacity was in question, the jury was as competent to form an opinion thereon, as the witnesses themselves. That the opinions of professional witnesses should be received, as they could judge with some degree of accuracy, from pathological symptoms, but as non-professional witnesses could only form their opinions from the actual demonstrations of the person, those demonstrations should be stated to the jury, and that body left to form their own opinion as to the cause and character of the appearances described. The fact has come, however, to be generally recognized, that it is impossible so to describe the appearance and demonstrations of a person, as to convey any accurate idea of their exact character, and to leave upon the mind of jurors the legitimate impressions which such demonstrations and appearances naturally leave upon the mind of the actual observer. The result has been that many of the earlier cases have been overruled, and the principle has come to be generally recognized that non-professional witnesses may give their opinions as to sanity, as a result of their personal observation of the person whose mental condition is in question, after first stating the facts which they observed.[1]

[1] Thomas v. State, 40 Texas, 65; Whitcomb v. State, 41 Texas, 125; McClackey v. State, 5 Tex. Ct. of App. 320; Webb v. State, 5 Tex. Ct. of App. 596; Hardy v. Merrill, 56 N. H. 227; Dennis v. Weeks, 51 Ga. 24; Choice v. State, 31 Ga. 424, 466; Berry v. State, 10 Ga. 511; People v. Sanford, 43 Cal. 29; Roe v. Taylor, 45 Ill. 486; Beller v. Jones, 22 Ark. 92; Clark v. State, 12 Ohio, 483; State v. Hayden, 51 Vt. 296; Crane v. Crane, 33 Vt. 15; Morse v. Crawford, 17 Vt. 499; Florey's Ex'rs v. Florey, 24 Ala. 247; Puryear v. Reese, 46 Tenn. 21; Gibson v. Gibson, 9 Yerg. (Tenn.) 329; People v. Finley, 38 Mich. 482, 484; Walker v. Walker, 14 Ga. 242; Fielder v. Collier, 13 Ga. 496; Dieken v. Johnson, 7 Ga. 484; Foster v. Brooks, 6 Ga. 290; Crowe Adm'r v. Peters, 63 Mo. 429; Sutherland v. Hawkins, 56 Ind. 343; Rush v. Megee, 36 Ind. 69; Hunt's Heirs v. Hunt, 3 B. Monr. (Ky.) 577; Rambler v. Tyron, 7 S. & R. 90; Wilkinson v. Pearson, 23 Penn. St. 117; McDougald v. McLean, 1 Winston (N. C.) Law, 120; Estate of Brooks, 54 Cal. 471; Williams v. Lee, 47 Md. 321; Dove v. State, 50 Tenn. 348; Waters v. Waters, 35 Md. 531; Pidcock v. Potter, 68 Penn. St. 342; State v. Newlin, 69 Ind. 108; State v. Klinger, 46 Mo. 224; Clary v. Clary, 2 Ired. (N. C.) 78; De Witt

§ 62. This Subject Continued.— This whole subject has been elaborately discussed in a recent case in New Hampshire, in which Mr. Chief Justice FOSTER states that; "A tolerably careful investigation authorizes me to repeat the language of Judge DOE, that 'in England no express decision of the point (the admissibility of such evidence) can be found, for the reason that such evidence has always been admitted without objection. It has been universally regarded as so clearly competent, that it seems no English lawyer has ever presented to any court any objection, question, or doubt in regard to it.'"[1]

It must be conceded, we think, that the interests of justice require that such testimony should be received. The inquiry does not seem to be one necessarily involving scientific evidence, as being one beyond the domain of common sense. And it is quite possible for non-professional witnesses to observe innumerable acts, motions and expressions, which it is impossible to communicate so as to convey any fair conception of their importance, and which are nevertheless sufficient to conclusively satisfy the observer as to a person's mental condition. While such opinions are admissible, yet no general rule can be laid down as to what shall be deemed a sufficient opportunity of observation in the witness, other than it has enabled him to form a belief or judgment thereon.[2] And in a recent case in the Court of Appeals of Texas, the idea is repudiated that it is within the province of the court to determine, upon the acquaintance and the sufficiency of the means of information, as to the facts stated upon which the conclusion of the witness is

v. Barley, 17 N. Y. 340; Beaublen v. Cicotte, 13 Mich. 459; Kelly's Heirs v. McGuire, 15 Ark. 555, 601; Stewart v. Redditt, 3 Md. 67; Dorsey v. Warfield, 7 Md. 65; Brooke v. Townshend, 7 Gill (Md.), 24; Burnham v. Mitchell, 34 Wis. 111; Kilgore v. Cross, 1 Fed. Rep. 582; People v. Wreden (Sup. Ct. of Cal.), 12 Reporter, 682; Pinney's Will, 27 Minn. 280.

[1] State v Pike, 49 N. H. 408, 409: Hardy v. Merrill, 56 N. H. 227, 240. See, too, Lord Denman's charge in Regina v. Oxford, 9 C. & P. 525; and Carew v. Johnston, 2 Sch. & Lef. 280, 285; Regina v. Nerville, Crawf. & Dix Ab. Not. Cas. 96.

[2] Choice v. State, 31 Ga. 424, 467.

based, and to determine upon the admissibility of the evidence, and to admit or exclude it, according as the facts should appear, as developed on the examination of the witness. It was said that " whether the means of information, or facts proved, or the conclusions drawn by the witness are of the satisfactory character required to base a finding upon, or not, is for the consideration of the jury, under proper instructions."[1] While the rule that non-professional witnesses shall not be permitted to give an opinion upon the question, seems to be still maintained in Massachusetts, yet such witnesses have been permitted to testify in that State, being acquainted with the person in question, whether they noticed any change in his intelligence, or any want of coherence in his remarks. Such inquiries, as it was said, did not call for the expression of an opinion upon the question whether the testator was of sound or unsound mind, and were therefore admissible.[2] So it has been held in the same State that one, who had been for many years the guardian of the testator, could be asked whether he ever observed any fact which led him to infer that there was any derangement of intellect.[3] In a case in Ohio the Supreme Court of that State ruled that the witness should be asked what opinion he entertained at the time of trial, and not as to the opinion which he may have entertained at the time of the acts referred to by him, inasmuch as subsequent reflection and consideration might have satisfied him that the opinion formed at the time of observation was erroneous.[4] And in Vermont the court held that, the fact that the witness did not form his opinion at the time he saw and observed the facts testified to by him, did not render his opinion on that account inadmissible.[5] The rule in New York has been laid down by the courts with great care and precision. Non-professional witnesses who have testified to facts tend-

---

[1] McClackey v. State, 5 Tex. Ct. of App. 331.
[2] Barker v. Comins, 110 Mass. 477.
[3] May v. Bradlee, 127 Mass. 414.
[4] Runyan v. Price, 15 Ohio St. 14.
[5] Hathaway's Admr. v. National Life Ins. Co., 48 Vt. 335.

ing to show mental unsoundness, are not permitted in the courts of that State to state what they thought of the person's condition of mind, or their impressions as to his state of mind.[1] But they are allowed to characterize as rational or irrational the acts and declarations to which they have testified, and to state the impression produced upon their minds by what they beheld or heard, their examination being limited to their conclusions from the specific facts they disclose, and so confined as to exclude any opinion on the general question of soundness or unsoundness of mind.[2]

§ 63. **Rape, Abortion, Pregnancy, etc.**— On the trial of an indictment for the rape of a child, the opinion of a physician that there had been actual penetration, is held admissible.[3] And upon such trials medical experts may be examined as to the health and physical condition of the prosecutrix at the time of the alleged offence, as bearing upon her ability to resist the defendant.[4] But it has been held incompetent to ask such witnesses the following questions: "From what you know of her health and strength, in your opinion could the defendant have had carnal connection with her against her will, without resort to other means than the exercise of his ordinary physical powers?" And whether, in the opinion of the witness, "a rape could be committed on a female who had borne children, and was in ordinary health and strength, without resort to other means than the exercise of ordinary physical powers."[5] It has been held proper for an expert to state what effect a rape would have on the sexual organs of the female, and that upon an examination of the prosecutrix several days after

[1] Real v. People, 42 N. Y. 282; Sisson v. Conger, 1 N. Y. Sup. Ct. 569.
[2] Hewlett v. Wood, 55 N. Y. 635; O'Brien v. People, 36 N. Y. 276; Clapp v. Fullerton, 34 N. Y. 190; Howell v. Taylor, 18 N. Y. Sup. Ct. 214; Higbee v. Guardian Mutual Life Ins. Co., 53 N. Y. 603; People v. Lake, 12 N. Y. 358.
[3] State v. Smith, Phillips (N. C.) Law, 302.
[4] State v. Knapp, 45 N. H. 148.
[5] Woodin v. People, 1 Parker Cr. Cas. 464. And see Cook v. State, 24 N. J. L. 843.

an alleged rape, he found her sexual organs inflamed.[1] But the witness cannot usurp the province of the jury, said the court in the case cited, by expressing the opinion that such inflammation "was produced by having a violent connection." The opinions of medical experts are received upon the question of whether an abortion has been performed,[2] and that certain medicines are known as abortives, and that it would be a dangerous thing to give certain drugs, in almost any dose, to a pregnant woman, and as to how large a dose would be required to produce an abortion.[3] It has been held that the parts of the person upon whom instruments were alleged to have been used for the purpose of procuring an abortion, and which had been preserved in alcohol, could be submitted to the jury in connection with the testimony of the physician who made the *post-mortem* examination.[4] And medical experts have been held competent to testify that certain surgical instruments found in the house of the defendant, indicted for an abortion, were adapted to produce an abortion.[5] Physicians are permitted to express an opinion upon the question of pregnancy.[6] A medical witness has been allowed to testify that pregnancy was just as likely to take place in case of rape as in the case of a voluntary sexual connection.[7] But a witness who has had no peculiar experience and possesses no peculiar skill, is not competent to express an opinion as to pregnancy.[8]

In a prosecution for seduction the opinion of medical experts has been held admissible, who testified to the effect that it was highly improbable, if not impossible for intercourse to have occurred under the circumstances described by the complainant (*i. e.*, in a buggy); and also as to the pain and suffering the complainant would have expe-

[1] Noonan v. State, 14 The Reporter, 320. (Sup. Ct. of Wis., May, 1882.)
[2] State v. Smith, 32 Me. 370; State v. Wood, 53 N. H. 484, 495.
[3] Regina v. Still, 30 Upper Canada (C. P.), 30.
[4] Commonwealth v. Brown, 14 Gray, 419.
[5] Commonwealth v. Brown, 121 Mass. 69.
[6] State v. Wood, 53 N. H. 484, 495.
[7] State v. Knapp, 45 N. H. 148, 152.
[8] Boies v. McAlister, 12 Me. 308.

rienced had such an act taken place.[1] And it has been held that a woman who had experience as a nurse in childbirth, and as such had been in attendance at premature births, might express an opinion as an expert as to whether the birth of a child was premature.[2] "The witness, by her experience and observation," said the court, "appears to have acquired knowledge of the subjects about which she was testifying, that persons generally do not have. To the extent of this peculiar knowledge, she was a person of skill and science, and her opinion, founded upon it, was evidence to go to the jury."

§ 64. **Opinions in Miscellaneous Cases.**—A medical expert has been permitted to express an opinion as to the permanency of a person's loss of vision.[3] It has been held proper to ask a physician who made a *post-mortem* examination as to the condition of the body of the deceased as to fulness or paucity of blood.[4] Upon the question of whether it be good medical practice to withhold from a patient in a particular emergency, or under given or supposed circumstances, a knowledge of the danger and extent of his disease, medical practitioners are allowed to give testimony.[5] Experts have been allowed to testify as to the condition of human remains after burial; as to how long before decay would set in, and when it would be complete.[6] Medical witnesses have testified that a certain routine of diet was injurious to the health of children.[7] A physician has been permitted to state his opinion as to the manner in which *prolapsus uteri* would be caused, and the degree of violence that would produce it.[8] It has been held that a physician who made the *post-mortem* examination, could be asked whether the appearance of the extravasated blood in

[1] People v. Clark, 33 Mich. 112.
[2] Mason v. Fuller, 45 Vt. 29.
[3] Tinney v. New Jersey Steamboat Co., 12 Abb. Pr. (N. S.) 1.
[4] O'Mara v. Commonwealth, 75 Penn. St. 424.
[5] Twombly v. Leach, 11 Cush. 405.
[6] State v. Secrest, 80 N. C. 450, 453.
[7] Crowley v. People, 83 N. Y. 464, 471.
[8] Napier v. Ferguson, 2 P. & B. (New Brunswick) 415.

the neck was an indication of mechanical violence or disease, and whether the clot of blood found could have existed twelve hours without causing death.[1] Whether a child was a "full time child," may be shown by any physician of ordinary experience who attended at the birth.[2] Where a body was found in the water, it has been held proper to ask a medical expert, who made the *post-mortem* examination, as to what indications would have been found if the person had been suffocated first, and then had fallen into the water.[3] A physician may be asked as to the curability of a disease, the nature and cause of which he has described.[4] So a surgeon may be asked whether a certain wound given on the chest endangered life.[5] So expert testimony is admissible as to the injuries likely to be produced under a given state of facts, the precise facts being stated, on which he is to base his opinion.[6] A physician being skilled in anatomy, may testify as to the sex of a person from an examination of the skeleton, but it is an error to receive the opinion of a non-professional witness on such a question.[7]

§ 65. **Opinions of Medical Experts in Malpractice Cases.**—In actions of malpractice brought against physicians or surgeons, for the improper treatment of a patient, the opinions of medical experts, who have heard the testimony as to the manner in which the case was treated, are received in evidence upon the question whether such treatment was proper or not.[8] But their opinions will not be received as to the general skill of the physician or surgeon on trial,[9]

---

[1] State v. Pike, 65 Me. 111, 114.
[2] Young v. Makepeace, 103 Mass. 50.
[3] Erickson v. Smith, 2 Abb. App. Decis. (N. Y.) 64.
[4] Matteson v. New York etc. R. R. Co., 35 N. Y. 487.
[5] Rumsey v. People, 19 N. Y. 41.
[6] Wendell v. Troy, 39 Barb. (N. Y.) 329.
[7] Wilson v. State, 41 Tex. 320, 321.
[8] Wright v. Hardy, 22 Wis. 348; Hoener v. Koch, 84 Ill. 408; Mertz v. Detweiler, 8 W. & S. (Penn.) 376; Heath v. Glisan, 3 Oregon, 67; Roberts v. Johnson, 58 N. Y. 613, 615.
[9] Boydston v. Giltner, 3 Oregon, 118; Williams v. Poppleton, 3 Oregon

although it has been said that they may state facts within their knowledge as to such person's skill.[1] Neither can the general reputation of the medical institution at which the defendant attended lectures, be introduced in evidence in such cases.[2] And it is no error to exclude an inquiry of a physician as to what the defendant had told him about the symptoms in cases the defendant had been treating, and the course of treatment he had been pursuing, and the opinion of the witness from these statements of the defendant, and the symptoms he himself saw in the cases, as to the propriety of the course the defendant said he had been pursuing, as showing his skill.[3] But medical experts may be asked as to the nature and properties of the medicines employed by the defendant in the particular instance in question ;[4] and also as to the practice of physicians in regard to consultations.[5] It is also competent to ask whether the treatment in the particular case was in conformity with the rules and practice of the medical profession.[6] And a physician who attended a patient who had been under the care of another physician, can testify as to what, so far as he could judge, had been the first physician's treatment ; in what respects it differed from his own ; what effect, so far as he could judge, it had upon the plaintiff, and whether or not he saw any evidence that the plaintiff had been injured by his treatment.[7] A medical expert may be asked whether, in his opinion, the death of the patient was or was not the result of any neglect or want of skill in the attending physician.[8] Where the action was brought for a personal injury to the patient's

---

139; Leighton v. Sargent, 11 Foster (N. H.), 120; Mertz v. Detweiler, 8 W. & S. 376.

[1] Williams v. Poppleton, 3 Oregon, 139. And see Boydston v. Giltner, 3 Oregon, 118.
[2] Leighton v. Sargent, 11 Foster (N. H.), 120.
[3] Leighton v. Sargent, *supra.*
[4] Mertz v. Detweiler, 8 W. & S. 376.
[5] Mertz v. Detweiler, *supra.*
[6] Twombly v. Leach, 11 Cush. (Mass.) 405.
[7] Barber v. Merriam, 11 Allen, 322.
[8] Wright v. Hardy, 22 Wis. 348.

limb, caused by the negligence of the surgeon, it was held proper to ask a medical expert as to the permanent effects of the injury, and whether the patient would ever recover the use of his limb.[1] But an expert cannot express an opinion as to whether, from all the evidence in the case, the defendant was guilty of malpractice or not.[2] That is the very question which the jury is to try and determine for themselves.[3] In an action for damages for injury to the eyes, producing blindness, for negligent and unskillful treatment, it was held that the following question might be properly asked of an expert: " Within your experience, have you ever known a case where contagion of this kind was communicated, of gonorrheal opthalmia, by the use of the brush?" The question was proper as showing the improbability of such an occurrence.[4]

§ 66. **Right to Order an Examination of the Person by Medical Experts in Cases of Alleged Impotency.** — Wherever impotency has been acknowledged as an impediment to marriage, the courts have compelled the parties, in proceedings to obtain a decree of nullity, to submit their persons to an examination by experts, whenever such an examination was necessary for the purpose of determining the fact of impotency. This arises from the necessity of the case, especially in the case of females, for impotency on the part of the female, which cannot be cured by proper medical treatment or a surgical operation, is said to be very rare. And divorce for the impotency of the female is limited to cases of an impervious or supposed impervious vagina, from an original malformation, or the effect of some supervening infirmity or disease, as mere sterility is not sufficient ground for a decree of nullity. "From the very nature of the case, it appears to be impossible to ascertain the fact of incurable impotency, especially where

---

[1] Wilt v. Vickers, 8 Watts (Penn.), 227; See too, Roberts v. Johnson, 58 N. Y. 613, 615.
[2] Hoener v. Koch, 84 Ill. 408.
[3] See § 24, chap. III.
[4] Doyle v. New York Eye and Ear Infirmary, 80 N. Y. 631.

the husband is the complaining party, except by a proper surgical examination by skillful and competent surgeons in connection with other testimony. * * * And I have no doubt as to the power of this court to compel the parties, in such a suit, to submit to a surgical examination, whenever it is necessary to ascertain facts which are essential to the proper decision of the cause."[1] As it is essential that the impotency should be incurable,[2] it is necessary that the fact of incurability should be made out by the evidence of experts who have made a personal examination. The right of the court to order such an examination, and the necessity for making such order, can no longer be considered as involved in any doubt whatever.[3] And when the wife is the plaintiff, and the libel states her to have been a spinster at the time of the marriage, it is usual to order an inspection of her person, as well as that of the husband, because her virginity and capacity implies his impotency.[4]

§ 67. **Who should be Appointed to make the Examination.**—According to the English practice the inspection was intrusted to three medical experts, either two physicians and a surgeon, or two surgeons and a physician, the adverse party having the privilege of naming one or more.[5] But in *Welde* v. *Welde*,[6] decided in 1830, the inspection of the wife was made by midwives, while that of the husband was by physicians. In this country we find Chancellor WALWORTH declaring that the examination should be made by "physicians of intelligence or skill, who by study or practice have made themselves well acquainted with the nature and progress of the disease which has caused the defendant's incapacity."[7] And in this same case the Chancellor said:

---

[1] Devenbagh v. Devenbagh, 5 Paige, 554.
[2] Brown v. Brown, 1 Haggard, 523.
[3] Briggs v. Morgan, 3 Phillimore, 325; Welde v. Welde, 2 Lee, 580; H——— v. P——— (L. R.), 3 Prob. & Div. 126; G——— v. G——— (L. R.), 2 Prob. &. Div. 287; Newell v. Newell, 9 Paige, 26.
[4] Coote's Ecc. Pr. 307. And see Norton v. Seton, 3 Phillimore, 147.
[5] Coote's Ecc. Prac. 388. And see Dean v. Aveling, 1 Robertson, 279.
[6] 2 Lee, 580.
[7] Newell v. Newell, 9 Paige, 26.

"The defendant must therefore submit to such an examination by one or more respectable gentlemen of the medical profession, who may be named for that purpose by the husband, with the sanction of the court. * * * Such medical attendants as she may think proper to call in are also to be present at the time of her examination by the complainant's professional witnesses." In another case it is said that in the selection of the experts due regard will be paid to the feelings and wishes of the defendant.[1] Proper respect for the feelings of the party to be examined, requires that the number of the experts appointed to make the examination should be restricted to the smallest number consistent with the interests of justice.

§ 68. **When Compulsory Examination in such Cases will not be Ordered.**— Where the party against whom impotency is alleged, has already submitted to an examination of competent physicians, whose testimony can be readily obtained, it is said that a further examination will not be insisted on.[2] But where the wife claimed that her incapacity existed now, but not at the time of the marriage, and to prove her claim produced the certificate of two medical gentlemen who had examined her recently, expressing their belief that the incapacity had arisen since the marriage, Chancellor WALWORTH, upon the application of the husband, ordered another examination, declaring that under the peculiar circumstances of the case, the complainant ought not to be compelled to leave the decision of his cause to rest solely upon the *ex parte* examination made by the physicians selected by the wife.[3]

§ 69. **Summoning Experts to assist in Determining the Proper Interrogatories.**—The usual practice in such cases has been to direct a reference to a master, to take the testimony and report thereon. And when the parties do not agree as to the interrogatories to be propounded on the ex-

---

[1] Devenbagh v. Devenbagh, 5 Paige, 554, 558.
[2] Brown v. Brown, 1 Haggard, 523, note *a*; Devenbagh v. Devenbagh, 554, 558.
[3] Newell v. Newell, 9 Paige, 26.

amination, they must be settled by the master, who may summon physicians or surgeons to assist him in determining the necessary interrogatories. It is necessary that the defendant, in connection with the examination by the experts, should answer all needful inquiries propounded by them, and the answers should be given under oath. This subject was considered by Chancellor WALWORTH at an early day in New York. "The interrogatories to be propounded to her (the defendant)," he says, "must be such only as relate to this alleged incapacity, and the commencement and progress of the disease by which it has probably been produced. And if the parties cannot agree upon the proper interrogatories, after having consulted with their physicians on the subject, the master in settling the interrogatories to be propounded to the defendant in connection with her examination by medical gentlemen, is to be at liberty to summon before him, and examine on oath, any physicians or surgeons, to enable him to decide what interrogatories may be necessary or proper to be allowed."[1]

§ 70. **The Subject of Inquiry—Structural Defect—Impracticability of Consummation.**—The inquiry of the experts is to be directed not merely to the discovery of whether a structural defect exists. It is possible that although no structural defect exists, the case may show the impracticability of consummation. In a recent case in England,[2] a divorce was obtained, where the professional witnesses swore that no structural defect existed, but there was an impracticability of consummation. As this is important, we quote the language of the court: "The impossibility must be practical. It cannot be necessary to show that the woman is so formed that connection is physically impossible, if it can be shown that it is possible only under conditions to which the husband would not be justified in resorting. The absence of a physical structural defect cannot be sufficient to render a marriage valid, if it be shown that connection is practically impossible, or even if it be

[1] Newell v. Newell, 9 Paige, 26, 27.
[2] G—— v. G——, 2 Prob. & Div. (L. R.) 287.

shown that it is only practicable after a remedy has been applied, which the husband cannot enforce, and which the wife, whether wilfully or acting under the influence of hysteria, will not submit to."[1] But a merely wilful and wrongful refusal of marital intercourse will never justify a decree of nullity by reason of impotence, although if persisted in long enough, the court may infer that it arises from incapacity.[2]

§ 71. **The Testimony of the Experts in such Cases to be Received with Caution.**—After the experts have made their examination and given their testimony, it is to be received and weighed with great caution, and Sir John Nichol goes so far as to declare, that he is " not aware that it has ever been held sufficient alone,"[3] to justify a decree of nullity.

§ 72. **Defraying the Expenses of the Examination by the Experts.**—The husband must, of course, furnish all the necessary funds to pay the expenses of the surgical examination.[4] If the wife refuses to submit herself to the examination ordered by the court, the allowance of her alimony may be suspended until she consents to the examination as directed.[5] And either party refusing to submit to such an examination, might undoubtedly be punished for contempt of court.[6] But as a refusal to submit to the examination has been regarded as evidence of incapacity,[7] a party will perhaps ordinarily hesitate before refusing compliance with the order of the court in such cases.

---

[1] See also P—— v. L——, 3 Prob. Division (L. R.), 73, note 2; H—— v. P——, 3 Prob. & Div. (L. R.) 126.
[2] S—— v. A——, 3 Probate Division (L. R.), 72.
[3] Norton v. Seton, 3 Phillimore, 147.
[4] Devenbagh v. Devenbagh, 5 Paige, 554, 558.
[5] Newell v. Newell, 9 Paige, 26.
[6] See Schroeder v. The C., R. I. etc. R. Co., 47 Iowa, 375.
[7] Harrison v. Harrison, 4 Moore, P. C. 96, 103, Lord Brougham's opinion. See too, H—— v. P——, 3 Prob. & Div. (L. R.) 126. The court should be satisfied, however, that there was no collusion between the parties. Pollard v. Wybourn, 1 Hagg. Ecc. R. 725; Sparrow v. Harrison, 3 Curteis, 16.

§ 73. Compulsory Examination in Criminal Cases.—. Whether the court has power to order a compulsory examination by experts of the person of a defendant in a criminal proceeding, is an important question which has been somewhat considered by the courts. The question turns on the construction to be placed on the constitutional provisions which provide that the accused shall not be compelled to give evidence against himself in any criminal case. Such a provision is found in the Constitution of the United States, and in the Constitutions of the several States, with hardly an exception. In *Jacob's Case*[1] the Supreme Court of North Carolina, in 1858, held that a defendant could not be compelled to exhibit himself to the inspection of a jury for the purpose of enabling them to determine his status as a free negro. And this ruling was approved by the same court in *Johnson's Case*[2] in 1872. Two years later the subject again came up in the same court in *Garrett's Case*.[3] In that case it appeared that the defendant had stated to persons present on the night of the homicide, that the deceased came to her death by her clothes accidentally catching fire while the deceased was asleep, and that she, the defendant, in attempting to put out the flames burnt one of her hands. At the coroner's inquest the defendant was compelled to unwrap the hand which she had stated was burnt, and exhibit it to a physician, in order that he might see whether there was any indication of burn upon it. And it was held that the actual condition of her hand, although she was ordered by the coroner to exhibit it to the doctor, was admissible evidence. *Jacob's Case* was distinguished as follows: " The distinction between that and our case is that in *Jacob's Case*, the prisoner himself, on trial, was compelled to exhibit himself to the jury, that they might see that he was within the prohibited degree of color; thus he was forced to become a witness against himself. This was held to be error. In our case, not the prisoner, but the witnesses, were called to

[1] 5 Jones, 259.
[2] 67 N. C. 58.
[3] 71 N. C. 58.

prove what they saw upon inspecting the prisoner's hand, although that inspection was obtained by intimidation." In Nevada it has been held that the court could lawfully compel a criminal defendant, against his objection, to exhibit his bare arm, for the purpose of determining whether it had on it certain tatoo marks. The question of identity was raised, and a witness had testified that he knew the defendant, and knew that he had tatoo marks (describing them) on his right forearm.[1] This is one of the best considered cases on this side of the question. The court declared that the Constitution prohibited the State from compelling a defendant to be a witness against himself, because it was believed that he might, by the flattery of hope or suspicion of fear, be induced to tell a falsehood, and that this reason was inapplicable to an examination of the person, which could not in the very nature of things lead to a falsehood. "The Constitution means," said the court, "just what a fair and reasonable interpretation of its language imports. No person shall be compelled to be a witness, that is to testify, against himself. To use the common phrase, ' it closes the mouth' of the prisoner. A defendant in a criminal case cannot be compelled to give evidence under oath or affirmation, or make any statement for the purpose of proving or disproving any question at issue before any tribunal, court, judge, or magistrate."

§ 74. **Compulsory Examination in Criminal Cases—The Subject Continued.**— The same question was similarly decided in the Court of Appeals of Texas, in 1879, although the question was presented in a different form. In that case testimony was held admissible that the footprints, which the prisoner was compelled to make in an ash heap, corresponded with those made on the night of the murder about the premises of the deceased.[2] And a similar ruling on a similar state of facts was made in North Carolina.[3] But a different conclusion has been reached in

---

[1] State v. Ah Chuey, 14 Nev. 79; s. c., 1 Crim. Law Mag. 634.
[2] Walker v. State, 7 Tex. Ct. of App. 245, 265.
[3] State v. Graham, 74 N. C. 646; s. c., 21 Am. Rep. 493.

Georgia,[1] and in Tennessee[2] on a like state of facts.

But in New York the subject was presented in a case which involved the question whether the prisoner had been delivered of a child. The coroner directed two physicians to go to the jail and make an examination of the woman, and determine whether she had recently been delivered of a child or not. She denied having been pregnant, and objected to being examined by the physicians. But on being told that if she did not submit to the examination, she would be compelled to submit by force, she yielded, and her private parts were examined by the physicians with a speculum, and they examined her breasts. The court refused to allow the physicians to testify, declaring that such an examination was a violation of the spirit and meaning of the Constitution, which declares that "no person shall be compelled in any criminal case to be a witness against himself." "They might as well have sworn the prisoner, and compelled her by threats, to testify that she had been pregnant and been delivered of the child, as to have compelled her, by threats, to allow them to look into her person, with the aid of a speculum, to ascertain whether she had been pregnant and had been recently delivered of a child."[3] It will be observed that in some of the cases in which the question has been considered, the right to order an examination of the person by experts was not directly involved, but they all involve the same principle, and it has been necessary to consider them all in this connection. The result of the examination of the cases shows a decided conflict of authorities, and that the question is still unsettled and open.

§ 75. **Compulsory Examination in Actions for Damages.**—It has been held, too, that in an action for damages for personal injuries, the plaintiff may be required by the court, upon an application of the defendant, to submit his person to an examination by physicians and sur-

---
[1] Day v. State, 63 Ga. 667; Blackwell v. State, 13 Reporter, 271; *s. c.*, 3 Crim. Law Mag. 394.
[2] Stokes v. State, 5 Baxt. 519; *s. c.*, 30 Am. Rep. 72.
[3] People v. McCoy, 45 How. Pr. 216.

geons for the purpose of ascertaining the character and extent of his injuries.[1] The court in this case declared that refusal to submit to an examination so ordered, would render the party liable to punishment for contempt of court, and if continued so long as to effectively obstruct the progress of the case, all allegations as to personal injury might be stricken from the pleadings. And it is declared that, "under the explicit directions of the court, the physicians should have been restrained from imperiling, in any degree, the life or health of the plaintiff. The use of anæsthetics, opiates or drugs of any kind, should have been forbidden, if indeed it had been proposed, and it should have prescribed that he should be subjected to no tests painful in their character." The above case was decided in 1877, and the conclusion reached was arrived at irrespective of authority, the court declaring that it was unable to find any case in which the question had been considered. But the same question had been considered in New York in 1868, and it was there held that the court, in an action for malpractice against a surgeon, could compel the plaintiff to submit her person to an examination at the hands of the defendant's experts.[2] "It is not proper," said the court, "that the cause should be left to be deter-

[1] Schroder v. The R. I. & P. R. R. Co., 47 Iowa, 375.
[2] Walsh v. Sayre, 52 How. Pr. 334. The complaint alleged that the defendant, in treating the plaintiff for an injury in the neighborhood of her hips, had so negligently and unskillfully, as to puncture the joint, causing the synovial fluid which lubricates the cartilaginous surface of the joint to escape, thereby seriously and permanently injuring the hip, and rendering the whole leg useless, and perhaps rendering its amputation necessary. The defendant petitioned the court, stating that since the commencement of the action, he had endeavored to obtain leave to make a professional examination of the affected part, but had been refused permission so to do. That he could not safely proceed to trial, nor properly defend the action, unless he could have a personal inspection and professional examination of the affected parts, and praying that said examination and personal inspection by himself and such other skillful and eminent surgeons as he might name, might be had under the direction of the sheriff, or a referee appointed for that purpose, at such time and place, and in such form or manner, as to the court might seem just and proper.

mined on the evidence of two or three surgeons, selected by the plaintiff out of the whole body of surgeons, perhaps because their views are adverse to the defendant's ; but it is eminently proper that defendant should have the benefit of the testimony of one or two surgeons of his own selection, and that these surgeons should have the requisite means of forming a correct judgment, one of which is the examination of the affected part."

The question, too, was considered in Missouri in 1873, in an action against a railroad company for personal injuries. The point raised was, however, very summarily disposed of in the opinion, and the right to order the examination denied. The court merely said: " The proposal to the court to call in two surgeons, and have the plaintiff examined during the progress of the trial, as to the extent of her injuries, is unknown to our practice and to the law. There was abundant evidence on this subject on both sides ; any opinion of physicians or surgeons at that time would have only been cumulative evidence at best, and the court had no power to enforce such an order."[1]

§ 76. **Detection of Poisons by Chemists.**—It is said that there is no poison accessible to the public, which cannot be detected by modern methods of research, and oftentimes months and years after it has slain its victims. " There is probably no limit to the time when the metallic poisons might not be discovered after the demise of the victim."[2] Experts are, therefore, allowed to testify, after having made a chemical analysis of the contents of the stomach, as to the presence of poison in the internal organs of the body.[3] And a person who is a chemist and toxicologist, may testify as an expert concerning the effect of a certain poison upon the human system, and it is not necessary that he should be a physician or surgeon.[4] A physician is also competent to

---

[1] Loyd v. Hannibal etc. R. R. Co., 53 Mo. 509, 515, 516.
[2] Crim. Law Mag. 294. Article by R. Ogden Doremus, M. D., LL. D., Prof. Chemistry and Toxicology in Bellevue Hosp. Med. Coll.
[3] State v. Bowman, 78 N. C. 509, 510.
[4] State v. Cook, 17 Kans. 394.

testify upon the same subject,[1] and may be asked to describe the symptoms which appear upon the administration of any particular poison.[2] They may express an opinion that death was caused by the administration of poison.[3] In the case last cited, a physician, after describing the symptoms, gave his opinion that the deceased died from the effects of arsenic, and in answer to an inquiry put to him, declared that he would not have formed such an opinion had he not been informed that there was arsenic in the house, but learning that fact, he reached his conclusion from observation of the symptoms of the case. Counsel sought to exclude the opinion upon the ground that it was not a medical opinion, but the objection was not sustained.

§ 77. **Chemical Analysis of Poison not Necessary When.**—It is held that it is not always essential that there should be a chemical analysis of a mixture, in order to qualify an expert to express an opinion as to its ingredients, and to its being a poison.[4] In the case cited; which was the trial of a prisoner indicted for administering a poisonous drug, a bottle was produced and shown to a medical expert, which contained the mixture administered by the defendant; he stated that he had made no chemical analysis of its contents, but thought he could tell its ingredients from its smell, taste and appearance. ‘He was allowed to give an opinion as to what the mixture was composed of, its effect upon a woman in pregnancy when taken, and the danger to life.

§ 78. **Chemical Analysis of Contents of Stomach.**—It has been held, however, that in a case of poisoning, chemical tests and an analysis of the contents of the stomach and bowels are essential to the ascertainment of the truth, and should be resorted to in all cases where there is no direct proof of the act. Symptoms of themselves, without other

[1] State v. Terrill, 12 Rich. 321.
[2] People v. Robinson, 2 Parker Cr. Cas. 236; Polk v. State, 36 Ark. 117, 124.
[3] Mitchell v. State, 58 Ala. 418.
[4] State v. Slagh, 83 N. C. 630.

circumstances, are pronounced unreliable, and said to be inconclusive evidence of guilt.[1] But in all cases where the opinions of experts are to be received as to the chemical contents of the stomach and bowels, it is necessary that there should be preliminary proof of the identity of the stomach and its contents and that the same have not been improperly tampered with. Such proof should be first submitted, and passed upon by the court, before the opinions of the experts should be received.[2] In the case last cited it is declared that the evidence should show that the stomach taken from the deceased was the identical stomach whose contents were analyzed, and that no foreign substance could have been introduced into the stomach, or into its contents, subsequent to the death of the deceased and prior to the chemical analysis. The court proceeded to say: "It was not necessary that the stomach should have been kept continuously under lock and key from the time it was taken from the body of the deceased until the final analysis, or that it should have been kept continuously sealed up. * * * And it was not necessary that all possibility of its being tampered with should have been excluded." After it is made to appear that no mistake has been made as to the identity of the stomach and its contents, the opinions of practicing physicians, who are not professional chemists, are received as to the analysis of the stomach, and the tests usually applied for detecting poison in such cases. Although it is said that the opinions of those who are not practical chemists, are entitled to less weight than those given by that class of experts whose conclusions are based upon experience as well as books.[3]

§ 79. **Order of Research in Analysis for Poisons.**— In the analysis of a poison case it is essential that the toxicologist should have followed a scientific order of research, as

---

[1] Joe v. State, 6 Fla. 591.
[2] State v. Cook, 17 Kan. 394.
[3] State v. Hinkle, 6 Iowa, 380. In this case the opinions of two practicing physicians were received. One of them stated that he was not a professional chemist, but understood some of the practical details of

otherwise it is quite possible for him to fail to discover the presence of the poison. It is important for counsel in the examination of such witnesses to bear this fact in mind, and we, therefore, append this order of research. The examination should be:

1. For the volatile poisons, such as hydrocyanic acid, chloroform, ether, etc. These poisons being most liable to escape detection, as they may be lost by evaporation.

2. For the vegetable poisons, such as strychnine, morphia, belladona, etc., as the tests employed for the detection of mineral poisons are often destructive of the vegetable poisons.

3. For the various acids, alkalies, metallic poisons, etc.[1]

§ 80. **Chemical and Microscopic Examination of Blood.** —Persons accustomed to make chemical and microscopic examination of blood and blood stains, are, of course, allowed to testify whether human blood can be distinguished from animal blood, and, if so, whether a particular blood stain was made by human or animal blood.[2] Such evidence has been received in numerous cases, and without any objection. It has been admitted lately in two especially notable cases, those of Rubenstein in New York, and of Hayden in Connecticut. The controversy is not over the admissibility of such testimony, but has been as to the possibility of distinguishing human from animal blood. The possibility of so doing is asserted on the one hand,[3] and

chemistry—that portion at least which belonged to his profession; that he had no practical experience in the analysis of poisons, until he analyzed the contents of the stomach of the deceased; that he was previously acquainted with the means of detecting poisons, and had since had some experience in that way. The other declared that he was not a practical chemist, but understood the chemical tests by which the presence of poison could be detected: that he had never experimented with the view of detecting strychnine by chemical tests, but that he had seen experiments by professors of chemistry, and that there was one test much relied on, the trial of which he had witnessed.

[1] See 1 Crim. Law Mag. 309.
[2] See Commonwealth v. Sturtivant, 117 Mass. 122, 124; State v. Knight, 43 Me. 1, 133.
[3] See 19 Am. Law Reg. (N. S.) 529, where the subject is discussed with learning and ability.

denied on the other.[1] While it is not within our province to enter upon this discussion, we may be permitted to cite below, the opinion of a distinguished expert, in the latest discussion of this important question.[2] An expert may illustrate his testimony touching the properties of human blood, as ascertained by chemical tests and microscopic observation, by the use and exhibition to the jury of a diagram. "It would be very difficult for an expert of the most accurate and extensive observation, to exhibit in language with precision, so as to be understood, those delicate appearances which are appreciable only by the sense of vision. Nothing short of an exact representation to the sight can give with certainty, a perfectly correct idea to the mind. * * A diagram approximating in any degree to perfect representation, when exhibited by one qualified from knowledge and experience to give explanations, may do much to make clear his testimony without danger of misleading."[3] In a criminal trial it is, of course, proper that

[1] See 10 Cent. Law Journal, 183.

[2] "The whole question may be, I think, summed up as follows:

1. Human and other mammalian blood, the corpuscles of which are circular, can be distinguished by the criterion of form from that of all other red-blooded animals, with the exception of that of the monotremata (ornithorhyncbus and echidna), which, according to Gulliver, have circular corpuscles. The camel family, which belong to the class mammalia, have oval corpuscles, as do all those not belonging to the mammalia, with the exception noted above.

2. Human blood can be distinguished from that of other red-blooded animals having circular corpuscles, in every case of individual comparison, where the average size of the corpuscles is greater than those of the animal with which it is compared, or where the largest corpuscles are larger than the largest of those of the animal with which they are being compared.

3. Human blood may be distinguished in a given case, from that of an animal (the dog for example), in which the averages of the corpuscles, and the size of single corpuscles in individual cases, are equal to, or exceed that of the average human blood.

4. Under the same conditions of actual individual comparison, the blood of two individuals of the same species may be distinguished from each other.

5. Blood may be distinguished from the opposite conditions of disease and health, as between individuals of the same species, or between a human being and a lower animal." 19 Am. Law Register, (N. S.) 605.

[3] State v. Knight, 43 Me. 1.

the prisoner should be allowed to have the articles, which the prosecution allege to be smeared with blood, examined by his own experts. After such articles have been offered in evidence by the government, they are placed in the special custody of the court, to be dealt with as justice requires. Then, if the prisoner desires an examination to be made by his experts, it should be allowed under proper precautions. As Mr. Justice LUDLOW has expressed it, "the court should see to it that they are guarded from intentional or accidental injury, with the most scrupulous care, and they may be examined in open court by any persons selected by the prisoner or his counsel, or if, from necessity, the examination cannot be made accurately in open court, they should be placed in the hands of any respectable chemist or physician to be selected by the prisoner, with the consent of the court. They should be properly identified as the very articles offered in evidence by the Commonwealth, before they are delivered to the person who has been selected by the prisoner's counsel, and for this purpose, that person should receive them in open court, and they should then be examined in the presence of an officer or officers of the court."[1]

§ 81. **Whether Ordinary Witnesses may Testify as to Blood Stains.**—But it has been made a question in several cases, whether ordinary witnesses may testify as to blood stains, it being objected that no one but a chemist is qualified to state whether stains, apparently made by blood, are really blood stains or not. We cannot find that such an objection has been sustained in a single instance. And the rule is, that ordinary witnesses are competent to testify that they observed spots of blood upon the clothing, etc., and no chemical analysis of the substance supposed to be blood is necessary.[2] "The testimony of the chemist who has analysed blood, and that of the observer who has merely recognized it, belong to the same legal grade of evidence;

[1] Commonwealth v. Twitchell, 1 Brewster (Penn.), 562.
[2] Dillard v. State, 58 Miss. 368, 386; People v. Greenfield, 30 N. Y. Sup. Ct. 462; *s. c.* 85 N. Y. 75.

and though the one may be entitled to much greater weight than the other with the jury, the exclusion of either would be illegal. * * Either party in the present case had the right to resort to microscopic or chemical tests, but neither was bound to do it, and neither can complain of the other for the omission. * * The affairs of life are too pressing and manifold to have everything reduced to absolute certainty, even in the administration of justice. * * Microscopes, chemists and men of science are not always at hand; and criminals are neither anxious to court observation, nor careful to preserve the evidences of their guilt." [1]

§ 82. **Blood Stains—Proper Question Concerning.**—It is sometimes very important to determine whether blood stains upon clothing were occasioned by blood flowing upon the outer, or upon the inner surface of the fabric. If caused by blood flowing directly upon the outer surface of the fabric, the coloring matter of the blood, which is suspended in the blood, will, of course, remain on the outer surface, whereas it would be on the inner surface of the garment if it came from within. It is held, therefore, that one who is qualified by chemical observations and experiments, may testify whether a blood spot upon a garment could have been occasioned by blood flowing directly upon the outer surface thereof.[2] And an expert may testify as to the direction from which a blood stain came, as, for instance, that it came from below upwards.[3] But in a case in Mississippi, where it was proposed to ask the experts to give their opinions as to the relative positions of the combatants at the time of the difficulty, as indicated by blood upon the shirt, with a view of showing by the blood marks, that the prisoner was probably prostrate on the ground, and deceased on top of him when the stains on the shirt were received, the question was excluded upon the ground that it did not involve any matter of science or skill, and that the jury must judge for themselves.[4]

[1] People v. Ganzalez, 35 N. Y. 49, 61.
[2] State v. Knight, 43 Me. 1, 133.
[3] Commonwealth v. Sturtivant, 117 Mass. 122.
[4] Dillard v. State, 58 Miss. 368, 387.

§ 83. Other Cases in which the Opinions of Chemists have been received. — A chemist has been permitted to testify as to the safety of camphene lamps.[1] In this case the witness was held competent to express an opinion as to the safety of the lamp, although he had never experimented with lamps, or made or used camphene, or paid any particular attention to camphene lamps, but it appeared that he had studied chemistry with a distinguished chemist, that he was himself an instructor in chemistry, and acquainted with gases, having experimented with them, and also knew how camphene was made. And in an action which involved the question whether a certain fertilizer was merchantable, and reasonably suited to the use intended, the opinion of a chemist, who had made an analysis of the fertilizer, was considered competent evidence, although not conclusive as to the suitableness of the fertilizer for the use intended.[2] So in an action to recover damages for injury to land by working a copper mill producing noxious gases, from which poisonous substances are discharged, the testimony of experts has been received, showing that they had made experiments with gases taken from the land, by means of which they had obtained copper.[3] The testimony of a chemist has been received, that the point of drainage of surrounding lands by a filter basin, on land taken for that purpose, could be determined, and it has been held proper to ask him whether the level had been determined by experiment, at which water stood under soil generally, and that he could state the results of experiments made by him in his laboratory in proving that fact.[4] A chemist might properly be asked as to the probability of spirits evaporating while undergoing transportation in certain casks.[5] The opinions of

---

[1] Bierce v. Stocking, 11 Gray (Mass.), 174.
[2] Wilcox v. Hall, 53 Ga. 635. See too, Gossler v. Eagle Sugar Refinery 103 Mass. 331, that certain sugar contained 3 per cent. of sand.
[3] Lincoln v. Taunton Manuf. Co., 9 Allen (Mass.), 182. See too, Salvin v. North Brancepeth Coal Co., 9 Ch. App. (L. R.) 705.
[4] Williams v. Taunton, 125 Mass. 34.
[5] Turner v. The Black Warrior, 1 McAlister, 181, 184.

chemists are, of course, received as to the constituent parts of a compound.[1] We have elsewhere considered the admissibility of the opinions of chemists as to the nature of inks, and the age of writing, in cases involving the genuineness of handwriting.[2]

§ 84. **Diseases in Animals—Qualifications of Expert.**— In determining who are qualified to testify as experts in reference to disease in animals, it has been laid down as follows: "A liberal rule must be applied in regard to evidence as to diseases in animals, as it is rare that persons are found who make the treatment of diseases in domestic animals a distinct profession, or attain to great skill or science therein. The best skill and science that can be expected, all that can be practically admitted in such cases, will be the evidence of persons who have had much experience, and have been for years made acquainted with such diseases, and with their treatment. They may give their opinions upon such experience, and on statements of fact upon which their opinions are based, as some evidence to be considered and weighed."[3] And to the same effect was the language of Mr. Justice BLACKFORD in a case decided in Indiana in 1837. In that case, a witness, who was not a farrier, was called to testify as to the disease of the eyes of a horse. The witness professed to understand when he examined a horse whether his eyes were good or not, though he acknowledged that there might be diseases of the eyes of horses with which he was unacquainted. He was asked, whether, from his knowledge of the diseases of horses eyes, he believed the disease of the eyes of the horse in question had been of long standing, and had existed before the exchange of horses made by the parties. It was held that he should be permitted to answer, and it was said: "We have scarcely any veterinary surgeons in our country, and the opinions of men of such knowledge as this witness appears to have, must be admitted in cases like the present.[4]

[1] Allen v. Hunter, 6 McLean, 303, 310.
[2] See §§ 134, 135.
[3] Slater v. Wilcox, 57 Barb. 604, 608.
[4] House v. Fort, 4 Blackf. (Ind.) 293.

But the witness should be one who has some special knowledge and experience in relation to the diseases of animals. Hence, a witness who is not an expert cannot testify whether a horse is or is not sound, or as to what constitutes unsoundness in a horse.[1] And a witness who is not an expert, cannot be permitted to state the symptoms and appearance of cattle that die from want of feed.[2] Neither can such a witness be asked whether he had observed certain appearances in horses that had been hard driven and then exposed.[3] So the opinion of a witness that a wound which he saw inflicted on a horse, was sufficient to cause his death, is inadmissible, unless the witness has some peculiar skill or knowledge as to the effect of such wounds.[4] But any witness may testify whether a horse seemed well or not, that being matter of common experience.[5] It has been held that a medical witness, who has stated that he had read various standard authors on the subject of diseases, and who has given his opinion in respect to the character of the disease of which the animal in question died, may be asked for "his best medical opinion, according to the best authority."[6] Of course no question is raised as to the right of a veterinary surgeon to testify as an expert, in cases relating to the diseases of animals.[7]

[1] Spear v. Richardson, 34 N. H. 428.
[2] Stonam v. Waldo, 17 Mo. 489.
[3] Moulton v. Seruton, 30 Me. 288.
[4] Harris v. Panama R. R. Co., 3 Bosw. 7.
[5] Spear v. Richardson, *supra*. And see Willis v. Quimby, 11 Foster (N. H.), 489.
[6] Pierson v. Hoag, 47 Barb. (N. Y.) 243.
[7] Pinney v. Cahill, 12 N. W. Reporter, 862; s. c. 14 The Reporter, 337 (Sup. Ct. of Mich., June, 1882).

CHAPTER V.

EXPERT TESTIMONY IN THE SCIENCE OF LAW.

SECTION.
85. The Law as a Subject for the Testimony of Experts.
86. Of what Laws Courts take Judicial Notice, and Expert Testimony is not Received.
87. Of what Laws Courts do not take Judicial Notice, and Expert Testimony is Received.
88. Distinction between Written and Unwritten Law as to Mode of Proof by Experts.
89. Presumption that Law is Unwritten.
90. Expert Testimony in Connection with the Written Law.
91. Statutory Provisions in Delaware, Kentucky, Maine, Massachusetts and Wisconsin.
92. Proof of Written Law by Experts — The Practice in England.
93. Proof of Written Law by Experts — The Practice in England — The Subject Continued.
94. Verification of Written Law by Experts.
95. Presumption that the Law remains Unchanged.
96. Who are Qualified to Testify as Experts in Foreign Law.
97. Who are Qualified to Testify as Experts in Foreign Law — The Subject Continued.
98. Who are Qualified to Testify as Experts in Foreign Law — The Subject Continued.
99. Mere Knowledge of the Foreign Law is Insufficient.
100. Knowledge of the Foreign Law must have been Acquired where.
101. Right of Expert to Cite Text Books, Decisions, Codes, etc.
102. How the Citations are to be Regarded.
103. Testimony as to Usage and Practice of Courts of Another State.
104. Testimony as to Powers and Obligations of an Attorney in his Relations to his Client.

§ 85. **The Law as a Subject for the Testimony of Experts.** — From the earliest times it seems to have been the practice of the English judges to receive, in certain cases, the opinions of persons skilled in the law. As early as the time of Henry VI., in a case which involved a question relating to civil law, we find it laid down that the common law judges heard a bachelor of the civil law "argue and discourse upon the difference between *compulsione præcisa et causativa*, as men that were not above being instructed and made wiser by him."[1] And in another case during the same reign, where *ex commengement* had been pleaded, and the party answered that he ought not to be disabled thereby as an appeal was pending, the common law judges inquired of those who were well versed in the canon law, touching the question involved.[2]

§ 86. **Of what Laws Courts take Judicial Notice, and Expert Testimony is not Received.**—Since experts cannot, as a general rule, be examined concerning such laws as the courts take judicial notice of,[3] it is important to distinguish between the laws which will be judicially noticed, and those which must be proved as facts, when advantage of them is desired.

I. We shall consider first, then, those laws of which courts take judicial notice, and concerning which, therefore, the testimony of experts will not be received, as not being necessary for the information of the court. Such laws are:

1. The law of nations.[4]
2. The law merchant.[5]
3. The maritime law, so far at least as recognized by the law of nations.[6]

---

[1] 7 Henry VI., 11.
[2] 20 Henry VI., 25.
[3] Jewell v. Center, 25 Ala. 498, 505; The Clement, 2 Curtis, 363.
[4] The Scotia, 14 Wallace, 171, 188.
[5] Edie v. East India Co., 2 Burr. 1226; Jewell v. Center, 25 Ala., 498; Bradford v. Cooper, 1 La. Ann. 325; Goldsmith v. Sawyer, 46 Cal. 209. The case last cited holds that where a board of brokers have rules, which are not rules or usages of trade and commerce that would be recognized without their adoption by the board, these will not be judicially noticed, but must be shown by experts therein.
[6] Chandler v. Grieves, 2 H. Bl. 606, n; Maddox v. Fisher, 14 Moore,

4. The ecclesiastical law, for the purpose of determining how far it is a part of the common law.[1]

5. The courts of a State which has been carved out of another State, take judicial notice of the statutes of the latter State passed prior to the separation.[2]

6. All courts take judicial notice of their domestic law.[3] And the common law of a State which had no political existence before the Revolution, is the common law as modified and amended by the English statutes passed prior to the Revolution.[4] But it is held that in those States where colonies were established before the Revolution, with a power to legislate for themselves, English statutes passed after the colonies were thus established, but prior to the Revolution, are not a part of their common law.[5]

7. The State courts take judicial notice of the Federal Constitution, and of its amendments,[6] as well as of Federal statutes.[7]

8. The Federal courts take judicial notice of the laws of the several States composing the national government.[8]

P. C. 103; Zugasti v. Lamer, 12 Moore, P. C. 331; The Scotia, 14 Wallace, 171, 188; Taylor on Evidence, § 5; Wharton on Evidence, § 298.

[1] Sims v. Maryatt, 17 Q. B. (79 E. C. L.) 292; 1 Roll. Abr. 526; 6 Vin. Abr. 496.

[2] Delano v. Jopling, 1 Litt. (Ky.) 417; Stokes v. Macker, 62 Barb. (N. Y.) 145; Doe v. Eslava, 11 Ala. 1028; Chouteau v. Pierre, 9 Mo. 3; Ott v. Soulard, 9 Mo. 581; United States v. Turner, 11 Howard, 663, 668; City of Brownsville v. Cavazos, 2 Woods, 293.

[3] State v. Jarrett, 17 Md. 309; State v. O'Conner, 13 La. Ann. 486; Pierson v. Baird, 2 Greene (Iowa), 235; Berliner v. Waterloo, 14 Wis. 378; Springfield v. Worcester, 2 Cush. (Mass.) 52; Division of Howard County, 15 Kans. 194; Dolph v. Barney, 5 Oreg. 191.

[4] Coburn v. Harvey, 18 Wis. 147; Dutcher v. Culver, 24 Minn. 584.

[5] Sackett v. Sackett, 8 Pick. (Mass.) 309, 316; Commonwealth v. Knowlton, 2 Mass. 534.

[6] Graves v. Keaton 3 Coldw. (43 Tenn.) 8.

[7] Kessel v. Albetis, 56 Barb. (N. Y.) 362; Papin v. Ryan, 32 Mo. 21; Morris v. Davidson, 49 Ga. 361; Rice's Succession, 21 La. Ann. 614, 616; Bayly v. Chubb, 16 Grattan (Va.), 284; Mims v. Swartz, 37 Tex. 13; Jones v. Laney, 2 Texas, 342; Semple v. Hagar, 27 Cal. 163; United States v. De Coursey, 1 Pinney (Wis.), 508; Montgomery v. Deeley, 3 Wis. 709, 712.

[8] Junction Railroad Co. v. Bank of Ashland, 12 Wallace, 226, 229; Bennett v. Bennett, Deady, 299, 311; Merrill v. Dawson, Hempstead, 563;

§ 87. **Of what Laws Courts do not take Judicial Notice, and Expert Testimony may be Received.**—II. In passing, in the second place, to the consideration of those laws which will not be judicially noticed, and as to which experts may, therefore, testify, we find :

1. That courts do not take judicial notice of the laws of foreign States.[1] As said by Lord LANGDALE in England : " With foreign laws an English judge cannot be familiar ; there are many of which he must be totally ignorant ; there is in every case of foreign law, an absence of all the accurate knowledge and ready associations which assist him in the consideration of that which is the English law."[2] So in this country, Mr. Chief Justice MARSHALL remarked : " The laws of a foreign nation designed only for the direction of its own affairs, are not to be noticed by the courts of other countries, unless proved as facts."[3]

2. That the courts of one State will not take judicial notice of the laws of any other State. This is upon the theory that the separate States which together constitute the nation, are, as respects their political relations to each other, essentially foreign countries, whose laws must be proved as facts.[4] At an early day it was held in Vermont, that judi-

Smith v. Tallapoosa Co., 2 Woods, 574, 576; United States v. Turner, 11 How. 663, 668; Owings v. Hull, 9 Peters, 607.

[1] Freemoult v. Dedire, 1 P. Wms. 430; Feaubert v. Turst, Pre. Ch. 207; Mostyn v. Farrigas, Cowp. 174; Male v. Roberts, 3 Esp. 163; Smith v. Gould, 4 Moore, P. C. 21; Strother v. Lucas, 6 Peters, 763; Armstrong v. Lear, 8 Peters, 52; United States v. Wiggins, 14 Peters. 334; Damess v. Hale, 1 Otto, 13; Bowditch v. Soltyk, 99 Mass. 138; Owen v. Boyle, 15 Me. 147; Hosford v. Nichols, 1 Paige (N. Y.) 220; McCraney v. Alden, 46 Barb. (N. Y.) 274; Monroe v. Douglass, 5 N. Y. 447, 452.

[2] Nelson v. Bridport, 8 Beavan, 527.

[3] Talbot v. Seeman, 1 Cranch, 38.

[4] Drake v. Glover, 30 Ala. 382; Mobile Railroad Co. v. Whitney, 39 Ala. 468; Forsyth v. Preer, 62 Ala. 443; Newton v. Cocke, 10 Ark. 169; Hempstead v. Reed, 6 Conn. 480; Brackett v. Norton, 4 Conn. 517; Dyer v. Smith, 12 Conn. 384; Bailey v. McDowell, 2 Harrington (Del.), 34; Stanford v. Pruet, 27 Ga. 243; Mason v. Wash, Breese (Ill.), 39; Irving v. McLean. 4 Blackf. (Ind.) 52; Davis v. Rogers, 14 Ind. 424; Johnson v. Chambers, 12 Ind. 112; Carey v. Cincinnati etc. R. R. Co., 5 Iowa. 357; Taylor v. Runyan. 9 Iowa, 522; Shed v. Augustine, 14 Kans. 282; Beauchamp v. Mudd, Hardin (Ky.), 163; Stephenson v. Bannister, 3

cial notice would be taken of the laws of sister States.[1] But that doctrine was subsequently overruled.[2] In an early case in New Jersey, a similar doctrine was intimated,[3] but the *dicta* in that case have also been overruled in later cases in the same court.[4] A similar position was taken at an early day in Tennessee, and has been ever since maintained.[5] And now, under the code of that State, the Supreme Court takes judicial notice of all foreign laws and statutes.[6] In a recent case in Rhode Island, the court took judicial notice of a law of the State of New York.[7] An exception should perhaps be made to the general rule, in so far that where a State recognizes acts done in pursuance of the laws of another State, the courts of the first State should take judicial cognizance of the said laws, so far as may be necessary to judge of the acts alleged to be done under them. And it has been so held.[8] And in a case in Pennsylvania, it was held that a State court, when its judgment would be liable to review by the Supreme Court of the United States, in a case arising under the law

Bibb. (Ky.) 369; Dorsey v. Dorsey, 5 J. J. Marsh. (Ky.) 280; Tyler v. Trabue, 8 B. Monr. (Ky.) 306; Syme v. Stewart, 17 La. Ann. 73; Anderson v. Folger, 11 La. Ann. 269; Legg v. Legg, 8 Mass. 99; Knapp v. Abell, 10 Allen (Mass.), 485; Brimhall v. Van Campen, 8 Minn. 13; Hoyt v. McNeil, 13 Minn. 390; Hemphill v. Bank of Alabama, 6 Sm. & M. (Miss.) 44; Babcock v. Babcock, 46 Mo. 243; Morrissey v. Wiggins Ferry Co., 47 Mo. 521; Ball v. Consolidated Franklin etc. Co., 32 N. J. Law, 102, 104; Uhler v. Semple, 5 C. E. Green (N. J.), 288; Campion v. Kille, 1 McCarter (N. J.), 229; Hosford v. Nichols, 1 Paige (N. Y.), 220; State v. Twitty, 2 Hawks (N. C.), 248; State v. Surtly, 2 Hawks (N. C.), 441; Evans v. Reynolds, 32 Ohio St. 163; Ripple v. Ripple, 1 Rawle (Penn.), 386; Whitesides v. Poole, 9 Rich. (S. C.) 68; Jones v. Laney, 2 Texas, 342; Anderson v. Anderson, 23 Texas, 639; Rape v. Heaton, 9 Wis. 328; Territt v. Woodruff, 19 Vt. 183; Woodrow v. O'Conner, 28 Vt. 776; Walsh v. Dart, 12 Wis. 635.

[1] Middlebury Coll. v. Cheney, 1 Vt. 348.
[2] Territt v. Woodruff, 19 Vt. 182; Woodrow v. O'Conner, 28 Vt. 776.
[3] Curtis v. Martin, 2 N. J. Law, 290.
[4] Van Buskirk v. Mulock, 18 N. J. Law, 184.
[5] Foster v. Taylor, 2 Overton, 191; Coffee v. Neely, 2 Heisk. 311; Hobbs v. Railroad Co., 9 Heiskell, 873.
[6] See Hobbs v. Memphis etc. R. R. Co., 56 Tenn. 874.
[7] Paine v. Schenectady Ins. Co., 11 R. I. 411.
[8] Carpenter v. Dexter. 8 Wallace, 513.

of a sister State, would take judicial notice of such law.[1] It has been held in Kansas that the constitutions of sister States will be judicially noticed.[2] Where it is desired to introduce evidence of the laws of other States, it is necessary that they should be pleaded.[3]

§ 88. **Distinction between Written and Unwritten Law as to Mode of Proof by Experts.**—In this country a distinction is taken between the written and the unwritten law, and while the latter may be proven by the testimony of experts,[4] the former can, in general, only be shown by the production of the written law itself, duly authenticated.[5] In an early case, Mr. Chief Justice MARSHALL said: " That no testimony shall be received which presupposes better testimony attainable by the party who offers it, applies to foreign law, as it does to all other facts."[6] Upon this principle, the statute itself must be regarded as better evidence of what it contains, than is the testimony of any individual, who, though he may know the general purport of the law,

---

[1] State of Ohio v. Hinchman, 27 Penn. St. 479.
[2] Butcher v. Bank, 2 Kans. 70; Dodge v. Coffin, 15 Kans. 277.
[3] Roots v. Merriwether, 8 Bush. 401; Peck v. Hibbard, 26 Vt. 698.
[4] Baltimore & Ohio R. R. Co. v. Glenn, 28 Md. 287; Heberd v. Myers, 5 Ind. 94; People v. Lambert, 5 Mich. 349; Merritt v. Merritt, 20 Ill. 65; Ennis v. Smith, 14 How. (U. S.) 400, 426; McRae v. Mattoon, 13 Pick. (Mass.) 53; Owen v. Boyle, 15 Me. 147, 151; Tyler v. Trabue, 8 B. Monr. (Ky.) 306.
[5] Zimmerman v. Hesler, 32 Md. 274; Kermott v. Ayer, 11 Mich. 181; Woodbridge v. Austin, 2 Tyler (Vt.), 364; Danforth v. Reynolds, 1 Vt. 265; Territt v. Woodruff, 19 Vt. 184; McNeill v. Arnold, 17 Ark. 154, 167, explaining Barkman v. Hopkins, 11 Ark. 168; Bowles v. Eddy, 33 Ark. 645; Emery v. Berry, 8 Foster (N. H.), 473; Comparet v. Jernegan, 5 Blackf. (Ind.) 375; Line v. Mack, 14 Ind. 330; Hoes v. Van Alstyne, 20 Ill. 202; McDeed v. McDeed, 67 Ill. 545; Lee v. Matthews, 10 Ala. 682; Innerarity v. Mims, 1 Ala. 660; Spaulding v. Vincent, 24 Vt. 501, 505; Gardner v. Lewis, 7 Gill (Md.), 379; Robinson v. Clifford, 2 Wash. C. C. 2; United States v. Otega, 4 Wash. C. C. 533; Ennis v. Smith, 14 How. (U. S.) 400, 426; Toulandou v. Lachenmeyer, 1 Sweeny (N. Y.), 45; Isabella v. Pecot, 2 La. Ann. 387; Raynham v. Canton, 3 Pick. (Mass.), 293; Bryant v. Kelton, 1 Texas, 434; Willings v. Consequa, 1 Peters C. C. 225; Kenny v. Clarkson, 1 Johnson (N. Y.), 385; Lincoln v. Battelle, 6 Wend. (N. Y.) 475.
[6] Church v. Hubbart, 2 Cranch, 187.

may not carry in his mind so minute and exact a knowledge thereof, as is often necessary for its proper application.

§ 89. **Presumption that Law is Unwritten.**—It has been held that, in the absence of evidence to the contrary, it will be presumed that the foreign law is unwritten, and that parol testimony of experts in such law will be received upon this assumption. "These laws are generally difficult of proof. It would be a very expensive matter to prove them by copies authenticated. It, therefore, shall reasonably fall on the parties objecting to the parol proof, to show that the law was a written edict of the country."[1]

§ 90. **Expert Testimony in Connection with the Written Law.**—While the general rule excludes, in this country, the testimony of experts as to the written or statutory law, yet such testimony has been received when the question was, not so much as to the language of the written law, but as to what was the law altogether, "as shown by its exposition, interpretation and adjudication." In admitting such testimony in Alabama, as to the law of Louisiana, the court said: "The exposition, interpretation and adjudication may never have been evidenced by books or writings; but may, nevertheless, have become well understood, as the rule of law deduced by the court from the written words of the code upon a particular state of facts. Upon such a question, the testimony or opinions of competent witnesses instructed in the law of that State, may be resorted to."[2] In another case decided in Illinois, it is held that while the statute of a foreign State cannot be proved by parol, yet the construction given to such statute by the tribunals where they are in force, may be given in evidence by witnesses learned in such laws.[3] And the Supreme Court of Rhode Island has recently permitted a Spanish lawyer, formerly of Havana, to testify that a verbal special partnership was valid under the laws of Cuba; that he might state the written law without pro-

[1] Dougherty v. Snyder, 15 S. & R. (Penn.) 84, 87. And see Livingston v. Maryland Ins. Co., 6 Cranch, 274, 280.
[2] Walker v. Forbes, 31 Ala. 9.
[3] Hoes v. Van Alstyne, 20 Ill. 202.

ducing it.¹ The court declared that in the case of the Spanish colonies it was difficult to ascertain what their law was without the aid of an expert, their law being composed partly of the various codes of Spain, and partly of the various decrees contained in the *Recopilacion de las Indias*, and the various decrees of later date. In the course of its decision the court says: " There are many cases where the evidence of a professional person, or one skilled *virtute officii*, may be much more satisfactory evidence of what the law is, than the mere exemplification of the exact words of a foreign statute, which the court may not have the necessary knowledge to construe. And it seems to us, that the requiring an exemplified copy is pressing the rule of requiring the best evidence to an extent that would often defeat the ends of justice." Chancellor KENT, in an early case, also permitted a Spanish lawyer to testify that a will was executed according to the laws of Cuba, without the production of the written law.² And recently in Pennsylvania, a witness was permitted to testify as to the laws of Baden, though his testimony involved a statute.³ So in a late case in Maryland, a New York lawyer was held competent to testify, in the absence of opposing proof, whether a sale made by a receiver was made after due public notice and advertisement, as required by the laws of New York.⁴ In other cases, too, in this country, experts have been allowed to testify as to the law of another State, where a statute and its construction have been involved.⁵

§ 91. **Statutory Provisions in Delaware, Kentucky, Maine, Massachusetts and Wisconsin.**— In a few States statutory provision has been made with reference to the proof of foreign law, which seems to leave it to the discretion of the court, to require the production of a copy of the

[1] Barrows v. Downs, 9 R. I. 453.
[2] In the matter of Roberts' Will, 8 Paige (N. Y.), 446.
[3] American Life Ins. Co. v. Rosenagle, 27 P. F. Smith, 507.
[4] Consolidated Real Estate & Fire Ins. Co. v. Cashow, 41 Md. 59.
[5] Hooper v. Moore, 5 Jones Law (N. C.), 130; Barkman v. Hopkins, 6 Eng. (Ark.) 157.

written law, or to receive the testimony of experts therein. In Delaware, Massachusetts and Wisconsin, the provision is as follows: "The existence and the tenor or effect of all foreign laws may be proved as facts by parol evidence; but if it shall appear that the law in question is contained in a written statute or code, the court may, in their discretion, reject any evidence of such law that is not accompanied by a copy thereof." [1] The phraseology of the Kentucky and Maine statutes differ somewhat from the above provision. The Kentucky statute reads as follows: "The existence and the tenor or effect of all foreign laws beyond the limits of the United States, may be proved by the parol evidence of persons learned in those laws. But if it appear that the law in question is contained in a written statute, the court may reject such parol evidence, unless it be accompanied by a copy of the statute." [2] While in Maine it runs as follows: "Foreign laws may be proved by parol evidence, but when such law appears to be existing in a written statute or code, it may be rejected unless accompanied by a copy thereof. The unwritten law of any other State or territory of the United States may be proved by parol evidence, and by books of reports of cases adjudged in their courts." [3]

§ 92. **Proof of Written Law by Experts — The Practice in England.** — The practice in England, formerly was to require the production of the *written* law, and to exclude all proof of it by the testimony of experts. When it was proposed to call a person conversant with the law of Russia as to the right to stop goods *in transitu*, Lord KENYON refused to receive his testimony, and the distinction between written and unwritten law was taken. "Can the laws of a foreign country," he asks, "be proved by a person who may be casually picked up in the streets? Can a court of justice receive such evidence of such a matter? I shall expect it to be made out to me, not by such loose evi-

---

[1] Delaware Rev. Code (1874), p. 652, § 8; Massachusetts Gen. Stat. (1882), p. 903, § 73; Wisconsin Rev. Stat. (1878), p. 1002, § 4139.
[2] Gen. Stat. (1873), p. 413, § 18.
[3] Rev. Stat. (1871), p. 653, § 98.

dence, but by proof from the country whose laws you propose to give in evidence, properly authenticated."[1] Lord ELLENBOROUGH also refused to receive parol evidence as to the law of Surinam, and declared that the law being in writing, an authenticated copy of it ought to be produced.[2] Chief Justice GIBBS, in a subsequent case, took the same distinction between the written and unwritten law, declaring that a copy of the former must be produced.[3] And Sir GEORGE HAY had, in 1776, refused to accept proof of foreign laws "by the opinions of lawyers, which is the most uncertain way in the world," and required certificates of the laws to be laid before him.[4] But this doctrine is no longer observed in that country, and the rule is now to regard the law as being something distinct from statutory or common law taken by themselves merely. It is considered as a resultant of the *lex scripta* and *lex non scripta*, and as such it is to be proved as any other fact of science, by witnesses duly qualified by learning and experience. As early as 1811 the opinions of Scotch advocates were received to prove the law of Scotland, although they referred to printed authorities as forming the basis of their opinions.[5] It was not, however, until the year 1845 that the principle can be said to have become settled, of admitting expert testimony as to law considered as a complex resultant of the written law, and its interpretation and construction. In that year a French advocate was permitted to testify that the feudal law was abolished in Alsace, *de facto*, in 1789, by the revolution, and *de jure*, by the treaty of Luneville; and that a formal decree existed abrogating the feudal law.[6]

§ 93. **Proof of Written Law by Experts — The Practice in England — The Subject Continued.** — Lord Chief Justice DENMAN, in sustaining the admission of the testimony,

[1] Boehtlinck v. Schneider, 3 Esp. 58. This case criticised by Lord Denman, C. J., in Baron De Bode's Case. 8 Ad. & Ellis (N. S.) 208.
[2] Clegg v. Levy, 3 Camp. 166.
[3] Millar v. Heinrick, 4 Camp. 155.
[4] Harford v. Morris, 2 Hagg. 430.
[5] Dalrymple v. Dalrymple, 2 Hagg. 54.
[6] Baron De Bode's Case, 8 Ad. & Ellis (N. S.) 208.

in the above case, said: "There is another general rule: that the opinions of persons of science must be received as to the facts of their science. That rule applies to the evidence of legal men; and I think it is not confined to unwritten law, but extends also to the written laws which such men are bound to know. Properly speaking, the nature of such evidence is not to set forth the contents of the written law, but its effect and the state of the law resulting from it. The mere contents, indeed, might often mislead persons not familiar with the particular system of law. The witness is called upon to state what law does result from the evidence." The same principle is laid down in *Earl Nelson* v. *Lord Bridport*,[1] where the court declares that although the written law is produced, and due proof made that it has not been repealed, varied, or fallen into disuse, and that the words have been accurately translated, " still the words require due construction, and the construction depends on the meaning of words to be considered with reference to other words not contained in the mere text of the law, and also with reference to the subject matter, which is not insulated from all others. The construction may have been, probably has been, the subject of judicial decision; instead of one decision, there may have been a long succession of decisions, varying more or less from each other, and ultimately ending in that which alone ought to be applied in the particular case." It is evident that as to such construction the evidence of experts is required for the instruction of the court. As Lord BROUGHAM declared in the House of Lords, in the celebrated *Sussex Peerage Case*:[2] " The witness may refer to the sources of his knowledge; but it is perfectly clear that the proper mode of proving a foreign law is not by showing to the House the book of the law; for the House has not organs to know and to deal with the text of that law, and therefore requires the assistance of a lawyer who knows how to interpret it. If the *Code Napoleon* was before a French court, that court

[1] 8 Beavan, 527.
[2] 11 Cl. & F. 85, 115.

would know how to deal with and construe its provisions, but in England we have no such knowledge, and the English judges must, therefore, have the assistance of foreign lawyers." So in another case the court declares that the proper course to be pursued, in ascertaining the laws of a foreign country, is to call a witness expert in such laws, and " ask him, on his responsibility, what the law is, and not to read any fragment of a code, which would only mislead."[1] A person skilled in the laws of Bohemia was therefore permitted, against objection, to testify as to the written laws of that country.

§ 94. **Verification of Written Law by Experts.**—When it is necessary to prove the language of the written law by producing a copy thereof, the question arises as to the manner in which the law is to be verified or authenticated. In a majority of the States express provision has been made for the admission of the printed statute books of any State. In some States it is provided that the statute books of another State, *purporting to be published by the authority of such State*, may be received in evidence without further proof.[2] In others, the provision is that statute books of a sister State, *purporting or proved to be published by authority, or proved to be commonly admitted in the courts of such State*, may be received in evidence.[3] In three of the States, that statute books of other States, *purporting to be published by authority or commonly admitted* in the courts of such State may be received.[4] In two of the States, that

---

[1] Cocks v. Purday, 2 C. & K. 269.
[2] Alabama Code of 1876, § 3045; Arkansas Dig. of Statutes (1858), ch. 67, § 2; Indiana. Rev. Stat. (1881), § 477; Illinois, Rev. Stat. (1874), p. 490, § 10; Maine, Rev. Stat. (1871), p. 653, § 97; Maryland, Rev. Code (1878), p. 759, § 46; Rhode Island, Public Statutes (1882), p. 589, § 144; Texas, Rev. Stat. (1879), p. 329, § 2250.
[3] Florida, Bush's Dig. (1872), p. 547, § 357; Iowa, Code of 1873, p. 573, § 3718; Massachusetts, Gen. Stat. (1882), p. 943, § 71; New York, Code of 1871, § 426, and new Code, § 942; North Carolina, Battle's Revisal (1873), p. 233; Ohio, 2 Rev. Stat. (1880), p. 1280, § 5244; Tennessee, 2 Statutes (1871), § 3800.
[4] Delaware, Rev. Code (1874), p. 652, § 6; Michigan, 2 Comp. Laws (1871), p. 1708, § 78; Minnesota Statutes (1878), p. 80), § 57.

statute books of other States, *printed by authority or proved to be commonly admitted* in the courts of such State, may be read in evidence.[1] While in a few others the provision is that statute books, *printed by authority*, may be received without further proof.[2] In Louisiana the statutory provision is that the published *digests* and *statutes* of other States shall be received in evidence.[3] While in New Jersey the provision is so different from those in the statutes of other States, that we give it entire.[4]

It is evident that in those cases in which provision is made for receiving the statute books of sister States, which are "commonly admitted," or "proved to be commonly admitted," in the courts of such States, the evidence of persons practicing in the courts of those States would be received to authenticate the law, by showing that the book containing it is received in evidence in the courts of the State whose law it purports to be. It has been held that these statutory provisions are to be regarded as cumulative, and that they do not repeal the common law mode of

[1] Oregon, Gen. Laws (1843-1872), p. 253, § 715; Wisconsin, Rev. Stat. (1878), p. 1002, § 4136.

[2] Colorado, Gen. Laws (1877), p. 405, § 1078; Connecticut, Gen. Stat. (Rev. of 1875), p. 438. § 19; Georgia, Code of 1873, p. 671, § 3824; Kentucky, Gen. Stat. (1873), p. 413, § 21. And see 1 Rev. Stat. of Missouri (1879), p. 379, § 2272.

[3] Revised Statutes of 1870, p. 283, § 1440.

[4] "The printed statute books and pamphlet session laws of any of the United States, printed and published by the direction or authority of such State, shall be received as evidence of the public laws of such State, in any court of this State; and the court may determine whether any book or pamphlet, offered as such, was so printed or published, either from inspection, or the knowledge of the judge or judges, or from testimony; and no error shall be assigned for the rejection of any book or pamphlet, offered as such, unless it be proved on error that such book or pamphlet is received as a statute book or pamphlet containing the session laws of said State, in the courts of such State whose statute book or pamphlet containing the session laws, it purports to be; nor shall any error assigned for the admission of such book or pamphlet be sustained, unless it be shown in support thereof, that the statute offered in evidence or some material part thereof, was not in force in such State at the time of the transaction or matter to which it was offered as pertinent or material." Revision (1709-1877), p. 381, § 22.

proof.¹ But, as the Supreme Court of Michigan has lately said, foreign statutes should, when possible, be proved, as provided for in the State laws and the Acts of Congress, rather than by the testimony of a lawyer who had practiced within the jurisdiction where they are in force.² And in the absence of all statutory provision regulating the mode of proof, it has been held that a copy of the foreign statute should be produced, which the witness can swear was recognized in the foreign country as authoritative.³ So in an early case in Pennsylvania, the court received a printed copy of Irish statutes to show the law of Ireland, an Irish barrister having testified that he received the same from the King's printer, and that it was good evidence in that country.⁴ And in England a book was received as evidence of the written law of France, which purported to be printed at the Royal Printing Office, and which the French Vice Consul produced, testifying that it contained the French code of laws upon which he acted, and that the office where it purported to be printed by authority of the government, was the government printing office.⁵ But in a case decided in New York, the court refused to receive a book in the French language, purporting to contain the commercial code of France, and which was produced by the Chancellor of the French Consulate at New York, who testified that it was an exact copy of the laws furnished by the French government to its consul in New York.⁶ And in New Jersey, prior to the adoption of any statutory provision regulating the matter, the courts held that parol proof by an attorney, that the book was read and received in the courts of the other State as an authentic copy of their statutes, was not

---

¹ Biesenthrall v. Williams, 1 Duval (Ky.), 330. And see Chamberlain v. Maitland, 5 B. Monroe (Ky.), 448.
² Kopke v. People, 43 Mich. 41.
³ Spaulding v. Vincent, 24 Vt. 501, 505.
⁴ Jones v. Maffett, 5 S. & R. 523.
⁵ Lacon v. Higgins, 3 Starkie (N. P.) 178. See also, Middleton v. Janverin, 2 Hag. Cons. R. 437.
⁶ Chanoine v. Fowler, 3 Wend. 173.

sufficient, but that it should be authenticated according to the Act of Congress, or by sworn copies from the original statutes.[1]

§ 95. **Presumption that the Law remains Unchanged.**— When a witness testifies as to the foreign law, the question has been raised whether it is sufficient for him to show the law as it existed at a period prior to the time of which the trial court is inquiring, or whether it is necessary that his testimony should be addressed directly to the very time of the transaction in question. It has been held, that where the statute of a sister State is shown to have existed at a time prior to that of the transaction in question, it will be presumed, in absence of proof to the contrary, that it continued unchanged to the period in controversy.[2] In a recent case in New York, when a printed copy of the French Code was presented, a witness testified that at the time he practiced in France, the book was commonly received by the judicial tribunals of that country as evidence of the existing law. The witness was licensed to practice in France in 1837, and ceased to practice in 1862. The period for the existing law of which the trial court was seeking, was in 1871, and the question was raised whether the law having been shown as it existed in 1862, could be presumed to have continued the same until the year 1871. This was not determined, but the court evidently had a serious doubt whether such presumption could be entertained.[3]

§ 96. **Who are Qualified to Testify as Experts in Foreign Law.**—In order to prove the law of a foreign country, it is necessary that the witnesses produced to testify in respect to it, should be more than ordinarily capable of speaking upon the subject. It does not, however, appear to be essential that the witnesses should in all cases be lawyers, and it has even been held to be unnecessary that they should have held an official appointment, in which it has

---

[1] Van Buskirk v. Mulock, 18 N. J. Law, 184, overruling, Hale v. Ross, 3 N. J. Law, 373. See Condit v. Blackwell, 19 N. J. Eq. 193, 196.
[2] Peck v. Hibbard, 26 Vt. 698; Raynham v. Canton, 3 Pick. (Mass.) 29.
[3] Hynes v. McDermott, 82 N. Y. 41.

been necessary for them, in the discharge of their official duties, to make themselves acquainted with the law. It has been declared that "all persons who practice a busines or profession which requires them to possess a certain knowledge of the matter in hand, are experts so far as expertness is required."[1] The question which this case involved, related to the Belgian law on the subject of the presentment of promissory notes, and the point raised was whether a witness called as an expert to testify as to such law, must be a professional man, one who, by virtue of his office, might be said to be *peritus*. It was held not, and one who had been a merchant and stock-broker at Brussels, was permitted to testify as an expert. "I think," said Mr. Justice MAULE, "that inasmuch as he had been carrying on a business which made it his interest to take cognizance of the foreign law, he does fall within the description of an expert." And in a case recently decided in the Supreme Court of Pennsylvania, it was held that the law of a foreign country on a given subject might be proven by any person, who, though not a lawyer, or not having filled any public office, was or had been in a position to render it probable that he would make himself acquainted with it. And a pastor of a church in a foreign country was permitted to testify that the church records had been kept according to the laws of that country.[2]

§ 97. **Who are Qualified to Testify as Experts in Foreign Law — The Subject Continued.** — So it has been held in England that a Roman Catholic bishop holding the office of coadjutor to a vicar-apostolic in England, was to be considered, by virtue of his office, as a person skilled in the matrimonial law of Rome, and, therefore, competent as a witness to prove that law.[3] And in this country it is held that a priest or minister of another State is a competent witness to prove the laws of such State as to marriage.[4] In another

[1] Vander Donckt v. Thellusson, 8 Man. G. & S. (65 E. C. L.) 812.
[2] American Life Ins. Co. v. Rosenagle, 77 Penn. St. 507.
[3] Sussex Peerage Case, 11 Cl. & F. 85.
[4] Bird v. Commonwealth, 21 Grattan (Va.) 800, 808. And in Phillips

case it is said that the foreign law "may be proved by professional men, or others conversant with, and having the *means of knowledge*."[1] In Texas the practice has long prevailed of receiving the evidence of intelligent Mexicans, not lawyers, as to the laws of Spain and Mexico in litigation pertaining to lands, and such evidence is pronounced by the courts of that State to have been "valuable in giving information as to the construction given to the laws of Spain and Mexico by the officers who executed them."[2] In New Hampshire the court declares that in proving the laws of a foreign country, the testimony of any person, whether a professional lawyer or not, is competent, provided he appears to the court to be well informed on the subject.[3] And in that State it has been held that a witness who was not a lawyer, but who for several years had acted as a magistrate in Canada, and had long been engaged in mercantile business there, and had become acquainted with the law in relation to notarial instruments, was competent to testify that according to the law of that country general powers of attorney must be executed before a notary, and that it was part of the sworn duty of every notary not to suffer any original paper executed before him to be taken out of his custody, and that notarial copies of such instruments are received in all the courts of Canada, without further proof of the execution of the original.[4] In an early case in New York Mr. Justice SPENCER declares that "courts of law will receive evidence of the common law, from intelligent persons of the country whose laws are to be proved,"[5] And in Illinois it is said that it may be proven by the testimony of competent witnesses instructed in its

---

v. Gregg, 10 Watts (Penn.), 158, 169, witnesses who were not lawyers, were received to testify as to what constituted a lawful marriage in Mississippi a half century before.

[1] Jones v. Maffett, 5 Serg. & R. (Penn.) 523, 532.
[2] State v. Cuellar, 47 Texas, 304.
[3] Hall v. Costello, 48 N. H. 179.
[4] Pickard v. Bailey, 6 Foster (N. H.), 169.
[5] Kenney v. Van Horne, 1 Johns. (N. Y.) 394.

laws.¹ In Tennessee, that it may be proven by jurists and legal characters experienced therein.² In Arkansas, it may be proven by witnesses skilled therein.³

§ 98. **Who are Qualified to Testify as Experts in Foreign Law — The Subject Continued.** — In the light of the foregoing decisions it must be regarded as the rule in this country, at least, that it is not necessary that an expert in foreign law should have been a member of the bar in the foreign State whose laws he is called to prove. This precise question was recently raised in the United States Court of Claims, where a witness who had never been admitted to the French bar, was held competent to testify as to the law of France.⁴ But it appeared that the witness had studied the law as a profession, had been graduated at the University of Paris, had since then been engaged in legal pursuits, and was then employed by the French government as legal adviser of the legation at Washington. In a still more recent case in England the Persian ambassador at Vienna was allowed to testify as an expert in the law of Persia; but this was after he had testified that in Persia there were no professional lawyers; that the administration of the law was left entirely to ecclesiastics, and that all persons in the diplomatic service of that country were required to be thoroughly versed in the law; and that he had, therefore, studied and become acquainted with it.⁵ And it is, undoubtedly, true, that in England a somewhat more rigid rule is applied, than is insisted on in this country, in determining who are qualified to give testimony as experts in foreign law. In one case the Master of the Rolls refused to act on the affidavit of one describing himself as a " Solicitor practising in the Supreme Courts of Scotland, Edinburgh," and required the opinion of an advocate as to the Scotch law.⁶

¹ Milwaukee & St. Paul R. Co. v. Smith, 74 Ill. 197.
² Wilson v. Smith, 13 Tenn. 399.
³ McNeill v. Arnold, 17 Ark. 154, 167.
⁴ Dauphin v. United States, 6 Ct. of Claims, 221.
⁵ The Goods of Dost Aly Khan, 6 Prob. Div. (L. R.) 6.
⁶ *In re* Todd, 19 Beavan, 582. The opinions of Scotch advocates were

In 1861, the British Parliament passed a very wise and useful act, by which it was intended that all questions of foreign law should be referred to the courts of the foreign country to be there decided and certified back. The act as yet remains a dead letter, no action having been taken in accordance with its provisions for carrying it into effect. We give the enactment in the note below.[1]

§ 99. **Mere Knowledge of Foreign Law is Insufficient.**—It was held in an English case that one who was not a lawyer, and who had no special qualifications, but who had resided in Scotland for twenty years, and who swore that he was acquainted with the law of marriage, was competent to state what the Scotch law of marriage was.[2] It did not appear that the witness had any peculiar means of information as to the law. This case has been disap-

---

also received in Williams v. Williams, 3 Beavan, 547; and in Hitchcock v. Clendinen, 12 Beavan, 534.

[1] "If, in any action depending in any court of a foreign country, or State, with whose government Her Majesty shall have entered into a convention as above set forth (*i. e.*, for the purpose of mutually ascertaining the law), such court shall deem it expedient to ascertain the law applicable to the facts of the case as administered in any part of Her Majesty's dominions, and if the foreign court in which such action may depend, shall remit to the court in Her Majesty's dominions whose opinion is desired, a case setting forth the facts and questions of law arising out of the same, on which they desire to have the opinion of a court within Her Majesty's dominions, it shall be competent to any of the parties to the action to present a petition to such last mentioned court, whose opinion is to be obtained, praying such court to hear parties or their counsel, and to pronounce their opinion thereon in terms of this act, or to pronounce their opinion without hearing parties or counsel; and the court to which such petition shall be presented shall consider the same, and if they think fit, shall appoint an early day for hearing parties or their counsel on such case, and shall pronounce their opinion upon the questions of law, as administered by them, which are submitted to them by the foreign court; and in order to their pronouncing such opinion, they shall be entitled to take such further procedure thereupon as to them shall seem proper, and upon such opinion being pronounced, a copy thereof, certified by an officer of such court, shall be given to each of the parties to the action by whom the same shall be required." 24 & 25 Vict., c. 11. See Law Magazine and Review, London, May, 1882, and 8 Southern Law Review, 153.

[2] Regina v. Dent, 1 Car. & K. (47 E. C. L.) 96.

proved, and cannot be regarded as the law. In the *Sussex Peerage Case*, in the House of Lords, the Lord Chancellor, in speaking of this case, said; "I ought to say at once that it is the universal opinion both of the Judges and the Lords that the case is not law."[1]

§ 100. **Knowledge of the Foreign Law must have been Acquired where.**—It has been held in several cases, that where the knowledge of a witness produced as an expert in foreign law, has not been acquired in the foreign country, such person is not to be regarded as competent, and his testimony cannot be received. Thus, it has been held in England, that a witness was incompetent to testify, who stated that he was a jurisconsult, and adviser to the Prussian Consul in England, and had studied law in the University of Leipsic, and that from his studies there, he was able to say that the Code Napoleon was the law of Cologne. The court declared, that one who never had been in the foreign state, and whose knowledge of the law was not derived there, was incompetent to testify as an expert in the foreign law.[2] And where one described himself as "a certified special pleader, and as familiar with Italian law," he was not allowed to testify that the office of curator in Italy was as nearly as possible identical with that of an administrator in England, the ground for his exclusion being that there was nothing "to show that he had any knowledge of Italian law, but from the study of it in this country," (England).[3] So an English barrister practicing in Canadian Appeals before the Privy Council, has been held incompetent in England, to give evidence as an expert as to the validity, according to the law of Canada, of a marriage solemnized in that country.[4] But in this country, a witness who showed himself to be instructed in the laws, customs and usages of Spain, and who was a legal practitioner in the Island of

---

[1] 11 Cl. & F. 85, 134. And see Vander Donckt v. Thellusson, 8 Man. G. & S. (65 E. C. L.) 812, where Regina v. Dent, *supra*, is distinguished.
[2] Bristow v. Sequeville, 5 Excheq. 272.
[3] The Goods of Bonnelli, 1 Prob. Div. (L. R.) 69.
[4] Cartwright v. Cartwright, 26 W. R. 684.

Cuba, which is governed by Spanish law, was held competent to prove the law of Spain, although he never resided or practiced in the latter country.[1]

§ 101. **Right of Expert to Cite Text Books, Decisions, Codes, etc.**—Where a lawyer or expert in foreign law is allowed to testify as to the law, assuming it to be a resultant of the *lex scripta* and the *lex non-scripta*, he may confirm his recollection of the law, or assist his own knowledge by reference to text books, decisions, statutes, codes, or other legal documents. And if he describes them as truly stating the law, they may be read, not as evidence *per se*, but as part and parcel of his testimony.[2]

§ 102. **How these Citations are to be Regarded.**—It is said that in the first instance, at least, the judge can only regard the citations of the laws and authorities contained in the opinions of the experts, as connected with the testimony, and that he cannot consider them as at all important, except with regard to the degree of weight given by the testimony. That if he reads them, they may appear to him to accord with the testimony, or to differ from it. "If, in his view, they accord with it, nothing is gained. If, in his view, they differ from it, he, being ignorant of the foreign law, cannot weigh his opinion against the clear and uncontradicted opinion of the witness, whose opinion ought to be derived, not only from the citation in question, but from all the sources of his knowledge of the law of which he is speaking."[3] In the *Duchess Di Siora's case* in the House of Lords, Lord CHELMSFORD declares that it seems contrary to the nature of the proof required, that the judge should be at liberty to search for himself into the sources of knowledge from which the witnesses have drawn, and produce for himself the fact which is required to be proved as a part of the case.[4] But where the opinions of the ex-

---

[1] Molina v. United States, 6 Ct. of Claims, 269.
[2] 2 Taylor on Evidence, § 1423; Nelson v. Bridport, 8 Beavan. 527, 538; Sussex Peerage Case, 11 Cl. & Fin. 114, 117.
[3] Nelson v. Bridport, 8 Beavan, 527. 541.
[4] 10 House of Lords Cases, 640.

perts are contradictory, the court is at liberty to examine for itself, the laws and authorities cited by the witnesses as the basis or foundation for their opinions.[1] Where the jury are the judges of the law, they, of course, are not at liberty to enter upon any independent investigation, and must of necessity, weigh the evidence of the experts when it is conflicting, giving to it such consideration as they deem it deserves. In some cases it has been held that the foreign law is a question of fact for the jury,[2] but the weight of authority in this country seems to be in favor of the theory that it is a question for the court, and not for the jury.[3] But a distinction has been made between the written and unwritten law; and it has been held, that where the law is unwritten, it is a question of fact for the jury, but where a statute or judicial decision is involved, the question of construction and effect is for the court.[4]

§ 103. **Testimony as to Usage and Practice of Courts of Another State.** — Lawyers are permitted to testify in the courts of another State, as to the usage and practice of the courts in the State in which they practice.[5] In the case cited, the depositions of lawyers and judges of Rhode Island were received in the courts of Massachusetts, to show that the service of a writ of arrest in the manner set forth in the officer's return, was a good and valid service under the practice and usage of the courts of Rhode Island, giving the courts of that State jurisdiction, and that a judgment concluded on such service would be valid there. It amounted to proof of the unwritten law. But the rule allowing

---

[1] Trimbey v. Vigner, 1 Bingham (N. S.) 158; Bremer v. Freeman, 10 Moore, P. C. 306.

[2] De Sobry v. Laistre, 2 H. & J. 191; Ingham v. Hart, 11 Ohio, 255; Holman v. King, 7 Met. 384.

[3] Sidwell v. Evans, 1 P. & W. (Penn.) 383; Ripple v. Ripple, 1 Rawle (Penn.), 386; Bock v. Lauman, 12 Harris (Penn.), 435; Inge v. Murphy, 10 Ala. 885; Hooper v. Moore, 5 Jones Law (N. C.) 130; Newell v. Newell, 9 Miss. 58.

[4] Ely v. James, 123 Mass. 36; Kline v. Baker, 99 Mass. 254. See Moore v. Guyner, 5 Me. 187.

[5] Mowry v. Chase, 100 Mass. 79.

experts to testify, does not enable a party to call lawyers to testify what is the practice of the profession, under a certain statute of the State, for the purpose of guiding the judge in the construction to be given to it, the question arising in the courts of the State which enacted the statute.[1]

§ 104. **Testimony as to Powers and Obligations of an Attorney in his Relations to his Clients.**—It is error to receive the opinions of lawyers as to the rights and duties of an attorney as between himself and his client.[2] In the particular case, it was held error to receive the opinions of such witnesses as to whether, in a certain state of facts, an attorney should, as a matter of course and of duty, have moved for a reference, and whether he had or had not a right, in the discharge of his legal and proper duty, to open a default.

[1] Gaylor's Appeal, 43 Conn. 82.
[2] Clussman v. Merkel, 3 Bosw. 402, 409.

CHAPTER VI.

EXPERT TESTIMONY IN THE TRADES AND ARTS.

SECTION.
105. Nautical Experts.
106. Nautical Experts—The Subject Continued.
107. Railroad Experts.
108. Railroad Experts—The Subject Continued.
109. Experts in Insurance.
110. Experts in Insurance—The Subject Continued.
111. Gardeners, Farmers and Stock Raisers.
112. Millers and Millwrights.
113. Surveyors and Civil Engineers.
114. Surveyors and Civil Engineers—The Subject Continued.
115. Machinists.
116. Mechanics, Masons and Master Builders.
117. Experts in Patent, Trade Mark and Copyright Cases.
118. Painters and Photographers.
119. Lumbermen.
120. Translation by Experts of Writings from a Foreign Language.
121. Expert Testimony as to Technical Terms and Unusual Words.
122. Expert Testimony as to Technical Terms and Unusual Words—The Subject Continued.
123. Expert Testimony as to Usage.
124. Opinions of Experts in Miscellaneous Cases.
125. Opinions of Experts in Miscellaneous Cases—The Subject Continued.
126. Opinions of Experts in Miscellaneous Cases—The Subject Continued.

§ 105. **Nautical Experts.**—The opinions of persons engaged in the navigation of vessels and boats are received on questions pertaining to nautical science. "Such men form their opinions from facts within their own experience, and not from theory or abstract reasoning. They come, therefore, even more properly within the definition of experts than men of mere science."[1] Their opinions have been received as to the seaworthiness of vessels;[2] as to what caused a vessel to leak;[3] as to the soundness of a chain cable;[4] as to the possibility of avoiding a collision by the use of proper care on the part of the officers and crew of one of the vessels;[5] as to whether a port could have been made by skillful management;[6] as to whether a vessel was stranded through unskillful and careless management, or inevitable accident;[7] as to the proper mode and time of changing the fastening of boats in a tow;[8] as to whether it would be safe or prudent for a tugboat, on any wide water, to tug three boats abreast, with a high wind;[9] and also as to the practical effect produced on a ship by cross seas and heavy swells, shifting winds and sudden squalls.[10] Experienced river navigators, who knew both boats, have been allowed to testify as to what would be the probable effect on one boat of the waves or swells of another and very large boat—that it would have a tendency to open the seams of the outriggers, and cause the caulking to fall out, which would have a tendency to let water in.[11] The opinions of

[1] Delaware etc. Steam Towboat Co. v. Starrs, 69 Penn. St. 36, 41.
[2] Beckwith v. Sydebotham, 1 Camp. 117; Baird v. Daly, 68 N. Y. 548; Patchin v. Astor Mutual Ins. Co., 13 N. Y. 268; Western Ins. Co. v. Tobin, 32 Ohio St. 77, 94. The certificate of a marine surveyor and inspector, made in the course of his business, is competent evidence of seaworthiness at that time, if supported by his oath that he examined the vessel, and has no doubt that the facts stated in it are true, although he has no independent recollection of the facts. Perkins v. Augusta Ins. Co., 10 Gray, 312.
[3] Parsons v. Manuf. etc. Ins. Co., 16 Gray, 463. See too, Zugasti v. Lamer, 12 Moore, P. C. 331, 336.
[4] Reed v. Dick, 8 Watts (Penn.), 479.
[5] Jameson v. Drinkald, 12 Moore, 148; Fenwick v. Bell, 1 Car. & Kir. (47 Eng. C. L. 311,) 312; Carpenter v. Eastern Transportation Co., 71 N. Y. 574.
[6] Dolz v. Morris, 17 N. Y. Sup. Ct. 202, 203.
[7] New England Glass Co. v. Lovell, 7 Cush. (Mass.) 319, 322.
[8] Delaware etc. Steam Towboat Co. v. Starrs, 69 Penn. St. 36, 41.
[9] Transportation Line v. Hope, 95 U. S. 297.
[10] Walsh v. Washington Marine Ins. Co., 32 N. Y. 427.
[11] Western Ins. Co. v. Tobin, 32 Ohio St. 77, 97.

nautical experts have also been received as to the proper management of a ship.[1] And experienced navigators who were acquainted with the nature and extent of obstructions in the waters navigated, and the dangerous character of their navigation, have been held competent to express an opinion as to the probable cause of the loss of a vessel.[2] In cases of collision, where the question is as to the direction from which the blow appeared to have come, the opinions of nautical experts have also been received.[3] In the case cited, the court say: "It may easily be perceived how an experienced boatman could judge of the direction of the body in motion, that displaced a portion of the plank and timbers of the injured vessel, as a surgeon can tell from what quarter a blow has been aimed that inflicts a wound upon the person; but a mere description of the broken fragments, in the one case, or the lacerated integuments in the other, will seldom, if ever, enable a jury to say how the disturbing cause made its approach."

§ 106. **Nautical Experts — The Subject Continued.** — Nautical experts may be permitted to testify as to what is a full cargo for a ship to carry with safety,[4] and to express an opinion as to the effect of a deck load upon the safety of a vessel.[5] They have been allowed to state that the opening of the garboard seam in a vessel was due to the working of the stem.[6] Upon the question of negligence in mooring a vessel, the ship's keeper has been held competent to testify as an expert, as to the conditions of the fastenings of the vessel as to safety.[7] A shipwright who has examined a decayed vessel may give his opinion, founded on the condition of the timbers at the time of his examination, whether a person could have removed a part of the "thick streak"

---

[1] Guiterman v. Liverpool etc. Steamship Co., 83 N. Y. 358.
[2] Western Ins. Co. v. Tobin, 32 Ohio St. 77, 92.
[3] Steamboat v. Logan, 18 Ohio, 375. And see Zugas i v. Lamer, 12 Moore, P. C. 331, 336..
[4] Ogden v. Parsons, 23 How. 167.
[5] Lapham v. Atlas Ins. Co. 24 Pick. (Mass.) 1.
[6] Paddock v. Commonwealth Ins. Co., 104 Mass. 521, 529.
[7] Moore v. Westervelt, 9 Bos. (N. Y.) 559.

some months before, without discovering that the timber under it was decayed.[1] The opinions of nautical experts are admissible as to the necessity of a jettison,[2] and upon the question whether an injured boat was worth repairing.[3] But it has been held that one experienced in raising sunken boats and repairing them, and who was acquainted with the boat in question, could not express an opinion as to what would be the expense of raising and repairing it; that he might state the particulars, but the jury should compute the expense, as it was a matter not lying peculiarly within the knowledge of experts.[4] On the other hand, one who had worked in a shipyard, and been the owner of vessels, has been permitted to testify as to the difference in value of a vessel as repaired, and what her value would have been, if repaired according to contract.[5] And an expert in the wrecking business has been allowed to state whether a sunken tug, which he had examined, could be raised as a whole, and to express an opinion as to its value when raised in comparison with the cost of raising it.[6] Sailing rules and regulations, prescribed by law, of course, furnish the paramount rule of decision upon questions of navigation. But where in any case, a disputed question of navigation arises, in regard to which neither the law nor the rules of the court regulating admiralty practice have made provision, then the evidence of nautical experts is admissible as to the general usage in such cases.[7] Experienced navigators and masters of vessels have been permitted to express an opinion that, a deposit of coin under the ballast, or under the cargo, was unusual, and increased the hazards and risk of loss to which the coin was exposed.[8] So one who has fol-

---

[1] Cook v. Castner, 9 Cush. (Mass.) 266.
[2] Price v. Hartshorn, 44 N. Y. 94.
[3] Steamboat v. Logan, 18 Ohio. 375.
[4] Paige v. Hazard. 5 Hill (N. Y.) 604.
[5] Sikes v. Paine, 10 Ired. (N. C.) Law, 282.
[6] Blanchard v. New Jersey Steamboat Co., 3 N. Y. Sup. Ct. 771.
[7] The City of Washington, 92 U. S. 31.
[8] Leitch v. Atlantic Mutual Ins. Co., 66 N. Y. 100, 106; s. c., 5 Ins. L. J. 775.

lowed the sea for forty years has been allowed to express an opinion as to whether an article was properly stowed on a boat.[1] "What is a competent crew for the voyage; at what time such crews should be on board; what is proper pilot ground; what is the course and usage of trade in relation to the master and crew being on board, when the ship breaks ground for the voyage; are questions of fact dependent on nautical testimony."[2]

A pilot who knew the place of the disaster, and the pilot in charge of the boat at the time, have been held competent to testify as to whether it was proper to suffer the pilot to pilot the boat at the time and place of the accident.[3] And a mate of a steamboat who had been engaged eight or ten years in navigation, and who saw the collision in question, has been allowed to testify that the sunken boat was not carrying a proper light at the time of the accident.[4] But one who is not an expert is incompetent to express an opinion as to the seaworthiness of a floating dock.[5] Where it was claimed that the length of the shaft caused a boat to settle by the stern, and the journals to heat and bind, it was held that an expert could be asked whether the boat settled more than it ought to, or than was usual.[6] In the same case it was held that an expert could not be allowed to express an opinion as to the course which the owner of a steamer ought, as a prudent man, to take as to the laying up for examination and repairs on discovering defects in the engine.

§ 107. **Railroad Experts.**—The running and management of railroad locomotives and trains is said to be so far an art, outside of the experience and knowledge of ordinary jurors, as to render the opinions of persons skilled therein admissible, such opinions being in the nature of expert

[1] Price v. Powell, 3 N. Y. 322.
[2] McLanahan v. Universal Ins. Co., 1 Peters, 170, 183, per Mr. Justice Story.
[3] Hill v. Sturgeon, 28 Mo. 323.
[4] Weaver v. Alabama, etc. Co., 35 Ala. 176.
[5] Marcy v. Sun Ins. Co., 11 La. Ann. 748.
[6] Clark v. Detroit Locomotive Works, 32 Mich. 348.

testimony.[1] Such witnesses have been permitted to testify within what distance such a train as that in question could be stopped with ordinary brakes, on an ascending grade, running at such a rate that a man could run faster than the train was going.[2] And it has been held that a person not connected with the management of a train of cars, but who had been for a long time in positions enabling him to observe the effect of checking a train, is competent to express an opinion as to how fast a train should have been moving at a certain point to be stopped at the usual place.[3] A locomotive engineer can testify as to the speed that is usual and considered safe in "backing" an engine drawing a train after dark; that he can state the effect of an engine striking an animal, when running backward, and that he may explain the structure of a locomotive tender.[4] An engineer in charge of a train of cars has been permitted to express an opinion as to the possibility of avoiding an injury to animals, struck by the locomotive, the opinion being given in view of the distance between the animals and the train, when the former came upon the track.[5] One who testified that he had charge of a stationary steam engine, and who did not claim to be a practical engineer, or a first class locomotive engineer, but who had fired and handled a locomotive, and understood an engine, has been held competent to testify as an expert, as to the effect of a leaky throttle valve upon the handling and operation of a locomotive.[6]

§ 108. Railroad Experts — The Subject Continued — A machinist connected many years with railroads has been held competent to express an opinion as to what threw a train of cars from the track.[7] Railroad conductors are competent to testify as to the means of stopping a train of

[1] Bellefontaine, etc. R. R. Co. v. Bailey, 11 Ohio St. 333, 335.
[2] Mott v. Hudson River R. R. Co., 8 Bos. (N. Y.) 345.
[3] Detroit, etc. R. R. Co. v. Van Steinburgh, 17 Mich. 99.
[4] Cooper v. Central Railroad of Iowa, 44 Iowa, 140.
[5] Bellefontaine, etc. R. R. Co. v. Bailey, 11 Ohio St. 333.
[6] Brabbitts v. Chicago & N. W. Ry. Co., 38 Wis. 289.
[7] Seaver v. Boston, etc. R. R. Co. 14 Gray (Mass.) 466.

cars.[1] Persons skilled in the running of railroad trains may be asked as experts, upon an assumed state of facts, whether in the case assumed, the brakemen were in their proper places.[2] The opinion of a railroad superintendent, upon a matter within the scope of his employment, " stands upon the footing of an opinion of an expert."[3] The road master of a railroad, whose duty it was to receive and inspect ties, has been allowed to testify as to the quality of certain railroad ties.[4]

Where the question was whether a rail was defective, or whether it had been maliciously cut, a newspaper editor, who had visited the scene of the accident for the purpose of reporting it, and had testified that during a period of twenty years he had visited " dozens of railroad accidents," and had examined them for the purpose of reporting the probable cause of the accident, was asked to state whether he had arrived at any conclusion as to the cause of the accident. The court held that it was no error to exclude his opinion.[5] And where the question was whether a certain accident would have been avoided provided there had been guard chains attached to the cars, the opinion of a railroad conductor was rejected, because, so far as the subject matter of inquiry was concerned, he " was not an expert, and had no peculiar knowledge on the subject."[6] So it has been held that a witness of long railroad experience cannot be allowed to testify whether the blowing of a steam-whistle was, under the circumstances of the case, prudent.[7] It has been held no error to refuse the testimony of switchmen to show that in their opinion it was not necessary for another switchman to have been where he was when he received the injury complained of. The opinions of the witnesses, though experts, were inadmissible as the subject matter of inquiry did

[1] Mobile, etc. R. R. Co. v. Blakeley, 59 Ala. 471.
[2] Cincinnati, etc. R. R. Co. Smith, 22 Ohio St. 227.
[3] Mason, etc. R. R. Co. v. Johnson, 38 Ga. 409.
[4] Jeffersonville R. R. Co. v. Lanham, 27 Ind. 171.
[5] Hoyt v. Long Island R. R. Co., 57 N. Y. 678.
[6] Bixby v. Montpelier, etc. R. R. Co., 49 Vt. 125.
[7] Hill v. Portland etc. R. R. Co., 55 Me. 438.

not partake of the nature of a science so as to require a course of previous habit or study to an attainment of a knowledge of it.[1] Other instances have been elsewhere given, where the testimony of railroad experts has been rejected for the same reason.[2] It has been held that railroad engineers or constructors are not the only persons competent to give an opinion as to how the running off of cars on the inside of a curve, instead of the outside, could be accounted for; but that *prima facie* the question could be answered by any person acquainted with the elementary principles of mechanism, and experts only in that branch of science.[3] One who had been the president of two or three city railroads, and had been engaged for some years in building such roads, has been allowed to give his opinion as to whether a street rail had been properly laid.[4]

§ 109. **Experts in Insurance.**— There has been a decided conflict of authority, both in this country and in England, on the right of underwriters, and others skilled in the business of insurance, to testify as to the materiality of concealed facts in applications for insurance. So marked has been the conflict of authority on this question in England, that one of the most eminent of the English writers on the law of evidence declares that no satisfactory answer can be given to it.[5] We believe, however, that the better rule is to consider the admissibility of such evidence as dependent on the nature of the facts concealed. It is evident that those facts may be of such a nature that ordinary jurymen would be perfectly competent to decide the question of their materiality, in which case there would be no justification for the admission of expert testimony. On the other hand, the facts may be so special and technical in their nature, especially in questions of marine insurance, that persons without previous experience in the business of insur-

---

[1] Pennsylvania Co. v. Conlan, 101 Ill. 93.
[2] See § 8, p. 14.
[3] Murphy v. New York, etc. R. R. Co., 66 Barb. 125.
[4] Carpenter v. Central Park etc. R. R. Co., 11 Abb. Pr. (N. S.) 416.
[5] 2 Taylor's Evid., 1420.

ance would be unable, from the very nature of the case, to arrive at any intelligent conclusion, in which case it seems that there would exist a necessity for the admission of expert testimony.[1]

As Mr. Justice RANNEY expressed it in a case decided in Ohio as long ago as 1853: "If the answer can be given from ordinary experience and knowledge, the jury must respond to it unaided; if the effects of such a cause are only known to persons of skill, and are to be determined only by the application of some principle of science or art, such persons may give the results of their own investigation and experience to the jury in the way of opinions, the better to enable them to come to a correct conclusion." [2]

So another distinction may be noted. It is held in Massachusetts that the testimony of experts, skilled in the business of insurance, that it increased the risk to allow a building to stand unoccupied, is inadmissible, as being a fact within the common experience and knowledge of men in general,[3] but that whether such a change in the occupation was material to the risk may be tested by the question whether underwriters generally would charge a higher premium.[4] "That," says Mr. Justice GRAY, "being a matter within the peculiar knowledge of persons versed in the business of insurance, testimony of such persons upon that point is admissible." [5]

And when the testimony of underwriters is received as to the materiality of facts, the question is not as to the effect which such facts, if disclosed, would have had on the particular witness, but on underwriters generally. "I do not allow you to ask the witness what he himself, as an underwriter, would have done; but whether, from his knowledge of the business, he is able to state that the facts in question would or would not have an influence with underwriters generally

[1] See 5 Am. Law Review, 237; 1 Arnold's Ins. 573; 2 Duer's Ins. 780, n; 1 Smith's Lead. Cas. 490, n; Hill v. Lafayette Ins. Co., 2 Mich. 476.
[2] Hartford Protection Co. v. Harmer, 2 Ohio St. 452, 457.
[3] Mulry v. Mohawk Valley Ins. Co., 5 Gray (Mass.), 545.
[4] Merriam v. Middlesex Ins. Co., 21 Pick. (Mass.) 162.
[5] Luce v. Dorchester Ins. Co., 105 Mass. 297.

in determining the amount of the premiums. If his knowledge and skill in this particular business does enable him to state this, I think it is legal evidence. * * * Here the inquiry is, in substance, whether the market value price of insurance is affected by particular facts. If the witness, being conversant with the business, has gained in the course of his employment a knowledge of the practical effect of these facts, or similar facts, upon premiums, he may inform the jury what it is."[1]

When the question is as to the materiality of concealed facts other witnesses than those experienced in insurance may be competent. For instance, in the case of life insurance, if the fact concealed were some bodily infirmity, it would certainly be competent to receive the testimony of medical experts on the question whether such infirmity was calculated to shorten the life of the insured. Or in the case of marine insurance it would be proper to receive the testimony of experienced mariners or ship carpenters on the question whether the defect was such as to endanger the safety of the ship.[2] And it has been laid down that insurance agents cannot be called as experts to prove what in their opinion would or would not be an increase of risk in a building, merely because they are insurance agents, unless it appears that in the course of their business they have acquired special knowledge upon the subject.[3]

§ 110. **Experts in Insurance—The Subject Continued.** —We have already stated that there is a conflict of authority as to the right to receive the testimony of experts in insurance, as to the materiality of concealed facts. However doubtful the question may be in England, we think the weight of authority is in favor of the reception of such evidence in this country, at least, in those cases in which the facts are

[1] Hawes v. N. E. Ins. Co., 2 Curtis C. C. 229. And see Berthon v. Loughman, 2 Starkie, 258, per Holroyd, J.; Hartman v. Keystone Ins. Co., 21 Penn. St. 466.

[2] Hartford Protection Co. v. Harmer, 2 Ohio St. 452, 457; Leitch v. Atlantic Mutual Ins. Co., 66 N. Y., 100.

[3] Schmidt v. Peoria, etc. Ins. Co., 41 Ill. 296; s. c., 5 Benn. Fire Ins. Cases, 90.

so technical and special, as not to lie within the common observation of men in general. We can do no more than to refer below to the cases in which the testimony of experts in insurance has been held inadmissible,[1] and those in which there has been a contrary ruling.[2] We may observe, however, that while in Massachusetts[3] and in Maine[4] experts are not allowed to testify directly to the fact, whether an unoccupied building is a more hazardous risk than one occupied, yet such testimony is received in New York[5] and Missouri.[6] Underwriters have been allowed to testify in New York, that the occupation of premises for certain purposes increased the risk,[7] and as to whether a livery stable is more exposed to conflagration, and a more hazardous risk, than a tavern barn.[8] So in Massachusetts, evidence has been received as to whether the existence of a partition in a story of a building, increased the risk.[9] In New

[1] Carter v. Boehm, 2 Burr. 1905; Durrell v. Bederly, Holt, N. P. Cases, 283; Campbell v. Rickards, 5 Barn. & Ad. 840; Milwaukee etc. R. R. Co. v. Kellogg, 94 U. S. 469; Hartford Protection Ins. Co. v. Harmer, 2 Ohio St. 452; Jefferson Ins. Co. v. Cotheal, 7 Wend. 72; Hill v. Lafayette Ins. Co., 2 Mich. 476; s. c., 3 Benn. Fire Ins. Cas. 325; Summers v. U. S. Ins. Co., 13 La. Ann. 504; s. c., 1 Bigelow Ins. Cas. 131.

[2] Seaman v. Fonerau, 2 Strange, 1183; Chaurand v. Angerstein, Peake N. P. C. 61; Haywood v. Rodgers, 4 East. 590; Littledale v. Dixon, 1 Bos. & Pul. 151; Rickards v. Murdock, 10 B. & C. 527; Elton v. Larkins, 5 C. & P. 385; Berthon v. Loughman, 2 Starkie, 258; Quinn v. National etc. Ins. Co., 1 Jones & Carey (Ir.) 316; s. c., 1 Benn. Fire Ins. Cas. 689; Hawes v. N. E. Ins. Co., 2 Curtis, C. C. 229; Moses v. Delaware Ins. Co., 1 Wash. C. C. 385; Marshall v. Union Ins. Co., 2 Wash. C. C. 357; Luce v. Dorchester Ins. Co., 105 Mass. 297; Daniels v. Hudson River Fire Ins. Co., 12 Cush. (Mass.) 416; Kern v. South St. Louis Mutual Ins. Co., 40 Mo. 19; Cornish v. Farm Buildings Fire Ins. Co., 74 N. Y. 295; Hobby v. Dana, 17 Barb. (N. Y.) 111; s. c., 3 Benn. Fire Ins. Cas. 581; M'Lanahan v. Universal Ins. Co., 1 Peters, 170, 187; Hartman v. Keystone Ins. Co., 21 Penn. St. 466.

[3] Mulry v. Mohawk Valley Ins. Co., 5 Gray, 545.

[4] Cannell v. Phoenix Ins. Co., 59 Me. 582; Joyce v. Maine Ins. Co., 45 Me. 168; State v. Watson, 65 Me. 74, 77; Thayer v. Providence Ins. Co., 70 Me. 539.

[5] See Cornish v. Farm Buildings Ins. Co., 74 N. Y. 295.

[6] Kern v. South St. Louis Mutual Ins. Co., 40 Mo. 19.

[7] Appleby v. Astor Fire Ins. Co., 54 N. Y. 253.

[8] Hobby v. Dana, 17 Barb. 111.

[9] Daniels v. Hudson River Fire Ins. Co., 12 Cush. 416.

Jersey, it has been held that a witness who was an experienced and practical fireman, could testify, whether in his opinion, the risk from fire was increased by certain alterations in a building.[1] In Pennsylvania, an insurance company's clerk has been allowed to testify that a risk would not be taken at any premium, on the life of one known to be engaged in a certain occupation.[2] In the case last cited, Mr. Chief Justice BLACK said: "But though the cases conflict seriously, I think none of them go so far as to say that one who knows the practice, not only of the particular office, but of insurance offices generally, may not give his opinion of the influence which a given fact would have had as an element in the contract. Certainly this is the opinion supported by the strongest authority and the best reasons." But in New York it has been held improper to prove by experts, that a person who was in the habitual use of intoxicating liquors, would not be considered an insurable subject.[3] It has been held in the Supreme Court of the United States, that experts in fire insurance, accustomed to estimating and calculating the hazard and exposures to fire from one building to another, could not testify that, owing to the distance between an elevator and a mill, and the distance between an elevator and some lumber piles, the elevator would not be considered as an exposure to the mill, and would not be considered in fixing a rate thereon, or in measuring the hazard of the mill or lumber.[4] In New York, it has been held that a medical examiner of an insurance company could not be asked as to what effect certain assumed facts would have had upon his answer to the propriety of taking the risk, if he had been advised of them.[5] And in a recent case in Indiana, it was held that insurance agents, being experts in the business of insurance, could be asked as to what

[1] Schenck v. Mercer Co. Mutual Ins. Co., 24 N. J. Law, 431; s. c., 3 Benn. Fire Ins. Cas. 714.
[2] Hartman v. Keystone Ins. Co., 21 Penn. St. 466.
[3] Rawls v. Am. Mut. Life Ins. Co., 27 N. Y. 282.
[4] Milwaukee etc. R. R. Co. v. Kellogg, 94 U. S. 469. And see State v. Watson, 65 Me. 74.
[5] Higbie v. Guardian Mutual Life Ins. Co., 53 N. Y. 603.

would be a reasonable time for an insurance agent to hold an agency for which he paid a consideration, no time having been fixed at the date of the appointment.[1]

§ 111. **Gardeners, Farmers and Stock Raisers.**—A witness who had used guano on all kinds of garden and field plants and crops, and who had closely and critically watched its effects, has been held competent to testify as to the proper method of using such fertilizers, and as to what would prevent them from acting beneficially.[2] A gardener and a farmer, who had attended to and practiced the draining of lands for the purpose of making them productive, have been held competent to testify to their opinion as experts, whether a certain piece of land, examined by and known to them, required draining to put it in fit condition for cropping.[3] The opinion of a gardener has been received as to the damage done to a garden and nursery by the smoke from a brick kiln.[4] The opinion of a farmer that a wagon loaded with hay in a certain manner was not safe to ride upon over ordinary roads, has been held inadmissible. The jury were competent to determine the question from the facts stated.[5] But the opinions of farmers have been received as to how many bushels of corn there would have been on certain land on which cattle had trespassed, had it not been for such trespass.[6] So it has been held that a farmer could be asked, " taking that hay as it stood then, what would it yield to the acre?" " A person," said the court, " conversant with the growth of grass, and accustomed to compare its appearance in different stages of such growth with its ultimate yield to the acre, may well be said to have such knowledge of that subject as to make him competent to testify how much, in his opinion, a given piece examined by him, will yield per acre. * * * The principle

[1] Niagara Ins. Co. v. Greene, 77 Ind. 595.
[2] Young v. O'Neal, 57 Ala. 566.
[3] Buffum v. Harris, 5 R. I. 250.
[4] Vandine v. Burpee, 13 Met. (Mass.) 288.
[5] Bills v. City of Ottawa, 35 Iowa, 109.
[6] Sickles v. Gould, 51 How. Pr. (N. Y.) 25; Seamans v. Smith, 46 Barb. (N. Y.) 320; Keith v. Tilford, 12 Neb. 271, 275.

is the same as that on which the opinion of an expert is received. The farmer, acquainted with the subject matter of such an inquiry as this under consideration, is an *expert*, and unless the witness has the peculiar knowledge which constitutes him an expert, his opinions would be excluded."[1] Farmers and dairymen have been held competent to express an opinion as to the adulteration of milk.[2] A farmer experienced in clearing up land has been allowed in New York to testify whether a fire was set on land at a proper time.[3] But in Vermont the court has held that the opinions of farmers who saw the fire set, and testified to its position, and to the force and direction of the wind, were inadmissible on the question whether the day on which the fire was set was a suitable and safe day.[4] It has been held in Minnesota that the opinion of a farmer experienced in clearing land was admissible, where the question was as to how many feet in width it would be necessary to plow to stop a fire on stubble land.[5] It has been held in Massachusetts that the opinion of a farmer was inadmissible on the question whether there was a liability that a fire set under certain circumstances would have spread to adjoining land.[6]

One who had experience as an overseer of a plantation, for some five or six years, has been held qualified as an expert to express an opinion that the overseer of another plantation had "managed pretty well."[7] And one who had served as overseer of a plantation for sixteen months, has been held competent, as an expert, to testify as to the amount of food which was sufficient for a plantation slave.[8]

The opinions of men, engaged in raising stock, and accustomed to riding through the same range in quest of

[1] Phillips v. Terry, 3 Abb. N. Y. Decis. 607, 609.
[2] Lane v. Wilcox, 55 Barb. (N. Y.) 615.
[3] Ferguson v. Hubbell, 26 Hun (N. Y.), 250.
[4] Fraser v. Tupper, 29 Vt. 409.
[5] Kipner v. Biebl (Sup. Ct. of Minn.), Alb. L. J., Sept. 3d, 1881.
[6] Higgins v. Dewey, 107 Mass. 494.
[7] Spiva v. Stapleton, 38 Ala. 171.
[8] Cheek v. State, 38 Ala. 227.

stock, have been received as to the number of stock of a particular brand running in the range.¹ And in a recent case in Texas it was held that an expert could testify as to the topography of the country, the number of cattle frequenting it, and whether they were wild or gentle, but that he could not testify as to the length of time which would be required to gather a certain number of cattle within the limits of a given range.² The opinions of experienced graziers have been received as to the condition of cattle, and as to the causes which affect their health and weight.³ Persons experienced in weighing cattle are permitted to express an opinion as to the weight of cattle.⁴ A stock raiser has been allowed to testify as to the damage done to cattle by falling through a wharf.⁵ And a shepherd will be permitted to give an opinion as to the age of a sheep, judging from its teeth,⁶ and so in respect to the age of a horse, or other animal, experienced persons will be permitted to express an opinion as to his age, from an examination of his mouth and the observation of other signs.⁷

§ 112. **Millers and Millwrights.**— Persons who have for many years been engaged in building and carrying on mills are qualified as experts, and entitled to give an opinion touching matters connected with their experience.⁸ The opinions of millers and millwrights have been received as to the quantity of grain a certain mill was capable of grinding, as to the value of the water for milling purposes, and as to the accuracy of the method of weighing and measuring adopted in the mill.⁹ A practical and professional millwright, who had taken the levels of the water and the

---

[1] Albright v. Corley, 40 Texas, 105.
[2] Tyler v. State, 11 Texas Ct. of App. 388.
[3] Baltimore, etc. R. R. Co. v. Thompson, 10 Md. 76.
[4] McCormick v. Hamilton, 23 Gratt. (Va.) 561; Carpenter v. Wait, 11 Cush. (Mass.) 257.
[5] Polk v. Coffin, 9 Cal. 56.
[6] Clague v. Hodgson, 16 Minn. 329.
[7] See Moreland v. Mitchell County, 40 Iowa, 401.
[8] Hammond v. Woodman, 41 Me. 177.
[9] Read v. Barker, 30 N. J. Law, 378; s. c., 32 Ib. 477.

water-wheel, has been permitted to testify that if the mill dam was a foot lower than it was, it would be impossible for the mill to grind in a proper manner.[1] Upon an issue as to the fitness of a shoal for a mill site, the opinions of millwrights have been received.[2] But it has been held that a witness may testify to the existence of a mill site without being an expert.[3] Where the identity of wheat was material, a miller and grower of wheat who was familiar with the different varieties, was permitted to testify that when his wheat was cut early it had a peculiar smell; that the wheat stolen had been cut early; that the grain found in the possession of the defendant had the same odor as that in the hogshead from which the grain had been stolen; and therefore that his opinion was that the wheat alleged to have been stolen was part of the wheat originally in his possession.[4] But where the question related to the freezing up of a mill, the court excluded the opinion of a millwright and a tender of mills, who had an experience of fourteen years, that a mill dam on one side of the river being some twenty rods further up the stream than the dam upon the other side, would "make it bad as regards anchor ice," and "that the dams being situated as they are, the anchor ice would naturally fall into the dead or still water." The court thought that it did not appear that his calling gave him means not ordinarily possessed by other persons of forming the opinion expressed.[5] Where the question was as to the skillfulness of work done on a mill, it was held that the opinion of a millwright was admissible, but not that of a miller.[6] And in an action for the rent of a mill, under a lease which provided that the lessor should put the mill in good running order, it was held competent to inquire of a millwright whether certain additions and repairs were neces-

---

[1] Detweiler v. Groff, 10 Penn. St. 376.
[2] Haas v. Choussard, 17 Texas, 592.
[3] Claggett v. Easterday, 42 Md. 617.
[4] Walker v. State, 58 Ala. 393.
[5] Woods v. Allen, 18 N. H. 28.
[6] Walker v. Fields, 28 Ga. 237.

sary to put the mill in such condition.¹ One who for a number of years had been the owner of mills has been permitted to give his opinion as to the capacity of a person as a millwright.²

§ 113. **Surveyors and Civil Engineers.**— A surveyor, who is familiar with the peculiar marks used by the government surveyors in their public surveys, may give his opinion as an expert whether a particular line was marked by them.³ The opinion of a practical surveyor has been received as to whether certain piles of stones, and marks on trees were monuments of boundary.⁴ And in a contest as to the true location of lines between adjacent lot owners, a practical surveyor, who has made an actual survey and plat of the lots, has been allowed to testify as to the correctness of the plat, and to state the result of his survey as to the location of the lines, and of the buildings and fences on the lots with reference to such lines.⁵ Upon a question as to the boundary line between two counties, which had never been officially located,⁶ it has been held that while the opinion of a surveyor was competent evidence to show that certain marks on a tree, claimed as a corner, were corner or line marks, yet it could not be received for the purpose of showing that the tree was the corner of a particular grant.⁷ While in an early case it was held that the opinion of a surveyor was admissible as to a mistake in a survey,⁸ and where he would locate a warrant similar to that under which a person held,⁹ yet the rule is that the opinion of a surveyor is not evidence as to the construction to be given to a survey;¹⁰ that he cannot be permitted to give his

¹ Taylor v. The French Lumbering Co., 47 Iowa, 662; Cooke v. England, 27 Md. 14.
² Doster v. Brown, 25 Ga. 24.
³ Brantly v. Swift, 24 Ala. 390.
⁴ Davis v. Mason, 4 Pick. 156; Knox v. Clark, 123 Mass. 216.
⁵ Messer v. Reginnitter, 32 Iowa, 312.
⁶ Kinley v. Crane, 34 Penn. St. 146.
⁷ Clegg v. Fields, 7 Jones (N. C.) Law, 37.
⁸ Forbes v. Caruthers, 3 Yeates, 527.
⁹ Farr v. Swan, 2 Penn. St. 245.
¹⁰ Ormsby v. Ihmsen, 34 Penn. St. 462.

opinion as to what are the controlling calls of a deed,[1] the proper location of a grant.[2] The title to property claimed under a recorded plat cannot be unsettled by the testimony of a surveyor who has scaled the plat, that the scale is incorrect.[3] Nor is the opinion of an examiner of titles admissible to fix the location in case of conflicting and doubtful lines.[4] "Experts cannot be called to give their opinions on a subject of this character. Witnesses are competent to show lines and measurements, but the construction of written instruments is for the court alone."[5] It has been held that one who had been occasionally employed as a surveyor in laying out and grading, but not in constructing highways was not competent to testify as an expert as to the safety of a highway.[6]

§ 114. **Surveyors and Civil Engineers — The Subject Continued.** — The opinion of civil engineers, experienced in the construction of bridges, has been received as to the strength of construction and safety of a bridge.[7] And a civil engineer, experienced in judging of the soundness of timbers in bridges, has been allowed to express an opinion as to whether one of the sleepers in a bridge had rotted recently, or whether the decay was of some length of time.[8] A civil engineer and surveyor, who had made a survey and map of the land in question has been allowed to testify how much ground would be overflowed at a given height of water.[9] Such witnesses have also been permitted to state the rules for the construction of cuts and embankments.[10] While in a controversy as to what constituted an approach

[1] Whittlesey v. Kellogg, 28 Mo. 404.
[2] Schultz v. Lindell, 30 Mo. 310; Blumenthal v. Roll, 24 Mo. 113; Randolph v. Adams, 2 W. Va. 519.
[3] Twogood v. Hoyt, 42 Mich. 609.
[4] Public Schools v. Risley's Heirs, 40 Mo. 356.
[5] Norment v. Fastnaght, 1 McArthur, 515.
[6] Lincoln v. Inhabitants of Barre, 5 Cush. (Mass.) 590.
[7] Hart v. Hudson River Bridge Co., 84 N. Y. 56, 60.
[8] City of Indianapolis v. Scott, 72 Ind. 196, 203.
[9] Phillips v. Terry, 3 Abb. N. Y. Decis. 607.
[10] Central R. R. Co. v. Mitchell, 63 Ga. 173; s. c., 1 Am. & Eng. R. R. Cases, 145.

to a railroad bridge, where the land adjoining the river bank was low and often overflowed, and the track was, in consequence, elevated and rip-rapped, and as to whether such rip-raps and dikes constituted such an approach, the opinions of experienced engineers have been admissible.[1] So engineers have been permitted to testify, judging from the situation of the banks, the course of the winds and tides, and the shifting of the sand, that a certain bank was not the occasion of a harbor's choking and filling up by stopping the back water.[2] And engineers who had taken the comparative levels of a fountain of water, and of certain agricultural drains in the same lot, and who had examined the intervening subsoil, have been allowed to express an opinion that the drains did not lessen the quantity of water in the fountain.[3] An engineer and landscape gardener has been permitted to express an opinion as to what certain land was suitable for.[4] The opinion of an expert has been held admissible as to the liability of a city to inundation, as well as to the injury to a harbor by the removal of the sand along the shore.[5] But a civil engineer is not necessarily an expert as to the construction of a highway.[6] It is well known that the declarations of persons, since deceased, are received in evidence as to the boundaries of lands, where from their situation they had the means of knowing where the boundaries were. In a case in New Hampshire it was sought to extend the principle to the declarations made by a surveyor since deceased. But the court held that the principles on which such evidence was admitted would not comprehend the declarations of a deceased expert. It was not necessary that such declarations should be received, inasmuch as other experts could be

[1] Union Pacific R. R. Co. v. Clopper, U. S. Sup. Ct., 1880; s. c. 2 Am. & Eng. R. R. Cases, 649.
[2] Folkes v. Chadd. 3 Douglas (26 Eng. C. L. 63), 157. See also Grigsby v. Clear Lake Water Works Co., 40 Cal. 396.
[3] Buffum v. Harris, 5 R. I. 250.
[4] Chandler v. Jamaica Pond Aqueduct, 125 Mass. 544, 551.
[5] Clason v. City of Milwaukee, 30 Wis. 316.
[6] Benedict v. City of Fond du Lac, 44 Wis. 495.

called, whose testimony would be equally valuable.[1] The opinion that the surveyor had expressed was that a certain tree was not an original monument, because the marks on it were not old enough.

§ 115. Machinists.— A machinist is competent to give an opinion as an expert, in relation to the construction of machinery.[2] The evidence of such experts has been received to show that a machine was not constructed in a workmanlike manner.[3] So where the question involved related to the merits of various machines, as whether one machine was equal in all respects to another machine of different make, persons having superior knowledge and experience with such machines have been permitted to express an opinion — as to whether a certain cotton gin was equal in all respects to the best saw gin then in use.[4] And a witness who had knowledge of the mechanism and working of knitting machines, and who was familiar with the operation of a needle called the latch needle, but who had no experience in the use of the spring needle, and did not know of its operation, has been permitted to show the facility and perfection of operation of the latch needle to the jury, to testify to its merits, and to express an opinion that its use could not be superseded by the spring needle, giving his reasons therefor.[5] It is not necessary in all cases that the witness should be a machinist by trade; if he has had practical experience in operating a particular machine, or machines of a similar character, he is competent to express an opinion as to the kind of work such machine can perform.[6] Where the question was as to the proper mode of testing the strength of leathern fire hose, a manufacturer of steam gauges, who had repeatedly tested hose, was held competent to express an opinion, and to state what constituted "a fair and satisfac-

---

[1] Wallace v. Goodall, 18 N. H. 439, 453.
[2] Sheldon v. Booth, 50 Iowa, 209.
[3] Curtis v. Gano, 26 N. Y. 426.
[4] Scattergood v. Wood, 79 N. Y. 263.
[5] James v. Hodsden, 47 Vt. 127.
[6] Sheldon v. Booth, 50 Iowa, 209.

tory test," such as was provided for by the contract.[1] And where an issue involved the question of how much work a machine could do, a person acquainted with the machine and its construction was allowed to express an opinion.[2] One employed in a railroad machine shop as a master mechanic, has been permitted to express an opinion that a certain spark-arrester was the best known.[3] So machinists and brass finishers of large experience have been allowed to state, that from common observation and without close inspection, it could not be told whether certain brass couplings were perfect or imperfect, and whether they were of any use for the purpose for which they were intended.[4]

§ 116. **Mechanics, Masons and Master Builders.** —A mechanic has been permitted to testify as to the injury done to a house by defects in the construction of the cellar under it.[5] So where a contract for the construction of a building stipulated that it should have a wood cornice with brackets, but failed to specify whether the cornice should be placed on the wall above the upper joist or below that point, or what width of cornice or length of bracket there should be, it was held competent to admit the testimony of house builders and mechanics as to these matters, and to show by them, that in order to properly place a cornice of a proper width on the building according to contract, it was necessary that the walls should have been built up to the point they were built to, and for which the contractor and builder claimed extra compensation.[6] And in an action for labor and materials in erecting a house, the testimony of master builders who had examined the building and made an estimate of the cost, has been held admissible for the purpose of ascertaining the amount of the damages.[7] The testimony of practical mechanics, who show themselves fully acquainted

[1] Chicago v. Greer, 9 Wallace, 726, 733.
[2] Burns v. Welch, 8 Yerger, (Tenn.) 117.
[3] Great Western R. R. Co. v. Haworth, 39 Ill. 349.
[4] Jupitz v. People, 34 Ill. 516, 521.
[5] Moulton v. McOwen, 103 Mass. 587.
[6] Haver v. Tenney, 36 Iowa. 80.
[7] Tebbetts v. Haskins, 16 Me. 283.

with the custom as to measuring, have been allowed to testify as to the measurement of masonry,[1] and as to the proper mode of measuring the angles of an octagonal cellar.[2] And a practical brick mason, who had aided in the construction of the plaintiff's wall, was allowed to express an opinion as an expert, as to whether the quantity of rain which fell on the premises within the wall was sufficient to wash it down.[3] So the opinions of masons have been received as to the length of time required to dry the walls of a house so as to make it fit for habitation.[4] But it has been held that the effect of water in disintegrating the mortar of a wall is not a matter of science, and that other persons than masons, who have had an occasion to observe it, are competent to express an opinion concerning it.[5] The opinion of one having a long and thorough acquaintance with the construction of berths on steamboats, has been received as to whether the berths on a certain steamboat were constructed in the manner usual upon the best boats built at the time of its construction.[6] When an application for insurance contained a warranty that the buildings insured were brick, and in an action on the warranty it was contended that the buildings were partly brick and partly wood, it was held that an experienced builder might be asked whether such buildings would be properly denominated "brick" buildings.[7] Builders and contractors have been held equally competent with architects, to show that the employment of an architect to make plans and designs for a building, carried with it an employment to superintend its construction.[8]

§ 117. **Experts in Patent, Trade Mark and Copyright Cases.** — It has been laid down that in actions for the in-

[1] Shulte v. Hennessy, 40 Iowa, 352.
[2] Ford v. Tirrell, 9 Gray (Mass.), 401.
[3] Montgomery v. Gilmer. 33 Ala. 116.
[4] Smith v. Gugerty, 4 Barb. (N. Y.) 619.
[5] Underwood v. Waldron, 33 Mich. 232.
[6] Tinney v. New Jersey Steamboat Co., 12 Abb. Pr. (N. S.) 1.
[7] Mead v. Northwestern Ins. Co., 3 Selden (N. Y.) 530; s. c., 3 Bennett Fire Ins. Cas. 483.
[8] Wilson v. Bauman, 80 Ill. 493.

fringement of patent rights, the testimony of experts is admissible for the purpose of explaining the drawings, models and machines exhibited, as well as for the purpose of explaining their operation, and pointing out the resemblance or difference in the mechanical devices involved in their construction.[1] But the court cannot be compelled to receive the evidence of experts as to how a patent ought to be construed, and whether it has been violated.[2] Neither will an expert be allowed to testify, that from investigations made by him in scientific works, he has ascertained that an invention patented long before, was well known prior to the application for letters patent thereon.[3] "The question," said the court, "proposed to the defendant, as an expert, sought to establish an historical fact, under the guise of a scientific opinion. It was properly excluded." In actions for the infringement of trade marks, it is said that the probability of deception is generally shown by resemblance, and by the opinions of experts.[4] And in the case of an alleged violation of a copyright, it has been held that experts could testify, and state the results of comparisons made by them of the notes and citations of authorities contained in the two law books in question, together with their opinion as to whether the several notes and citations were of the same character.[5]

§ 118. **Painters and Photographers.**—The opinion of an artist in painting is competent evidence as to the genuineness of a painting.[6] An ambrotypist and daguerreotypist has been held competent to express an opinion as to whether photographs were well executed.[7] And an expert in photography has been allowed to testify, from what he knew and

---

[1] Abbott's Trial Evid. 760; Corning v. Burden, 12 How. 252; Hudson v. Draper, 5 Fisher's Pat. Cas. 256, 259; s. c., 4 Clifford, 181; Cahoon v. Ring, 1 Clifford, 592; Winans v. N. Y. & Erie R. R. Co., 21 How. 88.
[2] Waterbury Brass Co. v. N. Y. etc. Co., 3 Fisher Pat. Cas. 43, 54.
[3] McMahon v. Tyng, 14 Allen, 167.
[4] Abbott's Trial Evidence, 752.
[5] Lawrence v. Dana, 4 Clifford, 1, 72.
[6] Folkes v. Chadd, 4 Dougl. 157.
[7] Barnes v. Ingalls, 39 Ala. 193.

saw of a photograph painter's work and capacity, how many photographic pictures such person could paint in the course of a month.[1] In the same case it was announced, that although experts might be alone competent to testify whether a photograph was well executed, yet it required no special skill in or knowledge of the photographic art to determine whether the picture resembled the original, and any person for whom the picture was taken could testify that it was a good likeness.

§ 119. **Lumbermen.**— One employed in getting out logs has been permitted to testify as an expert, whether a person with the force of men he had employed could have continued to deliver a certain amount of logs per day.[2] One who had experience in floating logs in a certain stream has been allowed to express an opinion as to the proper manner of floating logs through a dam and flume. "The running of the logs in that stream, and through that bulkhead, was not a matter of common knowledge, nor of adequate common-judgment upon the facts shown by the other evidence. The experience and observation of the plaintiff gave him the grounds and faculty of an opinion peculiar to himself, and not common to men who had no such experience or observation. In a substantial sense he may be regarded as an expert having peculiar knowledge and skill, which renders his opinion worthy of consideration as the ground of judgment and opinion in others who have not such knowledge and skill."[3] The opinion of a lumber dealer has been received as to the quality of certain lumber.[4] And one engaged in lumbering has been permitted to state whether a raft was properly moored.[5]

§ 120. **Translation by Experts of Writings from a Foreign Language.**— The rule is that when an instrument is written in a foreign language, one skilled in such language

[1] Barnes v. Ingalls, *supra*.
[2] Salvo v. Duncan, 49 Wis. 157.
[3] Dean v. McLean, 48 Vt. 412.
[4] Moore v. Lea's Admr. 32 Ala. 375.
[5] Hayward v. Knapp, 23 Minn. 430.

is to be called to translate it.[1] But it is not competent for a witness called to translate such a writing to give any opinion as to its construction, that being a question for the court.[2]

If the court, however, should undertake to translate a writing without the aid of experts, and should translate it correctly, it is probable that a new trial could not be obtained. In one of the cases we find the following upon this point: "Indeed, if the whole libel had been published in a foreign language, and the court had assumed to translate and define its meaning to the jury without the aid of experts, it is difficult to see how this error could be made the ground for a new trial. It is only error that prejudices, which justifies setting aside the verdict; and if the translation is in fact correct, it is difficult to see wherein the prejudicial error lies."[3]

§ 121. **Expert Testimony as to Technical Terms and Unusual Words.**—It is laid down as clearly within the province of the court to define technical words to the jury.[4] The courts take judicial notice of the meaning of words and idioms in the vernacular of the language.[5] And where foreign words have been so far Anglicized by common use as to have become substantially a part of our language, it is within the province of the court to define them to the jury.[6]

[1] Di Sora v. Phillips, 10 H. L. Cas. 624; Stearine v. Hentzman, 17 C. B. (N. S.) 56; Sheldon v. Benham, 4 Hill, 129; Geylin v. Villeroi, 2 Houston (Del.), 311.

[2] A Belgian consul was called to translate the following: "Les informations sur Gustave Sichel sont telles que nous ne pouvons lui livrer les 2500 cuisses que contre connaisement. Si vous voulez, nous vous enverrons les connaisements, et vous ne les lui dé livrerez que contre payment." He was asked to what the article "les" referred, and said it was applicable to the "counaisements." This was held to be error. Stearine v. Hentzman, *supra*.

[3] Gibson v. *Cincinnati Enquirer* (U. S. Cir. Ct.), 5 Cent. L. J. 380.

[4] Thompson's Charging the Jury, § 18.

[5] 1 Grenl.'s Evidence, § 5.

[6] Townshend on Slander & Libel, 160, note 2; Homer v. Taunton, 5 H. & N. 661, 667; Barnett v. Allen, 3 H. & N. 376; Hoare v. Silverlock, 12 Ad. & El. (N. S.) 624; Gibson v. *Cincinnati Enquirer*, 5 Cent. L. J. 380 (U. S. Circuit Ct., Southern District of Ohio).

Instances of such words are "*habeas corpus*," "*bona fide*," "*prima facie*," "*a fortiori*," "*flagrante delicto*." The general rule undoubtedly is that the meaning of an English word, not a technical term, cannot be made known to the jury by an examination of witnesses. It has, therefore, been held error in an action for libel to allow a physician to testify as to the meaning of the word "malpractice."[1] But this rule does not apply "where a known English word or phrase has acquired a local meaning different from its ordinary acceptation, nor where it has acquired a peculiar meaning in a particular science, art or trade, or among a particular sect, and where it seems to have been used in such local or peculiar sense."[2] Hence it may be laid down that when a new or unusual word is used in a contract, or when a word is used in a technical or peculiar sense, as applicable to any trade or business, or to any particular class of people, it is proper to receive the testimony of witnesses having special knowledge of such words as to the meaning attached to them.[3] The rule has been well stated by the Supreme Court of Massachusetts in the following language: "The general rule of law is, that the construction of every written instrument is matter of law, and, as a necessary consequence, that courts must, in the first instance, judge of the meaning, force and effect of language. The meaning of words, and the grammatical construction of the English language, so far as they are established by the rules and

---

[1] Rodgers v. Kline, 56 Miss. 818. See, too, Haley v. State, 63 Ala. 89; Campbell v. Russell, 9 Iowa, 337.

[2] Rodgers v. Kline, *supra*.

[3] Eaton v. Smith, 20 Pick. (Mass.) 156; Daniels v. Hudson River Fire Ins. Co., 12 Cush. (Mass.) 416, 429; Collender v. Dinsmore, 55 N. Y. 200; Sturm v. Williams, 38 N. Y. Superior Ct. 325; Hearn v. New England Mutual Ins. Co., 3 Clifford C. C. 318; Prather v. Ross, 17 Ind. 495; Silverthorne v. Fowle, 4 Jones (N. C.) Law 362; James v. Bostwick, Wright (Ohio), 142; Harris v. Rathbun, 2 Abbott (Ct. of App. Decis.), 328; Williams v. Poppleton, 3 Oregon, 139; Pollen v. Le Roy, 10 Bos. (N. Y.) 38; First Baptist Church v. Brooklyn Fire Ins. Co., 28 N. Y. 153, 155; Reynolds v. Jourdan, 5 Cal. 108; Reamer v. Nesmith, 34 Cal. 627; Callahan v. Stanley, 57 Cal. 479; Evans v. Commercial Ins. Co., 6 R. I. 47.

usages of the language, are, *prima facie*, matter of law, to be construed and passed upon by the court. But language may be ambiguous, and used in different senses; or general words, in particular trades and branches of business — as among merchants, for instance — may be used in a new, peculiar or technical sense; and, therefore, in a few instances, evidence may be received, from those who are conversant with such branches of business, and such technical or peculiar use of language to explain or to illustrate it."[1] In that case the court held that the testimony of experienced persons could not be received to show that stones of a considerable size were universally known as, and called gravel.

§ 122. **Expert Testimony as to Technical Terms and Unusual Words — The Subject Continued.** — A gas fitter has been permitted to testify whether *gas meters* were usually classified as *gas fixtures*, in an action for the price of gas meters alleged to have been furnished to fulfill a contract for gas fixtures.[2] The opinion of one engaged in the oil business has been received, to show that in a contract for the sale of a certain number of "barrels" of petroleum oil, the word "barrel" meant a vessel of a certain capacity, and not the statute measure of quantity.[3] So the opinion of an expert has been received to show that the meaning of the term "horn chains," used in a contract, meant chains made of hoof and horn;[4] and that the term "port risk," as used by underwriters in policies of marine insurance, had a special signification.[5] Where a contract was for the sale of "one hundred and fifty casks of one ton each, best madder, 12¼," dealers in madder were allowed to testify that the figures as used in the contract, meant 12¼ cents per pound.[6] The opinions of stock brokers have been received to

[1] Brown v. Brown, 10 Met. 373.
[2] Downs v. Sprague, 1 Abbott's Ct. of App. Decis. (N. Y.) 550.
[3] Miller v. Stevens, 100 Mass. 518.
[4] Sweet v. Shumway, 102 Mass. 365.
[5] Nelson v. Sun Mutual Ins. Co., 71 N. Y. 453.
[6] Dana v. Fiedler, 12 N. Y. 40.

explain the meaning among brokers and dealers in stock of the words, "settled at the market 72¾."[1] And the opinion of iron merchants has been received as to what was meant by "No. 1 Shott's Scotch pig iron."[2] Persons engaged in the construction and operation of mills and factories run by water, and acquainted with the application of water to machinery, have been permitted to testify as to the technical meaning of the term "raceway."[3] And experts may be called to decipher abbreviated and elliptical entries in the book of a deceased notary.[4]

§ 123. **Expert Testimony as to Usage.**—On a question of usage in a particular trade or business, the opinions of persons experienced therein will be received in evidence.[5] "Usage is proved," says the court in Massachusetts, "by witnesses testifying of its existence and uniformity from their knowledge, obtained by observation of what is practised by themselves and others in the trade to which it relates. But their conclusions or inferences as to its effect, either upon the contract or the legal title, or rights of parties, are not competent to show the character or force of the usage."[6] That the opinions of experts in a particular business as to the existence of a usage in that particular business, are inadmissible when the effect would be to contradict the express terms of the contract, is well settled upon the authorities.[7] Neither can such evidence be received

[1] Storey v. Salomon, 6 Daly (N. Y.) 532.
[2] Pope v. Filley, 9 Federal Reporter, 65, 69.
[3] Wilder v. Decou, 26 Minn. 10.
[4] Sheldon v. Benham, 4 Hill, 129.
[5] Wilson v. Bauman, 80 Ill. 494; Kershaw v. Wright, 115 Mass. 361; The City of Washington, 92 U. S. 31.
[6] Haskins v. Warren, 115 Mass. 514, 535. And see Barnes v. Ingalls, 39 Ala. 193.
[7] Malcolmson v. Morton, 11 Irish Law R. 230 (Q. B.); Peters v. Stavely, 15 L. T. (N. S.) 151; Reading v. Menham, 1 Moo. & R. 234; Savings Bank v. Ward, 100 U. S. 195, 206; Partridge v. Insurance Co., 15 Wall. 375; Thompson v. Riggs, 5 Wall. 663, 679; Snelling v. Hall, 107 Mass. 134; Brown v. Foster, 113 Mass. 136; Dickinson v. Gay, 7 Allen, (Mass.) 29, 31; Randall v. Rotch, 12 Pick. (Mass.) 107; Barlow v. Lambert, 28 Ala. 704; Polhemus v. Heinman, 50 Cal. 438; Bank of Commerce v. Bissell, 72 N. Y. 615; Collender v. Dinsmore, 55 N. Y. 200; Frith v.

when it would result in violating a positive requirement of law, or some principle of public policy.[1] It is not to be supposed, however, that a custom or usage cannot be shown in any case, if it is simply different in its effect from some general principle of law. To have this effect, it must conflict with some rule of public policy, or be unjust and oppressive in its character.[2]

It is held that a witness is competent to testify as to usage whose only knowledge of it is derived from his own business, if that has been sufficiently extensive and long continued.[3] The testimony of those engaged in a particular business, that they never heard of such a usage, is admissible.[4] On the issue whether an alleged commercial usage exists, a witness may be asked to describe how, under the usages in force, a transaction like the one in question would be conducted by all the parties thereto, from its inception to its conclusion.[5] It has been held in England that a London *stock broker* is a competent witness as to the course of business of London *bankers*.[6] And it is to be observed that a person may be competent to testify as to the usage which prevails in a certain business, without himself being engaged in that business. So that when the question was as

---

Barker, 2 Johns. (N. Y.) 334; Corbett v. Underwood, 83 Ill. 324; Wilson v. Bauman, 80 Ill. 493; Dixon v. Dunham, 14 Ill. 324; Stultz v. Locke, 47 Md. 562, 568; Bodfish v. Fox, 23 Me. 90; Exchange Bank v. Coleman, 1 W. Va. 69; Randolph v. Holden, 44 Iowa, 327; Erwin v. Clark, 13 Mich. 10, 18; Bedford v. Flowers, 7 Humph. (Tenn.) 242; Atwater v. Clancy, 107 Mass. 369.

[1] Barlow v. Lambert, 28 Ala. 704, 710; Antomarchi v. Russell, 63 Ala. 356; Wilson v. Bauman, 80 Ill. 493, 495; Bissell v. Ryan, 23 Ill. 570; Homer v. Dorr, 10 Mass. 26; Reed v. Richardson, 98 Mass. 216; Lockhart v. Dewees, 1 Texas, 535; Jackson v. Beling, 22 La. Ann. 377; Barnard v. Kellogg, 10 Wallace, 383; Brown v. Jackson, 2 Wash. C. C. 24; Southwestern Freight etc. Co. v. Standard, 44 Mo. 71; Raisin v. Clark, 41 Md. 158; Minnesota Central R. R. Co. v. Morgan, 52 Barb. (N. Y.) 217, 221; Inglebright v. Hammond, 19 Ohio. 337.

[2] See Lawson on Usages and Customs, Chapter V, §§ 225, 248.

[3] Hamilton v. Nickerson, 13 Allen (Mass.) 351.

[4] Evansville etc. R. R. Co. v. Young, 28 Ind. 516.

[5] Kirshaw v. Wright, *supra*.

[6] Adams v. Peters, 2 Car. & Kir. (61 E. C. L.) 722.

to the custom of the New York banks in paying the checks of dealers, it was held proper to call as witnesses persons who were not employed in banks. "Although not employed in banking business, the witnesses were dealers with the banks, and had knowledge of the ordinary course of dealing with them. There is no necessity for showing a man to be an expert in banking in order to prove a usage. He should know what the usage is, and then he is competent to testify, whether he be a banker, or employed in a bank, or a dealer with banks. There is no reason why a dealer should not have as much knowledge on such a subject as a person employed in a bank." [1]

§ 124. **Opinions of Experts in Miscellaneous Cases.**— The opinion of an ethnologist has been received upon the question of race,[2] the opinions of persons having a peculiar and special knowledge of iron, upon the question of the quality and strength of iron, the breaking of which caused an accident;[3] the opinion of a paver as to the number of bricks laid in a pavement, ascertained from a computation by the square yard according to usage of the craft, without reckoning them by tale;[4] the opinions of witnesses having knowledge of the geological structure and formation of the neighborhood, as to the existence of coal seams, and of the quality and quantity on the lands in question;[5] the opinions of persons engaged in the wool trade, as to the liability of wool waste to ignite spontaneously;[6] the opinion of a practical miner as to the safety of a particular blasting powder which he had used.[7] So one employed in manufacturing explosive compounds, and who had made blasts in all kinds

---

[1] Griffin v. Rice, 1 Hilton (N. Y.) 184.

[2] White v. Clemens, 39 Ga. 232; Nave's Admr. v. Williams, 22 Ind. 308; State v. Jacobs, 6 Jones (N. C.) Law, 284.

[3] Claxton's Admr. v. Lexington, etc. R. R. Co., 13 Bush (Ky.), 636; King v. New York Central, etc. R. R. Co., 72 N. Y. 607; Pope v. Filley, 9 Fed. Reporter, 65, 66.

[4] Mayor, etc. v. O'Neill, 1 Penn. St. 342.

[5] Stambaugh v. Smith, 23 Ohio St. 584, 594.

[6] Whitney v. Chicago & N. W. R. R. Co., 27 Wis. 327.

[7] Snowden v. Idaho Quartz Manuf. Co., 55 Cal. 450.

of rocks and stones, in every kind of blasting, has been held qualified "as a most competent expert," to state whether portions of a rock could have been thrown 280 feet from the point of discharge, the blast being exploded in the excavation of a sewer.[1] The opinions of experienced persons have been received as to whether two pieces of wood were parts of the same stick of natural growth.[2] And it has been held that an expert may be asked what the condition of a water pipe, as described by another witness, indicated as to the original construction of the joint.[3] A well-digger, who from the exercise of his busines in the vicinity has become acquainted with the character of the soil and subsoil, has been allowed to testify to his opinion, whether a given thickness of subsoil, if undisturbed, was impervious to water.[4] A witness who had been engaged for years in measuring and selling water to miners, was held sufficiently qualified to give his opinion as to the effect which a dam across a stream would have in raising the water in the channel above.[5] When the question was as to the cause of the settling and cracking of the surface of the earth, the opinions of experts were received, they having examined the premises, and being qualified by learning, observation and experience to form an intelligent judgment in the matter.[6]

§ 125. **Opinions of Experts in Miscellaneous Cases— The Subject Continued.**— The opinion of an expert has been received as to the quantity of stone furnished for a water works reservoir, where the average amount could only be estimated approximately.[7] The testimony of experts has been received as to whether it is possible to examine all the layers in a case of old tobacco without injuring the tobacco, and as to what is the proper method of examining such a case for the purpose of determining the kind and

[1] Koster v. Noonan, 8 Daly (N. Y.) 232.
[2] Commonwealth v. Choate, 105 Mass. 451.
[3] Hand v. Brookline, 126 Mass. 324.
[4] Buffum v. Harris, 5 R. I. 250.
[5] Blood v. Light, 31 Cal. 115.
[6] Clark v. Willett, 35 Cal. 534, 544.
[7] Eyerman v. Sheehan, 52 Mo. 221.

quality of the tobacco.[1] Experts have been allowed to testify that a certain quality of steel was not considered suitable for the manufacture of steel rails.[2] One who had made and sold railroad ties has been held competent to testify as to the quality of certain ties.[3] And in general skilled witnesses are allowed to testify as to the quality of goods.[4] The testimony of a tailor has been received as to whether a pocket book could have been taken out through a cut made by a pickpocket in a coat, it appearing that the coat had been mended subsequently to his examination of it.[5] The genuineness of a post mark may be shown by the testimony of a postmaster,[6] and perhaps by the testimony of any one who has been in the habit of receiving letters with that mark.[7] An expert has been permitted to express an opinion as to the contents of a tree from the size of its stump.[8]

Where books and schedules of the assets and debts of a party are put in evidence, an accountant may give the results of computations therefrom.[9] Witnesses who stated that they were accustomed to handling and driving horses, and knew their habits, have been allowed to express an opinion that certain obstructions on a bridge were of such a character as would be likely to frighten horses of ordinary gentleness. "The nature, habits, and peculiarities of horses," said the court, "are not known to all men. Persons who are in the habit of handling and driving horses, from this experience, learn their habits, nature, etc., and are, therefore, better able to state the probable conduct of a horse under a given state of circumstances, in which they have in their experience witnessed their conduct under simi-

[1] Atwater v. Clancy, 107 Mass. 369.
[2] Booth v. Cleveland Mill Co., 74 N. Y. 27.
[3] Jeffersonville R. R. Co. v. Lanham, 27 Ind. 171.
[4] Myers v. Murphy, 60 Ind. 282; Brown v. Leach, 107 Mass. 384.
[5] People v. Morrigan, 29 Mich. 5.
[6] Abbey v. Lill, 5 Bing. 299, 304,
[7] Woodcock v. Houldsworth, 16 M. & W. 124.
[8] Frantz v. Ireland, 66 Barb. 386.
[9] Jordan v. Osgood, 109 Mass. 457.

lar circumstances, than persons having no experience whatever with horses."[1]

§ 126. **Opinions of Experts in Miscellaneous Cases— The Subject Continued.** — The opinions of persons accustomed to witness the agility and power of certain fish, in overcoming obstructions in the ascent of rivers, and who have acquired superior knowledge upon that subject, have been held admissible for the purpose of showing that a certain stream, in its natural state, would or would not be ascendible by such fish. "The witnesses had acquired from observation, superior knowledge upon this subject. It appears to us to fall within that class of cases in which the opinions of persons skilled in any art, science, trade or business are received."[2] A brick and tile maker, having had some years experience in his trade, has been held competent to give an opinion as an expert on the proper mode of burning tiles, and as to what would be the effect of burning in one way or another.[3] An architect has been permitted to testify that the work done on a building was performed in compliance with the contract.[4] One who had been engaged for over twenty years in the manufacture of paper, has been held competent to testify as to what the condition of a paper mill and its machinery was at a certain time.[5] The opinion of a witness experienced in the use of guns, has been received as to the length of time since the weapon was discharged.[6] And it has been held that witnesses who saw a pistol immediately after it had been discharged, and who were familiar with such weapons, could be asked their opinion on the question, whether the appearances indicated how many barrels had been fired, and which ones.[7] A witness accustomed to packing marbles for transportation, has been permitted, against objection, to state whether cer-

[1] Moreland v. Mitchell County, 40 Iowa, 401.
[2] Cottrill v. Myrick, 12 Me. 222, 231.
[3] Wiggins v. Wallace, 19 Barb. (N. Y.) 338.
[4] Tucker v. Williams, 2 Hilton (N. Y.), 562.
[5] Blodgett Paper Co. v. Farmer, 41 N. H. 401.
[6] Monghon v. the State, 57 Ga. 102.
[7] Wynne v. State, 56 Ga. 113.

tain marbles were properly packed, the court declaring that such a question was a proper one for the testimony of experts.[1] An expert has been allowed to testify as to the usual manner in which zinc is imported.[2] A witness who is an expert in the curing and care of meats, may testify whether hams prepared in a certain prescribed way and shipped for transportation to a specified point, if properly stowed and cared for, "ought to have borne transportation" to that point.[3] Such a witness may also be asked whether hams shipped in a specified condition, would arrive at their destination in as good condition as when shipped, and as to what would likely be the effect of the weather upon provisions so shipped.[4]

§ 127. **Opinions of Experts in Miscellaneous Cases— The Subject Continued.**—The owner of a tan yard, who had been engaged in the business of tanning for twenty-three years, "seeing the work going on and knowing how it was done," has been allowed to testify as an expert as to matters connected with such business, although he was not himself a practical tanner, but employed others to do the work for him.[5] Where the question was as to the quality of the soap stone in a particular quarry, one who had been engaged for forty years in quarrying soap stone, and who had been employed in manufacturing soap stone into pipe for aqueducts for half that time, was allowed in the court below to testify as an expert as to the quality of the stone. But on appeal, the court held that his testimony should not have been received, saying: "It did not appear that he had ever devoted any time or study to an investigation of the composition and characteristics of soap stone, or made any particular observations on that subject, so as to be better qualified to give an opinion on the scientific question propounded to him, than any member of the jury."[6] In an action to

[1] Shriver v. Sioux City etc. R. R. Co., 24 Minn. 506
[2] Richards v. Doe, 100 Mass. 524.
[3] Leopold v. Van Kirk, 29 Wis. 548.
[4] Kershaw v. Wright, 115 Mass. 361
[5] Nelson v. Wood, 62 Ala. 175.
[6] Page v. Parker, 40 N. H. 59

recover compensation for an injury caused by the explosion of an oil still, a witness who was a steam fitter, and who had no knowledge of stills except such as he had derived from working with them, and fitting them up after they were put up, has been allowed to state whether, in his opinion, the iron of which the tank was composed was sufficiently strong."[1] Where the question was whether a sewer constructed along the walls of a building was properly constructed, the Supreme Court of Indiana, reversing the court below, held a witness not qualified to testify on that subject, who, on his preliminary examination, stated: "I have superintended the laying of some sewer pipe along the sides of walls. I have noticed some little such work, but have not specially noticed such work. I have put in sewers here in streets, and have seen some such work as this done in Indianapolis."[2] A witness who had on two occasions examined cotton that had been under water, but who did not know how long such cotton had been under the water, has been held incompetent to testify as to the injury which would probably be done to cotton by remaining from 12 to 24 hours under water.[3] In an action against a tender of a draw bridge, to recover damages by reason of his neglect to have due regard and caution for public travel, it has been held improper to receive the opinion of another draw tender as to the necessity of keeping a gate shut and lanterns lighted while the draw was open in the night time. The question was not one of science or skill.[4] For the same reason, it is error to allow experts to testify whether a certain cattle guard was suitable and sufficient to prevent cattle from getting on a railroad track.[5] And for the same reason, farmers cannot be allowed to express an opinion as to the sufficiency of a fence to restrain cattle.[6]

---

[1] Ardesco Oil Co. v. Gilson, 63 Penn. St. 146.
[2] Hinds v. Harbon, 58 Ind. 124.
[3] Weaver v. Alabama etc. Co., 35 Ala. 176.
[4] Nowell v. Wright, 3 Allen (Mass.), 166.
[5] Swartout v. N. Y. Central R. R. Co., 14 Hun (N. Y.), 575.
[6] Enright v. Railroad Co., 33 Cal. 230.

CHAPTER VII.

EXPERT TESTIMONY IN HANDWRITING.

SECTION.
128. The Scientific Investigation of Handwriting.
129. Experts in Handwriting — Who are such.
130. Experts in Handwriting — Who are such — The Subject Continued.
131. Experts in Handwriting — The Rule as stated in Iowa.
132. The Testimony of Experts in Handwriting.
133. The Testimony of Experts in Handwriting — The Subject Continued.
134. The Testimony of Experts Based on the Nature of the Ink.
135. The Qualifications of Experts in such Cases.
136. Comparison of Writings in Juxtaposition.
137. Statutory Provisions in England and the United States concerning Comparison of Writings.
138. Comparison of Writings in the Absence of Statutory Provisions.
139. Comparison of Writings in the Absence of Statutory Provisions— The Subject Continued.
140. Comparison of Writings in the Absence of Statutory Provisions— Comparison by Experts with Writings Admitted to be Genuine.
141. Comparison of Writings in the Absence of Statutory Provisions— Comparison by Experts with Writings Proved or Admitted to be Genuine.
142. Proof of the Genuineness of the Writings offered for Comparison.
143. The Expert should have before him in Court the Writings Compared.
144. The Writing Compared should be the Original, and not a Photographic Copy.
145. Comparison with Photographic Copies Allowed when.
146. Writings Admissible for Comparison in Orthography.
147. Comparison with Writings made on the Trial.
148. Comparison of Writings — Testing Accuracy of Expert on Cross-Examination.
149. Detection of Counterfeit Bank Notes.
150. Regulation of such Evidence by Statutory Provision.

§ 128. **The Scientific Investigation of Handwriting.**— Calligraphic experts have for years asserted the possibility of investigating handwriting upon scientific principles, and the courts have consequently admitted such persons to testify in cases of disputed handwriting. Judicial experience has justified to a certain extent the claims made by the experts. It may be asserted, therefore, that experiment and observation have disclosed the fact that there are certain general principles which may be relied upon in questions pertaining to the genuineness of handwriting. For instance, it seems to be established that in every person's manner of writing, there is a certain distinct prevailing character, which can be discovered by observation, and being once known can be afterwards applied as a standard to try other specimens of writing, the genuineness of which is disputed.[1] Handwriting, notwithstanding it may be artificial, is always, in some degree, the reflex of the nervous organization of the writer. Hence there is in each person's handwriting some distinctive characteristic, which, as being the reflex of his nervous organization, is necessarily independent of his own will, and unconsciously forces the writer to stamp the writing as his own. Those skillful in such matters state that it is imposssble for a person to successfully disguise in a writing of any length this characteristic of his penmanship; that the tendencies to angles or curves developed in the analysis of this characteristic may be mechanically measured by placing a fine specimen within a coarser specimen, and that the strokes will be parallel if written by the same person, the nerves influencing the direction which the will gives to the pen.

So, too, it is claimed that no two autograph signatures, written in a natural hand, will be perfect *fac similes*. In the famous Howland will case,[2] Prof. Pierce, a very distinguished mathematician, at that time the professor of mathematics in Harvard University, testified that the odds were

[1] See Plunkett v. Bowman, 2 McCord, 139.
[2] 4 Am. Law Review, 625, 649.

just exactly 2,866,000,000,000,000,000,000 to 1 that an individual could not with a pen, write his name three times so exactly alike as were the three alleged signatures of Sylvia Ann Howland, the testatrix, to a will and two codicils. The experts, therefore, claim, that if, upon superimposition against the light, they find that two signatures perfectly coincide, that they are perfect *fac similes*, that it is a probability, amounting practically to a certainty, that one of the signatures is a forgery.

It thus appears that there is abundant justification for the holding of the courts that there is a science of handwriting, and that experts who have qualified themselves by study and experience, should be received to testify to the genuiness and identity of handwriting.

§ 129. **Experts in Handwriting—Who are such.**— It is, of course, error to receive the opinion of any witness, offered as an expert, until he has first been examined touching his skill and experience in the examination and comparison of handwriting; to the end that the court may be satisfied that he is really possessed of skill in that department of inquiry.[1] The necessity of such a preliminary examination in all cases, has been elsewhere fully considered.[2]

The principle has been laid down in general terms, that whenever handwriting is a subject of controversy in judicial proceedings, the opinions of " witnesses who by study, occupation and habit have been skillful in marking and distinguishing the characteristics of handwriting," may be received in evidence.[3] Hence writing engravers, accustomed accurately to examine the formation of letters in different handwritings, and who had acquired skill from their occupation of making engravings of handwritings, have been allowed to testify as experts in such cases.[4] In the same

---

[1] State v. Ward, 20 Vt. 225, 236; McCracken v. West, 17 Ohio, 16.
[2] See §§ 15, 16, 17, 18.
[3] Sweetser v. Lowell, 33 Me. 450.
[4] Spear v. Bone, MSS. (cited in 5 A. & E. 709); Regina v. Williams. 8 Car. & P. 34; Norman v. Morell, 4 Vesey Ch. 768; Turnbull v. Dodds, 6 D. (Sc.) 901.

way tellers[1] and cashiers[2] of banks have been received as experts, having acquired skill in passing on the genuineness of signatures to notes and checks. And in general any officer of a bank whose business it is to examine papers with a view of detecting alterations and erasures, and ascertaining genuine from spurious writings, is an expert in questions pertaining to handwriting.[3] So a clerk in the postoffice, accustomed to the inspection of franks for the detection of forgeries, has been deemed to possess the qualifications of an expert.[4] So has a sheriff of a county,[5] and a county clerk,[6] each having been accustomed to pass on the genuineness of signatures. One who for some years had been the bookkeeper and cashier of a commercial house, and as such had experience in the examination of handwriting to determine its genuiness, has been held sufficiently qualified to give evidence as an expert.[7] A writing master has testified as an expert, the question being whether a writing was in a natural or simulated hand.[8] A person, by profession a lawyer, was held a competent witness, his preliminary examination showing that he had occasion to examine handwriting with a view to a comparison of writings; that he had been called to the stand as a witness in regard to them, a good many times; that he had never made a business of criticising writing, but had been accustomed to do it, and supposed he could identify handwriting pretty well.[9]

§ 130. **Experts in Handwriting — Who are such — The Subject Continued.**— It is evident from the cases referred to in the foregoing section that great importance attaches to the avocation in life of the witness. If it has been such as

[1] Spelden v. State, 3 Texas Ct. of App. 159.
[2] Dubois v. Baker, 30 N. Y. 355, 361; People v. Hewitt, 2 Parker's Cr. Cas. 20; State v. Phair, 48 Vt. 366, 369; Lyon v. Lyman, 9 Conn. 59, 60; Murphy v. Hagerman, Wright (Ohio), 293.
[3] Pate v. People, 3 Gilm. 644, 659.
[4] Revett v. Braham, 4 Term, 49.
[5] Yates v. Yates, 76 N. C. 142.
[6] State v. Phair, 48 Vt. 366, 369.
[7] State v. Ward, 39 Vt. 225.
[8] Moody v. Rowell, 17 Pick. (Mass.) 490.
[9] State v. Phair, 48 Vt. 366, 369.

naturally qualifies him to judge of handwriting, the court will allow him to testify as an expert. If, however, his business experience has not been such as to give him any special skill in the examination of disputed writings, he will not be permitted to testify as an expert, unless it is made to appear that he has in some other way acquired actual skill and scientific knowledge.[1] The rule is well laid down in a recent case in the Supreme Court of California, where it is said that the witness "must have been educated in the business about which he testifies; or it must first be shown that he has acquired actual skill and scientific knowledge upon the subject."[2] If the witness has really acquired actual skill and scientific knowledge upon the subject of handwriting, he is none the less an expert because he has not happened to have been in situations where his duty required him to distinguish between genuine and counterfeit handwriting.[3]

The fact that the expert has no other knowledge of the writing in dispute than that derived by a comparison of the disputed writing with others that are genuine, is not regarded as any disqualification whatever.[4] This must be regarded as the rule, although it was laid down at one time in the inferior courts of New York, that an expert who had never seen the party write could not give his opinion as to the genuineness of the writing in question based solely on a comparison of writings, but that he was to testify to the condition and appearance of the words, and of the letters and characters contained in the writings, and point out and explain similarities and differences.[5] When an expert acquires a knowledge of the handwriting of a person by simply observing him write several times, and this for the pur-

[1] State v. Tompkins, 71 Mo. 616; Wagner v. Jacoby, 26 Mo. 530.
[2] Goldstein v. Black, 50 Cal. 464.
[3] Sweetser v. Lowell, 33 Me. 450.
[4] Miles v. Loomis, 75 N. Y. 287; State v. Shinborn, 46 N. H. 497; Calkins v. State, 14 Ohio St. 222; Macomber v. Scott, 10 Kans. 335; Moody v. Rowell, 17 Pick. (Mass.) 490.
[5] Roe v. Roe, 40 N. Y. Superior Ct. 1; Frank v. Chemical National Bank, 37 Ib. 30.

pose of testifying, it is laid down that he is incompetent to give an opinion as to the genuineness of that person's signature.[1] It is quite possible that the party may have written differently through design.[2]

Mere opportunity afforded for observation of handwriting does not of itself qualify one to give testimony as an expert in the science of handwriting, and the mere fact that a witness has sometimes compared the signatures of individuals, where disagreements as to their genuineness have arisen, has been held not sufficient to render him competent to testify as an expert in disputed writings.[3]

§ 131. **Experts in Handwriting — The Rule as Stated in Iowa.**— In Iowa the court has been somewhat liberal in its determination of what is necessary to qualify one as an expert in handwriting. According to the view taken by that court it would appear that almost any business man is qualified to express an opinion as an expert in such cases. A witness has there been held competent, who testified on his preliminary examination that he did not consider himself an expert in handwriting, and had never made it a business to compare or detect feigned or forged handwriting. That he presumed he had some skill in comparing handwriting, but did not pretend to any extra skill, simply thinking that he was *as good a judge as business men generally*. He had been a clerk in a store, the editor of a newspaper, and for the last fifteen years a lawyer. He had examined a good deal of writing, and said he had been in the habit of examining bank bills to test their genuineness. So, in the same case, a merchant was held competent, who did not profess to be an expert, but had examined bank bills to detect counterfeits.[4] A witness who merely professed to be as good a judge of handwriting as business men generally, would certainly not be regarded in some courts as possessing the peculiar skill of an expert. But the court say that, "It is

---
[1] Reese v. Reese, 90 Penn. St. 89.
[2] Stranger v. Searle, 1 Espinasse, 14.
[3] Goldstein v. Black, 50 Cal. 464.
[4] Hyde v. Woolfolk, 1 Iowa, 159.

true that persons giving evidence on a matter pertaining to their particular science, trade or art, come most strictly and technically under the term 'experts,' but we cannot consent to the proposition that no others come within it, and are allowed to be witnesses in any case. It may very probably be true, that none are to be taken as experts on matters pertaining to a particular calling, art or science, but those who are, or have been practiced, in such art or science. But there are many subjects of inquiry which do not belong to a particular art, etc., but on which a greater or less degree of knowledge is common to many men in different callings." And the court concluded that a comparison of writings did not present such an inquiry as required a witness of a particular calling as an expert, but that his competency depended on his means of knowledge as a business man and his intelligence.

§ 132. **The Testimony of Experts in Handwriting.**— Experts in handwriting are permitted to express an opinion on the question whether a writing is in a natural or a simulated hand;[1] whether it appears more cramped and confined than the hand which the writer usually wrote;[2] and as to which of two instruments exhibits the greater ease and facility of writing.[3] They have been permitted to testify that a certain writing bore the appearance of having been touched by a pen a second time, as if done by some one attempting to copy or imitate the handwriting of another.[4] And on an indictment for uttering a forged will, which, together with writings in support of it, it was suggested had been written over pencil marks which had been rubbed out, the testi-

---

[1] Queen v. Shepherd, 1 Cox Cr. Cas. 237; Goodtitle v. Braham, 4 Term 497; Rex v. Cator, 4 Esp. 117; Spear v. Bone (MS.) cited in 5 A. & E. 709; Reilly v. Rivett, 1 Cases in Eng. Eccls. Cts. 43, note a; Moody v. Rowell, 17 Pick. (Mass.) 490; Commonwealth v. Webster, 5 Cush. (Mass.) 295; Burdick v. Hunt, 43 Ind. 381; Miles v. Loomis, 17 Hun (N. Y.), 372; Goodyear v. Vosburgh, 63 Barb. (N. Y.) 154; People v. Hewitt, Parker Cr. Cas. 20.

[2] Dubois v. Baker, 30 N. Y. 355, 362.

[3] Demerritt v. Randall, 116 Mass. 331.

[4] Spear v. Bone, *supra*.

mony of an engraver was received, who had examined the paper with a mirror and traced the pencil marks.[1]

It has been held competent to ask an expert whether certain parts of a writing could have been made with a pen, but not whether it could have been made with an instrument which was found in the possession of the defendant.[2] So an expert may testify whether two documents were written with the same pen and ink, and at the same time.[3] And when it is alleged and denied that the body and signature of an instrument are in the same handwriting, he may be asked to express an opinion whether the two parts were written by the same person.[4]

Where one writing crosses another, an expert may testify which in his opinion was written first.[5] His opinion has also been taken on the question, whether certain words on a paper shown him, were written before or after the paper was folded.[6] And the judicial committee and lords of the privy council have called an expert for the purpose of obtaining his opinion as to whether a circumflex line, surrounding the names of the witnesses to a will, was made before or after the signature.[7]

In consequence of a deed having been drawn up "in an unusual and slovenly manner, and so as at first sight to cause doubt as to the genuineness of a part of it," Chief Justice MEREDITH ordered an *expertise* in the Quebec Court of Review, and this course was not disapproved of either by the Court of Appeals or the Lords of the Privy Council.[8]

§ 133. **The Testimony of Experts in Handwriting—The Subject Continued.**—It is well settled that expert testimony

---

[1] Regina v. Williams, 8 Car. & P. 34.
[2] Commonwealth v. Webster, 5 Cush. (Mass.) 295.
[3] Fulton v. Hood, 34 Penn. St. 365; Quinsigmond Bank v. Hobbs, 11 Gray (Mass.) 250.
[4] Reese v. Reese, 90 Penn. St. 89.
[5] Cooper v. Bockett, 4 Moore P. C. 433; Dubois v. Baker, 30 N. Y. 355.
[6] Bacon v. Williams, 13 Gray (Mass.), 525.
[7] Cooper v. Bockett, 4 Moore P. C. 433.
[8] See Hamel v. Panet, 3 Quebec Law R. 173, 175.

is admissible upon the question of the alteration[1] or erasure of writings.[2] A holograph will, in which alterations and interlineations appeared, has been admitted to probate upon the testimony of an expert, that in his opinion, the alterations were written at the same time as the rest of the will.[3] An expert accustomed to the use of the microscope, having examined the note in question through that instrument, has been allowed to testify that the word "year" in the body of the note had been erased, and the word "day" written upon the erasure.[4] So an expert has been permitted to express an opinion, that a note has been altered by the substitution of one figure for another,[5] and whether certain words in a writing had been cancelled.[6]

An engraver has been examined as to an illegible writing,[7] and, in general, the testimony of experts is admissible whenever the writing is obscure and difficult to be deciphered.[8] If the writing is ancient, an expert may state his belief as to the probable period at which it was written.[9] It has been held that an expert could not express an opinion that certain words were interpolated into a written agreement after the signature was affixed, if such opinion was founded on the situation and crowded appearance of the words.[10] And how much a man can improve his handwriting in a short time, is not a subject for the testimony of experts. It has been held, therefore, improper to ask an expert

[1] Moye v. Herndon, 30 Miss. 118; Vinton v. Peck, 14 Mich. 287; Pate v. The People, 3 Gilm. (Ill.) 644.

[2] Edelin v. Sanders Ex'r. 8 Md. 118; Yates v. Waugh, 1 Jones (N. C.) Law, 483. See Swan v. O'Fallon, 7 Mo. 231; Wagner v. Jacoby, 26 Mo. 530.

[3] In the Goods of Hindmarch, 1 P. & M. 307.

[4] Dubois v. Baker, 30 N. Y. 355.

[5] Nelson v. Johuson, 18 Ind. 329.

[6] Beach v. O'Riley, 14 W. Va. 55.

[7] Norman v. Morell, 4 Vesey, ch. 768.

[8] Masters v. Masters, 1 P. Wm. 425; Stone v. Hubbard, 7 Cush. (Mass.) 595. It is a question for the jury and not for the court to decipher illegible letters or figures. Armstrong v. Burrows, 6 Watts. 266, 268.

[9] Tracy Peerage Case. 10 Cl. & Fin. 154; Doe v. Suckermore, 5 Ad. & Ellis, 703, 718, per Coleridge, J.

[10] Jewett v. Draper, 6 Allen (Mass.), 434.

whether a man could, within a short time, so improve his handwriting, as shown by the standard signatures of the testator, as to make a signature of as good a handwriting as that of the will.[1]

§ 134. **The Testimony of Experts Based on the Nature of the Ink.**— Where a writing purports to be of ancient or recent date, the testimony of experts, who have made a micro-chemical examination of the ink in which the instrument is written, is received to show the nature of the ink, whether it was found fresh or old, and whether it was of such a nature as to grow old rapidly.[2] Such testimony is also received when the question arises whether a portion of the writing was made at a time different from that at which the rest of the instrument was written, or whether different inks were employed.[3] Cases have been referred to in the sections immediately preceding this, showing that experts are permitted to express an opinion as to the probable time at which an instrument was written, whether different parts of the same instrument were written at the same time, and with the same ink, and where two writings cross each other, as to which was written first. In all these inquiries much light can be obtained from experts skillful in the micro-

[1] McKeone v. Barnes, 108 Mass. 344, 347.
[2] See 18 Am. Law Register (N. S), 273, 282.
[3] Ibid. 288. A distinguished expert in the scientific investigation of handwriting, there gives an interesting account of a case of this nature, which happened to come within his personal experience. It shows how the difference in inks may often be ascertained by means of a photographic copy of the writing. He says; "The photograph is able to distinguish shades of color which are inappreciable to the naked eye; thus where there is the least particle of yellow present in a color it will take notice of the fact by making the picture blacker, just in proportion as the yellow predominates, so that a very light yellow will take a deep black. So, any shade of green, or blue, or red, where there is an imperceptible amount of yellow, will print by the photographic process more or less black; while either a red or blue, verging to a purple, will show more or less faint. as the case may be. Here is a method of investigation which may be made very useful in such cases, and which will give no uncertain answer." In Goodyear v. Vosburgh, 63 Barb. (N. Y.) 154. the difference in the color of the ink used was taken into consideration.

chemical examination of inks. The importance of such testimony is well illustrated by a case very recently decided in the Supreme Court of Michigan, where an exact similarity in the inks used in executing two different instruments, bearing different dates, was treated in connection with other suspicious facts, as tending to indicate that both writings were made at the same time.[1]

When two writings cross each other, if the writing was done with a different kind of ink, the question which was the superposed ink may be easily determined by wetting a piece of paper with a compound which acts as a solvent of ink. By pressing the paper upon the writing in question, a thin layer of the superposed ink will be transferred to the prepared paper, thereby furnishing an answer to the question propounded. If the same kind of ink was used, the case presents greater difficulties, and other methods are resorted to. But to attempt to determine the question, as is often done, by the aid of the eye or the magnifying glass, is said to be no better than guess work.[2]

§ 135. **The Qualifications of Experts in such Cases.**— In all cases where opinions are desired predicated upon the nature of the ink used, an expert microscopist and chemist, accustomed to the examination of inks for the purpose of determining the nature and properties of different inks,

[1] Sheldon v. Warner, 45 Mich. 638.
[2] 18 Am. Law Reg. (N. S.) 273, 287, where R. U. Piper, M. D., of Chicago, a microscopic and chemical expert in the examination of writings, says: "I took for the purpose of my experiment ten of the most common kinds of ink found in the market, and drew a series of lines, three in number, with each kind of ink, across a sheet of paper. This was followed by a similar series drawn diagonally across the first, thus forming a hundred points of crossing, and placing each kind of ink above and also under all the others. In thirty-seven cases out of the hundred, the eye, with or without the glass, saw the under ink as if it were on the surface; in forty cases nothing could be decided in this respect; the balance told the truth of the matter. By the other method, that is, by the use of the solvent, the true facts could be made plain in every one of these cases. This experiment, as will be seen, was made with ten kinds of ink more or less differing from each other in color and in chemical composition, and it certainly proves that all such testimony, as I have said, has been thus far no better than guess work."

and the age of writings, would unquestionably be competent to express an opinion. But whenever the question relates to the age of a writing, an expert who has simply been in the habit of studying the genuineness of handwriting, for the mere purpose of determining whether it was in the handwriting of the person by whom it purported to have been written, would not be competent to express an opinion.[1] For that involves a question in a very different department of inquiry, and it is necessary that the witness should have made that subject a matter of special study and investigation. The courts cannot be too careful in passing on the qualifications of witnesses offered as experts in this particular line of inquiry.[2]

There are two cases to be noticed in this connection. The first was decided in the Supreme Court of North Carolina in the year 1854. In that case the defendant contended that although the instrument declared on was in the handwriting of his testator, yet the body of it was a forgery, the original having been removed by some chemical process, and the present writing substituted. To show this a witness was introduced who was not a professed chemist, and who knew little or nothing about the science. The trial court permitted him to testify that he had just seen an experiment performed, whereby legible writing with ordinary ink, had been erased and extracted from a piece of paper (which he then held in his hand), by the application of certain chemicals. The object of the testimony was to show that ink might be removed from paper without injuring its

[1] Clark v. Bruce, 19 N. Y. Sup. Ct. (12 Hun), 271, 273. See, too, Ellingwood v. Bragg, 52 N. H. 488.

[2] "I have repeatedly," says Dr. Piper. "examined papers which have been made to appear old by various methods, such as washing with coffee, with tobacco water, and by being carried in the pocket near the person, by being smoked and partially burnt, and in various other ways. I have in my possession a paper which has passed the ordeal of many examinations by experts and others, which purports to be two hundred years old, and to have been saved from the Boston fire. The handwriting is a perfect *fac simile* of that of Thomas Addington, the town clerk of Boston two hundred years ago, and yet this paper is not over two years old." 18 Am. Law Register (N. S.), 273, 289.

texture. The Supreme Court held that he was not properly qualified.[1] That the witness was not qualified to give testimony as an expert is entirely clear, but it is somewhat difficult to understand why he was not competent to testify in the character of an ordinary witness, to the fact which he had observed, namely, that certain effects followed the application of the chemicals to the paper in the instances which he witnessed.

The other is a case decided in the Supreme Court of California, which was an indictment for forgery. The testimony showed that a powder, composed of three parts of hydro-carbonate of soda to one part of chlorate of potash, was found in the baggage of one of the defendants. And a police officer was permitted to testify that he had used a portion of the powder found by him in the defendant's baggage, in connection with muriatic acid, for the purpose of extracting ink from paper; and that, with the use of a camel's hair brush, he had extracted the ink from two checks — one prepared by counsel of defendant, and the other written in imitation of the original check and with the same kind of ink. That the ink was extracted from the body of the checks without affecting the signatures, and leaving the parts where the ink was extracted perfectly white, the texture of the paper being uninjured.[2] Here the witness was not an expert, but he was permitted to testify to the facts which he had observed.

§ 136. **Comparison of Writings in Juxtaposition.**— There are two distinct methods of judging of the genuineness of handwriting by means of comparison. According to one method, a witness who has acquired personal knowledge of another's handwriting, by having seen such person write, or by having received letters from him in due course of business, may have formed in his mind an exemplar of the individual's handwriting, so that, upon the presentation of a signature, he can say, by comparing it with the exemplar in his mind, whether it corresponds or not with such

[1] Otey v. Hoyt, 2 Jones (N. C.) Law, 70.
[2] People v. Brotherton, 47 Cal. 395, 402.

exemplar. According to the other method, a witness who has no personal knowledge of another's handwriting, and therefore no exemplar in his mind, has before him in juxtaposition, the writing in dispute with other writings admitted or proved to be genuine, and from a comparison of such writings expresses an opinion whether the writings were made by the same person. The first is the comparison which the ordinary witness makes, when testifying from personal knowledge. The second is the comparison which an expert makes, testifying without such personal knowledge.

In France, papers admitted to be genuine, and writings of a public nature, such as signatures written in the presence of a notary or judge, or written or signed in a public capacity, are submitted to sworn experts, appointed by the court, for comparison with the disputed writing.[1]

In England, a comparison of handwriting placed in juxtaposition, has always been permitted in the ecclesiastical courts.[2] But in the common law courts a different rule was adopted, and experts were not allowed in those courts to express an opinion based on a comparison of hands placed in juxtaposition,[3] until the year 1854, when Parliament passed an act, hereafter set forth, which authorized such comparison to be made. But in the case of ancient documents, so old that they could not be authenticated by living witnesses, opinions based on a comparison of hands in juxtaposition, were admitted from necessity, even in the common law courts.[4]

[1] Code de Procedure Civile, Part I., § 2, tit. 10, § 200.
[2] Beaumont v. Perkins, 1 Phillimore, 78; Reilly v. Rivett, Prerog. 1792, 1 Cases in Eng. Ecc. Cts. 43, note a; Heath v. Watts Prerog. 1798, Ibid. note b; Saph v. Atkinson, 2 Eng. Ecc. R. 64, 88, 89; Machin v. Grindon, 2 Cas. temp. Lee, 335; s. c., 2 Addams, 91, note a; 1 Oughton's Ordo Judiciorum, tit. 225. De Comparatione Litterarum, etc., §§ 1, 2, 3, 10, 11 (1728).
[3] Doe v. Suckermore, 5 Ad. & Ellis, 703.
[4] Morewood v. Wood, 14 East, 327, note a; Rowe v. Rawlings, 7 East, 282, note a; Taylor v. Cook, 8 Price. 650; Doe v. Tarver, R. & M. 141; Doe v. Suckermore, 5 Ad. & Ellis, 703, 717, 724. So in Canada, Thompson v. Bennett, 22 Upper Canada (C. P.) 393, 405, 406.

In this country a difference of opinion has prevailed, and some of our State courts have denied, while others have maintained the right to introduce the testimony of experts based on a comparison of writings placed in juxtaposition. But in this country, as in England, there has been unanimity in holding that such evidence is admissible in the case of ancient documents.[1]

§ 137. **Statutory Provisions in England and in the United States Concerning Comparison of Writings.**— All dispute as to the right to receive the testimony of experts based on a comparison of hands, has been put to rest in England, and in some of the States of this country by statutory provisions adopted for that purpose. These provisions differ somewhat, some of them being more restricted than others. They are as follows:

England.— "Comparison of a disputed writing with any writing proved to the satisfaction of the judge to be genuine, shall be permitted to be made by witnesses, and such writings, and the evidence of witnesses respecting the same, may be submitted to the court and jury as evidence of the genuineness or otherwise of the writing in dispute."[2]

[1] West v. State, 22 N. J. Law, 241, 242; Clark v. Wyatt, 15 Ind. 271; Willson v. Betts, 4 Denio (N. Y.), 201; State v. Givens, 5 Ala. 754; Kirksey v. Kirksey, 41 Ala. 626, 640; Strother v. Lucas, 6 Peters, 763, 767.

[2] 28 and 29 Victoria, ch. 18, § 8. In 1854 a similar provision was passed, but it was confined in its operation to the admission of evidence in civil cases. 17 and 18 Vict., ch. 125. But in 1865 the provision was made applicable alike to civil and criminal cases. In reference to this provision it is laid down as follows: "Under this statutory law it seems clear, first, that any writings, the genuineness of which is proved to the satisfaction, not of the jury, but of the judge (see Eagan v. Cowan, 30 Law Times, 223, in Ir. Ex.), may be used for the purposes of comparison, although they may not be admissible in evidence for any other purpose in the cause (Birch v. Ridgway, 1 Fost. & Fin. 270; Cresswell v. Jackson, 2 Fost. & Fin. 24); and next, that the comparison may be made either by witnesses acquainted with the handwriting, or by witnesses skilled in deciphering handwriting, or, without the intervention of any witnesses at all, by the jury themselves (Cobbett v. Kilminster, 4 Fost. & Fin. 490, per Martin, B.), or in the event of there being no jury, by the court." 2 Taylor's Evidence, § 1668. It is to be observed, however, that this statute expressly provides that it is not to apply to Scotland.

California.— "Evidence respecting the handwriting may also be given by a comparison, made by the witness or the jury, with writings admitted or treated as genuine by the party against whom the evidence is offered or proved to be genuine to the satisfaction of the judge."[1]

Georgia.— "Other writings, proved or acknowledged to be genuine, may be admitted in evidence for the purpose of comparison by the jury. Such other new papers, when intended to be introduced, shall be submitted to the opposite party before he announces himself ready for trial."[2]

Iowa.— "Evidence respecting handwriting may be given by comparison made by experts or by the jury, with writings of the same person which are proved to be genuine."[3]

Nebraska.— "Evidence respecting handwriting may be given by comparisons made by experts or by the jury, with writings of the same person which are proved to be genuine."[4]

New Jersey.— "In all cases where the genuineness of any signature or writing is in dispute, comparison of the disputed signature or writing with any writing proved to the satisfaction of the court to be genuine, shall be permitted to be made by witnesses; and such writings, and the testimony of witnesses respecting the same, may be submitted to the court or jury as evidence of the genuineness or otherwise of the signature or writing in dispute, *provided*, *nevertheless*, that where the handwriting of any person is sought to be disproved by comparison with other writings made by him, not admissible in evidence in the cause for any other purpose, such writings, before they can be compared with the signature or writing in dispute, must, if sought to be used before the court or jury by the party in whose handwriting they are, be proved to have been written before any dispute arose as to the genuineness of the signature or writing in controversy."[5]

[1] Code of Civil Procedure, § 1944.
[2] Revised Code (1873), p. 674, § 3840.
[3] Code (1873) § 3655; 2 McClain's Annotated Statutes (1880), p. 922, § 3655.
[4] Compiled Statutes (1881), p. 576, § 344.
[5] Revision (1877), p. 381, § 19.

New York.—"Comparison of a disputed writing with any writing proved to the satisfaction of the court to be genuine, shall be permitted to be made by witnesses in all trials and proceedings, and such writings, and the evidence of witnesses respecting the same, may be submitted to the court and jury as evidence of the genuineness, or otherwise, of the writing in dispute." [1]

Oregon.—"Evidence respecting the handwriting may also be given, by a comparison made by a witness skilled in such matters, or the jury, with writings admitted or treated as genuine by the party against whom the evidence is offered." [2]

Rhode Island.—"Comparison of a disputed writing with any writing proved to the satisfaction of the judge to be genuine, shall be permitted to be made by witnesses, and such writings, and the evidence of witnesses respecting the same, may be submitted to the court and jury as evidence of the genuineness, or otherwise, of the writing in dispute." [3]

Texas.—"It is competent in every case to give evidence of handwriting by comparison, made by experts or by the jury; but proof by comparison only shall not be sufficient to establish the handwriting of a witness who denies his signature under oath." [4]

§ 138. **Comparison of Writings in the absence of Statutory Provisions.**— Where the question has been decided in this country independently of any statutory regulation, a marked difference of opinion has existed as to the rule which should be adopted.

I. According to one theory comparison of writings placed in juxtaposition is improper, and the opinions of scientific wit-

---

[1] Laws of 1880, ch. 36, p. 141.
[2] General Laws (1843-1872), p. 259, § 755.
[3] Public Statutes (1882), p. 588, § 42.
[4] Revised Statutes (1879), Code of Crim. Procedure, Art. 754. This is construed so as to admit comparison with writings admitted to be genuine or proved to be so. Heard v. State, 9 Texas Ct. of App. 1, 19; Phillips v. State, 6 Texas Ct. of App. 331; Hatch v. State, 6 ib. 384; Eborn v. Zimmerman, 47 Tex. 503.

nesses based thereon are inadmissible. It is the adoption of the English rule as finally agreed on before that rule was changed by the act of parliament already referred to. This theory has been adopted in the Supreme Court of the United States,[1] and it has been held in one of the inferior Federal Courts that the statute of a State permitting a comparison of writings for the purpose of determining the genuineness of handwriting, has no effect in a criminal case in the courts of the United States.[2] It has been adopted also in Alabama,[3] Illinois,[4] Kentucky,[5] Maryland,[6] Pennsylvania,[7] Texas,[8] Virginia[9] and Wisconsin.[10] This was the theory which was adopted in New Jersey,[11] and in Rhode Island,[12] by the courts of these respective States prior to the enactment of the statutory provisions already set forth, and adhered to by them up to the time of such enactment.

There are, however, certain exceptions to the rule. For instance, we find the Supreme Court of the United States declaring that "the general rule of the common law, disallowing a comparison of handwriting as proof of a signature, has exceptions equally as well settled as the rule itself. One of these exceptions is, that if a paper admitted to be in the handwriting of the party, or to have been subscribed by him, is in evidence for some other purpose in the cause,

[1] Strother v. Lucas, 6 Peters, 763; Moore v. United States, 91 U. S. 270.
[2] United States v. Jones, 10 Federal Reporter, 469.
[3] Little v. Beazley, 2 Ala. 703; State v. Givens, 5 Ala. 747; Kirksey v. Kirksey, 41 Ala. 640.
[4] Jumpertz v. People, 21 Ill. 374; Kernin v. Hill, 37 Ill. 209.
[5] Hawkins v. Grimes, 13 B. Monr. 267; McAlister v. McAlister, 7 B. Monr. 270.
[6] Miller v. Johnson, 27 Md. 36; Tome v. Parkersburg, etc. R. R. Co., 39 Md. 36.
[7] Amnick v. Mitchell, 82 Penn. St. 211; Haycock v. Greup, 57 Penn. St. 438; Travis v. Brown, 43 Penn. St. 9, 15; Lodge v. Pipher, 11 S. & R. 334; Bank of Pennsylvania v. Jacobs, 1 Penn. 178.
[8] Handley v. Gandy, 28 Texas, 211.
[9] Rowt. Adm'x. v. Kile's Adm'r., 1 Leigh, 216.
[10] State v. Miller, 47 Wis. 530; Hazleton v. Union Bank, 32 Wis. 34.
[11] West v. State, 22 N. J. Law, 241, 242.
[12] Kinney v. Flynn, 2 R. I. 319.

the signature or paper in question may be compared with it by the *jury*."[1]

§ 139. **Comparison of Writings in the Absence of Statutory Provisions — The Subject Continued.** — But what is more to our purpose, there are exceptions to the rule, which permit the testimony of experts in some cases to be received. And perhaps we cannot do better than to transcribe the language of the Supreme Court of Alabama, which is as follows: " That the doctrine as to experts, as applicable to signatures or writings, relates to ancient writings, which are not proved by their antiquity; and to giving their opinion as to the genuineness of a signature or writing, or its being a counterfeit, founded on a knowledge of the handwriting of the party by whom it is said to be written, or in the case of bank bills, on a knowledge of the genuineness of bills of the character in dispute, and some skill and experience that the witness may possess in detecting counterfeits, not possessed by the mass of men; and, perhaps, to an opinion as to whether a signature is genuine or counterfeit, without having any acquaintance with the hand in dispute, but not by comparison."[2]

The language of the Supreme Court of Pennsylvania on the same general subject is as follows:

" 1st. That evidence touching the genuineness of a paper in suit may be corroborated by a comparison, to be made by the jury, between that paper and other well authenticated writings of the same party.

2nd. But mere experts are not admissible to make the comparison, and to testify their conclusions from it.

3d. That witnesses having knowledge of the party's handwriting are competent to testify as to the paper in suit; but they, no more than experts, are to make comparison of hands, for that were to withdraw from the jury a duty which belongs appropriately to them.

4th. That test documents to be compared should be

[1] Moore v. United States, 91 U. S. 270.
[2] Kirksey v. Kirksey, 41 Ala. 626.

established by the most satisfactory evidence before being admitted to the jury.

5th. That experts may be examined to prove forgery or simulated writings, and to give the conclusions of skill in such cases as have been mentioned, and their like."[1]

Although the fourth of the above propositions does not relate to the particular subject we are considering, it may be remarked in passing that it goes farther than most of the cases warrant, which profess to adopt the English rule, and which limit the comparison to writings already in the case, and admitted to be genuine.[2] So in many of the States which receive the testimony of experts based on comparison, the comparison is limited to papers already in evidence and admitted to be genuine.[3]

§ 140. **Comparison of Writings in the Absence of Statutory Provisions — Comparison by Experts with Writings Admitted to be Genuine.**— II. According to a second theory a comparison of writings placed in juxtaposition is proper, the writings being in evidence for another purpose and admitted to be genuine, and the opinions of scientific witnesses based on such comparison are admissible in evidence. Such is the theory held by the courts of Colorado,[4] Indiana,[5] Kansas,[6] Michigan,[7] Missouri[8] and New York prior

---

[1] Travis v. Brown, 43 Penn. St. 9, 17 and 18.

[2] See Moore v. United States, 91 U. S. 270; Bishop v. State, 30 Ala. 34; Bestor v. Roberts, 58 Ala. 331; Miller v. Jones, 32 Ark. 337; Brobston v. Cahill, 64 Ill. 358; Hawkins v. Grimes, 13 B. Monr. (Ky.) 267; Clark v. Rhodes, 40 Tenn. 206; Fogg v. Dennis, 3 Hum. (Tenn.) 47; Hazleton v. Union Bank, 32 Wis. 34; State v. Miller, 47 Wis. 530; Clay v. Robinson, 7 W. Va. 348; Clay v. Alderson, 10 W. Va. 49.

[3] See the cases cited in succeeding section.

[4] Miller v. Eicholtz, 5 Colorado, 243.

[5] Hazzard v. Vickery, 78 Ind. 64; Forgery v. First National Bank, 66 Ind. 123, 125; Burdick v. Hunt, 43 Ind. 381; Chance v. Indianapolis, etc. Co., 32 Ind. 472.

[6] Macomber v. Scott, 10 Kans. 335.

[7] Vinton v. Peck, 14 Mich. 287; Matter of Alfred Foster's Will, 34 Mich. 21; First National Bank v. Robert, 41 Mich. 709.

[8] Corby, Exr. v. Weddle, 57 Mo. 452; State v. Clinton, 67 Mo. 380; State v. Tompkins, 71 Mo. 616; Pourcelly v. Lewis, 8 Mo. App. 593.

to legislative enactment already noted,[1] and North Carolina.[2] But in this case, as in all others where there is a comparison of writings, the rule excludes a comparison by ordinary witnesses. If the comparison by juxtaposition of writings is made by witnesses, it must be by those who are experts.[3] The rule being that a witness who is not an expert must speak from his knowledge of having seen the party write, or from authentic papers derived in the course of business.[4]

§ 141. **Comparison of Writings in the Absence of Statutory Provisions — Comparison by Experts with Writings Proved or Admitted to be Genuine.**— According to the third theory, experts are permitted to express an opinion, based not merely on a comparison of writings conceded to be genuine, but on writings the genuineness of which has been proved on the trial for the express purpose of comparison. Such testimony has been received in Connecticut,[5] Maine,[6] Massachusetts,[7] Mississippi,[8] New Hampshire,[9] and Ohio.[10]

The objections to the introduction of specimens of handwriting not admitted to be genuine and not otherwise in the case, are succinctly stated by the Supreme Court of Kansas, and may be repeated here in this connection: "The principal, if not the only objections urged against this kind of evidence are as follows: 1st. The writings

[1] Dubois v. Baker, 30 N. Y. 355.
[2] Yates v. Yates, 76 N. C. 142; McLeod v. Bullard, 84 N. C. 515.
[3] Forgery v. First National Bank, 66 Ind. 123, 125; Chance v. Indianapolis, etc. Co., 23 Ind. 472; Woodman v. Dana, 52 Me. 9; State v. Owen, 73 Mo. 440; First National Bank of Omaha v. Lierman, 5 Neb. 247.
[4] See Strother v. Lucas, 6 Peters, 763; Rogers v. Ritter, 12 Wall. 317.
[5] Tyler v. Todd, 36 Conn. 222; Lyon v. Lyman, 9 Conn. 59, 60.
[6] Sweetser v. Lowell, 33 Me. 446; Woodman v. Dana, 52 Me. 9; Page v. Homans, 14 Me. 478.
[7] Moody v. Rowell, 17 Pick. 490; Richardson v. Newcomb, 21 Pick. 315; King v. Donahue, 110 Mass. 155, 156; Martin v. Wallis, 11 Mass. 309, 312; Martin v. Maguire, 7 Gray, 177.
[8] Wilson v. Beauchamp, 50 Miss. 24.
[9] State v. Hastings, 53 N. H. 452.
[10] Pavey v. Pavey, 30 Ohio St. 600; Bragg v. Colwell, 19 Ohio St. 412; Calkins v. State, 14 Ohio St. 222; Hicks v. Person, 19 Ohio, 426.

offered in evidence as specimens, may be manufactured for the occasion. 2nd. Fraud may be practiced in the selection of the writings. 3d. The other party may be surprised; he may not know what documents are to be produced, and therefore he may not be prepared to meet the inferences sought to be drawn from them. 4th. The handwriting of a person may be changed by age, health, habits, state of mind, position, haste, penmanship, and writing materials. 5th. The genuineness of the specimens of handwriting offered in evidence may be contested, and others successively introduced, to the infinite multiplication of collateral issues, and the subversion of justice. 6th. Juries are too illiterate, and are not competent to judge of this kind of evidence."[1]

§ 142. **Proof of the Genuineness of the Writing Offered for Comparison.**— In the English statute it is expressly provided that the writing offered as a standard, if not admitted to be genuine, must be proved genuine to the satisfaction of the court. And so it is provided in the statute of California, of New Jersey, of New York and of Rhode Island. But the statutes of the other States contain no such provision. The question is then presented whether in such cases the proof of the genuineness of the instrument is addressed to the court or the jury. In New Hampshire it seems the question rests solely with the jury, and if they determine that the proof is insufficient, it becomes their duty to lay the writing, and all the evidence of the experts based on its genuineness, entirely out of the case.[2] But elsewhere the courts have held such proof to be addressed in the first instance to the court,[3] yet the fact that the court has adjudged the papers genuine does not debar the jury from ultimately determining the question for themselves.[4]

And the general rule is that the proof of the genuineness of the instrument thus offered must be positive. It should

---

[1] Macomber v. Scott, 10 Kans. 339.
[2] State v. Hastings, 53 N. H. 452, 461.
[3] Bragg v. Colwell, 19 Ohio St. 412; State v. Ward, 39 Vt. 225.
[4] State v. Ward, *supra*.

be proved either by the admission of the party when the standard is not offered by himself, or else by the testimony of persons who testify directly and positively to having seen the party write the paper.[1] This was the rule, too, in the English ecclesiastical courts, where the maxim was: *Testes qui poterint deponere, quod viderunt testatorem subscribentem hujus modi scriptis*, etc.[2]

As the Supreme Court of Massachusetts has expressed it, the genuineness of a writing to be used as a standard of comparison, " must be shown beyond a doubt."[3]

And the court in the case last cited held that it could not be shown by producing a paper which had been witnessed, and then proving the handwriting of the subscribing witness, upon due proof being made that such witness resided out of the State. So the same court in a subsequent case has held that letters received from the testator in answer to letters to him, could not be received as standards.[4] Where a receipt was offered as a standard, and the witness testified that the defendant gave him a receipt that looked very similar to the one offered, but could not positively say that it was the identical one, the Supreme Court of Ohio held the proof too uncertain to admit of the reception of the paper.[5]

§ 143. **Expert should have Before him in Court the Writings Compared.**— The rule is that an expert in handwriting, when speaking as a witness only from a comparison, should have before him in court the writings compared.[6] The reason being that their presence is essential to an intelligent examination in chief, as well as to an intelligent cross-examination ; nor can there be any fair means of

---

[1] Hyde v. Woolfok, 1 Iowa, 159; Pavey v. Pavey, 30 Ohio St. 600; Calkins v. State, 14 Ohio St. 222, 228; Bragg v. Colwell, 19 Ohio 412; Eborn v. Zimpleman, 47 Texas, 503, 518.

[2] Oughton's Ordo Judiciorum, tit. 225; De Comparatione Litterarum, § 3; Beaumont v. Perkins, 1 Phillimore, 78.

[3] Martin v. Maguire, 7 Gray, 177. And see Baker v. Haines, 6 Wharton (Penn.) 291; De Pue v. Place, 7 Penn. St. 429.

[4] McKeone v. Barnes, 108 Mass. 344.

[5] Pavey v. Pavey, 30 Ohio St. 600.

[6] Hynes v. McDermott, 82 N. Y. 41; Woodman v. Dana, 52 Me. 9.

meeting the testimony of the witness by that of other witnesses, unless the writings upon which the opinion of the expert is based are in court to be presented to other experts for their opinion. But where the original writing is lost, and the loss has been clearly proved, the opinion of an expert has been received as to the genuineness of the signature to the lost instrument, he having examined the signature prior to its loss, and compared his recollection of such signature with the admitted genuine signatures of the same person, on papers already in the case.[1] And an expert has been allowed to testify that entries upon hotel registers, which he had seen and examined, were in the handwriting of the person who wrote certain other signatures, which were produced and proved or admitted to be genuine, although the entries were not before the jury, the registers having been destroyed, by the person whose signature was in question, for the purpose of suppressing the evidence.[2] So where the State, upon an indictment for forgery, was unable to produce the check alleged to have been forged by the prisoner, an expert, called by the State, and who had seen the alleged forged check several months previously, was permitted to testify as to the genuineness of the signature, a genuine signature of the accused having been shown on the trial.[3]

§ 144. **The Writing Compared should be the Original and not a Photographic Copy.**— In a late case in New York the Court of Appeals refused to permit the comparison of a signature in dispute with photographic copies of other writings, for the purpose of getting the opinion of an expert as to whether a signature was real or feigned.[4] But stress was laid upon the fact that the originals from which the copies were made were not brought into court, and could not be shown to other witnesses. And no proof had been presented as to the manner and exactness of the photo-

---
[1] Abbott v. Coleman, 21 Kans. 250.
[2] State v. Shinborn, 46 N. H. 497.
[3] Koons v. State, 36 Ohio St. 195.
[4] Hynes v. McDermott, 82 N. Y. 41.

graphic method used. "We may recognize," said the court, "that the photographic process is ruled by general laws that are uniform in their operation, and that almost without exception a likeness is brought forth of the object set before the camera. Still somewhat for exact likeness will depend upon the adjustment of the machinery, upon the atmospheric conditions, and the skill of the manipulator. And in so delicate a matter as the reaching of judicial results by the comparison of writings through the testimony of experts, it ought to be required that the witness should exercise his acumen upon the thing itself which is to be the basis of his judgment; and still more, that the thing itself should be at hand, to be put under the eye of other witnesses for the trial upon it of their skill. The certainty of expert testimony in these cases is not so well assured as that we can afford to let in the errors or differences in copying, though it be done by howsoever a scientific process." The objections to the use of photographic copies in such cases were very ably stated in a decision excluding the opinions based on such evidence, in a case decided some ten years before in the Surrogate's Court of the county of New York. It was said that such evidence would raise many collateral issues, as, for instance, the correctness of the lens, the state of the weather, the skill of the operator, the color of the impression, the purity of the chemicals, the accuracy of the focusing, the angle at which the original to be copied was inclined to the sensitive plate, etc. "When we reflect that by placing the original to be copied obliquely to the sensitive plate, the portion nearest to the plate may be distorted by being enlarged, and that the portion furthest from the plate must be correspondingly decreased, whilst the slightest bulging of the paper upon which the signature is printed may make a part blurred, and not sharply defined, we can form some idea of the fallacies to which this subject is liable. * * * In what manner can photography make the signature, in any practical sense, more apparent to the observer than the signature itself? The operator may, moreover, through fraud or skill, make some particular lines in the reproduced signature stand forth more prominently than in the original signature. If the photograph be an absolutely perfect reproduction of the original signature — the former being the same as the latter — there can be no necessity for the study of the reproduction. If, through the fraud or skill of the operator, some lines be brought out with undue prominence, then it should not be considered proper evidence on which to base an opinion, for it is not a correct reproduction." [1]

The right to make a comparison with photographic copies of handwriting, has also been denied in Maryland,[2] but the force of these cases is weakened by the fact that a comparison of hands is not permitted in that State, the old English rule being still adhered to. But the question was fairly raised in Texas in *Eborn* v. *Zimpelman*,[3] where an attempt was made to introduce in evidence the opinion of a witness, living in another State, as to the genuineness of a disputed handwriting, the opinion being based on a photographic copy of the instrument in dispute, attached to the interrogatories. In support of the admissibility of the evidence, it was urged that the court should take judicial notice that the photographic process secured a mathematically exact reproduction of the original, and that therefore, evidence as to the handwriting of such a copy, was as satisfactory as though it referred to the original. The conclusion reached by the court was that photographic copies of instruments sued on, could only be used as secondary evidence, and rejected the testimony upon the ground that no foundation had been laid for it.

The Supreme Court of Michigan, speaking of this kind of evidence, said in the *Matter of Alfred Foster's Will*,[4] decided in 1876: "If the court had permitted photographic copies of the will to be given to the jury, with such precau-

---

[1] Taylor Will Case, 10 Abb. Pr. (N. S.) 300, per Surrogate Hutchings.
[2] Miller v. Johnson, 27 Md. 36; Tome v. Parkersburg, 39 Md. 36.
[3] 47 Texas, 503.
[4] 34 Mich. 23.

tions as to secure their identity and correctness, it might not, perhaps, have been error. Nevertheless, it is not always true that every photographic copy would be safe on any inquiry requiring minute accuracy. Few copies can be so satisfactory as a good photograph, but all artists are not competent to make such pictures on a large scale, and all photographs are not absolutely faithful resemblances. It is quite possible to tamper with them, and an impression which is at all blurred would be very apt to mislead on questions of handwriting where forgery is claimed. Whether it would or would not be permissible to allow such documents to be used, their use can never be compulsory. The original, and not the copy, is what the jury must act upon, and no device can be properly allowed to supersede it. Copies of any kind are merely secondary evidence, and in this case they were intended to be used as equivalent to primary evidence in determining the genuineness of the primary document."

§ 145. **Comparison with Photographic Copies Allowed, when.**— In a case where the original papers were on file in the War Department, and could not be removed without public detriment and inconvenience, Mr. Justice BRADLEY held that photographic copies could be received, as being the best evidence the case admitted of.[1] A comparison with photographic copies of handwriting has been held to be proper in Massachusetts, where the copies had first been verified by the oath of the photographer as being accurate in all respects, excepting only in relation to size and color.[2] It was thought to be not dissimilar to an examination of the writing with a magnifying glass. "Under proper precautions," said the court, "in relation to the preliminary proof as to the exactness and accuracy of the copies produced by the art of the photographer, we are unable to perceive any valid objection to the use of such prepared representations

---

[1] Leathers v. Salvor Wrecking Co., 2 Wood, 680, 682.
[2] Marcy v. Barnes, 16 Gray, 161. The photograph ought to be verified by the oath of the photographer. Hollenbeck v. Rowly, 8 Allen, 473.

of original and genuine signatures as evidence competent to be exhibited and weighed by the jury."

§ 146. **Writings Admissible for Comparison in Orthography.**— Although prior to the act of 1854 writings could not be introduced in evidence in the English courts, for the purpose of showing a similarity in the formation of letters, or figures and modes of writing, yet it was held they could be introduced for the purpose of proving a particular mode of spelling. For such a purpose specimens of the party's handwriting containing that particular orthography were admissible.[1] A peculiar case of this kind occurred at the Greenwich County Court. The party denied most positively that a certain receipt was in his handwriting. It read, " Received the Hole of the above." He was asked to write a sentence containing the word " whole." He took pains to disguise his hand, but adopted the above phonetic style of spelling, even retaining the capital H.[2] But in Wisconsin a different view seems to have been taken of the subject, although the preceding cases were not brought to the attention of the court. In that case, which was an indictment for arson, the prosecution desired to show that a letter, containing threats of arson, was written by the prisoner. It contained words of peculiar form, style and orthography, and was repeated to him orally and verbally by the police officers at the station, who requested him to write as they read. The copy thus made was found to be an exact *fac· simile* of the original in the peculiarities above noted. The court excluded it on the ground that a comparison of hands was not allowable. The letter, however, might perhaps have been inadmissible on other grounds, as that it was compelling the prisoner to give evidence against himself; but this was not referred to by the court.

§ 147. **Comparison with Writings made on the Trial.**— A party cannot be compelled on cross-examination, to write his name in court for the purpose of having it compared

---

[1] Brookes v. Tichborne, 5 Exch. 929.
[2] Taylor on Evidence, 1552, note *a*.

with the disputed writing.[1] But if he writes his name as requested, it has been held that it may be used as a standard of comparison, for the purpose of contradicting him.[2] Hence in a recent case in Nebraska, where the defendant denied the genuineness of a promissory note, and called his son as a witness, who testified in chief that certain words in the note which his father actually gave were written by himself, and on cross-examination was requested to write the same words in the presence of the jury, it was held that such writing could be used for purposes of comparison, the party conducting the examination taking the risk whether the writing was dissimilar or not.[3] But a party is not entitled to write his signature in the presence of the jury for purposes of comparison with a signature puporting to be his, the genuineness of which he denies.[4] So it has been held error to permit a witness, who confesses to having written the forged instrument under the direction and request of the prisoner, to write a similar instrument in the presence of the court and jury, for purposes of comparison.[5]

§ 148. Comparison of Writings—Testing Accuracy of Expert on Cross-Examination.—It is not competent, on cross-examination of an expert in handwriting, who has testified to the genuineness of a signature, to submit to him a disputed signature for the purpose of testing his accuracy.[6] That it is not submitted for purposes of comparison, but simply to test the accuracy of the witness, renders it none the less inadmissible.[7] And a genuine signature is as inadmissible for this purpose as a spurious one would be.[8]

[1] First National Bank of Houghton v. Robert, 41 Mich. 709.
[2] Cobbett v. Kilminster, 4 Fos. & Fin. 490; Doe v. Wilson, 10 Moore, P. C. 502, 530; Chandler v. LeBarron, 45 Me. 534.
[3] Huff v. Nims, 11 Neb. 364.
[4] King v. Donahue, 110 Mass. 155.
[5] Williams v. State, 61 Ala. 33.
[6] Tyler v. Todd, 36 Conn. 222; Bacon v. Williams, 13 Gray, 525; Howard v. Patrick. 43 Mich. 128.
[7] Van Wyck v. McIntosh, 14 N. Y. 439; Bank of Commonwealth v. Mudgett, 44 N. Y. 514.
[8] Fogg v. Dennis, 3 Humph. (Tenn.) 47.

§ 149. **Detection of Counterfeit Bank Notes.** — Books known as bank note detectors, are not competent evidence as to the genuineness or worthlessness of bank bills, neither is the testimony of a witness who does not profess to be an expert.[1] One who is not acquainted with the handwriting of the president or cashier of the bank, but who has studied and learned the system by which it is believed counterfeit bank notes can be detected, and who has such knowledge of the marks and devices used in etching and engraving as enables him to detect gross counterfeits, is competent to testify as an expert concerning the genuineness of bank notes.[2] So where a witness has been in the habit of receiving and paying out notes of the bank, and believes that he has thereby become acquainted with the handwriting of its president and cashier, he is considered qualified by his experience, although he has never seen these officers write, to testify as to the genuineness of notes purporting to have been issued by the bank.[3] One who is a bank officer, engaged in banking, and a judge of counterfeit money, is competent to give his opinion as an expert as to the spuriousness of a bank note.[4] A cashier who has received and passed a great number of the notes of the bank in question, and believes he can distinguish between a genuine and counterfeit note, is competent to give his opinion as an expert.[5] The same principle governs in the case of tellers.[6] But bank officers are not the only witnesses who are qualified to testify in such cases. And it has been said that the opinion of any one, who is familiar with the notes of the bank in question, may be received.[7] Hence the testimony of mer-

[1] Payson v. Everett, 12 Minn. 216.
[2] Jones v. Finch, 37 Miss. 468.
[3] Allen v. State, 3 Humph. (Tenn.) 367; Commonwealth v. Carey, 2 Pick. (Mass.) 47; State v. Candler, 3 Hawk's Law & Eq. (N. C.) 393; Sasser v. State, 13 Ohio, 453; Hess v. Ohio, 5 Ohio, 6; Kirksey v. Kirksey, 41 Ala. 626; State v. Allen. 1 Hawk's L. & Eq. (N. C.) 6.
[4] May v. Dorsett, 30 Ga. 116; State v. Hooper, 2 Bailey (S. C.) Law. 37; Atwood v. Cornwall, 28 Mich. 339.
[5] State v. Harris, 5 Ired. (N. C.) Law, 287.
[6] Hess v. Ohio, 5 Ohio. 6; Kirksey v. Kirksey, 41 Ala. 626.
[7] State v. Hooper, 2 Bailey, (S. C. Law, 37; State v. Tutt, Ib. 44.

chants, brokers and others, who are in the habit of receiving, scrutinizing and paying out the notes of the bank, is received as coming from witnesses whose experience renders them qualified to express an opinion.[1] In New Hampshire it is said that a bill may be proved to be a counterfeit by persons who know the signatures of the president and cashier, by having seen the bills in circulation.[2] Experts are allowed to testify as to the false character of bank bills, without first proving that the bank purporting to issue them had an existence,[3] or that it had issued genuine bills of which those in question might be counterfeits.[4] In the case of bills of exchange, it has been held that one who had presented to the firm many notes which had been paid by them, was qualified by his experience to testify, that, in his opinion, the handwriting of the bill in question was the same as that upon the bills which the firm had paid.[5] Although it cannot be considered as laying down a correct principle of law, it is worthy of note that in an early case in the New York court of sessions, it was ruled that experts should not be allowed to swear as to the genuiness of bank bills, if witnesses could be produced who had seen the president and cashier write.[6]

§ 150. **Regulation of such Evidence by Statutory Provision.**— In some of the States statutory provision has been made as to the reception of evidence in the cases considered in the preceding section. Such provision has been made in Illinois, Indiana, Kansas, Pennsylvania, and perhaps elsewhere.

Illinois.— "Persons of skill shall be competent to testify as to the genuineness of any bill, note or other instrument alleged to be forged or counterfeited." [7]

[1] State v. Cheek, 13 Ired. (N. C.) 114; Watson v. Cresap, 1 B. Monr. (Ky.) 196.
[2] State v. Carr, 5 N. H. 369, 373.
[3] Jones v. State, 11 Ind. 357.
[4] Crawford v. State, 2 Ind. 132.
[5] Gordon v. Price, 10 Ired. (N. C.) 385.
[6] People v. Badger, 1 Wheeler, Cr. Cas. 543.
[7] Revised Statutes (1880), ch. 38, § 109.

Indiana.— "Persons of skill may be called to prove the genuineness of a note, bill, draft, or certificate of deposit, but three witnesses, at least, shall be required to prove the fact, except in the case of a larceny thereof, the simple evidence of the cashier of a bank purporting to have issued the same may be received as sufficient."[1]

Kansas.— "Persons of skill or experts may be called to testify as to the genuineness of a note, bill, draft, certificate of deposit, or other writing, but three witnesses, at least, shall be required to prove the fact, except in the case of a larceny thereof, the single evidence of the president, cashier, or teller of the bank purporting to have issued the same, or the maker thereof, may be received as sufficient."[2]

Pennsylvania.— "Upon the trial of any indictment for making, or passing and uttering any false, forged or counterfeit coin, or bank note, the court may receive in evidence to establish either the genuineness or falsity of such coin or note, the oaths or affirmations of witnesses who may by experience and habit have become expert in judging of the genuineness or otherwise of such coin or paper, and such testimony may be submitted to the jury without first requiring proof of the handwriting or the other tests of genuineness, as the case may be, which have been heretofore required by law."[3]

In Maine it is provided that in the case of forged bank notes, etc., if the president or cashier reside out of the State, or more than forty miles from the place of trial, the opinions of other witnesses may be received.[4] And in Rhode Island it is provided that the opinions of skilled persons may be received in such cases, provided the persons whose names are forged are out of the State, or reside thirty miles distant from the place of trial.[5]

---

[1] 2 Revised Statutes (1876), p. 396, § 91.
[2] General Statutes (1868), p. 854, § 216.
[3] 1 Brightly's Purd. Dig. (1700-1872), p. 631, § 63.
[4] Revised Statutes. (1871), p. 836, § 8.
[5] Public Statutes (1882), p. 589, § 44.

CHAPTER VIII.

VALUE.

SECTION.
151. Value as a Subject for the Testimony of Experts.
152. The Amount of Damages.
153. Opinions of Non-Professional Witnesses.
154. Qualifications of the Expert in Values.
155. Not Necessary that Expert should see the Property.
156. Time of Examination of Property by Expert.
157. Competency in Particular Cases.
158. Competency in Particular Cases—The Subject Continued.
159. Value of Legal Services.
160. Value of Services Rendered by Physicians and Nurses.
161. Value of Services in other Callings.
162. Opinions as to Value of Real Estate.
163. Value of Annuities.
164. Value of Foreign Currency and Negotiable Securities.
165. Opinions of Merchants and Brokers.

§ 151. **Value as a Subject for the Testimony of Experts.**—The opinions of experts are received in evidence on the question of value.[1] "It is every day's practice," said Mr. Chief Justice NELSON of New York, "to take the opinion of witnesses as to the value of property—persons who are supposed to be conversant with the particular article in question, and of its value in the market: as a farmer, or dealer

[1] Brown v. Providence & Springfield R. R. Co., 12 R. I. 238; Buffum v. N. Y. Cent. etc. R. R. Co., 4 R. I. 221; Forbes v. Howard, 4 R. I. 366; Cantling v. Hannibal etc. R. R. Co., 54 Mo. 385; Hough v. Cook, 69 Ill. 381; Shaw v. City of Charlestown, 2 Gray (Mass.), 109; Edmonds v. City of Boston, 108 Mass. 535; Dickenson v. Fitchburg, 13 Gray (Mass.), 546; Cobb v. City of Boston, 109 Mass. 438; Burger v. Northern Pacific R. R. Co., 22 Minn. 343, 347; Crawford v. Wolf, 29 Iowa, 568; Tebbetts v. Haskins, 16 Me. 283, 289.

in, or person conversant with the article, as to the value of lands, cattle, horses, produce, etc. These cases all stand upon the general ground of peculiar skill and judgment in the matters about which opinions are sought."[1] This rule however, did not commend itself to the courts of New Hampshire, and the practice there was to exclude the opinions of witnesses on questions of value, in cases where it was customary in the courts of other States to unhesitatingly receive them, provided only, the witnesses were duly qualified to testify in relation to the subject of inquiry. For example, the practice in that State was to exclude the opinions of witnesses as to the value of real estate, irrespective of any question as to their qualifications.[2] The exclusion was based on the assumption that the ordinary value of land of a particular description, within the county, was a matter of public notoriety, and was, therefore, such a question as the jury, required by statute to be composed of freeholders, would be fully conversant with, and abundantly able to decide. So in the same State the courts have held that there was nothing in the study, or ordinary observation of horses, which entitled a witness to be introduced as an expert as to their value.[3] This practice of excluding opinions in such cases, was found not to work well, and was embarrassing to the jury, as well as prejudicial to the rights of the parties interested in the litigation. The legislature accordingly interfered, and provided as follows: "The opinions of witnesses as to the value of any real estate, goods or chattels, may be received as evidence thereof, when it appears to the court that they are qualified to judge of such value."[4]

The rule that the opinions of witnesses are admissible on questions of value, is, of course, inapplicable in those cases

[1] Lincoln v. Saratoga etc. R. R. Co., 23 Wend. 425, 433.
[2] Rochester v. Chester, 3 N. H. 364; Petterborough v. Jaffrey, 6 N. H. 462; Holtt v. Moulton, 1 Foster, 586; Marshall v. Columbian Mutual Fire Ins. Co., 7 Foster, 157.
[3] Robertson v. Stark, 15 N. H. 109; Low v. Connecticut etc. R. R. Co., 45 N. H. 370, 381.
[4] General Laws of New Hampshire (1878), p. 532, § 23.

in which the subject of value is susceptible of specific proof. Hence, in a recent case in the United States Court of Claims, the court declared that the testimony of experts could not be received to show the value of a cotton factor's outlays for insurance, freight, rebating, etc., inasmuch as specific proof could be given of the outlays actually made by the factor.[1] And in a case in New York where a witness, who stated that he knew the effect on fat cattle of getting out of an inclosure and wandering about, was asked what, in his opinion, would be the shrinkage of certain cattle, which he had not seen, resulting from such a tramp, it was held that he could not answer. The court said: "To admit this, was to extend the admissibility of evidence by experts too far. There could be no difficulty, in this case, in showing the actual injury to the cattle which followed their escape and their wandering about. If they had shrunk in weight, or had been injured in appearance, these facts could have been proved by those who saw them. For these were plain and conspicuous results. To prove what is the usual effect of such an escape on such cattle, is to substitute conjecture for certainty."[2] The object, of course, was to show the depreciation in value of the cattle. The opinions of witnesses will be incompetent wherever the data upon which the conclusions of the experts are based, do not have that certainty of relation which entitles them to authority as a law of science. It has, for this reason, been held that a conjectural deduction, or generalization, made by experts upon the operation of other railroads, was incompetent evidence for the purpose of showing the worth of the government's right to use the plaintiff's road.[3] The experts were persons specially familiar with railroads and railroad accounts, and the claimants contended that they had proven by them that 20 per cent. of the gross transportation earnings of a railroad, was a reasonable and proper deduction for the use of

[1] Patten v. United States, 15 Ct. of Cl. 288. See too, Page v. Hazard, 5 Hill (N. Y.), 603.
[2] Schernerhorn v. Tyler, 11 Hun, 551.
[3] Atchison etc. R. R. Co. v. United States, 15 Ct. of Cl. 126.

a railroad, and that they were, therefore, entitled to recover 80 per cent. of their tariff rates. The court refused to consider the evidence, on the ground that inasmuch as railroads differed in their essential features, the data were too uncertain to entitle them to authority as a law of science. While, on the other hand, it has been held that the opinions of witnesses specially acquainted with the business of the railroad in question, and of the expenses of operating it, would be competent evidence as to the value of the use of the particular road during a given time.[1] There may be inquiries as to value which, from their very nature, cannot be answered by any one as an expert. Such would be an inquiry into the value of the reversion of land over which a railroad is located; the value of which necessarily depends on the length of time that the public easement over it may continue. As the essential element on which the inquiry turns is one in relation to which there has been no experience, it follows that an expert could not be heard to express an opinion thereon.[2]

§ 152. **The Amount of Damages.**— We find it laid down generally in the authorities, that on questions as to the amount of damages resulting from a particular transaction, witnesses are not permitted to express an opinion, but are confined to a description of the injuries; it being the duty of the jury to estimate the damages from the facts proven as to the nature and character of the injuries.[3] It is, how-

[1] Sturgis v. Knapp, 33 Vt. 486.
[2] Boston etc. R. R. Co. v. Old Colony etc. R. R. Co., 3 Allen (Mass.), 142, 147.
[3] Lincoln v. Saratoga, etc. R. R. Co., 23 Wend. (N. Y.) 433; Norman v. Wells, 17 Wend. (N. Y.) 136; Dunham v. Simons, 3 Hill (N. Y.), 609; Fish v. Dodge. 4 Denio (N. Y.), 311; Thompson v. Dickhart, 66 Barb. (N. Y.) 604; Terpenning v. Corn Exchange Ins. Co., 43 N. Y. 279; Whitmore v. Bischoff, 5 Hun (N. Y.), 176; Fleming v. Delaware, etc. Canal Co., 8 Hun (N. Y.), 358; Evansville R. R. Co. v. Fitzpatrick, 10 Ind. 120; Sinclair v. Roush, 14 Ind. 450; Mitchell v. Allison, 29 Ind. 43; Bissell v. Weir, 35 Ind. 54; Ohio, etc. R. R. Co. v. Nickless, 71 Ind. 271; Pierson v. Wallace, 7 Ark. 282; Central Railroad, etc. Co. v. Kelly, 58 Ga. 107; Wilcox v. Leake, 11 La. Ann. 178; Atlantic, etc. R. R. Co. v. Campbell, 4 Ohio St. 583; Cleveland, etc. R. R. Co.

ever, well settled that a competent witness may be asked to state his opinion as to the value of property before and after the injury complained of.[1] So that practically the same result is attained, as though the witness expressed an opinion in answer to a direct inquiry as to the amount of damages. The only difference seems to be, that in the one case, the jury make the subtraction, in the other, the witness. It certainly seems to be a very immaterial distinction, which is of no consequence whatever. And in some States witnesses are permitted to express an opinion in answer to a direct inquiry, in all cases where the value of property is in issue. Such is declared to be the well settled law in Massachusetts,[2] and the courts elsewhere are recognizing and asserting the same doctrine.[3] There seems to be a growing tendency to permit witnesses to express an

---

v. Ball, 5 Ohio St. 568; Roberts v. Commissioners of Brown County, 21 Kans. 248; Whitmore v. Bowman, 4 G. Greene (Iowa) 148; Anson v. Dwight, 18 Iowa, 244.

[1] Schuylkill Navigation Co. v. Thoburn, 7 S. & R. (Penn.) 411, 422, 423; Watson v. Pittsburgh, etc. R. R. Co., 37 Penn. St. 469, 481; East Pennsylvania R. R. Co. v. Hottenstine, 47 Penn. St. 30; Shaw v. City of Charleston, 2 Gray, 107; Inhabitants of West Newbury v. Chase, 5 Gray (Mass.), 421; Swan v. Middlesex, 101 Mass. 173; Sexton v. North Bridgewater, 116 Mass. 201; Simmons v. St. Paul, etc. R. R. Co., 18 Minn. 184, 189, 190; Colvill v. St. Paul, etc. R. R. Co., 19 Minn. 283, 285; Smalley v. Iowa Pacific R. R. Co., 36 Iowa, 571, 574; Snow v. Boston, etc. R. R. Co., 65 Me. 230, 231; Whiteley v. Inhabitants of China, 61 Me. 199; Haskell v. Mitchell, 53 Me. 466; Carter v. Thurston, 58 N. H. 104; Houston, etc. R. R. Co. v. Knapp, 51 Texas, 592; Curtis v. St. Paul, etc. R. R. Co., 20 Minn. 28; Churchill v. Price, 44 Wis. 542. In Morehouse v. Mathews, 2 N. Y. 514, it was held improper to permit a witness to state the amount of damage which cattle suffered by improper feeding, but the court held that he might state how much less valuable the cattle were when taken away, than they were when taken to the defendant's.

[2] Shattuck v. Stoneham Branch R. R. Co., 6 Allen (Mass.), 116, 117.

[3] Rochester, etc. R. R. Co. v. Budlong, 10 How. Pr. (N. Y.) 289; Snow v. Boston, etc. R. R. Co., 65 Me. 230, 231; Keithsburg, etc. R. R. Co. v. Henry, 79 Ill. 290; Cooper v. Randall, 59 Ill. 317; White & Deer Creek, etc. Co. v. Sassaman, 67 Penn. St. 415, 421; Ottawa Gas Light Co. v. Graham, 35 Ill. 346; Curtis v. St. Paul, etc. R. R. Co., 20 Minn. 28; Snyder v. Western Union R. R. Co., 25 Wis. 60, 66, 70. In Mississippi River Bridge Co. v. Ring, 58 Mo. 492, witnesses appear to have testified to the damage, no objection being made thereto.

opinion on the amount of damages, where the value of property is in issue.[1] The true principle would seem to be, and has been so laid down in a carefully considered case, that whenever the question of value and the question of damages are identical, that then the opinions of witnesses may be received as to the amount of damages. That there is no such inherent distinction between questions of value and questions of damages, if from the latter is excluded all idea of any legal rule or measure of damages, as brings the one within and the other without the province of the opinions of witnesses.[2] And the rule is that where the injury sustained is of such a nature that only an expert can properly form an opinion in reference to it, or when the character of the property is such that only experts can properly form an opinion as to its value, an ordinary witness is incompetent to express an opinion as to the amount of damages, and experts must be called for that purpose.[3]

§ 153. **Opinions of Non-Professional Witnesses.**—The opinions of persons acquainted with the value of property are sometimes received in evidence, although such knowledge may not be the result of any peculiar skill in any particular branch of business, or department of science.[4] They are received upon the ground of necessity.[5] "These opinions are admitted, not as being the opinions of experts,

[1] See Mills on Em. Domain, § 165.
[2] Rochester, etc. R. R. Co. v. Budlong, 10 How. Pr. (N. Y.) 289.
[3] See 1 Wharton on Evidence, § 450.
[4] Swan v. Middlesex. 101 Mass. 173; Wyman v. Lexington. etc. R. R. Co., 13 Met. (Mass.) 216, 326; Dalzell v. City of Davenport, 12 Iowa, 437, 440; Whitfield v. Whitfield, 40 Miss. 352, 358; Cantling v. Hannibal, etc. R. R. Co., 54 Mo. 385; Continental Ins. Co. v. Horton. 28 Mich. 173; Printz v. People, 42 Mich. 144; Richardson v. McGoldrick, 43 Mich. 476; Keables v. Christie. 47 Mich. 595; Whitesell v. Crane, 8 W. & S. (Penn.) 372; McGill v. Rowand. 3 Penn St. 452; Mish v. Wood, 34 Penn. St. 451, 454; Thatcher v. Kaucher, 2 Col. 698; Cooper v. State, 53 Miss. 393; Cooper v. Randall, 59 Ill. 317, 320; Washington, etc. Co. v. Webster, 68 Me. 449; Anson v. Dwight, 18 Iowa, 244; Foster v. Ward, 75 Ind. 594; Pittsburgh. etc. R. R. Co. v. Rose, 74 Penn. St. 368, 362; Chamness v. Chamness, 53 Ind. 304.
[5] Wyman v. Lexington, etc. R. R. Co., 13 Met. (Mass.) 316, 326; Dalzell v. City of Davenport, 12 Iowa, 437, 440.

strictly so called, for they are not founded on special study or training, or professional experience, but rather from necessity, upon the ground that they depend upon knowledge which any one may acquire, but which the jury may not have, and that they are the most satisfactory, and often the only attainable evidence of the fact to be proved.[1]

A distinguished writer has stated the rule as follows:

"Two essentials, therefore, exist to a proper estimate of value:

"*First*. A knowledge of the intrinsic properties of the thing.

"*Secondly*. A knowledge of the state of the markets. As to such intrinsic properties as are occult, and out of the range of common observers, experts are required to testify; as to the properties which are cognizable by an observer of ordinary business sagacity, being familiar with the thing, such an observer is permitted to testify."[2]

But whenever it is desired to have the opinions of a witness on the subject of value, it is always necessary, whether the witness is offered as an expert or not, to lay some foundation for the introduction of his opinion, by showing that he has had the means to form an intelligent opinion, "derived from an adequate knowledge of the nature and kind of property in controversy, and of its value."[3]

§ 154. **Qualifications of the Expert in Values.**—Where a witness is produced to testify, in the character of an expert, as to the value of property, it should appear that he has some special skill or experience, or peculiar knowledge of the value of the class of property about which it is proposed to question him, such skill or knowledge having been acquired by him in the line of his business or profession.

---

[1] Swan v. Middlesex, 101 Mass. 173, per Gray. J.
[2] 1 Wharton's Evidence, § 447.
[3] Whitney v. City of Boston, 98 Mass. 315. In this case it was held no error to exclude the opinion of a shoemaker as to the value of land, who had hired one of several buildings on the land, occupying the upper stories and underletting the lower. And see Chambovet v. Cagnet, 3 J. & S. (N. Y.) 474; Haight v. Kimbak, 51 Iowa, 13.

Where the question was as to the value of a house, a witness, whose business was the loaning of money on real estate, was held incompetent to testify as an expert concerning the value of the house, for the reason that it did not appear that his experience in the matter of houses was such as to make him from the nature of his profession, an exact judge in such matters.[1] So it has been held that witnesses are not competent to testify as experts to the effect of dampness in the cellar of a store in lessening the value of the annual rent of the building, whose experience consisted merely in hiring stores, and being acquainted with their value. "Two witnesses," said the court, "were allowed to testify as experts after objection, as to the effect of the state of the cellar upon the value of the premises in question, when their only stock and extent of experience consisted of having hired stores, and being acquainted with their value. They do not appear to have been acquainted with the effect on a yearly rent of dampness in a basement or water in a sub-cellar. A mere knowledge of the value of stores which never had a damp basement would not assist any one in determining the extent of its deteriorating effects on such value."[2]

Where the inquiry related to the value of the services rendered by a broker in effecting the sale of a colliery, the Supreme Court of Pennsylvania has lately held that a real estate broker, whose business consisted in the sale of city real estate, and who had no experience in and knew of no sales of collieries, or of commissions paid on such sales, was incompetent to testify as to the value of the services.[3] And in another case, the value of a mill being in issue, the Supreme Court of Maine held that a witness could not testify as an expert, where the testimony showed that he had resided many years in the vicinity of the mill privilege; that he was the owner of real estate in the vicinity; had been an assessor in the town; and was something

[1] Naughton v. Stagg, 4 Mo. App. 271.
[2] Benkard v. Babcock, 2 Robt. (N. Y.) 175, 186.
[3] Potts v. Achternacht, 93 Penn. St. 142.

of a judge of the value of real estate in that vicinity; but had never bought, sold, owned, or operated a mill, and had no special knowledge of the value of mills and mill privileges.[1] So, a farmer has been held incompetent to express an opinion as to the value of a fishing privilege.[2] And such a person has been held to be incompetent to express an opinion as to the value of the services rendered by a clerk in a country store.[3]

It is impossible, however, to define with any precision the degree of special knowledge which the witness should possess in order to render him competent.[4] The witness should have peculiar knowledge of the property and of its value, is the language of the decisions.[5] "The evidence of experts is received on the ground of science or skill, and witnesses may speak on the value of property or labor, where it appears they have peculiar sources of knowledge to guide them on these subjects, and which are not presumed to be equally within the reach of the jury."[6]

§ 155. **Not Necessary that Expert should See the Property in Question.**— As experts may testify where they have no personal knowledge of the facts in controversy, basing their opinions upon the facts which have been testified to by other witnesses, so the opinion of an expert may be received as to the value of articles similar to one which has been described by witnesses having personal knowledge of it, although such expert has never seen the particular article in question which has been lost or destroyed. No reason is perceived why an expert, testifying in respect to value, should be governed by a different principle in this respect than that which applies to experts testifying upon other subjects.

In a case in Pennsylvania this question was considered, and the conclusion was reached that it was unnecessary that

---

[1] Clark v. Rockland Water Power Co., 52 Me. 68.
[2] Boston, etc. R. R. Co. v. Montgomery, 119 Mass. 114.
[3] Lamoure v. Caryl, 4 Denio (N. Y.), 373.
[4] Bedell v. Long Island R. R. Co., 44 N. Y. 367, 370.
[5] Terpenning v. Corn Exchange Ins. Co., 43 N. Y. 279.
[6] Lamoure v. Caryl, 4 Denio (N. Y.), 373.

the expert should have personal knowledge of the particular article. "What is there," asked Mr. Justice THOMPSON, "to prevent a merchant from testifying, in corroboration of an invoice, as to values, where no values are given, when goods are lost? The fact of the existence or loss of the goods is not touched by such testimony. That remains to be established by other evidence. I think I have known many instances of this kind. If a trunk should be packed by a servant, incapable of placing a value on the wardrobe of his or her master or mistress, although able to testify to each article, and describe its quality, yet wholly incompetent to give the slightest idea of the real value of the articles; in case of loss how is the value to be ascertained, but by the testimony of a tradesman acquainted with the value of such articles, based upon a description of them? So in regard to furniture insured, and lost by fire, it can hardly be doubted, but that it would be competent to fix the value, by persons acquainted with such matters, and competent as such to testify, after its quality had been described.

If the rule be, that only persons who have seen the articles which have been lost, can give an estimate of their value, then, in all the cases suggested, there would be a failure to recover for a loss, or the jury would be left to guess at their value."[1] It has been held that a nurseryman could testify as to the value of trees which had been destroyed, and which he had not seen, but had heard described.[2] And the courts elsewhere have taken a similar view of this question.[3] But where a millwright had neither seen the mill in question, nor a drawing of it, and where he testified that it was hard to estimate the cost of the mill without seeing or knowing what the work was, it was held

[1] Mish v. Wood, 34 Penn. St. 451.
[2] Whitbeck v. N. Y. etc. R. R. Co., 36 Barb. 644.
[3] Orr v. Mayor, etc., 64 Barb. 106; Miller v. Smith, 112 Mass. 470, 475; Beecher v. Denniston, 13 Gray (Mass.), 354. In Miller v. Smith, *supra*, a witness possessing special knowledge and experience was permitted to express an opinion as to the value of fast trotting horses of a certain age, size, gait, speed, and other qualities, although he had not seen the horse in question.

that he could not testify to its value, although he stated he thought he could come within five or ten per cent. of its value if he had a right view of the mill.¹

§ 156. **Time of Examination of Property by the Expert.**— Where an expert testifies as to the value of the property from a personal examination made of it, the question has arisen whether the time of examination was so remote to the time of inquiry as to render the opinion inadmissible. In the case in question the expert had examined the property, real estate, six months before he was called on to testify, and his knowledge had reference to that time. The court held his opinion admissible, and Mr. Justice AMES said: "In an inquiry as to the value of property at any given time, it is impossible to say that evidence as to its value at an earlier date is incompetent and inadmissible, unless that earlier date is so remote as to have no importance or relevance in the inquiry. It cannot be said to be too remote in this instance."²

It is evident that much must depend on the nature of the property. A period of time which would not be remote as to real estate might be too remote as to personalty, or what would be remote as to realty in one part of the country, would not be remote in another part, where the value of such property changes slowly.

§ 157. **Competency in Particular Cases.**— The opinion of an author is received as to the value of his literary production, based upon the time and labor employed in its preparation.³ An artist may testify as an expert as to the value of a portrait.⁴ Millwrights are competent witnesses as to the value of work done on a mill,⁵ and machinists as to the value of particular machinery.⁶ Where

[1] Westlake v. St. Lawrence Co. Ins. Co. 14 Barb. (N. Y.) 206; s. c., 3 Bennett Fire Ins. Cases, 404.
[2] Cobb v. City of Boston, 109 Mass. 438.
[3] Babcock v. Raymond. 2 Hilt. (N. Y.) 61.
[4] Houston etc. R. R. Co. v. Burke, 55 Texas, 324.
[5] Adams v. Dale, 29 Ind. 273.
[6] Steam Packet Co. v. Sickles. 10 Howard (U. S.) 419; Haskins v. Hamilton Ins Co., 5 Gray (Mass.). 432; Winter v. Burt, 31 Ala. 33.

the question was as to the value of a particular threshing machine, a witness who testified that he had run a threshing machine for six or eight years, and had seen the particular machine in operation, was adjudged competent to express an opinion as to how much less such machine was worth than other machines that would run and do first class work.[1] A superintendent of locomotive works, who was familiar with the cost of building, rebuilding and repairing locomotives, and with the value of the materials used therein, and the labor employed thereon, has been permitted to answer the following question: "Could the engine (which you have seen) by any possibility have been so damaged by wear and tear, or by accident, that with the parts or materials as testified to by Mr. F., $20,000 would have been a reasonable charge for rebuilding her?"[2] So one who had purchased and sold machinery of a peculiar kind, and owned and run it, and had made estimates of the cost of building such machinery, and had procured such estimates of other machinists for the purpose of having such machines manufactured, has been held competent to testify as to the value of such machinery.[3]

A witness who had experience and knowledge of sales by retail of such articles as sugar, whisky, tobacco and ale, and of the losses which, according to his own experience in the course of several years, were the results of sales of such goods in small quantities, has been allowed to testify that it would be impossible to realize by small sales, the amount of the retail prices on the entire quantity of articles sold, and to give his reasons therefor, and to testify that, as the result of his own experience, his opinion was that small retail sales of such articles would cause, in ordinary cases, a loss of five per cent. upon the total account of goods so sold.[4] Real estate agents accustomed to value and sell real estate in the neighborhood or city where the

[1] Sheldon v. Booth. 50 Iowa, 209.
[2] Tyng v. Fields. 5 Sup. Ct. (N. Y.). 672.
[3] Haskins v. Hamilton Mutual Ins. Co., 5 Gray (Mass.), 432.
[4] M'Fadden v. Murdock, 1 Irish R. (C. L.) 211.

land in question is situated, are competent to testify as to its value.[1] A real estate agent, engaged in letting houses, testifying as an expert to rental value, may be asked on cross-examination as to where the houses were situated which he had let, what they were, and what rent they were let for.[2] A real estate expert testifying as to the rental value of a lot, cannot base his opinion upon a computation of the annual interest upon what he believes to be the value of the fee; he must have other means of knowledge.[3] Farmers, graziers and drovers have been held competent to testify as to the value of growth and increase of weight which certain cattle might reasonably have been expected to attain, but for the over-feeding of the pasture where they grazed.[4] A farmer has been permitted to testify as to the loss in value of a cow by allowing her to become dry.[5] So he has been held competent to express an opinion as to the value of a mare of common blood,[6] and as to the value of grass destroyed by cattle.[7]

§ 158. **Competency in Particular Cases—The Subject Continued.**—Persons experienced in building railroads may testify what, in their opinion, will be the probable cost of completing a railroad.[8] An architect is allowed to testify as to the value of houses; and in the case cited, such a witness was permitted to testify as to the depreciation in value of buildings in a neighborhood, as caused by a nuisance.[9] A carpenter, engaged in buying lumber and building houses, is a competent witness as to the value of the lumber in a particular house.[10] And carpenters have been

---

[1] Bristol County Savings Bank v. Keavy, 128 Mass. 298.
[2] Drucker v. Simon, 4 Daly (N. Y.), 53.
[3] Maguire v. Labeaume, 7 Mo. App. 185.
[4] Gilbert v. Kennedy, 22 Mich. 117.
[5] Smith v. Wilcox, 4 Hun (N. Y.), 411.
[6] Brown v. Moore, 32 Mich. 254.
[7] Townsend v. Brundage, 6 Thomp. & C. (N. Y.) 527.
[8] Waco Tap R. R. Co. v. Shirley. 45 Texas, 355.
[9] Gauntlett v. Whitworth. 2 C. & K. 720.
[10] Simmons v. Carrier, 68 Mo. 416; Shepard v. Ashley, 10 Allen (Mass.), 542.

permitted to testify as to the value of a house which had been destroyed by fire, it appearing that they possessed a general acquaintance with the house in question, having a knowledge of its shape, location, external appearance, and to some extent, its internal condition.[1] Such persons have also been allowed to express an opinion as to the cost of building a house in the vicinity of the town where they worked, their opinions being based on an examination of the plans and specifications of the house.[2] In a recent case in New York, it is laid down that a carpenter and builder, an architect, or an insurance and real estate agent engaged in appraising similar property, would be competent to express an opinion as to the value of replacing a house destroyed by fire, their opinion being based on knowledge which they had acquired as dealers or builders.[3] So, too, it has been held that a carpenter and builder who had seen the buildings in question, and knew the kind and quality of lumber put into them, was qualified to testify what it was reasonably worth to put the lumber into the buildings.[4] Dealers in articles are competent witnesses as to the value of such articles.[5] "When persons are engaged in any particular trade, the presumption is, that they are acquainted with the value and intrinsic worth of the articles which they are engaged in buying and selling."[6] For this reason, in the case cited, it was said that bankers and brokers were presumed to be better acquainted with the genuineness and value of the circulation of banks, than the community generally. "Their opportunities are better, and the interest of their business necessarily leads them to inform themselves in this respect, beyond other persons." So a dealer in hay

[1] Bedell v. Long Island R. R. Co., 44 N. Y. 367.
[2] Hills v. Home Ins. Co., 129 Mass. 345.
[3] Woodruff v. Imperial Fire Ins. Co., 83 N. Y. 133, 138; s. c. 10 Ins. Law J. 125. See also Tebbetts v. Haskins, 16 Me. 283.
[4] Hough v. Cook, 69 Ill. 581.
[5] Cantling v. Hannibal etc. R. R. Co., 54 Mo. 385; Luse v. Jones, 39 N. J. Law, 708; Sturm v. Williams. 38 N. Y. Superior Ct. 325; Illinois Central R. R. Co. v. Copeland, 24 Ill. 336.
[6] Hinckley v. Kersting, 21 Ill. 217.

may testify as to the value of hay.¹ And one who had been engaged for many years in sawing, buying and selling box board logs, and who had erected a mill for the purpose of sawing them, has been held a competent witness as to their value.² A gunsmith is, by reason of his acumen and knowledge of firearms, a competent witness as to the value of a gun.³ A broker is competent to testify to the value of stocks.⁴

§ 159. The Value of Legal Services.—At common law the rewards of an advocate's services were deemed, not *merces*, but *honoraria*, and could not be recovered by means of legal proceedings.⁵ But in this country the rule of the common law does not prevail, and a right of action exists for the recovery of counsel fees.⁶ In the absence of some express contract fixing the amount of the attorney's compensation, if an action is instituted to enforce payment, it is necessary to determine the value of the services rendered. The rule therefore is that in such an action an attorney may be called as an expert to testify as to the value of the services in question.⁷ It has been well said, that "the very best means of adjusting this value are the opinions of those who, in earning and receiving compensation for them, have

---

¹ Burger v. Northern Pacific R. R. Co., 22 Minn. 343.
² Lawton v. Chase, 108 Mass. 238.
³ Cooper v. State, 53 Miss. 393; Beecher v. Denniston, 13 Gray (Mass.), 354.
⁴ Jonan v. Ferrand, 3 Rob. (La.) 366.
⁵ Kennedy v. Brown, 13 C. B. (N. S.) 677; 32 L. J. 137. And see Brown v. Kennedy, 33 L. J. Ch. 71: 33 Beav. 133; 4 D. J. & S. 217.
⁶ See 13 Central Law Journal, 43, where the subject is considered and the cases collected. The English rule, however, is still recognized in New Jersey. Seeley v. Brown, 15 N. J. L. 35; Van Atta v. McKinney, 16 N. J. L. 235; Schoup v. Schenck, 40 N. J. L. 195. And counsel fees cannot be recovered unless an express contract fixing the fees is shown. Hopper v. Ludlum, 41 N. J. Law, 182 (1879).
⁷ Harnett v. Garvey, 66 N. Y. 641; Williams v. Brown, 28 Ohio St. 547, 551; New Orleans etc. R. R. Co. v. Albreton, 38 Miss. 242, 246, 273; Allis v. Day, 14 Minn. 516; Anthony v. Stinson, 4 Kans. 211; Ottawa University v. Parkinson, 14 Kans. 159; Head v. Hargrave, 14 Cent. L. J. 388 (Sup. Ct. of U. S.); Llussman v. Merkel, 3 Bos. (N. Y.) 402; Beekman v. Platner, 15 Barb. (N. Y.) 550; Jevne v. Osgood, 57 Ill. 340.

learned what legal services in their various grades are worth."[1] And the opinion has been expressed that one who is not an attorney is incompetent to prove the value of an attorney's services.[2] But it does not seem to be necessary that the attorney should be at the time, actually engaged in the active practice of his profession.[3] The witness may base his opinion in part on his personal knowledge, and in part on the testimony of others;[4] and if he has no personal knowledge of the services rendered, his testimony must be based upon a hypothetical question submitted to him.[5] In determining the value of the attorney's services, it is proper to show by the witness, the character and professional standing of the person rendering the services in question,[6] as well as the nature and importance of the services rendered.[7] And it has been held proper to propound the following inquiry: "From the character of the case set out in the complaint filed, what would be a reasonable fee for defending said suit?"[8] The value of the services of counsel under circumstances of general similarity to those under which the services in question were rendered, may also be shown.[9] But what an attorney receives in a case is no criterion of the value of the services of another attorney in the same case, in the absence of any showing that the services were similar, the skill equal, and the time spent the same.[10] It has been held, that upon the cross-examination of an attorney testifying as an expert in such cases, it is within the discretion of the trial court to reject a

[1] Thompson v. Boyle, 85 Penn. St. 477.
[2] Hart v. Vidal, 8 Cal. 56.
[3] See Blizzard v. Applegate, 61 Ind. 371.
[4] Garfield v. Kirk, 65 Barb. (N. Y.) 464; Brown v. Huffard, 69 Mo. 305.
[5] Williams v. Brown, 28 Ohio St. 547, 551; Central Branch etc. R. R. Co. v. Nichols, 24 Kans. 242.
[6] Jackson v. N. Y. Cent. R. R. Co., 2 Sup. Ct. 653.
[7] Harland v. Lilienthal, 53 N. Y. 438; Garfield v. Kirk, 65 Barb. (N. Y.) 464.
[8] Covey v. Campbell, 52 Ind. 158.
[9] Thompson v. Boyle, 85 Penn. St. 477.
[10] Ottawa University v. Parkinson, 14 Kans. 160.

question as to the income derived by the witness from the practice of his profession.[1]

§ 160. **The Value of Services Rendered by Physicians and Nurses.**— In a case decided as early as 1791, Lord KENYON declared that he understood that the fees of physicians and surgeons were merely honorable and not demandable of right.[2] And such was undoubtedly the law of England.[3] In this country the courts, however, have not recognized the English rule, and physicians may recover for the value of their services.[4] And this right is now secured to them in England by statute adopted in 1858.[5]

As the value of services rendered by lawyers may be shown by the testimony of those engaged in the same profession, so the value of the services rendered by physicians and surgeons in the practice of their profession, is to be shown by the testimony of their professional brethren. And it has been laid down that one who is not a physician, is incompetent to testify as to the value of medical services.[6] But it seems it is not necessary that the witness should know just what physicians were in the habit of charging for services similar to those in question, and for what such services could be procured.[7] In the Indiana case last cited the facts were as

[1] Harland v. Lilienthal, 53 N. Y. 438.
[2] Chorley v. Bolcot, 4 Term, R. 317.
[3] Lipscombe v. Holmes, 2 Camp. 441.
[4] Judah v. McNamee, 3 Blackf. (Ind.) 269; Mooney v. Lloyd, 5 S. & R. (Penn.) 416; Rouse v. Morris, 17 S. & R. (Penn.) 328; Simmons v. Means, 8 S. & M. (Miss.) 397; Mock v. Kelly, 3 Ala. 387; Smith v. Watson, 14 Vt. 332.
[5] 21 and 22 Vict. Ch. 90, § 31. See too, Gibbon v. Budd, 32 L. J. Ex. 182; s. c., 2 H. & C. 92.
[6] Mock v. Kelly, 3 Ala. 387. And see Wood v. Brewer, 57 Ala. 515.
[7] Board of Commissioners v. Chambers, 75 Ind. 409. In this connection it is interesting to note the language of the Supreme Court of Minnesota in Elfelt v. Smith, 1 Minn. 126: "The value of services upon a *quantum meruit* stands in regard to the proof, upon the same principle as the value of chattels upon a *quantum valebant*. The value of chattels in such a case is always regulated by the usual or market value of such chattels, of like quality, at the time and place of sale; and before a witness can, in such a case, be permitted to testify to such value, it must appear by his own, or other competent evidence, that he knows with

follows: Certain physicians were called to testify as to the value of the services of a physician in making a *post mortem* examination under the employment of a coroner. The witnesses testified on their direct examination that they were physicians and surgeons, and considered themselves competent to testify as to the value of services rendered in making *post mortem* examinations. But it appeared on their cross-examination that they did not know what physicians had charged for making such examinations, and that they knew nothing of the prices at which such services could be procured, but formed their judgment of the value of the services from what they thought such services would be worth. The court held it proper that their testimony should be received, saying: "The testimony was competent, for the witnesses were shown to be experts, and to possess such knowledge, skill and acquaintance with the subject under investigation as entitled them to express their opinions to the jury. They may have had some knowledge of the value of such services, without knowing anything at all about what others were charging for like services."

In an action by a physician to recover for medical services, it is competent for him to prove the nature of the disease, and the character of the treatment given; and such evidence is not rendered incompetent by the provision of the statute, forbidding the disclosure of confidential communications made by a patient to his physician.[1] As to the value of services rendered in nursing and caring for the sick, the rule is that the witnesses should be persons who have had experience in nursing and caring for the sick. Physicians [2]

reasonable certainty what such usual or market value is. He then testifies to the value as a fact, and not as a mere matter of opinion. So in regard to services: it must appear that the witness knows the usual value of, or rate of compensation paid for such or the like services at the time when, and place where, they were rendered, before he can be properly permitted to testify what such value or rate is."

[1] Kendall v. Gray, 2 Hilton (N. Y.), 302.
[2] Woodward v. Bugsbee, 4 N. Y. Sup. Ct. 393; Reynolds v. Robinson, 64 N. Y. 589; Shafer v. Dean's Adm'r, 29 Iowa, 141.

and nurses[1] are competent witnesses in such cases. And it has been held that one who had long had the care of an insane person, and provided for his table, and who had been for a considerable period of time in another family while such person was boarding there, was qualified to express an opinion as to the value of taking care of him and boarding him in the latter place.[2]

§ 161. **Value of Services in other Callings.**— The general rule is that it is competent for a witness to state the value of another's services in all cases where he has knowledge of the matter in controversy, and is acquainted with the value of services such as those rendered in the particular case.[3] For instance, an expert accountant may testify as to what would be a fair compensation for the services of a competent accountant in keeping the account books of a business of a certain character, and as to the usual charge per day for the services of an accountant in fixing up complicated accounts.[4] And where the plaintiff, who was not a real estate broker, sued for services rendered in effecting the purchase of a mill, the evidence of a real estate broker was held admissible as to the commissions which he charged for such services, and as to what he would have charged in the case in question.[5] Elsewhere it has been held that the statements of what the witness himself would have charged for similar services, were inadmissible.[6] In a case in Indiana, it was held no error on the cross-examination, to ask the witness what he would have undertaken the work for.[7]

But if the witness is unacquainted with the value of services such as those rendered in the particular case, he is not an expert in that particular matter of inquiry, and cannot

---

[1] Shafer v. Dean's Adm'r., *supra*.
[2] Kendall v. May, 10 Allen (Mass.), 59.
[3] Bowen v. Bowen, 74 Ind. 470; Johnson v. Thompson, 72 Ind. 167; Parker's Heirs v. Parker's Admr., 33 Ala. 459.
[4] Shattuck v. Train, 116 Mass. 296.
[5] Elting v. Sturtevant. 41 Conn. 176.
[6] Fairchild v. M. C. R. R. Co., 8 Bradw. (Ill.) 591.
[7] Gilman v. Gard, 29 Ind. 291. 293.

testify as such. Hence, in a suit by a broker to recover commissions for the sale of a colliery, a broker whose business was the sale of real estate in Philadelphia, and who had no experience and knew of no sales or commissions paid on sales of colleries, was held an incompetent witness as to the value of the services rendered.[1] In an action brought for services in planning, preparing and organizing for the erection of a factory, and in superintending the mounting and putting in operation of its machinery, the Supreme Court of Georgia has permitted witnesses, who were not experts, and who knew nothing of the particular services sued for, except from a general description of the same contained in the interrogatories in answer to which their evidence was given, to testify as to what in their opinion would be a reasonable salary for the services performed. The court held that witnesses who had employed the person rendering the services, or who had been employed with him, and who had seen the results of his skill, and who knew his professional standing, could testify in such cases.[2] It was conceded, however, that the evidence was barely admissible. So it has been held that neighbors, who have employed servants to do like work, are competent to testify to the value of services of a girl employed to do housework.[3] And the value of the services of a farm laborer may be shown by the testimony of those who had employed him.[4]

§ 162. **Opinions as to the Value of Real Estate.**— On questions of the valuations of real property it is frequently found necessary to take the opinions of witnesses who are not experts. "'The market value of land is not a question of science or skill, upon which only an expert can give an opinion.'"[5] But a strange inconsistency is seemingly found in the rules laid down in the different courts as to the qualifications of those who may express opinions in such cases.

[1] Potts v. Aechternacht, 93 Penn. St. 142.
[2] Eagle & Phœnix Manuf. Co. v. Browne, 58 Ga. 240.
[3] Carter v. Carter, 36 Mich. 207.
[4] Ritter v. Daniels, 47 Mich. 617.
[5] Pennsylvania, etc. R. R. Co. v. Bunnell, 81 Penn. St. 426.

In Illinois it is said that the value of real estate is to be ascertained from the opinions of those who profess to be familiar with the subject of inquiry, and whose business in life has afforded them an opportunity of acquiring information and of judging accurately on such questions.[1] While in Massachusetts witnesses are competent to testify as to the value of land, whose knowledge is derived from sales or purchases made by themselves, or by others, although upon their cross-examination they say they know no more concerning the value of land than citizens generally.[2] In Pennsylvania it is said that, "Persons living in the neighborhood may be presumed to have a sufficient knowledge of the market value of property with the location and character of the land in question. Whether their opinion has any proper ground to rest upon, or is mere conjecture, can be brought out upon cross-examination."[3] And in Missouri it is said that, "Property holders and residents in the neighborhood where land is situated are competent witnesses to fix the price of land in that neighborhood."[4] While in Rhode Island the court say opinions are not admissible simply because the witness resides near the land and is acquainted with it.[5] Then again we find the rule laid down in general terms, that witnesses having a personal knowledge of the property, and who possess the necessary information to enable them to form a proper estimate of the value of the land, are competent to express the opinion which they have formed.[6] However differently the rule may be laid down, the inconsistencies of expression are more apparent than real. And it is believed that the courts are practically unanimous in holding that residents in the immediate vicinity, who are acquainted with the property in question, and know the value of land in that neighborhood, are com-

[1] Green v. City of Chicago, 97 Ill. 372.
[2] Swan v. Middlesex, 101 Mass. 173.
[3] Pennsylvania, etc. R. R. Co. v. Bunnell, 81 Penn. St. 426.
[4] Thomas v. Mallinckrodt, 43 Mo. 65.
[5] Buffum v. N. Y., etc. R. R. Co., 4. R. I. 221.
[6] Frankfort, etc. R. R. Co. v. Windsor, 51 Ind. 238; Ferguson v. Stafford, 33 Ind. 162; Crouse v. Holman, 19 Ind. 30.

petent to testify as to the value of the land in controversy. This is the principle in accordance with which farmers and residents in the neighborhood of the property, have been held qualified in many cases to testify as to the value of the land in their vicinity.[1] It is not necessary that the witness should have bought or sold land in that vicinity,[2] or should have known of sales of exactly such tracts as the one in question,[3] or that his knowledge of sales should have been personal,[4] or that it should have been derived from the buyer or seller of the land sold.[5] And it has been laid down that, "The knowledge requisite to qualify a witness to testify to his opinion of the value of lands may either be acquired by the performance of official duty, as by a county commissioner or selectman, whose duty it is to lay out public ways, or by an assessor, whose duty it is to ascertain the value of lands for the purpose of taxation; or it may be derived from knowledge of sales and purchases of other lands in the vicinity, either by the witness himself, or by other persons."[6]

In a recent case in Rhode Island the court holds that while a farmer living in the vicinity of farming land, and familiar with it, may, as an expert, give his estimate of its

[1] Robertson v. Knapp, 35 N. Y. 91; Snyder v. Western Un. R. R. Co., 25 Mo. 60; West Newbury v. Chase, 5 Gray (Mass.), 421; Clark v. Baird, 9 N. Y. 183; Lehmicke v. St. Paul, etc. R. R. Co., 19 Minn. 464; Simmons v. St. Paul, etc. R. R. Co., 18 Minn. 184; Crouse v. Holman, 19 Ind. 30; Thomas v. Mallinckrodt, 43 Mo. 58; Brainard v. Boston, etc. R. R. Co., 12 Gray (Mass.), 407; Hayes v. Ottawa, Oswego, etc. R. R. Co., 54 Ill. 373; Galena, etc. R. R. Co. v. Haslem, 73 Ill. 494; Wallace v. Finch, 24 Mich. 255; Hanover Water Co. v. Ashland Iron Co., 84 Penn. St. 284; Keithsburg, etc. R. R. Co. v. Henry, 79 Ill. 290; Selma, etc. R. R. Co. v. Keith, 53 Ga. 178; Hudson v. State, 61 Ala. 334; Milwaukee, etc. R. R. Co. v. Eble, 4 Chand. (Wis.), 72; Erd v. Chicago, etc. R. R. Co., 41 Wis. 64; Ferguson v. Stafford, 33 Ind. 162; Tate v. M. K. & T. R. R. Co., 64 Mo. 149; Russell v. Horn Pond, etc. R. R. Co., 4 Gray (Mass.), 607; Stone v. Covell, 29 Mich. 362.

[2] Whitman v. Boston, etc. R. R. Co., 7 Gray (Mass.), 313; Lehmicke v. St. Paul, etc. R. R. Co., 19 Minn. 464, 482.

[3] Frankfort, etc. R. R. Co. v. Windsor, 51 Ind. 240.

[4] Hanover Water Co. v. Ashland Iron Co., 84 Penn. St. 284.

[5] Whitman v. Boston, etc. R. R. Co., 7 Gray (Mass.), 313.

[6] Swan v. Middlesex, 101 Mass. 177, per Mr. Justice Gray.

value as *farm* land, yet that his opinion generally of the value of such realty would be inadmissible, since the market value of such realty might be much greater than its agricultural value.[1]

While a real estate agent accustomed to value and sell real property in the city or neighborhood where the land is situated, is competent to testify in reference to its value, although he may never have sold land on the particular street upon which the land is located,[2] yet it is essential that he should be acquainted with the value of land in the vicinity of the property in question.[3] And it is said that a speculator in real estate, who buys and sells real property for himself, is competent, provided he is conversant with the property in question, and with other property of the same character in the vicinity, and knows at what prices such property is held by persons owning and controlling it.[4] Where it was desired to show a depreciation in the value of certain real property, it was held that the secretary of an insurance company, who had been in the habit of examining buildings in reference to insurance, might express the opinion that the passage of locomotive engines within a certain distance of a building, would diminish the rent and increase the rate of insurance against fire, and that he might state that his company had declined to take the risk at any rate of insurance on applications for insurance on buildings in that vicinity.[5]

§ 163. **Value of Annuities.**— Stock brokers who have been engaged in buying and selling life annuities, and who have thereby become acquainted with the value and market price of annuities, have been allowed to testify as to the market price of an annuity for the life of a person of a certain age.[6] So, actuaries, experienced in the business of

---

[1] Brown v. Providence, etc. R. R. Co., 12 R. I. 238.
[2] Bristol County Savings Bank v. Keavy, 128 Mass. 298.
[3] Haulenbeck v. Cronkright, 23 N. J. Eq. 413.
[4] Jarvis v. Furman, 25 Hun (N. Y.), 393.
[5] Webber v. Eastern R. R. Co., 2 Met. (Mass.), 147.
[6] Heathcote v. Paignon, 2 Brown's Ch. 167, 169.

life insurance, are permitted to testify as to the value of an annuity.[1] And an accountant, who was acquainted with the business of insurance companies, has been examined as to the average duration of human lives.[2] With the view of ascertaining the probable duration of a particular life at a given age, it is material to know what is the average duration of the life of a person of that age. "The particular life on which an annuity is secured may be unusually healthy, in which case the value of the annuity would be greater than the average, or it may be unusually bad, in which case the value would be less than the average; but it must be material to know what, according to the experience of insurance companies, the value of an annuity secured on an average life of that age would be." For the purpose of determining this, the witnesses are permitted to refer to standard tables used by insurance companies in the course of their business.[3] And it has been held that the Carlisle Tables of Mortality, being standard tables on this subject, are admissible evidence for the purpose of showing the expectation of life at a particular age.[4] The Northampton Tables have been received for the same purpose.[5] And in a recent case in Kentucky, in determining the value of the potential right of dower, the court adopted the table prepared by Professor Bowditch, on that subject, declaring that it furnished a safer and more convenient guide than the

---

[1] *Ex parte* Whitehead, 1 Merivale, 127, 128; *Ex parte* Thistlewood, 19 Vesey, 235; Heathcote v. Paignon, 2 Brown's Ch. 167, 169; Griffith v. Spratley, 1 Cox Ch. 389.

[2] Rowley v. London, etc. R. R. Co., 8 Exch. (L. R.) 221. In the case cited Brett, J., did not think it necessary to say whether such a witness was competent, but thought it doubtful, as he was not an actuary. Blackburn, J., said that as he gave evidence that he was experienced in the business of life insurance, his opinion was admissible.

[3] See Davis v. Marlborough, 2 Swanston, 113, 150; Nichols v. Gould, 2 Vesey, 423; Rowley v. London, etc. R. Co., *supra*.

[4] Donaldson, v. Mississippi, etc. R. R. Co., 18 Iowa, 281.; Simonson v. C., R. I. & P. R. Co., 49 Iowa, 87.

[5] Schell v. Plumb, 55 N. Y. 598; Sauter v. N. Y. Cent. & H. R. R. Co., 13 N. Y. Sup. Ct. 451; Wager v. Schuyler, 1 Wend. (N. Y.) 553; Jackson v. Edwards, 7 Paige Ch. (N. Y.) 386, 408.

opinions of witnesses.[1] For the purpose of determining the value of the life of a decedent, an expert may be asked, "From your knowledge of the decedent's age, habits, health, and physical condition," how long, in your opinion, would he have been useful to his family?[2] And an expert in life insurance may be asked as to the relative hazard of different occupations.[3]

§ 164. **Value of Foreign Currency and Negotiable Securities.**— In order to ascertain what is the lawful money of a foreign country it is considered unnecessary that the law of such country, regulating the subject, should be produced.[4] And witnesses who have had business transactions in such country, having had occasion in that way to learn the value of the currency in common use, are competent to testify as to such value, and to state its equivalent in our own currency.[5] So it has been held that the value of the stock of a railroad company at a specified date, could be shown by the testimony of one who dealt in such stock at or near that date.[6] And it has even been held that the testimony of a witness as to the market value of negotiable securities, at a somewhat remote period, was competent and sufficient *prima facie* evidence, although it was founded on a general recollection based on his keeping the run of the market price in consequence of being very much interested in the company which issued the securities.[7]

§ 165. **Opinions of Merchants and Brokers.**— The experience which merchants and brokers acquire in the ordinary conduct of their business is such as qualifies them to testify as to the value of articles with which they are required by the necessities of their business to be familiar. And if in the course of their business they are kept informed as to the market value of any particular thing, by

[1] Lancaster v. Lancaster's Trustees, 78 Ky. 200.
[2] Pennsylvania Railroad Co. v. Henderson, 51 Penn St. 320.
[3] Hartman v. Keystone Ins. Co., 21 Penn. St. 478.
[4] Comstock v. Smith, 20 Mich. 338.
[5] Kermott v. Ayer, 11 Mich. 181; Comstock v. Smith, *supra*.
[6] Noonan v. Ilsley, 22 Wis. 27.
[7] Smith v. Frost, 42 N. Y. Superior Ct. 87.

price current lists duly furnished them for use in their business, opinions derived from such information will be received in evidence.¹ But in an action for work and labor done, and materials furnished, it was held that the price list itself could not be received in evidence.² And there is no error in excluding the testimony of a witness, whose knowledge as to market price was derived wholly from statements of his partner as to the prices at which his firm had sold, entries of which it was his duty to make in the books of the firm.³

¹ Whitney v. Thacher, 117 Mass. 526. *In re* Cliquot's Champagne, 3 Wall. 114; *In re* Fennerstein's Champagne, 3 Wall. 145; Sisson v. Toledo R. R. Co., 14 Mich. 489; Cleveland, etc. R. R. Co. v. Perkins, 17 Mich. 296; Sirrine v. Briggs, 31 Mich. 443; Lush v. Druse, 4 Wend. (N. Y.) 317; Terry v. McNeil, 58 Barb. (N. Y.) 241. See Whelan v. Lynch, 60 N. Y. 469, and Schmidt v. Herfurth, 5 Robertson (N. Y.) 124, 145.

² County of Cook v. Harms, 10 Bradw. (Ill.) 24.

³ Flynn v. Wohl, 10 Mo. App. 582.

234 EXPERT TESTIMONY.

CHAPTER IX.

THE RELATION OF SCIENTIFIC BOOKS TO EXPERT TESTIMONY.

SECTION.
166. The Relation of Scientific Works to Expert Testimony.
167. The Admissibility of Scientific Works in Evidence.
168. The Inadmissibility of Medical Treatises in Evidence. The Rule in England.
169. Their Admissibility in Alabama.
170. Their Inadmissibility in Indiana.
171. Their Admissibility in Iowa.
172. Their Inadmissibility in Maine.
173. Their Inadmissibility in Maryland.
174. Their Inadmissibility in Massachusetts.
175. Their Inadmissibility in Michigan.
176. The Doctrine in New York.
177. Their Inadmissibility in North Carolina.
178. Their Inadmissibility in Rhode Island.
179. Their Inadmissibility in Wisconsin.
180. Dicta in California and New Hampshire—The Result of the Authorities.
181. The Contradiction of Experts by Medical Treatises.
182. Testing Knowledge of Experts on Cross-examination.
183. Views of Writers on Medical Jurisprudence as to the Exclusion of Medical Treatises.
184. Reading from Scientific Books in Argument.
185. Reading from Scientific Books in Argument—The Subject Continued.
186. Reading the Testimony of Experts as Contained in Official Reports.

§ 166. **The Relation of Scientific Works to Expert Testimony.**— As we have already seen,[1] experts are permitted to express opinions on subjects connected with their particular departments of science, or of art, although their opinions are based on information derived by them from

[1] §§ 19, 20.

the study of books, and not from their own experience or observation. They are also permitted to refresh their memories by the use of standard authorities.[1] But a marked distinction exists between permitting a witness to refresh his memory by reference to an authority or writing, and the introduction of the writing itself in evidence. It may be wholly improper that the writing should be introduced in evidence, and yet entirely proper for the witness to refresh his recollection by a reference to it. An equally well marked distinction exists between the admissibility of opinions based on a study of authorities, of standard writings, and the reception of the writings themselves in evidence. It is fair to assume that the expert has weighed the assertions and opinions of the different authorities, and that he has reached an independent judgment thereon. The opinion which he expresses is given in a court of justice, and under the solemnity of an oath. While it can hardly be presumed that a standard writer would give expression in his public writings to a dishonest opinion, yet the fact remains that the opinion was not expressed under oath, and may have subsequently been modified. The writer is not presented in court. No opportunity is given for his cross-examination, and the jury cannot observe the witness. The question, therefore, arises are scientific works admissible in evidence? Can the opinions of scientific writers, as expressed in their writings, be received in evidence as the opinions of experts, or must the writers themselves be called as witnesses, and give expression to their opinions under oath, in the presence of the court, the jury, and the parties? This is an important question, which we are now to consider.

§ 167. **The Admissibility of Scientific Works in Evidence.**— Attention has elsewhere in this work been called to the fact that standard tables of mortality have been received in evidence for the purpose of showing the expecta-

---

[1] Taylor on Evidence, 1230; 1 Wharton's Evid. 438; People v. Wheeler, 9 Pac. Coast L. J. 584; Hoffman v. Click, 77 N. C. 555.

tion of life at a particular age.[1] There are other instances in which scientific tables and works have been received in evidence, and which remain for us briefly to notice. Thus in a case in the Mayor's court of New York, in the year 1816, it was held that tide tables could be received for the purpose of showing that the time of high water at New York and New London was the same.[2] So in a case in Maryland in 1880, the court held that an almanac was admissible in evidence for the purpose of proving at what hour the moon rose on a certain night. "An almanac," said the court, "forecasts with exact certainty planetary movements. We govern our daily life by reference to the computations which they contain. No oral evidence or proof which we could gather as to the hours of the rising or setting of the sun or moon, could be as certain or accurate as that which we may obtain from such a source."[3] So in Connecticut and California it has been held that an almanac may be used for this purpose.[4] But whether it could be received in England for such a purpose may be somewhat doubtful.[5] It has been said by one of the most distinguished writers on the law of evidence that "The hour at which the moon rose is a fact, and it can fairly be argued upon the general principles of the law of evidence, that the best evidence of that fact is the testimony of some one who observed its occurrence."[6]

It has been held, too, in this country, that a record of the weather, kept for a number of years at the State Insane Asylum, was competent evidence to prove the temperature of the weather on a given day included in such record.[7] Are

---

[1] § 163, and Donaldson v. Mississippi, etc. R. R. Co., 18 Iowa, 281; Schell v. Plumb, 55 N. Y. 598; Sauter v. N. Y. Cent. & H. R. R. Co., 13 N. Y. Sup. Ct. 451; Wager v. Schuyler, 1 Wend. (N. Y.) 553; Jackson v. Edwards, 7 Paige Ch. 386, 408.
[2] Green v. Aspinwall, 1 City Hall Recorder, 14.
[3] Munshower v. State, 55 Md. 11.
[4] State v. Morris, 47 Conn. 179; People v. Cheekee, 14 Rep. 582.
[5] See Sutton v. Darke, 5 H. & W. 647.
[6] Taylor on Evidence, 1230.
[7] De Armand v. Neasmith, 32 Mich. 231.

these cases in accordance with the general rule, or do they constitute an exception to the rule? Do they establish the principle that scientific treatises may be received in evidence?

§ 168. **The Inadmissibility of Medical Treatises in Evidence — The Rule in England.** — The question whether scientific treatises may be read in evidence, has generally been raised in cases where an effort has been made to introduce as evidence the opinions expressed in medical treatises. And it is in this connection that we shall now consider the question. So far as England is concerned the rule was definitely settled in that country in the year 1831, and in the well known case of *Collier* v. *Simpson*.[1] The action was one of slander, the defendant having charged that the plaintiff, who was a physician, had prescribed improper medicines for a child suffering from water on the brain. The question being whether certain prescriptions were proper under the circumstances of the case, counsel proposed to put in evidence certain medical books of recognized authority, to show the received opinion of the medical profession on the subject. But Mr. Chief Justice TINDAL held that medical treatises could not be thus received. So more recently, as late as 1875, the question was again raised when counsel proposed to read to the jury a case from Taylor's Medical Jurisprudence. Mr. Justice BRETT refused, however, to allow counsel to proceed with the reading, and said : "That is no evidence in a court of justice. It is a mere statement by a medical man of hearsay facts of cases at which he was in all probability not present. I cannot allow it to be read." [2]

§ 169. **Their Admissibility in Alabama.** — Such treatises are considered in this State as admissible in evidence, such a conclusion having been reached in the year 1857,[3] and subsequently adhered to, once in 1861,[4] and again in 1879.[5]

[1] 5 Carr v. Payne, 73 (24 Eng. C. L. 219).
[2] Regina v. Thomas, 13 Cox's Cr. Cases, 77.
[3] Stoudenmeier v. Williamson, 29 Ala. 558, 565.
[4] Merkle v. State, 37 Ala. 139.
[5] Bates v. State, 63 Ala. 30.

The court concluded that inasmuch as judges in determining matters of law, could consult legal treatises of authority, the jury should have the same right to consult medical treatises laid before them in evidence, for the purpose of enabling them to determine matters of fact. The books themselvês were said to be as safe guides for the jury as the opinions derived from their perusal and deposed to by witnesses.

§ 170. **Their Inadmissibility in Indiana.**—Twenty years after *Collier* v. *Simpson* was decided in England, the question came up in Indiana, and the authority of that case was fully recognized and followed. The circumstances were as follows: It was proposed to have a physician testify as to the effects of poison upon the human system, his information being derived from standard medical treatises. Thereupon the objection was made that his evidence was not admissible, but that the authors themselves should be produced as witnesses, or if dead, that their books should be offered in evidence. The court held that the books could not be received, but that the opinions of a physician based on them, were admissible.[1]

§ 171. **Their Admissibility in Iowa.**—The earliest case recognizing the right to introduce medical treatises in evidence, so far as we have been able to discover, is that of *Bowman* v. *Woods*,[2] decided in the Supreme Court of Iowa in 1848. The reasoning by which the court reached its conclusion was quite similar to that, which, as we have seen, subsequently induced the Supreme Court of Alabama to lay down the same rule. In an action for malpractice, the defendant offered certain medical books in evidence which competent witnesses had pronounced standard works, and from which they declared they had derived much of their knowledge. The court said it saw no reason for their exclusion. "The opinions of an author as contained in his works, we regard as better evidence than the mere state-

[1] Carter v. State, 2 Carter, 619. See, too, Jones v. Trustees, etc. Ind. R. 47.
[2] 1 G. Greene, 441.

ment of those opinions by a witness, who testifies as to his recollection of them from former reading." In 1865 the court again announce the same rule.[1] In a more recent case a Herd Book was held inadmissible, as there was no evidence by experts that its correctness was recognized by cattle breeders.[2]

§ 172. **Their Inadmissibility in Maine.**— The question was first considered in this country in the Supreme Court of Maine, and it is somewhat curious that the subject was disposed of in this State in the same year in which *Collier v. Simpson* was decided in England, and that a similar conclusion was reached in both cases, each court being ignorant of the ruling of the other. The question was carefully considered, and much stress was laid on the fact that the reception of such works would be to receive evidence not sanctioned by an oath, without any opportunity for cross-examination, which was justly deemed a matter of great importance in any search after truth. "The practice if by law allowed, would lead to endless inquiries and contradictory theories and speculations. In a word, if one book is evidence, so is another, and if all are admitted, it is to be feared that truth would be lost in the learned contest of discordant opinions."[3]

§ 173. **Their Inadmissibility in Maryland.**— The rule that medical treatises are inadmissible in evidence was adopted in Maryland in 1873, when it was held that the rules prescribed by medical authors for making *post-mortem* examinations could not be received in evidence. It was said that if it was desired to show that an examination had not been made by the physicians in a skillful and proper manner, it could be done only through the testimony of witnesses competent to testify on that subject.[4] And the doctrine was broadly laid down that medical treatises could not be received to sustain or contradict an expert. The

[1] Donaldson v. The Mississippi, etc. R. R. Co., 18 Iowa, 291.
[2] Crawford v. Williams, 48 Iowa, 249.
[3] Ware v. Ware, 8 Maine, 42.
[4] Davis v. State, 38 Md. 15, 36.

court has in a case lately decided held that a book entitled "The Principles and Practice of Life Insurance," containing the rules and modes of adjusting life insurance, was not admissible in evidence.[1]

§ 174. **Their Inadmissibility in Massachusetts.**— A witness who had expressed an opinion as an expert that it was impossible to distinguish human blood from the blood of animals, was asked whether he concurred with the views expressed in Taylor's Medical Jurisprudence on that subject, the book being passed to him, counsel proposing that the witness should read therefrom to the jury a certain paragraph with which he coincided in opinion. The court held that this could not be done.[2] In a subsequent case counsel again claimed the right to read to the jury books of medical authority, as to any matter of which medical experts might testify, but the court again denied the right.[3] These cases were in accordance with an earlier case in the same court in which Mr. Chief Justice SHAW, in denying the right to read from medical treatises, had stated that facts or opinions could not be laid before a jury "except by the testimony under oath of persons skilled in such matters."[4]

§ 175. **Their Inadmissibility in Michigan.**— There is no doubt that medical treatises cannot be introduced in evidence in Michigan.[5] "Medical writers are by no means a unit upon the various questions of medical jurisprudence. A passage may be found in some work favorable to a particular opinion, which in another may be successfully controverted and overthrown, although not known to counsel or the court, who are not presumed to be particularly versed in that branch of science, and, therefore, the counsel should have the opportunity of eliciting from an expert upon the witness stand, that peculiar information which he

---

[1] Mutual Life Ins. Co. v. Bratt, 55 Md. 200.
[2] Commonwealth v. Sturtivant, 117 Mass. 122.
[3] Commonwealth v. Brown, 121 Mass. 69, 75.
[4] Commonwealth v. Wilson, 1 Gray, 337.
[5] See Fraser v. Jennison, 42 Mich. 206, 214; Pinney v. Cahill, 12 N. W. Rep. 862.

alone is presumed to possess, and which would be imparted in language easily understood, and not in those technical terms so common in medical books, where even common words are sometimes used in a peculiar manner, distinct from their received meaning in the general use of the language."[1]

§ 176. **The Doctrine in New York.**— In New York the question does not appear to have been ruled on in either the Court of Appeals, or in the Supreme Court. The New York Superior Court, however, as early as 1858, laid down the rule that the matters alleged in standard treatises, must be proved in the same manner as any other facts, and that the books themselves were no evidence of the truth of the assertions of fact contained in them.[2]

§ 177. **Their Inadmissibility in North Carolina.**—The subject has been twice considered in this State, and in each instance a conclusion was reached adverse to the admissibility of such treatises in evidence. It was first presented in 1854, and the conclusion was grounded upon the fact that the writers had not been sworn and could not be cross-examined.[3] It was again before the court in 1877, when much importance was attached to the fact that medicine is an inductive science, and that medical treatises are based on data constantly shifting with new discoveries and more accurate observation. "The medical work which was a 'standard' last year becomes obsolete this year. Even a second edition of the work of the same author is so changed by the subsequent discovery and grouping together of new facts, that what appeared to be a logical deduction in the first edition, becomes an unsound one in the next. So that the same author at one period may be cited against himself at another."[4]

§ 178. **Their Inadmissibility in Rhode Island.**— In holding such treatises inadmissible in Rhode Island, the

---

[1] Barrick v. City of Detroit, 1 Mich. N. P. 135.
[2] Harris v. Panama R. R. Co., 3 Bosw. 1, 18.
[3] Melvin v. Easley, 1 Jones Law, 338.
[4] Huffman v. Click, 77 N. C. 55.

court remarked that, "scientific men are admitted to give their opinions as experts, because given under oath; but the books which they write containing them, are, for want of such an oath, excluded."[1] It was said that such books were not rendered any the more admissible by the fact that the experts had read passages from them, to which in cross-examination they had been referred, and in relation to which they had answered questions. And counsel cannot read from them for the purpose of contradicting the experts.

§ 179. **Their Inadmissibility in Wisconsin.** — In a case decided in 1848, counsel had proposed to read to the jury certain standard medical works " as *evidence*, or by way of instruction to the jury." Objection was made, which the trial court sustained. "This is a matter," said the Supreme Court, "generally within the discretion of the court, and, therefore, not a subject of a writ of error. In many cases, no doubt, it would be proper to allow books of science to be read, though generally, such a practice would lead to evil results."[2]

But in a very recent case the same court has overruled its earlier decision that the admissibility of such treatises is discretionary with the trial court; and placed itself in line with the weight of authority on this subject, and declared the rule to be that medical books cannot be read to the jury as evidence, although such books have been shown by expert testimony to be standard works in the medical profession.[3]

§ 180. **Dicta in California and New Hampshire — The Result of the Authorities.** — In a case in California Mr. Justice McKinstry, in delivering the opinion of the court, declared that medical treatises were not admissible in evidence, and said that if such treatises were to be held admissible, the question at issue might be tried, not by the testimony, but upon excerpts from works presenting partial

[1] State v. O'Brien, 7 R. I. 336, 338.
[2] Luning v. State, 1 Chandler, 178.
[3] Stilling v. Town of Thorp, to appear in 54 Wis.; Knoll v. State, The Reporter, Sept. 20th, 1882, p. 381.

views of variant and perhaps contradictory theories.[1] The question in the case, however, was whether counsel had a right to read from such treatises in argument, so that the above expression of opinion must be regarded as *dicta*. In another part of this work, and in another connection, we have had occasion to quote *dicta* to the same effect from an opinion of the Supreme Court of New Hampshire.[2] The result of the cases on this subject shows clearly that the very decided weight of authority is against the admissibility in evidence of standard medical treatises. Such is the rule in England, Indiana, Maine, Maryland, Massachusetts, Michigan, North Carolina, Rhode Island and Wisconsin, supported by *dicta* in California and New Hampshire, and opposed by decisions in Alabama and Iowa.

The objections to the reception of such books in evidence have been concisely and forcibly stated by a distinguished writer as follows: "In the first place, a sound induction last year is not necessarily a sound induction this year, and as a matter of fact, works of this class, when they do not become obsolete, are altered, in material features from edition to edition, so that we cannot tell, in citing from even a living author, whether what we read is not something that this very author now rejects. In the second place, if such books are admitted as a class, those which are compilations must be admitted as well as those which contain the result of original research; the purely speculative must come in side by side with the empirical; so that if such treatises are admitted at all, it will be impossible to exclude those which are secondary evidence of the facts they state. In the third place, such books, without expert testimony, cannot generally be pointed to the concrete case; with expert testimony, they become simply part of such testimony, and lose their independent substantive character as books.

"In the fourth place, the authors of such books do not write under oath, and hence the authorities on which they

---

[1] People v. Wheeler, 9 Pacific Coast Law J., 581, 583. (1882.)
[2] See pp. 31 and 33, for an extract from Dole v. Johnson, 50 N. H. 452. And see Ordway v. Haynes, 50 N. H. 159.

rest cannot be explored, nor their processes of reasoning tested.

"Lastly, such books are at best hearsay proof of that which living witnesses could be produced to prove."[1]

§ 181. **The Contradiction of Experts by Medical Treatises.**—It is clear then, that the weight of authority is against the admission of medical treatises in evidence. And we think it equally clear that the weight of authority is sustained by the better reason. The Supreme Court of North Carolina, which, as we have seen, holds medical treatises inadmissible in evidence, nevertheless recognizes an exception to the rule. It is there laid down that if a physician has cited such works in his testimony, those works may be put in evidence for the purpose of discrediting him.[2] Such a conclusion has also been reached in Wisconsin, on principle and without affirming the correctness of a former decision of the same court, holding the admission of such treatises discretionary with the trial court.[3] So in a case decided in Michigan in 1882, there was a similar ruling, and the court said: "He (the expert) borrowed credit for the accuracy of his statement on referring his learning to the books before mentioned, and by implying that he echoed the standard authorities like Dodd. Under the circumstances it was not improper to resort to the book, not to prove the facts it contained, but to disprove the statement of the witness, and enable the jury to see that the book did not contain what he had ascribed to it. The final purpose was to disparage the opinion of the witness, and hinder the jury from being imposed upon by a false light. The case is a clear exception to the rule which forbids the reading of books of inductive science as affirmative evidence of the facts treated of."[4]

These cases are certainly distinguishable from the case in Massachusetts, in which it was held that an expert could not

[1] Wharton's Evidence, § 665.
[2] Huffman v. Click, 77 N. C. 55.
[3] City of Ripon v. Bittel, 30 Wis. 614.
[4] Pinney v. Cahill, 14 The Reporter, 337; s. c., 12 N. W. Reporter, 862.

read from a treatise a paragraph laying down propositions in which he concurred.[1] But in Maryland,[2] and also in Rhode Island,[3] it seems to be laid down that such treatises cannot be read from to contradict an expert in such cases. It seems, however, these cases to the contrary notwithstanding, that an exception should be recognized to the general rule, and that medical treatises may be introduced in evidence for the sole purpose of contradicting an expert who has been permitted to testify, on his direct examination, that they contained certain statements, which are not to be found therein.

§ 182. **Testing Knowledge of Experts on Cross-Examination.**—Another distinction has been taken in a case decided in Illinois in 1878, in which the right of counsel is sustained, to read, on the cross-examination of a physician, paragraphs from standard authors treating of the disease of which he had stated the deceased died, at the same time asking him whether he agreed with the statements therein contained.[4] This the court considered to be different from reading the books to the jury as evidence in the case. Counsel had a right, said the court, to test the knowledge of the expert by any fair means that promised to elicit the truth. "It will be conceded it might be done by asking proper and pertinent questions, and what possible difference could it make whether the questions were read out of a medical book, or framed by counsel for that purpose. * * Assuming to be familiar with standard works that treat of *delirium tremens*, it was not unfair to the witness to call his attention to the definitions given in the books, of that particular disease, and ask him whether he concurred in the definitions. How could the knowledge of the witness of such subjects be more fully tested? That is in no just sense reading books to the jury as evidence, or for the purpose of contradicting the witness." It seems doubtful

---

[1] Commonwealth v. Sturtivant, 117 Mass. 122.
[2] Davis v. State, 38 Md. 15.
[3] State v. O'Brien, 7 R. I. 336, 338.
[4] Conn. M. L. Ins. Co. v. Ellis, Adm'r., 89 Ill. 516.

whether the distinction which the court undertook to draw in this case was not, after all, a distinction without a difference. For how was the knowledge of the witness tested, but by comparing his answers with the statements read from the book in the presence of the jury? And what was this but practically introducing the book in evidence as a standard to discredit the witness if he disagreed therewith? The recognition of such a principle enables counsel, under the color of a cross-examination of an opposing witness, to practically introduce affirmative evidence in his own behalf from medical authorities. For while the books are not formally offered in evidence, an impression may be made on the minds of the jury which will be equally effective.

§ 183. **Views of Writers on Medical Jurisprudence as to the Exclusion of Medical Treatises.**—The medical experts seem to have been inclined to disprove, if not to actually resent, the exclusion of medical treatises from the evidence. In the famous case of *Spencer Cowper*, when objection was made to a reference to medical authorities, Dr. Crell, a witness in the case, is reported to have exclaimed: "My lord, it must be reading, as well as a man's own experience, that will make any one a physician; for without the reading of books in that art, the art itself cannot be attained to. I humbly conceive, that in such a difficult case as this, we ought to have a great deference for the reports and opinions of learned men; neither do I see any reason why I should not quote the fathers of my profession in this case, as well as you, gentlemen of the long robe, quote Coke upon Littleton in others."[1]

In Beck's Medical Jurisprudence the learned author strenuously maintains the right of the professional witness to refer to medical treatises. He has manifestly fallen into error in laying down the following proposition:

"In this country, I believe, the objection to medical books has never been made. There is scarcely a case of any note, where testimony has been required, in which fre-

---

[1] 2 Beck's Med. Jurisprudence, 919; Hargrave's St. Trials.

quent reference has not been had to medical works. They are quoted and commented on by the bench and bar, and by the professional witnesses."[1]

The later writers on medical jurisprudence have taken a more just view of this question, and appreciate the reasonableness and justice of the rule. In Elwell's Medical Jurisprudence we find that distinguished writer saying: "The medical witness, therefore, has no just grounds of complaint, because his books are not received in evidence. The court honors his individual opinion as of higher value than that of an outside author. The court presumes, that from reading these authors, close thought and actual observation and experience, the witness under oath, subject to cross-examination, will more certainly enlighten the case than if it depends upon the published opinions of authors, who perhaps had a favorite theory to support, or an old prejudice to influence them, on a question or subject constantly advancing. Then the author himself may have changed his opinions since the book was written."[2]

So in Ordonaux's Jurisprudence of Medicine it is said: "The reason of this rule is founded, in the principle, that the expert is called to express a personal opinion upon a state of facts of variable interpretation, and if a book could pronounce it as well, it would be superfluous to call him. * * * The justice of excluding scientific books from the field of evidence becomes immediately apparent, when we reflect that they deal necessarily only with universal propositions, and inasmuch as every particular case wears a complexion of its own, it is indispensable to its correct interpretation that some living witness, skilled in experience, and able to detect laws of common agreement, should be called in as an expert umpire. As no dictionary of human thoughts will ever be written, so no dictionary of physical laws will ever be compiled, that shall provide with strictest fidelity, the necessary interpretation for all the variously complex and conflicting manifestations of muta-

[1] 2 Beck's Med. Jurisprudence, 919.
[2] Elwell's Med. Jurisprudence, 335.

tional phenomena, not to speak of the more puzzling sphere of antinomies and apparent contradictions."[1]

§ 184. **Reading from Scientific Books in Argument.**— The same objections which have been deemed sufficient to exclude scientific treatises as evidence, would seem to be equally potent against the right of counsel to read extracts therefrom as a part of their argument to the jury. It is difficult to see how any just distinction can be made between the two cases. And it is not believed that any such right will be recognized by any court which maintains the inadmissibility of the treatises in evidence. We think the better rule is not to allow counsel to read to the jury as a part of their argument extracts from scientific works, though shown to be standard authorities. Such is the rule in England, as we shall presently see, and such is the rule in this country as recognized by the better authorities. There are, however, some cases to the contrary, which we shall first consider.

In Connecticut, where the question of the admissibility of treatises in evidence has not yet been determined, the right of counsel is recognized to read extracts from such treatises as by the testimony of experts have been accepted as authority.[2] Counsel it seems had been permitted by tacit consent for a long series of years, in that State, to exercise that right. The court, therefore, decided, when the right was formally questioned, that the practice must be regarded as having, by repetition, hardened into a rule.

In Indiana the doctrine was stated in an early case as follows: "It would, no doubt, be improper to permit matters which are objectionable as evidence, to be introduced in evidence in that way. That is, if the extracts referred to contained the opinions or expositions of learned or scientific witnesses upon a point in issue, and such extracts were inadmissible when offered as evidence during the introduction of testimony by the parties, the court should not have per-

---

[1] Ordonanx's Jurisprudence of Medicine, 153, 154.
[2] State v. Hoyt, 46 Conn. 330.

mitted them to be read at any time. But if the extracts were merely argumentative and contained no opinions or expositions, which could be regarded as properly matters of evidence, we cannot perceive any valid objection to their being read or adopted as argument, subject, of course, to the instructions of the court as to the law of the case."[1] To the same purpose are the decisions in Ohio[2] and Texas,[3] as we understand them. In a subsequent case in Indiana,[4] and another in Delaware,[5] it has been held proper to allow counsel to read from standard medical authorities, the jury being instructed that the extract was not to be regarded as evidence. The objections to the practice pointed out in the later and better considered cases do not seem to have occurred to the courts announcing these opinions.

§ 185. Reading from Scientific Books in Argument — The Subject Continued.— In a case in England, where counsel in his address to the jury attempted to quote from a work on surgery, it was held he was not justified in doing so, and ALDERSON, B., said; "You surely cannot contend that you may give the book in *evidence*, and if not, what right have you to quote from it in your address, and do that indirectly which you would not be permitted to do in the ordinary course?"[6]

In Massachusetts when counsel for the defendant in his opening to the jury, contending that cribbing was not an unsoundness in a horse, but a habit, proposed to read from a work on Veterinary Surgery, a description of the habit "as a better mode of showing what cribbing was, but not as evidence in the case," it was held no error to refuse to allow him to proceed.[7] So in an earlier case

[1] Jones v. Trustees, etc., Indiana R., 47.
[2] Legg v. Drake, 21 Ohio, 286.
[3] Wade v. De Witt, 20 Texas, 398.
[4] Harvey v. State, 40 Ind. 516.
[5] State v. West, 1 Houston Cr. Cas. 371.
[6] The Queen v. Crouch, 1 Cox Cr. Cas. 94. And see Regina v. Taylor, 13 Cox Cr. Cases, 77.
[7] Washburn v. Cuddihy, 8 Gray, 430.

the same court denied the right, on the ground that the extracts would, in effect, be used as evidence.[1]

In North Carolina the question has been carefully considered, and the language of the court in denying the right, warrants repetition in this connection. "It sounds plausible to say, you do not read it as evidence, but that you adopt it as part of your argument. But in so doing the counsel really obtains from it all the benefits of substantive evidence fortified by its 'standard' character. He first proves by the medical expert that the work is one of high character and authority in the profession, and then he says to the jury, 'here is a book of high standing, written by one who has devoted his talents to the study and explanation of this special subject of nervous diseases. He expresses my views with so much more force than I can, that I will read an extract from his work and adopt it as a part of my argument.' It is evident that the effect of this manœuvre is to corroborate the evidence of the medical expert, or other witnesses, by the authority of a great name testifying, but not under oath, to the same thing as the expert, but with this difference, that the author has not heard the evidence upon which the expert based his opinion."[2]

And in Michigan the Supreme Court has lately sustained the trial court in refusing to allow counsel in his opening to read a passage from Griesenger on Mental Diseases, to the effect that grief, loss of fortune and disappointed ambition were among the causes of insanity.[3]

So in a recent case in the Circuit Court of the United States for the Northern District of New York, when counsel stated that he desired to read from Ericson on Railway Injuries, as a part of his argument, Mr. Justice WALLACE declared that he could not read any portion or extract from the book.[4]

---

[1] Ashworth v. Kittridge, 12 Cush. 194.
[2] Huffman v. Click, 77 N. C. 54.
[3] Fraser v. Jennison, 42 Mich. 206, 214.
[4] Robinson v. New York Central, etc. R. R. Co., Albany Law J., Oct. 29th, 1881, p. 357.

The latest case in which the subject has been considered was decided in the Supreme Court of California in 1882. Counsel in the trial court was permitted, against objection, to read as a portion of his argument from a book called "Browne's Medical Jurisprudence of Insanity." No testimony was introduced to show that this was a standard authority, and while stress was laid on this fact, the reasoning of the court leads to the conclusion that had such testimony been introduced it could not have affected the judgment announced. Judgment was reversed, and a new trial granted.[1] It seems difficult to understand why any stress should be laid on the fact that the work was not shown to be a standard authority. The right to read from the work at all is predicated upon the fact that counsel has adopted the extract as his own, and made it a part of his argument. The theory is that it comes before the jury, not as the opinion of the writer, for as such it would be inadmissible, but as the opinion or argument of counsel. The right of counsel, therefore, to make the argument cannot depend upon the fact that it is sustained by standard authorities, or by any authorities at all. This fact the court overlooked, although it reached a correct conclusion on the facts.

§ 186. **Reading the Testimony of Experts as Contained in Official Reports.**— It sometimes happens that expert testimony given in another case is set out at length in the official reports, appearing either in the decision of the court, or in the statement of the case by the reporter. While the opinions of the experts have in such cases been expressed under oath, counsel have no right to make use of them in another case, as no opportunity is afforded in such case for any cross-examination. Such a case arose in Illinois, where the State's attorney undertook to read to the jury on a murder trial, the testimony of a professor of chemistry, as found in an official report of another case, concerning the symptoms of poisoning by arsenic. This was pronounced to be the height of injustice, and judgment was reversed.[2]

[1] People v. Wheeler, 9 Pac. Coast Law J. 581.
[2] Yoe v. People, 49 Ill. 410, 412.

CHAPTER X

COMPENSATION OF EXPERTS.

SECTION.
187. Statutory Provisions Concerning the Compensation of Experts.
188. The Effect of Making Extra Compensation.
189. Experts need not Make a Preliminary Examination, unless Special Compensation is Made.
190. Whether Special Compensation must be Made to Experts Testifying as Such.
191. Opinions of Writers on Medical Jurisprudence — As to Additional Compensation.
192. American Cases Favoring Extra Compensation.
193. American Cases Denying the Right to Extra Compensation.
194. Extra Compensation Allowed in England.
195. Special Compensation to Experts Employed by the State in Criminal Cases.
196. Special Compensation to Experts Summoned for the Defense — Paid out of the Public Treasury.

§ 187. **Statutory Provisions Concerning the Compensation of Experts.**— In some of the States the law expressly provides that when a witness is summoned to testify as an expert, he shall be entitled to extra compensation. Such a provision may be found in the laws of Iowa, of North Carolina, and of Rhode Island. They are as follows:

Iowa: Witnesses called to testify only to an opinion founded on special study or experience in any branch of science, or to make scientific or professional examinations, and state the result thereof, shall receive additional compensation, to be fixed by the court, with reference to the value of the time employed, and the degree of learning or skill required." [1]

[1] Code of 1873, § 3814. See Snyder v. Iowa City, 40 Iowa, 646.

North Carolina: "Experts when compelled to attend and testify, shall be allowed such compensation and mileage as the court may, in its discretion, order."[1]

Rhode Island: "In addition to the fees above provided, witnesses summoned and testifying as experts in behalf of the State before any justice of the Supreme Court, trial justice or coroner, may be allowed and paid such sum as such justice of the Supreme Court, trial justice or coroner may deem just and reasonable: *Provided*, that the allowance so made by any trial justice or coroner, shall be subject to the approval of a justice of the Supreme Court."[2]

In Indiana, on the other hand, is has been provided by statute that experts may be compelled to testify to an opinion without any extra compensation. The provision is as follows: "A witness who is an expert in any art, science, trade, profession, or mystery, may be compelled to appear and testify to an opinion, as such expert, in relation to any matter, whenever such opinion is material evidence, relevant to any issue on trial before a court or jury, without payment or tender of compensation other than the *per diem* and mileage allowed by law to witnesses, under the same rules and regulations by which he can be compelled to appear and testify to his knowledge of facts relevant to the same issue."[3]

In the absence of all statutory provision authorizing it, the compensation of experts, beyond the regular witness fees, is not a necessary disbursement, and cannot be taxed as a part of the costs. It is considered as having been incurred for the party's own benefit, and is no more a disbursement in the cause than the fees paid to an attorney."[4]

§ 188. **The Effect of Making Extra Compensation.**— It is undoubtedly the practice in all important cases, for the parties calling experts, or professional witnesses, to pay them an additional compensation. And it is not considered

---

[1] Laws of 1871, ch. 139, § 13. See State v. Dollar, 66 N. C. 626.
[2] Public Statutes (1882), p. 733. § 15.
[3] Indiana Revised Statutes (1881), p. 94, § 504.
[4] Mask v. City of Buffalo, N. Y. Ct. of App., Dec. 1881, 13 Reporter, 251. And see Haynes v. Mosher, 15 How. Pr. 216.

contrary to the policy of the law, that these witnesses should be specially feed. For if special compensation was not made or permitted, the testimony of such witnesses could not be procured without great pecuniary loss, and perhaps could not be secured at all. While the question as to the amount paid, or agreed to be paid in such cases, cannot affect in the least the regularity of the trial, yet it is stated that it may, perhaps, properly affect the credit of the witness with the jury.[1]

§ 189. **Experts Need not Make a Preliminary Examination, unless Special Compensation is Made.**— An expert cannot be compelled to make any preliminary investigation of the facts involved in a case, in order to enable him to attend on the trial and give a professional opinion. For instance, if the State desires the opinion of medical experts as to the cause of death, it cannot compel them to make a *post mortem* examination of the body of the deceased, for the purpose of qualifying them to express an opinion as to what was the cause of death.[2] And it has been said that an expert cannot be required to attend during the entire trial, for the purpose of attentively considering, and carefully listening to the testimony, in order that he may be qualified to express a deliberate opinion upon such testimony.[3] In all such cases special compensation should be made.

§ 190. **Whether Special Compensation Must be Made to Experts Testifying as Such.**—There can be no doubt that professional men are not entitled, in this country, to claim any additional compensation when testifying as ordinary witnesses to facts which happened to fall under their observation.[4] But another question arises, when they are summoned to testify as to facts of science with which they have become familiar by means of special study and investigation, and to express opinions based upon the skill

---

[1] See People v. Montgomery, 13 Abb. Pr. (N. S.) 207, 240.
[2] See Summers v. State, 5 Texas Ct. of App. 374.
[3] See People v. Montgomery, 13 Abb. Pr. (N. S.) 220.
[4] Snyder v. Iowa City, 40 Iowa, 646. And see Buchman v. State, 59 Ind. 1.

acquired from such researches, as to conclusions which ought to be drawn from certain given facts. Whether they can be compelled to testify in such cases, when no other compensation has been tendered than the usual fees of witnesses testifying to ordinary facts, is a point upon which the cases are not in harmony. In this country the cases are so nearly balanced, that the question must be regarded as still an open one. But in England it seems to be settled that additional compensation is required. The practical importance of the question requires that the subject be examined somewhat at length.

§ 191. **Opinions of Writers on Medical Jurisprudence as to Additional Compensation.**— And before examining the decisions of the courts, attention is called to the opinions of the writers on Medical Jurisprudence. For, while these opinions cannot be regarded as authoritative, they are important, and entitled to the respectful consideration of the profession and the courts. In Ordonaux's Jurisprudence of Medicine,[1] that learned and distinguished writer says: "It is evident that the skill and professional experience of a man are so far his individual capital and property, that he cannot be compelled to bestow it gratuitously upon any party. Neither the public, any more than a private person, have a right to extort services from him, in the line of his profession, without adequate compensation. On the witness stand, precisely as in his office, his opinion may be given or withheld at pleasure; for a skilled witness cannot be compelled to give an opinion, nor committed for contempt if he refuse to do so. Whoever calls for an opinion from him in chief, is under obligation to remunerate him, since he has to that extent employed him professionally; and the expert, at the outset, may decline giving his opinion until the party calling him either pays or agrees to pay him for it. When, however, he has given his opinion, he has now placed it among the *res gestæ*, and cannot decline repeating it or explaining it on cross-examination. Once uttered to the

[1] §§ 114, 115.

public ear of the court, it passes among the facts in evidence."

So in Beck's Medical Jurisprudence the eminent author, in considering this subject, comments as follows:

"If the duties on which I have enlarged are important to the community, in promoting the proper administration of justice, ought not the individuals engaged in them to receive adequate compensation? I advert to this, not only because it is just in principle, but because it would remove all imputation of volunteering in criminal cases. No one can refuse being a witness when legally summoned; every one, I presume, may decline the dissection of a dead body, or the chemical examination of a suspected fluid; and yet there is not, I believe, an individual attending on any of our courts, who is not paid for his time and services, with the exception of such as are engaged in these investigations. * * * It is quite time that the medical profession in this country should rouse itself to a demand of its just rights."[1]

§ 192. **American Cases Favoring Extra Compensation.**— The earliest of the American cases upon this subject seems to have arisen in the District Court of the United States for the District of Massachusetts, in 1854. The question came up before SPRAGUE, J., in the following manner: During a trial upon an indictment, a motion for a *capias* was made by the district attorney, for the purpose of bringing in a witness subpœnaed to act as an interpreter of some German witnesses, but who had refused or neglected to attend. In answer to this application, the court said: "A similar question has heretofore arisen, and I have declined to issue process to assist in such cases. When a person has knowledge of any fact pertinent to the issue to be tried, he may be compelled to attend as a witness. In this all stand upon an equal ground. But to compel a person to attend, merely because he is accomplished in a particular, science, art, or profession, would subject the same

---

[1] Beck's Medical Jurisprudence, 920, 921.

individual to be called upon in every cause in which any question in his department of knowledge is to be solved. Thus, the most eminent physician might be compelled, merely for the ordinary witness fees, to attend from the remotest part of the district, and give his opinion in every trial in which a medical question should arise. This is so unreasonable, that nothing but necessity can justify it. The case of an interpreter is analogous to that of an expert. It is not necessary to say what the court would do if it appeared that no other interpreter could be obtained by reasonable effort. Such a case is not made as the foundation of this motion. It is well known that there are in Boston many native Germans, and others skilled in both the German and English languages, some of whom, it may be presumed, might, without difficulty, be induced to attend for an adequate compensation."[1]

The question came before the Supreme Court of Indiana in 1877, in *Buchman* v. *The State*,[2] the statutory provision above noted not having been enacted at that time, and that court held that while a physician or surgeon could be required to attend as a witness to facts without other compensation than that provided by law for other witnesses, yet he could not be required to testify as to his professional opinion, without the compensation of a professional fee. In the opinion of the court the professional knowledge of an attorney or physician is to be regarded in the light of property, and his professional services are no more at the mercy of the public, as to remuneration, than are the goods of the merchant, or the crops of the farmer, or the wares of the mechanic. "When a physician testifies as an expert, by giving his opinion, he is performing," says the court, "a strictly professional service. To be sure, he performs that service under the sanction of an oath. So does the lawyer, when he performs any services in a cause. The position of a medical witness, testifying as an expert, is much more like that of a lawyer than that of an ordinary witness, tes-

[1] In the matter of Roelker, 1 Sprague, 276.
[2] 59 Indiana, 1.

tifying to facts. The purpose of his service is not to prove facts in the cause, but to aid the court or jury in arriving at a proper conclusion from facts otherwise proved." The court then goes on to say that if physicians or surgeons can be compelled to render professional services by giving their opinions on the trial of causes, without compensation, then an eminent physician or surgeon may be compelled to go to any part of the State, at any and all times, to render such service without other compensation than is afforded by the ordinary witness fees. And this the court does not think he can be compelled to do. This conclusion is based both upon general principles of law, and the Constitution of the State, which provides that "no man's particular services shall be demanded without just compensation."

The latest case in which this subject has been considered seems to be the case of the *United States* v. *Howe*, recently decided in the United States District Court for the Western District of Arkansas.[1] In this case, which was a prosecution for murder, a physician summoned as an expert, being sworn refused to testify, unless first paid a reasonable compensation for giving the results of his skill and experience. The court declined to regard this refusal as a contempt of court. The distinction was sustained between a witness called to depose to a matter of opinion depending on his skill in a particular profession or trade, and a witness called to depose to facts which he saw. When he has facts within his knowledge, the public have a right to those facts, but the skill and professional experience of a man are so far his individual capital and property, that he cannot be compelled to bestow them gratuitously upon any party. That the public cannot, any more than a private person extort services from a person in the line of his profession or trade without adequate compensation.

§ 193. **American Cases Denying the Right to Extra Compensation.**— A different conclusion to that reached in the foregoing cases was arrived at in the Supreme Court of

[1] 12 Central Law Journal, 193.

Alabama in 1875, in *Ex parte Dement*.[1] The prisoner on trial was charged with murder, and the physician, after testifying that he had seen the deceased after he had received the wounds which the prosecution asserted had produced death, was asked to state the nature and character of the wound received, and its probable effect. This he declined to do upon the ground that "he had not been remunerated for his professional opinion, nor had compensation for his professional opinion been promised or secured." A fine was thereupon imposed upon him for contempt of court. A motion to have the fine set aside upon the ground that the court could not compel him to testify as a professional expert until compensation for his professional opinion had been first made or secured, having been overruled, the case was taken on appeal to the Supreme Court, which affirmed the ruling. In their decision, after an examination of the authorities, the court say: "It will be noticed that it has not been adjudged in any of the cases cited, that a physician or other person examined as an expert, is entitled to be paid for his testimony as for *professional opinions*. The reports contain nothing to this effect. The English cases only indicate, and it is implied by the decision of Judge SPRAGUE (*In the matter of Roelker*),[2] that persons summoned to testify as experts ought to receive compensation for their *loss of time*. And it is to be inferred that the judges delivering some of the opinions thought the time of such a witness ought to be valued, in the language of the English statute, 'according to his countenance and calling.' But it is not intimated by any of them, that a physician, when testifying, is to be considered as exercising his skill and learning in the healing art, which is his high vocation; or that a counsellor at law, in the same situation, is exerting his talents and requirements in professionally investigating and upholding the rights of a client. If this were so, each one should be paid for his testimony as a witness,

---

[1] 53 Alabama, 389.
[2] Sprague's Decisions, 276.

as he is paid by clients, or patients, according to the importance of the case and his own established reputation for ability and skill. But in truth he is not really employed or retained by any person. And the evidence he is required to give should not be given with the intent to take the part of either contestant in the suit, but with a strict regard to the truth, in order to aid the court to pronounce a correct judgment." It is to be observed that this case was decided two years prior to the case of *Buchman* v. *The State*, in which the right to extra compensation was grounded, not upon the *loss of time*, upon which the Alabama court comments disapprovingly, but upon the ground that professional knowledge constitutes *property* of which he cannot be deprived without just compensation.

In 1879, the question came up before the Court of Appeals of Texas in *Summer* v. *State*.[1] In this case, the defendant, being on trial for murder, the State called a medical practitioner, one Dr. Spohn, who testified that he had attended the deceased, and had made a *post mortem* examination, but declined to state the cause of his death. In his testimony he said: "I found the deceased breathing, but unconscious; had a contusion upon the left side of the head, but no exterior evidence of fractured skull; removed the patient to town, and attended him until the next day, when he died; after death, made a *post mortem* examination, but I decline to state the cause of the man's death, as my knowledge was obtained by professional skill and from the deductions of experience, which I consider my own property, and which the county of Nueces has persistently refused to pay for. I have no knowledge of the actual cause of the man's death, save through the *post mortem* examination alluded to." The trial court sustained this refusal to disclose the knowledge thus acquired, upon the ground that not having been paid, he could not be compelled to testify as to the same. But the Court of Appeals viewed the matter in a different light, and expressed itself

[1] 5 Texas Court of Appeals, 374.

as follows: "The court may compel a physician to testify as to the result of a *post mortem* examination; and it is to be regretted that a member of a profession so distinguished for liberal culture and high sense of honor and duty should refuse to testify in a cause pending before the courts of his country, involving the life and liberty of a fellow being, and the rightful administration of the laws of a common country. Dr. Spohn has doubtless been misled, in taking the position he did, by the misconception of certain writers on medical jurisprudence."

The court then refers to *Ex parte Dement*, and concludes as follows: "A medical expert could not be compelled to make a *post mortem* examination unless paid for it; but an examination having already been made by him, he could be compelled to disclose the result of that examination."

§ 194. **Extra Compensation Allowed in England.**—In *Betts* v. *Clifford*,[1] Lord CAMPBELL declared that a scientific witness, or expert, was not bound to attend upon being served with a *subpœna*, and that he ought not to be subpœnaed. If the witness, however, knew any question of *fact*, he might be compelled to attend, but he could not be compelled to attend to speak merely to matters of opinion. The same distinction was also taken in *Webb* v. *Page*,[2] which was a case in which a witness had been called by the plaintiff to testify as to the damage sustained by certain cabinet work, and the expense necessary to restore or replace the injured articles. The witness having demanded compensation, Mr. Justice MAULE said: "There is a distinction between the case of a man who sees a fact, and is called to prove it in a court of law, and a man who is selected by a party to give his opinion on a matter on which he is peculiarly conversant from the nature of his employment in life. The former is bound, as a matter of public duty, to speak to a fact which happens to have fallen within his own knowledge; without such testimony the course of justice must be stopped. The latter is under no such obli-

[1] Warwick Lent Assizes, 1858.
[2] 1 Car. & K. 23.

gation; there is no such necessity for his evidence, and the party who selects him must pay him." According to these cases, therefore, an expert is under no obligation to testify as to matters of opinion, at least in civil cases. If his testimony is desired, the party desiring it must first render him such compensation as his services are worth. It is also to be noticed that, in England, it has been held, in civil cases, at least, that a professional man, even though called to testify to facts, and not to opinions, is entitled to extra compensation on the higher scale allowed under the statute of Elizabeth,[1] which provides that the witness must "have tendered to him, according to his countenance or calling, his reasonable charges." In a case decided in 1862, the expenses of an attorney, called as a witness, but who did not give professional evidence, were allowed by the Master, on the higher scale allowed professional witnesses. This allowance was held proper on motion to show cause, and Mr. Chief Justice EARL said: "We do not approve of the rule which is said to prevail in criminal cases, that if a surgeon is called to give evidence not of a professional character he is only to have the expenses of an ordinary witness. We think the Master was quite right in allowing the expenses of this witness on the higher scale."[2] So also in *Turner* v. *Turner*,[3] the same principle was applied by the vice-chancellor in the case of a barrister. The theory seems to be that the time of professional men is more valuable than the time of non-professional men, and that they should be compensated accordingly. It has been suggested that the rule is a hard one,[4] and it may be considered doubtful whether it can stand the test of examination. It seems more correct to regard professional and scientific knowledge in the light of property which the public have no right to use without making a proper compensation.

[1] 5 Eliz. c. 9.
[2] Parkinson v. Atkinson, 31 L. J. (N. S.) C. P. 199.
[3] 5 Jur. (N. S.) 839.
[4] See Lonergan v. Royal Exchange Assurance, 7 Blng. 725, 727; Collins v. Godefroy, 1 Barn. & Adol. 930.

§ 195. **Special Compensation to Experts Employed by the State in Criminal Cases.**— And in the absence of express statutory provision authorizing it, it has been the practice in many of the States, in criminal cases, to make a proper compensation to the experts summoned by the government. As lawyers who are employed by the government to assist in the prosecution of the criminal, receive a special compensation, so the experts receive a special compensation ; and this is allowed under certain statutory provisions authorizing the allowance of accounts for necessary services and expenses.

§ 196. **Special Compensation to Experts Summoned for the Defence Paid out of the Public Treasury.**— The Supreme Court of Massachusetts, in 1870, had its attention called to the right to allow the prisoner's counsel, in the case of an indictment for murder, to tax as a part of the costs to be paid out of the public treasury, extra compensation to the experts employed by him, as a part of the necessary expense of the trial, and as such to be allowed under the statutes referred to in the preceding section. As the question is an important one, we quote from the decision, allowing such taxation, as follows :

" Whenever the prosecuting officer thinks the interests of justice require it, we do not doubt that he is authorized, by the statutes above mentioned, to employ experts to make proper investigations for ascertaining the truth of a case, and that it is proper for him in some capital cases to enable the prisoner's counsel to make similar investigations, and to procure the attendance of experts at the trial, if the prisoner is not able to do so ; and the court is authorized to allow a reasonable compensation to such experts for their services, both for attending the trial, and for their prior investigations. This is not on the ground that the statute has given to a prisoner the right to such aid at the expense of the public treasury ; but on the ground that it is for the interest of the Commonwealth, in the case then before the court, that all proper investigations should be made, in order to guard against the danger of doing injustice to the prisoner in a case where he is exposed to so great a penalty. * * * We do not think the prosecuting officer or the court would be authorized to allow the charges of all such persons as the prisoner would have a right to employ as experts at his own expense, without regard to their character, or to the need of employing them in the case. But the assent of the prosecuting officer should be obtained beforehand to the employment of such experts as may be selected and agreed upon, or, in the case of his refusal to assent, application should be made to the court to appoint the experts. This would be the more proper course of proceeding, if the prisoner desires to have the experts called by him paid out of the public treasury." [1]

[1] Attorney-General Petitioner, 104 Mass. 537.

APPENDIX

OF THE OPINIONS OF THE COURTS AS TO THE VALUE OF EXPERT TESTIMONY.

It has been considered advisable to note the opinions which have been expressed on the value of expert testimony. Some of these opinions refer to the value of such testimony in general, and are to be found in appendix "A"; others relate to the value of such testimony in the investigation of handwriting, and are to be found in appendix "B"; and others still refer to the value of the testimony of medical experts, and are to be found in appendix "C".

While this work has been running through the press, a few additional cases of value relating to expert testimony have appeared. References to these cases will be found in apppendix "D", with references to the appropriate sections in the body of the work.

"A."—EXPERT TESTIMONY IN GENERAL.

Taylor on Evidence.—" Perhaps the testimony which least deserves credit with a jury is that of skilled witnesses. These gentlemen are usually required to speak, not to facts, but to *opinions*; and where this is the case, it is often quite surprising to see with what facility, and to what an extent, their views can be made to correspond with the wishes or the interests of the parties who call them. They do not, indeed, wilfully misrepresent what they think, but their judgments become so warped by regarding the subject in one point of view, that, even when conscientiously disposed, they are incapable of expressing a candid opinion. Being zealous partisans, their belief becomes synonymous with faith as defined by the Apostle, and it too often is but 'the substance of things hoped for, the evidence of things not seen.'" (§ 58.)

And " as experts usually come with a bias on their minds to support the cause on which they are embarked, little weight will, in general, be attached to the evidence which they give, unless it be obviously based on sensible reasoning." (§ 1877.)

Best on Evidence.—There is " no evidence the value of which varies so immensely as that now under consideration, and respecting which it is so difficult to lay down any rules beforehand. * * * It would not be easy to over-rate the value of the evidence given in many difficult and delicate inquiries, not only by medical men and physiologists, but by learned and experienced persons in various branches of science, art and trade. * * * and there can be no doubt that testimony is daily received in our courts as 'scientific evidence,' to which it is almost profanation to apply the term, as being revolting to common sense, and inconsistent with the commonest honesty on the part of those by whom it is given." § 514.

Redfield on Wills.— " Medical experts are beginning to be regarded much in the light of hired advocates, and their testimony, as nothing more than a studied argument in favor of the side for which they have been called. So uniformly has this proved true, in our limited experience, that it would excite scarcely less surprise to find an expert called by one side, testifying in any particular, in favor of the other side, than to find the counsel upon either side arguing against their clients, in favor of their antagonists." Vol. I., p. 103.

Rolls Court of England.— In a case where surveyors were sworn as to the value of certain real estate, the Master of the Rolls said: "I have frequently had to comment upon the unsatisfactory nature of the evidence of value given by surveyors. Men of equal knowledge and respectability are constantly found giving very contradictory evidence on this subject, and always more or less favorable to the side on whose behalf they are adduced. This probably is inevitable, but the conclusion to which I have been compelled to come is, that in all these cases, I place very little reliance on the evidence of surveyors, who know beforehand on which side their evidence is intended or desired to be used." (Waters v. Thorn, 22 Beavan, 547, 556.)

Supreme Court of United States.— In a case involving the infringement of a patent, Mr. Justice Grier declares: " Experience has shown that opposite opinions of persons professing to be experts, may be obtained to any amount; and it often occurs that not only many days, but even weeks are consumed in cross-examinations, to test the skill or knowledge of such witnesses, and the correctness of their opinions, wasting the time and wearying the patience of both court and jury, and perplexing, instead of elucidating the questions involved in the issue." (Winans v. N. Y., etc. R. R. Co., 21 How. 88, 101).

Supreme Court of Michigan.— " The experience of Courts with the testimony of experts has not been such as to impress them with the conviction that the scope of such proofs should be extended." (People v. Morrigan, 29 Mich. 1, 8, per Campbell, J.)

Supreme Court of Maine.—"Any one who has listened to the 'vain babblings and oppositions of science so called,' which swell the record of the testimony of experts when the hopes of a party depend rather upon mystification than enlightenment, will see the wisdom of the rule (excluding opinions), and look carefully to the legitimacy of any exceptions that may be offered." (State v. Watson, 65 Me, 74, per Barrows, J.)

And, " While the opinion of the experienced, skillful and scientific witness, who has a competent knowledge of the facts involved in the case on which he speaks, affords essential aid to courts and juries, that of unskillful pretenders, quacks and mountebanks, who at times, assume the character of *experts*, not unfrequently serves to becloud and lead to erroneous conclusions. The rules under which this class of testimony is received should not, in my opinion, be relaxed. Such, I believe, would be the judgment of every intelligent person who has had any considerable experience in courts of justice." (Heald v. Thing, 45 Me. 392, 398, per Rice, J.)

"B."—EXPERT TESTIMONY IN HANDWRITING.

English and Scotch Courts.—Lord Campbell, speaking in the House of Lords, declares: "Hardly any weight is to be given to the evidence of what are called scientific witnesses; they come with a bias on their minds to support the cause in which they are embarked." (Tracy Peerage, 10 Cl. & Fin. 154, 191.)

And Lord President Boyle in the Scotch courts says: "A set of engravers have been examined on both sides, to whose testimony I pay very little attention, as their opinions are very little to be depended upon. In this as in all other cases they take different sides. It seems to be a part of their profession to take different sides." (Turnbull v. Dods, 6 Dunlop, 901.)

Michigan Supreme Court.—"Every one knows how very unsafe it is to rely upon any one's opinions concerning the niceties of penmanship. The introduction of professional experts has only added to the mischief, instead of palliating it, and the results of litigation have shown that these are often the merest pretenders to knowledge, whose notions are pure speculation. Opinions are necessarily received, and may be valuable, but at best this kind of testimony is a necessary evil. Those who have had personal acquaintance with the handwriting of a person, are not always reliable in their views, and single signatures, apart from some known surroundings, are not always recognized by the one who made them. Every degree of removal beyond personal knowledge, into the domain of what is sometimes called, with great liberality, scientific opinion, is a step toward greater uncertainty, and the science which is so generally diffused is of very moderate value." (Foster's Will, 34 Mich. 21, 25.)

Supreme Court of District of Columbia.—"The signatures of these papers are claimed not to be genuine, and here we are treated to the opinion of half a dozen men who claim to be experts, and who come up and give us their views as to the genuineness of these signatures. Of all kinds of evidence admitted in a court, this is the most unsatisfactory. It is so weak and decrepit as scarcely to deserve a place in our system of jurisprudence." And, notwithstanding the evidence of the experts, the court declared that it was satisfied as to the genuineness of the signatures. (Cowan v. Beall, 1 McArthur, 270, 274.)

Supreme Court of Vermont.—"It would be trite to repeat the very uniform expression of judges and the books as to the small value of this kind of evidence, yet it is warrantable to say that such expression is corroborated by our own observation and experience in judicial administration." (Wright v. Williams' Estate, 47 Vt. 222, 234.) In an earlier case the same court had declared such evidence to be of "but little weight, as proof of the disputed fact." (Pratt v. Rawson, 40 Vt. 183, 188.)

United States Circuit Court.— " Whether the signatures appear to be done by the same hand, that, I think, is a question you can put to an expert. Though the testimony is of rather a dangerous character, and not much to be relied on." (Grier, J., in U. S. v. Darnaud, 3 Wall. Jr. 143, 183.) And, " Opinions with regard to handwriting are the weakest and least reliable of all evidence as against direct proof of the execution of an instrument." (Grier, J., in Turner v. Hand, 3 Wallace Jr., 88, 115.)

Supreme Court of Indiana.— " Experience shows that the opinions of persons of skill, are often more reliable than the judgment of those who speak from knowledge of having seen the party write." (Chance v. Indianapolis, etc. R. R. Co., 32 Ind. 472, 474.)

New Jersey Court of Chancery.— All doubt respecting the competency of the opinion of experts in handwriting, based upon mere comparison, as evidence, have been removed by statute; but it still must be esteemed proof of low degree. Very learned judges have characterized it as much too uncertain, even when only slightly opposed, to be the foundation of a judicial decision." (Mutual Benefit Life Ins. Co. v. Brown, 30 N. J. Eq. 193, 201.)

Supreme Court of Mississippi.—Declares that the evidence of experts in handwriting "ought to be received and weighed cautiously by the jury," but adds: " An eye practiced in judging writings, may, at a glance, detect irregularities or counterfeits about it, which would entirely escape notice or detection from an unpracticed eye. * * To shut out the evidence which might be afforded by skilful persons in the art of writing, would be almost equivalent to saying that the law had provided no means by which well executed forgeries could be detected, and they must, therefore, be respected as genuine." (Moye v. Herndon, 30 Miss. 118.)

Supreme Court of Iowa.— The opinion of this court on the value of expert testimony in handwriting, may be found on page 63 of this work.

" C."— THE TESTIMONY OF MEDICAL EXPERTS.

The Supreme Courts of North Carolina, of Texas and of Pennsylvania.— The Supreme Court of North Carolina says: " The opinion of a well instructed and experienced medical man upon a matter within the scope of his profession, and based on personal observation and knowledge, is and ought to be carefully considered and weighed by the jury in rendering their verdict." (Flynt v. Bodenhamer, 80 N. C. 205.)

The Supreme Court of Texas, in a case involving a person's sanity, declares: " 'The opinions of medical men are received with great respect and consideration, and properly so." (Thomas v. State, 40 Texas, 65.)

To the same effect is the language of the Supreme Court of Pennsylvania: " It is well settled," says that court, " that the knowledge and experience of medical experts is of great value in questions of insanity." (Pannell v. Commonwealth, 86 Penn. St. 260.)

The Court of Appeals of West Virginia.— In a case which involved the mental capacity of a grantor to make a valid deed, said: " The evidence of physicians, especially those who attended the grantor, and were with him considerably during the time it is charged he was of unsound mind, is entitled to great weight." (Jarrett v. Jarrett, 11 W. Va. 627.)

St. Louis Court of Appeals.— In Slais v. Slais, 9 Mo. App. 96, it is said that the testimony of a physician as to the insanity of a person he did not know at the time, is entitled to but little weight.

The Supreme Court of Mississippi, says: " Prominent among the testimony made use of at this stage of investigation (a dead body having been found, to show death was caused by criminal act), is that of medical and scientific persons, surgeons, physicians and chemists, by whom the body or its remains have been inspected or examined either at the time of their discovery or shortly after. The testimony of these witnesses, as to the appearances observed on such examinations is always of the greatest value, and their opinions as to the causes of such appearances are entitled to much consideration." (Pitts v. State, 43 Miss. 472, 480.)

The Supreme Court of Georgia, speaking of the value of expert testimony in cases of insanity, says: " As it respects this species of testimony generally, the doctrine is this: It is competent testimony, and where the experience, honesty, and impartiality of the witnesses are undeniable, as in this case, the testimony is entitled to great weight and consideration. Not that it is so authoritative, that the jury are bound to be governed by it — it is intended to aid and assist the jury in coming to correct conclusions." (Choice v. State, 31 Ga. 424, 481.)

In the same case, Mr. Justice Lumpkin, speaking for himself, says: "As for myself, I would rely as implicitly upon the opinion of practical men, who form their belief from their observation of the appearance, conduct and conversation of a person, as I would upon the opinions of physicians, who testify from facts proven by others, or the opinions even of the keepers of insane hospitals." (p. 406.)

The Supreme Court of Ohio, in a criminal case involving the sanity of a person on trial for murder, said: " It would be but a farce to try such a question upon the strength of medical opinions, and to regard the weight of evidence always on the side which produced the greatest numbers. Sir John Nicholl, in *Evans* v. *Knight*, 1 Add. 239, observes that ' experience in the ecclesiastical courts taught him that evidence on questions of capacity, being commonly that of opinion merely, was almost always contradictory.' * * * The difficulties witnessed by Sir J. Nicholl, almost always occur when the opinions of physicians are required in cases of medical jurisprudence. Whenever they have enlisted on the side of either party, or of some favorite theory, and one portion of the profession is placed in array against another, the difficulties mentioned in the passage above quoted, are greatly multiplied, and, however honest or renowned for professional character the witnesses may be, such will be the conflict of their testimony, in nine cases out of ten, that it will be utterly unsafe for a jury or court to follow, or adopt, the conclusions of either side. * * * Medical testimony is of too much importance to be disregarded. * * * When delivered with caution, and without bias in favor of either party, or in aid of some speculation and favorite theory, it becomes a salutary means of preventing even intelligent juries from following a popular prejudice, and deciding a cause on inconsistent and unsound principles. But it should be given with great care and received with the utmost caution, and, like the opinions of neighbors and acquaintances, should be regarded as of little weight, if not well sustained by reasons and facts that admit of no misconstructions, and supported by authority of acknowledged credit." (Clark v. State, 12 Ohio, 483.)

The Supreme Court of Illinois.—In 1875, the Supreme Court of Illinois said: "These doctors were summoned by the contestants as 'experts,' for the purpose of invalidating a will deliberately made by a man quite as competent as either of them to do such an act; they were the contestants' witnesses and so considered themselves, Dr. Bassett especially, whose sole testimony is pregnant with such indications. The testimony of such is worth but little, and should always be received by juries and courts with great caution. It was said by a distinguished judge, in a case before him, if there was any kind of testimony not only of no value, but even worse than that, it was, in his judgment, that of medical experts. They may be able to state the diagnosis of the disease more learnedly, but, upon the question, whether it had, at a given time, reached such a stage that the subject of it was incapable of making a contract, or irresponsible for his acts, the opinions of his neighbors, if men of good common sense, would be worth more than that of all the experts in the country. * * * It must be apparent to every one, but few wills could stand the test of the fanciful theories of dogmatic witnesses, who bring discredit on science, and make the name of 'expert' a by-word and a reproach. We concur with the judge above referred to; we would not give the testimony of these common sense witnesses, deposing to what they know and saw almost every day for years, for that of so-called *experts*, who always have some favorite theory to support—men often as presumptuous as they are ignorant of the principles of medical science.," (Rutherford v. Morris, 77 Ill. 397, 404.)

And the same court in a subsequent case of *Carpenter* v. *Calvert*, 83 Ill. 62, 70, expressed itself in somewhat similar language.

The Scotch Courts.—The *London Lancet*, said to be the most eminent medical journal in the world, says in a recent issue: "Several cases which have recently been considered in the higher courts of Scotland have brought into unfortunate prominence the diversity of opinion regarding the cases in dispute so frequently manifested, even by the most distinguished members of our profession. A few months ago, in a murder trial at Aberdeen, the most contradictory opinions regarding the mental condition of the culprit were expressed, and Lord Deas signified his unwillingness to have his mental condition investigated by one of these medical men, evidently fearing that he himself might be incarcerated." And it quotes Lord Frazer as saying in another case that: "The evidence was as unsatisfactory as any he had seen. It left on the mind the distressing impression, that the science of medicine was simply the science of guessing and experts. Different doctors with equal confidence and equal dogmatism, expressed contrary opinions upon the same condition of things. He advised the jury to exercise their common sense, throw overboard the medical opinions, and go by the facts." (See 15 Central Law J. 61, July 28th, 1882.)

"D."— ADDITIONAL CASES.

§ 8. Upon a trial for murder an expert testified that certain hair which was found on a wheelbarrow and that taken from the skull of the deceased, was from the head of the same person. His conclusion was reached not from any scientific tests, but from the length, magnitude and color. It was held that the comparison made required no peculiar skill nor scientific knowledge. "It was no more in the province of an expert than of an ordinary person to make it. It related to a matter of common observation," and the opinion was inadmissible. (Sup. Ct. of Wisconsin, June, 1882, Knoll v. State, 14 The Reporter, 381.)

§ 75. In an action to recover for personal injuries caused by the negligence of the defendant, the court has power to require the plaintiff to submit his person to an examination by physicians and surgeons. On his refusal to comply with the order, the court may dismiss the action, or refuse to allow him to give evidence to establish the injury. The application for an order to submit to such an examination ought to be so made as not unnecessarily to prolong the trial, or to prejudice the plaintiff in proving his case. When the application is not made until after the close of the plaintiff's evidence in chief, and the commencement of the introduction of the defendant's evidence, and no reason is shown for the delay in the application, it may be refused on that ground. And it is not error to refuse to charge the jury that the refusal of the plaintiff "at any time *after the close of the testimony on his behalf*" to submit to an examination, affords a presumption against him. The refusal of the trial court to order an examination will not be presumed to have been made on the ground of a want of power to make the order, but in the absence of a showing to the contrary, on the ground that, under the circumstances, the order ought not to have been granted. (Turnpike Co. v. Baily, 37 Ohio St. 104.)

§ 31. A question calling for the opinion of a physician as to whether certain specified symptoms in connection with *other* testimony (not specified), indicated unsound mind, is held improper as referring to other testimony without specifying what the other testimony was. (Storer's Will, 28 Minn. 9.)

§ 48. The opinion of an expert physician derived from statements of the patient of *present* feelings and pains, and of *present* bodily condition is held admissible, and he may give in evidence such statements. But his opinion based upon the patient's *past* experience or history of the case is inadmissible, and he cannot give such past statements in evidence. (Railroad Company v. Frazier, 27 Kans. 463.)

§ 127. The opinions of witnesses who had been in the ice business for several years, were held admissible to show what per cent. of waste from melting, etc., there would be, the ice being properly handled and managed. (Sexton v. Lamb, 27 Kans. 426.)

§ 38. The jury are to exercise an independent judgment, and give such weight to the expert testimony as they deem it worth. And in an action for legal services, the opinions of attorneys as to their value is not to preclude the jury from exercising their own ideas and knowledge upon the subject. (Knapp v. Monell, (N. Y. Sup. Ct.), 15 Cent. Law J., 281).

§ 155. A dealer in clocks may testify as to the value of a clock which he has not seen, but has heard described. The fact that he has not seen the clock does not go to his competency, but only to the weight to be attached to his testimony. (Whiton v. Snyder, 88 N. Y. 299, 308).

INDEX.

☞ The figures refer to the pages.

A.

ABORTION.
opinions of medical experts as to, 95.
ABSTRACT QUESTIONS OF SCIENCE.
when opinions as to are inadmissible, 19.
ACCIDENT.
whether anything could have been done to prevent, 48, 142, 146.
opinion as to severity of injury by a railroad, 71, n. 2.
whether wound was inflicted by, 84.
ACCOUNTANT.
computations made by, 172.
opinion as to compensation for services of, 226.
opinion of as to average duration of life, 231.
ACTUARIES.
opinion of as to value of an annuity, 230.
ADMISSIBILITY OF EXPERT TESTIMONY. See INADMISSIBILITY OF OPINIONS.
the practice of admitting expert testimony an ancient one, 3.
when such testimony is admissible, 8, 12.
inadmissible, 12-21.
when admissible on questions of medical science, 68, 117.
of legal science, 118, 140.
relating to the trades and arts, 141.
relating to handwriting, 176.
to the value of property, 208.
ADULTERATION OF MILK.
opinion as to, 154.
AGE.
opinion as to by non-professional witnesses, 6.
opinion as to by professional witnesses, 155.
admissibility of standard tables of mortality to show expectation of life at a particular age, 231.

ALABAMA.
  statutory provision as to verification of written law, 129.
ALMANACS.
  admissibility of, in evidence, 236.
ANIMALS.
  who are qualified to testify as to diseases in, 116.
ANNUITIES.
  testimony as to the value of, 230.
ARCHITECT.
  opinion as to the employment of, 162.
    work done on a building, 173.
    value of houses, 220, 221.
ARGUMENT.
  reading from scientific books in, 248, 251.
ARKANSAS.
  statutory provision as to verification of written law, 129.
ART.
  · definition of the term, 12.
ART AND SKILL.
  opinions of experts received on questions of, 12.
ARTIST.
  opinion of as to genuineness of painting, 163.
    as to the value of a portrait, 218.
ASSUMING THE EXISTENCE OF FACTS.
  right of counsel as to, in framing the hypothetical question, 39.
  when the opinion of the expert must be asked on assumed state of facts, 39.
  when it need not be, 43.
  doctrine as to, on the cross-examination, 46.
ATTORNEY. See LAWYERS.
AUTHOR.
  opinion as to the value of a literary production, 218.

B.

BANKERS.
  opinion of as to genuineness of bank notes, 205.
  an inadmissible opinion of, 15.
  testimony of as to usage, 170.
BANK NOTES.
  detection of counterfeits, 205.
  statutory provisions as to proof of genuineness, 206.
BANK NOTE DETECTORS.
  such books are inadmissible in evidence, 205.

BLOOD STAINS.
  expert testimony as to, 111-113.
  testimony of non-professional witnesses as to, 113.
  proper questions to experts concerning, 114.
BOOKS OF SCIENCE.
  their relation to expert testimony, 234.
  their admissibility in evidence, 236.
  medical treatises inadmissible as evidence, 237.
  whether a witness is qualified as an expert by a study of, 28.
  the admissibility of opinions based on, 29.
BRAKEMAN.
  inadmissible opinion of, as to switching cars, 14.
  opinion as to proper place of, 147.
BRASS FINISHERS.
  opinion of, 161.
BRICK-MAKER.
  opinion of as to mode of burning tiles, 173.
BRICK MASON.
  opinion of, 162.
BROKERS.
  an inadmissible opinion of, 15.
  opinion of, as to course of business, 169.
  opinion of, as to counterfeit bank notes, 206.
  opinion of, as to the value of stocks, 222, 230, 232.
BUILDERS.
  opinions of, 161, 162.

C.

CALIFORNIA.
  statutory provision as to comparison of handwriting, 191.
CANAL BOATMAN.
  opinion of, as to seamanlike acts, 38.
CARLISLE TABLES.
  admissibility of to show expectation of life, 231.
CARPENTER. See MECHANICS.
  opinion of, 220, 221.
CASHIER.
  opinions of, 205.
CATTLE. See GRAZIER.
CHEMISTS.
  detection of poisons by, 108.
  chemical analysis of poison, whether necessary, 109.
  examination of blood and blood stains, 111.
  opinions of in some miscellaneous cases, 115.
  opinion as to the nature of the ink used in writing, 186.

CIVIL ENGINEER.
   opinion of, as to construction of embankments. 29, 158.
   construction and safety of bridge, 158.
   amount of ground overflowed, 158.
   cause of choking up of harbor, 159.
   what certain land was suited for, 159.
   construction of highway, 159.

CLEARING LAND.
   opinion as to proper time for, 17.

COLORADO.
   statutory provision as to verification of written law, 130.

COMPARISON OF HANDWRITING. See HANDWRITING.

COMPENSATION OF EXPERTS.
   husband must defray in examinations for structural defect, 103.
   statutory provisions concerning, 252.
   the effect of making extra compensation to experts, 253.
   experts need not make preliminary examination without extra compensation, 254.
   whether special compensation must be made, 254.
   opinions of writers on medical jurisprudence on, 255.
   paid out of the public treasury, 263.

COMPETENCY OF EXPERTS.
   must be shown before they can testify, 22.
   is a question addressed to the court, 23.
   when decision of trial court on, is deemed conclusive, 24, 25.
   rule by which the question of, is determined, 24.
   preliminary examination, to determine, 25.
   whether the witness must be actually engaged in the trade or art at the time of testifying, 26.
   whether he must possess the highest degree of skill, 27.
   mere opportunities for observation not sufficient, 27.
   when their knowledge is derived from the study of standard authorities only, 28-33.
   question of, is sometimes dependent on whether expert has heard the testimony, 33.
   when testifying as physicians, 68.
   statutory provision in Wisconsin, as to, 69, 71.
   statutory provisions in other States, 72.
   who are competent to testify to the nature and prevalence of a disease, 80.
   when testifying as to character of instrument producing a wound, 84.
   when testifying to mental condition, 85.
   when testifying concerning poisons, 108.
   when testifying concerning blood and blood-stains, 111, 113.
   when testifying concerning disease in animals, 116.
   when testifying as to foreign law, 132-137.
   when testifying as nautical experts, 141-145.

COMPETENCY OF EXPERTS—Continued.
  railroad experts, 145-148.
  experts in insurance. 148-152.
  gardeners, farmers and stock raisers, 153.
  millers and millwrights, 155, 156.
  surveyors and civil engineers, 157-159.
  machinists, 160.
  mechanics, masons and master builders, 161.
  painters and photographers, 163.
  lumbermen, 164.
  to technical terms and usage, 165, 170.
  in miscellaneous cases, 170-175.
  to handwriting, 178-182.
  to the nature and character of ink, 186.
  to value, 214-222.
  to the value of legal services, 222.
  to the value of medical services, 224.
  to the value of other services, 226.
  to the value of real estate, 227.
  to the value of annuities, 230.
CONCLUSIONS OF FACT.
  are to be drawn by the jury, 5.
  expert cannot draw from the evidence, 37.
CONCLUSIONS OF EXPERTS.
  jury not bound to accept, 59 *et seq.*
CONDUCTOR (RAILROAD.)
  an inadmissible opinion of, 14, 147.
  an admissible opinion of, 146.
CONFIDENTIAL COMMUNICATIONS.
  opinions based on, when made in professional confidence, 71.
  statutory provisions on this subject considered, 72-74.
CONNECTICUT.
  verification of written law, statutory provision, 130.
CONSTRUCTION.
  given to a foreign statute by a foreign tribunal, 124.
  to be given to a survey, surveyor cannot express an opinion on, 157.
  of machinery, opinion as to, 160.
  of writings, expert cannot express an opinion on, 165.
COPYRIGHT.
  opinions of experts, in questions of, 162.
COUNTERFEITS.
  opinions of experts in the detection of, 205.
COURT.
  must determine competency of witnesses, 23.
  discretion of, in passing on questions of competency. 23.
  right of, to examine witnesses, 25.
  right to exclude experts from court room, 53.

COURT—Continued.
right of, to limit number of witnesses, 54.
selection of experts by, 56.
instructions of, as to weight of testimony, 61-65.
right of, to order an examination of the person, 99-108.
takes judicial notice of what, 119-122.
construction of writings, a question for, 165.

CREDIBILITY OF EXPERTS.
is a question for the jury, 58.
what it depends upon, 59.
right of jury to exercise an independent judgment on, 60.
instructions as to 61-65.

CROSS-EXAMINATION.
what is a proper, 46.
refusal to allow on preliminary examination no error, 50.
right to reasons of expert on, 50, 51.
general rules as to, 52, 53.
what is improper in the investigation of handwriting, 204.
what is proper, on value of real estate, 220.
legal services, 223.
testing knowledge of experts on, by scientific books, 245.

CURRENCY.
value of, 232.

CUSTOM AND USAGE.
opinions as to, 168.

D.

DAMAGES.
the opinions of witnesses as to amount of, 211.
compulsory examination of the person, in actions for, 106.

DEATH.
opinions of experts as to cause of, 21, 77, 98, 81.
opinion of non-professional witness that a person was going to die, inadmissible, 80.

DEFINITIONS.
of the term "expert," 1-3.
of the terms "science" and "art," 12.
of the meaning of words is given by the court to the jury, 165.

DELAWARE.
statutory provision as to proof of foreign law, 125.
verification of the written law, 129.

DETECTIVES.
opinion of, 15.

DIMENSION.
opinion as to, 5.

DISCRETION OF COURT.
much is left to, in passing on competency of experts, 23.
DISEASE.
opinions of experts as to nature and symptoms of, 79.
non-professional witnesses, as to, 80.
as to, in animals, 116.
DISTANCE.
opinions as to, 5.
DIVORCE.
for impotency, examination of the person by experts in cases of, 99, 103.
DOWER.
admissibility of tables for computing potential right of, 231.
DURATION OF TIME.
opinion as to. 5.

E.

ENGINEER. See CIVIL ENGINEER AND SURVEYOR.
an inadmissible opinion, 38.
railroad, opinions of, 146, 148.
ENGRAVER.
opinions of, in handwriting, 178, 183, 184.
ETHICS.
opinions founded on a theory of, are inadmissible, 18.
ETHNOLOGIST.
opinion of, as to race, 170.
EVIDENCE. See TESTIMONY.
expert cannot draw conclusions from, nor pass on the weight of the, 37 et seq.
of collateral facts admissible when, 52.
EXAMINATION OF EXPERT WITNESSES. See CROSS-EXAMINATION.
preliminary to their testifying as experts, 25.
mode of their examination, 36.
by the hypothetical question, 39-43.
when it need not be by a hypothetical question, 43-46.
not to be asked questions of law, 47.
as to particular cases, 47.
on facts not stated by them, 48.
latitude of inquiry in, 49.
as to the reasons for their opinions, 51.
general rules as to examination of witnesses, 51-53.
excluding witnesses from court room, during, 53.
as to sanity, 87.
as to blood stains, 114.
whether it should be conducted by the court, 58.

EXAMINATION OF THE PERSON.
right of court to order a compulsory one, in case of impotency, 99.
in criminal cases, 104.
in actions for damages, 106.
EX PARTE INVESTIGATIONS.
opinions based on, 20.
EXPERIENCE.
degree of, required in experts, 27.
EXPERTS. See ADMISSIBILITY OF EXPERT TESTIMONY, COMPENSA-
TION OF EXPERTS, COMPETENCY OF EXPERTS, CREDIBILITY OF
EXPERTS, CROSS-EXAMINATION, DEFINITIONS, EXAMINATION
OF.
who cannot be considered as such, 3.
opinions as to reputation and skill of, 49, 50.
EYE.
expert testimony as to, 71, 99, 116.

F.

FARMERS.
opinion of, as to spreading of fire in clearing land, 17, 154.
condition of land for cropping, 153.
safety of wagon loaded with hay, 153.
yield of land to the acre, 153.
adulteration of milk, 154.
sufficiency of fence, 175.
value of cattle, 220.
value of real estate, 220.
FARRIER.
opinion of, 116.
FEDERAL CONSTITUTION.
State courts take judicial notice of, 120.
FEDERAL COURTS.
State statutes as to comparison of handwriting of no effect in, 193.
take judicial notice of State statutes, 120.
FEDERAL STATUTES.
State courts judicially notice, 120.
FENCE.
opinion as to sufficiency of, 175.
FIRE.
opinion as to proper time to set, 17.
FIRE ARMS.
opinion as to wadding, 16.
length of time since weapon was discharged, 173.
opinion as to which barrels had been discharged, 173.
opinion as to value of, 222.

FISH.
    opinion as to agility of, 173
FLORIDA.
    statutory provision as to verification of written law, 129.
FOREIGN LAW. See LAW.
    as a subject for the testimony of experts, 121.
    mode of proof, by experts in, 123.
    presumed to be unwritten, 124.
    statutory provisions as to verification of, 129.
    certification of questions of, to courts of foreign country, 136.
    qualifications of experts in, 132-138.
    right of expert in, to cite books, 138.
FRANCE.
    how experts are selected in, 55.
    submission to experts of disputed writings for comparison, 189.

G.

GARDENER.
    opinion as to method of using fertilizers, 153.
        condition of land for cropping, 153.
        damage to garden by smoke, 153.
        what certain land was suitable for, 156.
GAS-FITTER.
    opinion of, 167.
GEOLOGIST.
    opinion of, as to existence of coal seams, 170.
        settling and cracking of the earth, 171.
GEORGIA.
    statutory provision as to verification of written law, 130.
        comparison of handwriting, 191.
GERMANY.
    how experts are selected in, 56.
GIN.
    opinion as to whether certain liquor was, 5.
GOVERNMENTAL EXPERTS.
    a system of, considered, 56.
GRAZIER.
    opinion as to number of stock running in a range, 155.
        condition of cattle and causes affecting their health, 155.
        weight of cattle, 155.
        damage to cattle, 155.
        the value of cattle, 220.
GUN AND GUNSMITH. See FIRE-ARMS.
GUN-SHOT WOUNDS.
    who may testify as to, 83-85.

II.

HAIR.
opinion as to whether human or not, 6.

HANDWRITING. See WRITINGS.
the scientific investigation of, 177.
who are experts in, 178–182.
what they may testify to, 182-184.
testimony as to nature and quality of inks, 185.
who are qualified to testify as to the nature of ink. 186-188.
comparison of writings, 188.
    statutory provision as to, 190.
    in the absence of statutory provision, 192-195.
    with those admitted to be genuine, 195.
    with photographic copies, 199-202.
    with writings made on the trial, 203.
    in questions of orthography, 203.
proof of genuineness of writing compared, 197.
expert should have the writing before him, 198.
testing accuracy of expert in, 204.

HIGHWAY.
whether experts may testify as to sufficiency of. 17.

HORSES.
opinion as to health and disposition of, 6.
objects calculated to frighten, 6, 172.

HYPOTHETICAL QUESTION.
opinions of experts should be asked by means of, 39.
when the question need not be hypothetical, 43-46.
how it is to be framed. 39-43.
form of, on cross-examination, 46.
where jury may disregard opinion based on, 40.
should be submitted before rebutting evidence is heard, 46.

I.

IDENTITY.
opinions, as to, 5.
evidence of. 8.

ILLINOIS.
statutory provision as to verification of written law. 129.
statutory provision as to competency of experts in detection of counterfeits, 206.

IMPOTENCY.
right to order an examination of the person in cases of, 99.
who should be appointed to make an examination in cases of, 100.
when an examination will not be ordered in cases of, 101.
testimony in cases of, received with caution. 103.

INADMISSIBILITY OF BOOKS OF SCIENCE.
  as evidence, 234.
INADMISSIBILITY OF OPINIONS. See ADMISSIBILITY OF EXPERT
    TESTIMONY.
  opinions of witnesses in general inadmissible, 4.
  opinions of non-professional witnesses inadmissible on questions of
    science, art, or trade, 6.
  when opinions of experts are inadmissible, 12.
  opinions founded on a theory of morals or ethics, 18.
  opinions based on speculative data, 19.
  opinions of experts who have made *ex parte* investigations, 20.
  based on part of the testimony, 43.
  based on facts heard outside, 48.
INDIANA.
  statutory provision as to disclosure of professional communications
    by physicians, 72.
  statutory provision as to verification of written law, 129.
    extra compensation of experts, 253.
INK.
  whether two documents were written with the same, 183, 185.
  micro-chemical examination of, 185.
  qualifications of experts in, 186.
INSANITY.
  form of question as to, 38, 44, 87.
  opinions of medical experts on, 85.
  who are competent to testify as experts, 85-87.
  evidence bearing on questions of, 88-90.
  opinions of non-professional witnesses, 90, 94.
INSPECTION OF THE PERSON. See EXAMINATION OF THE PER-
    SON.
INSTRUCTIONS.
  as to the nature and weight of expert testimony, 61-65.
INSTRUMENT.
  by which wounds were inflicted, opinion as to character of, 84, 85.
INSURANCE EXPERTS.
  whether they may testify as to the materiality of concealed facts,
    148-150.
  who are competent to testify to such materiality, 150.
  what they may testify to, 151-153.
INTERROGATORIES.
  summoning experts to determine in cases of impotency, 101.
INTOXICATION.
  opinion as to whether a person is under, 5.
IOWA.
  statutory provision as to disclosure by physician of professional
    communications, 72.

IOWA—Continued.
    statutory provision as to comparison of handwriting by experts, 191.
    verification of written law, 129.
    compensation of experts, 252.

J.

JETTISON.
    opinion as to necessity of, 144.

JUDICIAL NOTICE.
    is taken of what laws, 119.
    is not taken of what laws, 121.
    of the meaning of words and idioms, 165.

JURY.
    province of jury to draw inferences from the facts, 5.
    is not selected with a view to its knowledge of science, art, or trade, 9.
    competency of experts cannot be referred to, 23.
    weight of expert testimony is to be determined by, 58.
    right of, to exercise an independent judgment in passing on the weight of expert testimony, 59-61.
    instructions to, on the nature and weight of expert testimony, 61-65.
    reading scientific books to, as evidence, 237.
        as argument, 248.
    inspection of the person by, 104.

K.

KANSAS.
    statutory provision as to competency of experts in detection of counterfeits, 207.

KENTUCKY.
    statutory provision as to verification of written laws, 130.
    proof of foreign law, 126.

L.

LAW. See FOREIGN LAW; JUDICIAL NOTICE; LAWYERS.
    as a subject for expert testimony, 118.
    distinction between written and unwritten as so mode of proof, 123.

LAWYERS.
    as experts in the science of law, 119.
    whether witnesses must be, to testify to foreign law, 132-136.
    where knowledge of the law must have been acquired, 137.
    right of to cite text books, decisions and codes, 138.
    testimony of, as to usage and practice of the courts, 139.
        powers and obligations of an attorney, 140.
        value of their services, 222.
    whether they may read from scientific books in argument, 248.

LIQUOR.
  non-professional witness may testify as to character of certain, 5.
LOUISIANA.
  statutory provision as to verification of written law, 130.
LUMBERMEN.
  opinion as to amount of logs could be delivered per day, 164.
  proper manner of floating logs, 164.
  quality of lumber, 164.
  whether a raft was properly moored, 164.

M.

MACHINERY.
  who can testify as to construction of mill machinery, 28.
  opinion that machine was constructed in workmanlike manner, 44.
  opinion as to the merits of, 160.
  need not be a machinest to testify as an expert in, 160.
  opinion as to how much work a machine could do, 161.
  opinions as to the value of, 218, 219.
MAINE.
  statutory provision as to verification of written law, 129.
  proof of foreign law, 125.
  opinion of witnesses in the detection of counterfeits, 207.
MALPRACTICE.
  testimony of medical experts in cases of, 97.
MARINE SURVEYOR.
  opinion as to seaworthiness, 142, n. 2.
MARYLAND.
  statutory provision as to verification of written law, 129.
MASONS AND MASTER BUILDERS.
  opinions of, 161, 162.
MASSACHUSETTS.
  statutory provision as to verification of written law, 129.
  proof of foreign law, 125.
MECHANICS.
  opinions of, 161.
MEDICAL EXPERTS.
  who are qualified to testify as such, 68-71, 80, 86.
  opinion as to physical condition, 42, 77, 94.
    cause of death, 44, 45, 77, 98, 109.
    nature and symptoms of disease, 79, 80.
    nature and effect of wounds, 81-85, 107.
    character of instrument used in inflicting, 84-85.
    mental condition, 85.
    whether a rape has been committed, and effect of, 94.
    whether an abortion has been performed, 95.
    pregnancy, 95.

MEDICAL EXPERTS—Continued.
  permanency of loss of vision, 96.
  questions of medical practice, 96-98.
  condition of remains after burial, 96.
  premature births, 97.
  sex of a skeleton, 97.
  miscellaneous cases, 96-97.
  curability of a disease, 97.
  skill of physician on trial, 97.
  nature and properties of medicine, 98.
  impotency, 99-102.
  effect of poisons, 108.
  diseases in animals, 116-117.
  opinions based on declarations of patients, 49, 75-77.
    statements out of court, 74.
  disclosure of confidential communications, 71.
  examination of the person by, in cases of impotency, 99.
    in criminal cases, 104-106.
    in actions for damages, 106-108.
  testimony of, as to the value of the services of physicians and nurses, 224.

MEDICAL TREATISES.
  their general inadmissibility in evidence, 237-243.
  when admissible for purpose of contradicting a medical expert, 244.
  testing knowledge of expert by means of, on the cross-examination, 245.
  views of writers on medical jurisprudence as to their exclusion, 246.
  reading from, in arguing to the jury, 248.

MENTAL CONDITION. SEE INSANITY.

MICHIGAN.
  statutory provision as to disclosure by physicians of professional communications, 72.
  statutory provision as to verification of written law, 129.

MICROSCOPIST.
  opinion of, in handwriting, 184.
    as to blood stains, 111.

MIDWIFE.
  inspection of the person by, 100.

MILLERS AND MILLWRIGHTS.
  opinion as to quantity of grain a mill could grind, 155.
    value of water power for mill purposes, 155.
    fitness of mill site, 156.
    identity of wheat, 156.
    anchor ice, 156.
    skilfulness of work on a mill, 156.
    necessity of repairing mill, 157.
    capacity of millwright, 157.

MILLERS AND MILLWRIGHTS—Continued.
 technical terms, 168.
 value of a mill, 217, 218.
 who can testify as to construction of mill machinery, 28.

MINER.
 opinion of, 170.

MINNESOTA.
 statutory provision as to disclosure by physicians of professional communications, 72.
 statutory provision as to verification of written laws, 129.

MISSOURI.
 statutory provision as to disclosure by physicians of professional communications, 72.
 statutory provision as to verification of written law, 130, n. 2.

MORALS.
 opinions based on a theory of, are inadmissible, 18.

MORTALITY TABLES.
 their admissibility in evidence, 231.

N.

NATIONALITY.
 opinion as to a persons, 6.

NAUTICAL EXPERTS.
 their opinion as to seaworthiness of vessels, 142, 145.
 cause of a leak in a ship, 142.
 the soundness of a chain cable, 142.
 the collision of vessels, 142, 143.
 the management of ships, 142, 143.
 the method of towing boats, 142.
 effect of cross-seas, 142.
 cause of the loss of a vessel, 143.
 what cargo can be safely carried, 143.
 negligence in mooring vessel, 143.
 the necessity of a jettison, 144.
 what would be the expense of raising and repairing a vessel, 144.
 sailing rules and regulations, 144.
 safe place for carrying cargo, 144.
 competency of crew, 145.
 piloting of a boat, 145.

NAVIGATION. See NAUTICAL EXPERTS.

NEBRASKA.
 statutory provision as to disclosure by physicians of professional communications, 72.
 statutory provision as to comparison of handwriting, 191.

NEGOTIABLE SECURITIES.
   value of, 232.
NEW HAMPSHIRE.
   statutory provision as to opinion evidence on the value of property, 209.
NEW JERSEY.
   statutory provision as to verification of written law, 130.
   comparison of handwriting, 191.
NEW YORK.
   statutory provision as to disclosure by physicians of professional communications, 72.
   statutory provision as to verification of written law, 129.
   comparison of handwriting, 192.
NON-PROFESSIONAL WITNESSES.
   are not in general allowed to express opinions, 4.
   when they may express opinions, 5.
   cannot express opinions on questions of science, skill or trade, 7.
   cannot testify as to prevalence of disease in a certain locality, 80.
   may testify whether a person appears sick or well, 80.
   may express an opinion as to necessity of medical services, 80.
   cannot testify as to the character of a disease, 80, 81.
   may describe the appearance of a wound, 82.
   may testify as to a person's mental condition, 90-94.
   cannot express opinion as to pregnancy, 95.
   whether they may testify as to blood stains, 113.
   whether they may testify as to diseases in animals, 116.
   whether they may testify as to foreign law, 132-136.
   cannot express an opinion based on a comparison of handwriting, 196.
   opinions of, in questions relating to value, 213.
   whether they may testify as to the value of an attorney's services, 223.
   whether they may testify to the value of medical services, 224.
   their opinions of the value of real estate, 227.
NORTH CAROLINA.
   statutory provision as to verification of written law, 129.
   statutory provision as to additional compensation to experts, 253.
NORTHAMPTON TABLES.
   admissibility of, to show expectation of life, 231.
NURSE.
   who may testify as to the value of their services, 225.
   opinion of, as to a premature birth, 96.
   opinion of physician founded on declarations of, 74.
NURSERYMAN.
   opinion of, as to the value of trees, 217.

O.

OBJECTION.
  to expert testimony may be general when, 23.
OCULIST.
  whether a physician must be, to testify in relation to the eyes, 71.
OHIO.
  statutory provision as to disclosure by physicians of professional communications, 72.
  statutory provision as to verification of written law, 129.
OPINION. See ADMISSIBILITY OF EXPERT TESTIMONY — INADMISSIBILITY OF OPINIONS — NON-PROFESSIONAL WITNESSES.
OREGON.
  statutory provision as to verification of written law, 130.
  comparison of handwriting, 192.
OVERSEER.
  opinion of, 154.

P.

PAINTER. See ARTIST.
  opinion of, 27.
PAPER. See WRITINGS.
  how made to appear old, 187, n.
  whether it had been used as gun wadding, 16.
PATENTS.
  opinions of experts in, 162.
PAVER.
  opinion of, 170.
PENNSYLVANIA.
  statutory provision as to admissibility of expert testimony in detection of counterfeits, 207.
PHOTOGRAPHS.
  comparison of handwriting should be with the original and not a photographic copy, 199.
  when a comparison of writings may be made with photographic copy, 202.
  opinions of experts as to, 163.
PHYSICIAN. See MEDICAL EXPERTS — PRIVILEGED COMMUNICATIONS.
  is an expert as to matters relating to his profession, 68.
  need not be a graduate or have a license, to testify as an expert, 68.
  whether he must be engaged in practice, 69.
  need not be a specialist to testify as an expert, 70.
  when not competent to testify as to sanity, 70, 86.
  need not be an oculist to testify as to the eye, 71.
  whether he may be asked for his impressions, 71.
  testimony of, on question of mental condition, 85.

PHYSICIAN. See MEDICAL EXPERTS — PRIVILEGED COMMUNICATIONS—Continued.
  testimony of, in poison cases, 108.
  value of services of, how shown, 224.
  medical treatises cannot be cited in general to sustain or contradict the testimony of, 237-247.
  cannot be compelled to make a *post mortem* examination without special compensation, 254.
  extra compensation of, when testifying as an expert, 256.
  opinion inadmissible as to whether he faithfully discharged his duty to his professional brethren, 19.

PILOT.
  opinion of, 145.

POISONS.
  detection of, by chemists, 108.
  a chemist need not be a physician to testify as to the effects of, 108.
  a physician may testify as to symptoms appearing on the administration of, 109.
  when a chemical analysis of, is not necessary, 109.
  order of research in analysis for, 110.

POST-MARK.
  genuineness of, how shown, 172.

POST MORTEM EXAMINATIONS.
  what is sufficient time in which to make, 19, 20.
  admissibility of testimony of physicians making, does not depend upon their thoroughness, 21, 81.
  interrogation of physicians who made, 96.
  rules prescribed for making cannot be introduced in evidence, 239.
  value of services in making, may be shown by whom, 225.
  physician need not make without extra compensation, 254.

PREGNANCY.
  an inadmissible opinion as to, 20.
  the testimony of medical experts on the question of, 95.
  examination of the person with a speculum, 106.

PRESUMPTIONS.
  persons are presumed to understand questions pertaining to their own business or profession, 2.
  that the law is unwritten, 124.
  that the law remains unchanged, 132.
  that dealers are acquainted with value of articles dealt in, 221.

PRIEST.
  a Roman Catholic, as an expert in questions of sanity, 86.
  an expert as to the matrimonial law, 133.
    law governing church records, 133.

PRIVILEGED COMMUNICATIONS.
communications to physicians not privileged at common law, 71.
statutory provisions as to disclosure of information acquired by physicians in attending patients, 71, 72.
these statutory provisions construed, 72-74.

PROVINCE OF THE JURY. See JURY.

PROXIMATE CAUSE.
the question of, is not one of science, 17.

Q.

QUALIFICATIONS OF EXPERTS. See COMPETENCY OF EXPERTS — PHYSICIANS.

QUALITY.
who are qualified to testify to quality of railroad ties, 147, 172.
lumber, 164.
iron, 170.
expert testimony as to quality of steel for rails, 172.

QUESTIONS OF FACT.
whether a witness possesses the requisite qualifications of an expert, 23-25.

QUESTIONS OF LAW.
whether the subject-matter of inquiry is such that expert testimony may be received, 18, 25.
what are the qualifications necessary to entitle a witness to testify as an expert, 18, 25.
are not to be embraced in questions to experts, 47.
construction of written instruments are, 158, 165, 166.

QUESTIONS OF SCIENCE, ART AND TRADE.
experts may testify on, 8-11.
meaning of the terms "science" and "art," 12.
opinions of experts are inadmissible except in relation to, 12-14.
illustrations of what are not, 14-18, 114, 147, 152, 153, 154, 155, 162, 175.

R.

RAILROAD EXPERTS.
opinions as to the management of trains, 145.
stoppage of trains, 146.
safe rate of speed, 146.
possibility of avoiding injury, 146.
effect of leaky throttle-valve, 146.
why train was thrown from track, 146.
whether brakemen were in their proper place, 147.
quality of railroad ties, 147.
whether rail was laid properly, 148.
questions upon which their testimony was inadmissible, 14, 147-148

RAPE.
  opinions of medical experts on questions relating to, 94.
REAL ESTATE AGENTS.
  value of their services shown how, 226, 227.
  opinions of, on value of real estate, 219.
REAL ESTATE.
  who are competent to testify as to the value of, 227-230.
RELIGION.
  opinions founded on a theory of are inadmissible, 18.
REPUTATION OF EXPERTS.
  when it can be impeached, 49.
  when other experts may testify to, 49, 50.
RHODE ISLAND.
  statutory provision as to verification of written law, 129.
  comparison of handwriting, 192.
  special compensation of experts, 253.
ROAD-BUILDERS.
  opinion of, 17.
ROBBERY.
  opinion of detectives as to the manner, of, 15.
ROMAN CATHOLIC PRIEST.
  an expert as to sanity, 86.
ROMAN LAW.
  practice of receiving expert testimony under, 3.
RUPTURE.
  who may testify to fact of, 81.

S.

SANITY. See INSANITY.
SEAWORTHINESS.
  opinions as to, 142, 145.
SCIENCE.
  the term defined, 12.
  questions to experts must partake of the nature of, 13.
  expert must have experience in, 2, 3.
SCIENTIFIC BOOKS. See BOOKS OF SCIENCE.
SHEPHERD.
  opinion as to age of sheep, 155.
SHIPWRIGHT.
  opinion of, 143.
SKILL.
  expert must be possessed of peculiar, 2, 8, 22.
  much is left to discretion of court in determining whether a witness
    is possessed of, 23.
  whether a witness has peculiar skill, a question of fact, 24.

SKILL—Continued.
  expert need not possess the highest degree of, 27.
  opinions of witnesses as to whether an expert has, 49.
  value of opinion of expert does not depend on degree of skill professed, 59.
  of physician, testimony as to in malpractice cases, 97.
SOBER.
  opinion to as to whether a person was, 5.
SOCIETY.
  whether a physician to testify as an expert should be a member of a medical, 68, 69.
SPECULATIVE DATA.
  the admissibility of opinions based on, 19.
SPIRITS.
  opinion as to evaporation of, 115.
STATUTES.
  of a State are taken judicial notice of by Federal courts, 120.
  of the Federal Government are taked judicial notice of by State courts, 120.
  of a State providing for a comparison of handwriting are not binding in a Federal court, 193.
  of Wisconsin providing for qualifications of physicians, 69.
  providing against the disclosure by physicians of information acquired while attending a patient, 71.
  providing as to proof of foreign law, 125.
    verification of written law, 129.
    comparison of handwriting, 190.
    detection of counterfeit notes, etc, 206.
    additional compensation to experts, 253.
  of New Hampshire providing for expert testimony in cases of value, 209.
STOCKBROKER.
  testifying as an expert as to the law of promissory notes, 133.
  opinion of as to technical terms, 167.
    the course of business, 169.
STOCK-RAISER.
  opinions of, 155.
STREET.
  whether experts may testify as to the sufficiency of, 17, 18.
SUICIDE.
  inadmissible opinion as to, 18.
SURVEYOR. See CIVIL ENGINEER.
  opinion inadmissible as the highest part of a hill, 15.
  opinion as to boundary marks, 157.
  cannot give a construction to a survey, 157.
  cannot testify as to safety of a highway, 158.

SYMPTOMS.
  opinion of medical experts based on patient's declaration of, 75.
  testimony of experts based on evidence of symptoms, 77, 78.
  of disease, medical testimony as to, 79.
  of poisoning, chemists and physicians may testify to, 108, 109.
  unreliability of, in cases of poisoning, 109.
  of disease in animals, who may testify to, 116.

T.

TAILOR.
  opinion of, 172.
TECHNICAL TERMS.
  testimony of experts as to, 165-168.
TELLERS.
  testify as experts in handwriting, 179.
    the detection of counterfeit bank notes, 205.
TENNESSEE.
  statutory provision as to verification of written law, 129.
TESTIMONY. See ADMISSIBILITY OF EXPERT TESTIMONY; INADMISSIBILITY OF OPINION; VALUE OF EXPERT TESTIMONY; WEIGHT OF EXPERT TESTIMONY.
  questions should not call for a critical review of, 37.
  expert not to reconcile conflicting, 38.
  whether an expert must hear all the, 39.
  should tend to establish every fact embraced in a hypothetical question, 39, 40.
  expert cannot express opinion as to value of testimony of other experts, 50.
  weight of, a question for the jury, 58.
  of experts, to be considered like any other testimony, 59.
  right of jury to exercise an independent judgment, 60.
  expressions of opinion by the court as to the weight of, 61.
  instructions as to the nature and weight of, 62-65.
  the value and weight of, 65.
  reference to a master to take, in cases of alleged impotency, 101.
  testimony of medical experts in cases of alleged impotency to be received with caution, 103.
  illustration of, by the use of diagrams, 83, 112.
  of experts as found in the reports, reading from, 251.
  relation of scientific books to expert testimony, 234.
TEXAS.
  statutory provision as to verification of written law, 129.
    to comparison of handwriting, 192.
TEXT BOOKS. See BOOKS OF SCIENCE.
  right of experts in legal science to cite, 138.

TRADE.
  one experienced in, an expert, 1.
  as an "art," 12.
  expert testimony admissible in questions of, 8.
  the testimony of experts in the various trades, 141-175.
TRADE MARKS.
  opinions of experts in, 162, 163.
TOBACCO.
  opinion of an expert in, 171.
TRANSLATION OF WRITINGS.
  by persons of skill, 164.

U.

UNDERWRITERS.
  when they may testify to the materiality of concealed facts, 148, 150, 151.
  opinion of, as to increase of risk, 149, 151.
USAGE OF COURTS.
  as shown by testimony of lawyers, 139.
USAGE OF TRADE.
  evidence as to, is inadmissible when, 168.
  who are competent to testify as to, 169.

V.

VALUE OF EXPERT TESTIMONY.
  is a question for the jury, 58, 65.
  upon what it depends, 59, 66.
  instructions as to the, 61-65.
  expressions of judicial opinion as to, in miscellaneous cases of appendix, "A."
  expressions of judicial opinion as to, in the investigation of handwriting, appendix "B."
  expressions of judicial opinion as to, in the case of medical experts, appendix, "C."
VALUE.
  as a subject for expert testimony, 208.
  the doctrine in New Hampshire, 209.
  when the opinion of experts are inadmissible on questions of, 210.
  opinions as to the amount of damages, 211-213.
  the admissibility of the opinions of non-professional witnesses on questions of, 213.
  qualifications of experts in value, 214-216.
  whether the expert should see the property, 216-218.
  time of examination of the property by the expert, 218.
  competency in particular cases, 218-222.

VALUE—Continued.
value of legal services, 222.
value of services of physicians and nurses, 224.
value of services in other callings, 226.
opinions as to the value of real estate, 227.
the value of annuities, 230.
the value of foreign currency and negotiable securities, 232.

VETERINARY SURGEON.
testimony as to disease in animals, 116.

VIOLENCE.
opinion as to whether death was caused by, 21.

VOICE.
identification by means of, 5, n. 2.

W.

WEIGHING TESTIMONY.
is the province of the jury, 58.
right of jury to exercise an independent judgment in, 60.

WEIGHT OF EXPERT TESTIMONY.
depends on what, 59.
instructions as to, 61-63.

WISCONSIN.
statutory requirements as to the qualifications of physicians, 69.
statutory provision as to disclosure by physicians of information acquired while attending a patient, 71.
statutory provision as to verification of written law, 130.
proof of foreign law, 125.

WITNESSES. See COMPETENCY OF EXPERTS — CREDIBILITY OF EXPERTS — EXAMINATION OF EXPERTS — CROSS-EXAMINATION.
exclusion of, from court room, 53.
right to limit number of, 54.
selection of expert, 55.
may be examined to determine the qualification of experts, 25.

WORDS.
defining technical words to jury, 165.
expert testimony as to technical words, 166-168.

WOUNDS.
opinions as to the natural and probable results of, 81.
which of two, caused death, 82.
that a wound was inflicted after death, 82.
opinion as to position of body when struck, 83.
experiments upon a dynamometer, 84.
by what instrument produced, opinion as to, 84.
whether they were produced accidentally, 84.
who are competent to express opinions as to instrument used, 85.
opinions of non-professional witnesses as to, 82.

WRITERS ON MEDICAL JURISPRUDENCE.
  views of, on exclusion of medical treatises from evidence, 246.
  views of, as to additional compensation to experts, 255.
WRITINGS. See HANDWRITING
  translation of, 164.
  expert cannot give construction to, 165, 166.
  whether in a simulated hand, 182.
  whether touched with a pen a second time, 182.
  whether made with a pen, 183.
  whether made by the same person and at same time, 183.
  which was written first, 183,
  opinion as to the alternation of, 184.
  opinions as to illegible, 184.
  whether of ancient or recent date, 185.
  who may testify to the age of, 186.
WRITTEN LAWS. See FOREIGN LAWS.
  distinction between written and unwritten law as to mode of proof, 123.
  law presumed to be unwritten, 124.
  expert testimony in connection with, 124.
  statutory provision as to, 125.
  rule in England as to proof of, 126-129.
  statutory provision as to verification of, 129.

www.ingramcontent.com/pod-product-compliance
Lightning Source LLC
Chambersburg PA
CBHW030750230426
43667CB00007B/909